ENZAGUA   22.50

Feminism and Its Discontents

Feminism and Its Discontents

A Century of Struggle
with Psychoanalysis

Mari Jo Buhle

Harvard University Press
Cambridge, Massachusetts
London, England
1998

Library of Congress Cataloging-in-Publication Data
Buhle, Mari Jo, 1943–
Feminism and its discontents : a century of struggle with
psychoanalysis / Mari Jo Buhle.
p.   cm.
Includes bibliographical references and index.
ISBN 0-674-29868-3 (alk. paper)
1. Psychoanalysis and feminism.   I. Title.
BF175.4.F45B84   1998
150.19'5'082—dc21   97-32397

Contents

Feminism and Its Discontents

Introduction

In 1909, to celebrate the twentieth anniversary of the founding of Clark University in Worcester, Massachusetts, Sigmund Freud joined other renowned scholars and delivered a series of lectures on psychoanalysis. The attentive audience comprised mainly professors and physicians, with one notable exception. Seated conspicuously in the front row, "chastely garbed in white" and with a rose pinned to her waist, according to a newspaper account, was Emma Goldman. The notorious anarchist and free lover had heard Freud speak in Vienna fifteen years earlier, and she continued to count herself among his most ardent admirers. Gladly, she interrupted her own lecture tour to be present at this historic event, Freud's only appearance in the United States.

Goldman undoubtedly hoped Freud would speak on some aspect of sexuality. His colleague Ernest Jones remembered a "lady"—perhaps Goldman herself—passing him a note asking the founder of psychoanalysis to address explicitly the question of sex. Upon hearing this request, Freud allegedly replied that he could no more "be driven *to* the subject than *away* from it." Soon, however, he fulfilled Goldman's expectations. Although Freud began cautiously by providing a simple outline of his theories, he wrapped up the series of lectures in a dauntless manner. "We ought not to exalt ourselves so high as completely to neglect," he warned, "what was originally animal in our nature. Nor should we forget that the satisfaction of the individual's happiness cannot be erased from among the aims of our civilization." Freud concluded by proclaiming the potential of psychoanalysis to free "a certain portion of the repressed libidinal impulses." For an anarchist who refused to assist any revolution forbidding her to dance, this counsel could not have been more pleasing. Goldman nevertheless pressed the issue. She turned to another speaker to demand an explanation for the failure of the women's colleges "to take up the most important subject, that of sex psychology."[1]

Not long after the Worcester meeting Goldman published a short essay specifying the affinity between psychoanalysis and feminism: the recognition of sexuality as preeminent in the makeup of women as well as men. Moreover, she added, Freud attributed the intellectual inferiority of so many women "to the inhibition of thought imposed upon them for the purpose of sexual repression." In short, according to Goldman, Freud had perceived the link between the private and public dimensions of man's subjugation of woman. Although successive generations of feminists would alternately laud and revile Freud's special insight into this relationship, Goldman never wavered in her faith in psychoanalysis or in the man she considered "a giant among pygmies."[2]

It was not merely the emphasis on sexuality that prompted Goldman to acclaim Freud's theories. Rather, she saw feminism and psychoanalysis as historically paired and standing together on the brink of modernity. No less than psychoanalysis, feminism heralded a definitive break with past endeavors. "We have grown accustomed in these years to something known as the Woman Movement. That has an old sound—it is old. Therefore, no need to cry it down," one of Goldman's contemporaries affirmed. Woman's rights to the ballot, economic self-support, and higher education—to equality in all spheres of civil society—extended into the twentieth century as campaigns still worthy of support. But feminism encompasses far more than these goals. Feminism promises nothing less than, another devotee instructed, "a changed psychology, the creation of a new consciousness in women."[3]

Goldman embraced psychoanalysis as a vital contribution to the historic quest for female subjectivity. As early as 1892, in her justly famous address "Solitude of Self," Elizabeth Cady Stanton had proclaimed the "individuality of each human soul." Stanton deftly described woman's wish to develop beyond "the incidental relations of life, such as mother, wife, sister, daughter," but she lacked a vocabulary to make her case in psychological terms. Her descendants, with access to a different range of scientific and philosophical discourses, broke the barriers of formalism and fashioned a new language to express female selfhood. "The new, wonderful, final step which woman must take," as one twentieth-century writer put it, "is to enter upon the free unfolding of her personality as an end in itself." With this goal in mind, Goldman judged Freud's theories a tributary of the specific project of women's emancipation.[4]

Feminism and psychoanalysis together share a large responsibility for what the historian Warren I. Susman described as the distinctly modern spectacle of "consciousness of self." Distantly grounded in the humanistic legacy of the Renaissance, psychoanalysis and feminism both concern the meaning of individuality in a secular society and, as philosophical systems, gained coherence only as this century began. Psychoanalysis took shape as a clinical or therapeutic method, feminism as a political strategy. The two systems occupied a common domain as theories of human liberation, even at subsequent moments of conflict or competition.[5]

It is sometimes alleged, though, that feminists more frequently discuss and dispute the merits of psychoanalysis in relation to their enterprise than psychoanalysts consider the value of feminism to theirs. I argue to the contrary. Whereas Freud may have played the more celebrated role in facilitating vast shifts in sensibility, feminists did their part in registering the significance of gender. There is no doubt that Freudian theories inspired feminists to refine their categories of analysis. But feminists in turn compelled psychoanalysts to consider the implications of one of Freud's own, most uncompromising propositions: "that human beings consist of men and women and that this distinction is the most significant one that exists." Both feminism and psychoanalysis build on this premise. Almost by necessity, their practitioners cross paths in performing the "ideological work" ongoing since the Enlightenment, in the historian Thomas Laqueur's notation, of defining woman as "not a lesser man, measured on a male scale of virtue, reason, or sensuality," but as *woman*.[6]

This book is based on the premise that feminism and psychoanalysis developed dialogically, that is, in continuous conversation with each other. It brings to light the spirited, ever changing, but surprisingly persistent relationship as their chief theorists tackle common problems.

The term "self" is heavily loaded with meaning. To many readers it signals either a postmodernist style of psychoanalysis derived from the writings of the late French analyst Jacques Lacan and made fashionable in the United States by feminist literary and film critics; or object-relations theory, developed in Great Britain and popularized in the United States by the heuristic writings of Nancy Chodorow. These two major variations of psychoanalytic theory as reinterpreted by American feminists figure prominently in the second half of this book. Their very celebrity since the 1970s inspired me to write the book. But rather than contributing to the abundant literature assessing the relative merits of Lacanian and object-relations theories, I place both variations within a century-long tradition of intellectual endeavor.

The story begins with Freud's original formulations or, more precisely, the reworking of his ideas in the United States. As Freud insisted, psychoanalysis began with him and received its first major public hearing when he presented his lectures at Clark University. Although he continuously revised his theories until he died in 1939, Freud set the standards of orthodoxy. He could not, however, prevent other psychoanalysts from traveling deviate paths. By 1909, just as his theories began to attract a sizable following, Freud endured the first attempts to overhaul them. Dissension soon fractured the ranks of the fledgling European psychoanalytic movement. Freud's prize pupils, Alfred Adler and Carl Gustav Jung, split off to form their own distinctive schools, while others began to tamper with basic tenets. In the United States, Freudian orthodoxy never took hold.

Freud himself forecast the alchemic fate of his doctrines on these alien shores. At first he looked to American scholars to confer upon psychoanalysis the commendation refused by the European scientific community. Soon he suspected that such success would be costly.

Many things about American culture made Freud uneasy. His only visit to the United States generated so much anxiety that he fainted several times in transit and suffered indigestion during his entire stay. Unable to summon the concentration to prepare his lectures in advance, Freud spoke extemporaneously in German. Even after encountering kudos from all sides, he remained suspicious. A Boston news reporter characterized his work as the "latest" and described Freud as "a man of great refinement, of intellect and of many-sided education." Another journalist praised "the father of psychoanalysis" as one of "the most attractive of the eminent foreign savants."[7] The trustees of Clark University bestowed an honorary doctorate on him. Despite these favors, Freud returned home in a dour mood. "America is a mistake; a gigantic mistake, it is true," he allegedly said to Jones on his arrival in Vienna, "but none the less a mistake." Of all its wonders, only Niagara Falls could charm the ambivalent tourist.[8]

Americans paid no attention to Freud's apprehensions. Soon after his visit, at the 1910 meeting of the American Psychological Association, one prominent scholar noted a "mad epidemic of Freudianism now invading America." The *American Journal of Psychology* quickly translated and published the Clark University lectures, while the *Journal of Abnormal Psychology* reviewed the fundamentals of Freudian theory. Adulation notwithstanding, virtually no one planned to toe a line. The *Psychoanalytic Review: A Journal Devoted to an Understanding of Human Conduct* debuted in the United States in 1913 with a determinedly eclectic editorial policy. Each issue abstracted articles from the leading European journals and thereby kept its English-language readers informed of the latest developments in continental theory. At the same time, its editors William A. White and Smith Ely Jeliffe welcomed writers far outside the Freudian camp and provided a forum for competing schools of psychoanalysis. The mass media abided even fewer restrictions. Essays on psychoanalysis in popular magazines soon outnumbered the ever abundant articles on other types of mind cure. *McClure's Magazine,* with nearly a half-million readers, introduced Freud's ideas in 1912, and theoretical rigor was nowhere in sight. Typical were the exploits of *Cosmopolitan's* fictional detective "Craig Kennedy" employing dream analysis to solve a crime. The United States proved remarkably fertile for the growth of psychoanalysis—but not for the orthodoxy its founder craved.[9]

Within a decade of Freud's visit, a loose network of assorted publicists had formed. One notable coterie comprised left-leaning journalists, novelists, playwrights, poets, critics, college professors, and physicians characterized by the historian Mark Sullivan as "a type of intellectual called, somewhat condescendingly, 'high-brows.'" The majority lived in the environs of New York City, frequented the coffeehouses and cabarets of Greenwich Village, and participated in common political and cultural endeavors. Max Eastman, editor of the radical magazine *The Masses,* for example, tried psychoanalysis with several practitioners, including Beatrice Hinkle, Jeliffe, and Abraham A. Brill. By his own account, Eastman proceeded "to read Freud and every book on Freud then available in English, rehearsing the doctrine point by point" with his analysts. Considering himself an "amateur specialist," Eastman wrote several essays on psychoanalysis, which he described as "a kind of magic." His friend and collaborator Floyd Dell underwent analysis with Samuel Tannenbaum and likewise emerged "sort of a missionary on the subject." The salon-host Mabel Dodge, who eventually serialized in the Hearst newspapers a report of her own experiences in analysis, brought all these folks together in her famed Fifth Avenue apartment. She once sponsored a well-attended "evening" with Doctor Brill. On other occasions, she engaged her guests in word-association parlor games and amateur dream analysis. Commenting on this scene, one of the first Freudian playwrights, Susan Glaspell, dryly remarked that one "could not go out to buy a bun without hearing of some one's complex."[10]

Having savored early translations of *Psychopathology of Everyday Life* and *The Interpretation of Dreams,* Freud's earliest American fans freely transposed his basic tenets. Eastman described the "unconscious mind" as "the place where those desires and fancies go which we are not willing to acknowledge even to ourselves." Psychoanalysis, Mabel Dodge wrote, "simplified all problems to name them. There was the Electra complex, and the Oedipus complex and there was the Libido with its manifold activities, seeking every chance for outlet, and then all that thing about Power and Money!" Dell did little better, explaining that psychoanalysis allowed him to understand why other people "acted as they did, and what they would do next, and—most magically of all—read their hidden secrets when I needed to do so, much to their astonishment." Heterodox to the core, these unbridled interpreters inaugurated a practice that would prove enduring.[11]

Psychoanalysis in the United States quickly became, as Freud predicted, the property of freewheeling intellectuals and popularists as well as of physicians. In the 1920s Freud himself received an invitation, which he declined, to become a script consultant to a Hollywood filmmaker; a nephew of his achieved spectacular success in the American advertising industry. Popular culture continued throughout the twentieth century to serve as a major conduit for psychoanalysis. The print media quickly gave rise to the commonplace caricature of the goateed therapist seated silently behind the couch. They also generated numerous jokes about complexes and neuroses and other ceaseless satires of therapy. Theories attributed to Freud inspired playwrights, novelists, and the personnel of the movie industry; filled the pages of women's magazines and middle-brow journals such as the *New Yorker* and the *Atlantic Monthly;* and dictated the perspectives of untold numbers of marriage manuals, self-help volumes, and childrearing advice books. Some of the responsibility for this process lay with psychoanalysts themselves and other scholars trained in the discipline. Karl Menninger wrote a column for the *Ladies' Home Journal* in the early 1930s; Margaret Mead picked up the thread decades later in her regular contributions to *Redbook*. After World War II the most prominent psychoanalysts enjoyed long runs on the nonfiction bestseller list and met with even greater success when their books were reprinted as mass-market paperbacks.

It must be said, too, that Freud himself prepared Americans to play fast and loose with his doctrines. At the Clark University conference, he realized immediately that his audience was not limited to such specialists as the introspective psychologist Edward Bradford Tichenor and the psychiatrist Adolph Meyer. He noted not only representatives of several academic disciplines but the news media. Aiming to please, Freud presented a simplified overview of psychoanalysis, uncharacteristically stressing its practical and positive sides. In the long run he succeeded perhaps too well. As one historian has noted, Freud could not see clearly enough "the strange links between American popular and professional cultures" that would carry his ideas forward. Just a little over ten years later, in 1920, when the American Psychoanalytic Association (APA) attracted a paltry ten members to its annual meeting, American writers were poised to produce by decade's end over two hundred books on the subject. Of this number, trained experts wrote only a minuscule portion, and they themselves preached a thoroughly heterodox doctrine.[12] In short, revisionism flourished across the board. In the 1930s, when scores of European psychoanalysts fled fascism in Central Europe, they found in this country a notable and, according to some, healthy respite from the Freudian rule.

This diverse field of participants did not keep American psychoanalysis from gaining at least one enduring characteristic that set it apart from European-hewn theory: an overpowering optimism. Freud's earliest enthusiasts, all neo-romantics, eagerly embraced his theories as a means to transcend the repressive mandates of "civilized" society. Whereas Freud hoped at best to temper these forces, his American fans were determined both to achieve happiness in their own lives and to bring about a comprehensive social harmony. Floyd Dell spoke for many in his therapy-inclined milieu when he claimed that psychoanalysis had supplied "a new emotional center" to his life, allowing him to feel "free for the first time." Dell also judged the ultimate appeal of psychoanalysis, the fact that it "deals with ourselves," entirely compatible with his political commitment to social change. Freud, of course, had admitted as much. In his popular essay " 'Civilized' Sexual Morality and Modern Nervous Illness" (1908), he stated that observations did not lead him to believe "that sexual abstinence helps to bring about energetic and self-reliant men of action or original thinkers or bold emancipators and reformers." Dell ran wild with this idea, depicting Freud's theories as a complement to Marx's. Psychoanalysis, he insisted, added a salutary subjective dimension to the socialist vision of human freedom.[13]

Over the decades Americans would distance themselves from the precise ideological mix promoted by Dell and his peers, but for many psychoanalysis would continue to raise the prospect of human liberation. To a large extent, psychoanalysis advanced in the United States at the behest of left-leaning and liberal intellectuals. Apparent at the time of Freud's visit, this pattern emerged even more clearly during the interwar period, when issues of bigotry, racial prejudice, and ethnocentrism fired new research strategies. During the tumultuous 1960s youthful celebrants of Eros embraced psychoanalysis as a theory of liberation. This dimension also provided—at times—a bridge to feminism.

The cultural terrain under investigation here is therefore not limited to the output of licensed psychoanalysts. I depart significantly from the line drawn by other interpreters who emphasize the allegiance of American psychoanalysts to the strict standards set by the medical profession.[14] As is well known, the APA, founded in 1914, ultimately ignored Freud's bidding and by the late 1930s made medical training a requirement for membership. This process of "medicalization" speeded up during World War II, when psychoanalysis began to flourish as a branch of psychiatry, and accounts, it is argued, for the allegedly crimped character of American theory. Perhaps. But, as I see it, even in excluding lay practitioners, psychoanalysts in the United States rarely restricted themselves to the practice of medicine. To the contrary, as a group they proved much more alert than their European contemporaries to developments outside their discipline and they more readily teamed up with other scholars. They also carefully monitored the contributions of fine and commercial artists, journalists, and unaffiliated intellectuals of all kinds. For several decades it was this expansive group that shaped the public perception of American psychoanalysis. Certainly the APA, which as late as 1940 enrolled fewer than two hundred members, could not alone claim credit for the widespread appeal of psychoanalysis by midcentury. Literary criticism, history, anthropology, and, to a lesser extent, sociology all spurred its development.

All these sources figure into this book because I am concerned equally with the professional status of psychoanalysis and the popular rendition of theories. For example, no genre is more informative than Hollywood feature films of the 1940s. At the time, the movie industry enjoyed close connections to the psychoanalytic profession. Numerous producers, writers, actors, and technicians were undergoing psychoanalysis. As converts to a cause, they proceeded to fill the silver screen with Freudian imagery. Meanwhile their analysts, based mainly in Los Angeles and Beverly Hills, frequently served as highly paid consultants.[15] Necessarily, this kind of evidence serves my purpose, which is to examine the interface of psychoanalysis not so much with medical or scientific theory but with another public discourse, feminism.

The neo-Freudians serve particularly well to illustrate the multifaceted quality of American psychoanalysis. While rejecting several basic premises of Freudian theory, including the primacy of sexuality, neo-Freudian psychoanalysts nevertheless revered the founder's writings as canonical and advanced their own theories in reference to them. It was the neo-Freudians, moreover, who not only widened the audience for Freud's works but established psychoanalysis on firm ground in the United States. Mainly European-trained analysts who immigrated after the rise of fascism in their homelands, they built the major training institutes and clinical practices. They also joined a diverse assortment of American-bred scholars and pushed psychoanalysis to the center of American intellectual life, where it remained for several decades. Much of what has passed as psychoanalysis reflects the opinions of such prominent contributors and bestselling writers as Erich Fromm, Karen Horney, Abram Kardiner, and Margaret Mead.

Since its high point at midcentury, neo-Freudianism has fallen into a disrepute bordering on contempt. Deemed a theoretical travesty or dismissed as immaterial, it rarely figures in any serious study of the field.[16] I overturn this received wisdom by illustrating the importance of the revisionist impulse to the trajectory of American psychoanalysis. Neo-Freudians not only retained but magnified the social element in psychoanalysis. They made the study of prejudice and bigotry the heart of a major interdisciplinary endeavor.

For my purposes, neo-Freudianism is especially relevant because it evolved from the first conflict between feminist principles and Freudian tenets. Before 1920 Freud wrote only incidentally on female psychosexual development, sketching at best a rough pattern derived from the male. Analysts within his inner circle, meanwhile, advanced their own hypotheses, eventually forcing the master to clarify his ideas and to expand his framework to incorporate their concerns. But it was not until the 1930s, when several leading dissenters immigrated to the United States, that an entirely new paradigm took hold. For better or worse, these revisionists rebuilt psychoanalysis from the ground up. In the process they asked salient questions about the meaning of gender and of Western civilization as a whole.

The neo-Freudians clarified the terms of the debate that continues to engage feminists to this day. They criticized Freud for overestimating biological factors in the shaping of personality. Diminishing the founder's emphasis on instincts and anatomy, the neo-Freudians privileged instead the indeterminate field of environmental and interpersonal influences, ranging from childrearing practices to ideological systems. They thereby sharpened the significance of two opposing points of reference in both feminism and psychoanalytic theory: biology and culture, nature and nurture. The chapter they opened has yet to be closed.

Neo-Freudianism did not remain, however, an unswerving complement to feminism or the principal form of American psychoanalysis. The revisionists themselves vacillated wildly in positioning their theories in relation to feminism, and their immediate successors, ego psychologists, proved to be strident anti-feminists. But it is precisely this instability that gives my narrative its distinctive and intricate shape.

By charting continually changing valences, I aspire to undermine all faith in either a predetermined affinity or a transcendent mutual antagonism between feminism and psychoanalysis. At its best, the complex story that unfolds here largely justifies Freud's suspicions about the Americans who, in their enthusiasm, totally transformed psychoanalysis. I seek, then, to assess the historical significance of, rather than to disparage, the successive revisionist tendencies, all the while realizing that each brand of psychoanalysis, like each brand of feminism, has produced its own share of true believers and truthseekers determined to define the omnipotent core.

Ultimately, the revisionist program more than orthodoxy undergirds the narrative structure of this book. In short, this book is not primarily about Freud's views of women. His specific theories of female sexuality and femininity play only a small part. Nor do they serve as a litmus test of either psychoanalytic elegance or misogyny. Acknowledging the heuristic importance of the founder's theories, I look even more closely at a far-reaching project that engaged an assortment of practitioners and critics residing mainly in the United States. Intentionally sidestepped are the major heresies of Adler and Jung. Although both theorists responded to feminist challenges in provocative ways, they deviated so thoroughly from Freud's principles as to write themselves out of the psychoanalytic movement. Adler and Jung established their own illustrious fields of, respectively, individual psychology and analytic psychology. I follow instead the twists and turns in American psychoanalysis across several generations of Freudians, neo-Freudians, and post-Freudians. Ego psychology, object-relations and Kleinian theories, the critical theory inspired by the Frankfurt School, self psychology, Lacanian formulations, and even the thick stew known simply as "contemporary psychoanalysis" all play their parts.

Just as psychoanalysis in this book inevitably lacks a stable referent, so too does feminism. If defined very broadly as a refutation of male authority, feminism enjoys an even longer history, dating perhaps to the fifteenth century and the emergence of the secular culture of the Western state. Historians routinely credit Christine de Pisan (1364–1430?) with inaugurating a kind of sexual politics amid a *Querelle des Femmes* at least four hundred years before the French Revolution.[17] But as an expression of collective discontent, feminism achieved a discernible presence only in the early nineteenth century, when woman's rights and other organizations promoting civil reform took shape. Yet, to be precise, much of this first wave, the so-called century of struggle culminating in the United States in the Nineteenth Amendment, functioned without a label and without political cohesion. Unlike psychoanalysis, which by Freud's fiat emanates from his original canon, feminism flows from no single source.

Before Freud's visit in 1909 neither "feminism" nor "psychoanalysis" figured in the day-to-day conversations of even the best-read and most politically astute Americans. One could still encounter phrases awkward to the modern ear, such as "woman's advancement" and "mind cure." But within a short time the two terms, both imported from continental Europe, helped to define not only the sensibilities of a generation of activist intellectuals but the modern meaning—indeed, the modern imperative—of selfhood.

For Goldman's generation, feminism encompassed the historic campaign for woman's rights such as suffrage. But unlike the century-old Woman Question, which focused mainly on woman's advancement into civil society, feminism signified a new existential reality, as one writer put it, "an inner revolution before it is an outer revolt, subjective before objective."[18] Psychoanalysis, with its focus on the individual psyche, emerged as a natural ally to these "feminists." In turn, Freud's theories in the hands of feminists received their first significant political application.

There was, however, another defining quality to "feminism" circa 1909. Most of its professors, including Goldman, believed that the female psyche must express its own, immanent laws of being because woman is fundamentally unlike man. Feminists therefore sought autonomy as a prerequisite for a massive restructuring of humanity on the basis of what much later generations would term "difference." Chapters 1 and 2 of this book focus on this initial attempt to define feminism as the intention to acknowledge "woman" as not lesser than but decidedly different from "man."

The moment passed quickly, however. The decades between the passage of the constitutional amendment enabling women to vote and the rise of the women's liberation movement in the 1960s provided an entirely different semantic setting. Despite agitation around the Equal Rights Amendment and the rise of the welfare state, the term "feminism" itself fell into widespread disrepute just as it became much more commonplace in the general lexicon. By the 1920s the meaning of feminism had turned inside out to acquire an unusually pronounced association with the rights, privileges, and roles enjoyed by men. In most middle-brow circles it narrowed even further, its meaning encapsulated in the pejorative "careerism." Feminism came to signify masculinism, and little else.

The significance of this semantic declension cannot be overestimated. Even those vocal neo-Freudians who led the campaign against the masculine bias in Freudian theory refused the label "feminist." The interpreter of these events finds herself, therefore, in an awkward position. It is easy enough to acknowledge the fragmentation of the historic women's movement in the aftermath of the suffrage campaign and to gauge its negative impact on subsequent attempts to challenge misogyny. It is much more difficult to characterize such defensive efforts when the actors themselves disavow the feminist label. Nevertheless, and despite their own rhetorical preferences, the era's luminaries, including Karen Horney, Margaret Mead, and Clara Thompson, were certainly not *anti*-feminists. This honor belongs to others in their ranks. Militant anti-feminists grew in number at a very fast rate during the interwar period to become major players by midcentury.

Everything changes again with the advent of second-wave feminism. By the 1960s, when the term began to regain some of its positive energy, "feminism" acquired a generic or universal quality. Historians themselves now use the term incautiously to cover a gamut of issues and ideologies bound by no particular chronology. Thus, such dissimilar types as Margaret Fuller, Frances Willard, Elizabeth Cady Stanton, Emma Goldman, and Betty Friedan all enjoy the attribution of "feminist" in the scholarly literature. Historically speaking, feminism has come to encompass woman suffrage, equal rights, sexual freedom, and even women's liberation a half-century later.

As if to counteract this tendency, second-wave feminists have produced as many qualifications as psychoanalysts have of their designations. Since 1965 a host of descriptive adjectives have taken hold: liberal, socialist, material, radical, lesbian, cultural, spiritual, maternal, eco-, social, and postmodern, among others derived from racial or ethnic identities. Several subsets stand, politically or philosophically, in stark opposition to others. The antagonism between, for example, socialist feminists and cultural feminists easily rivals that between classical Freudians and neo-Freudians. The nuances of contemporary feminism necessarily play a large part in the later chapters of this book.

In the broadest sense, though, the definitional axis of feminism swings between *difference,* meaning an emphasis on the qualities that distinguish "woman" from "man" and determine the distinctive roles, rights, and identities of each; and *equality,* meaning a claim to autonomy and justice based on the common humanity of men and women. The historian Karen Offen has sharpened this contrast. She calls our attention to the strain of feminism that acknowledges "both biological and cultural distinctions between the sexes, a concept of womanly or manly nature, of a sharply defined sexual division of labor, or roles, in the family, and throughout society following from that 'difference' and that 'nature,' and the centrality of the complementary couple and/ or the mother/child dyad to social analysis."[19] This strain, which Offen isolates by introducing yet another modifier, "relational," often escapes notice. She asks us, therefore, to be wary of Webster's definition, precisely because it standardizes the meaning of feminism as the theory that women should have political, economic, and social rights equal to men's. Yet even the most fastidious scholar must admit that the line marking off the two major variations of feminism is neither hard nor fast.

This book highlights the multiple possibilities inherent in feminism, especially as tailored by specific national traditions. Central is the well-known inheritance of the Enlightenment philosophies of natural rights and nineteenth-century liberalism. John Stuart Mill, Elizabeth Cady Stanton, Charlotte Perkins Gilman, Alice Paul, and Betty Friedan all gave witness, at various times, to this legacy. They commonly assumed that the creative capacities of men and women are, if not identical, comparable. With varying degrees of enthusiasm, they sought to grant women all rights of citizenship, including the franchise, education, access to the labor market, ownership of property, and political office. To many scholars, this brand of feminism, with equality its core, has flourished as the quintessential Anglo-American version. By contrast, feminists on the European continent shaped an alternative metaphysics, one premised on the immanent differences between the sexes. This dualistic schema, overdrawn as it is, shapes my interpretations.

This book begins and ends with an examination of imported doctrine. In 1909, Freud's Germanic philosophy was not the only one floating across the Atlantic. New perspectives on women's emancipation, also emanating from Central Europe, were finding their way to these shores. Those Americans such as Goldman, Dell, and Dodge who embraced Freudianism did so precisely to enrich their understanding of feminism, itself an articulation mainly of European writers and activists who exalted the differences between the sexes. In a stunning return engagement, something eerily similar accompanied the more recent (if not necessarily more familiar) case of Lacanian psychoanalysis and French feminism, the synthetic matrix that marks my closure.

This is not to suggest, however, that home-grown American feminism has consistently expressed the principles of equal rights above all others. The largest mobilization of women, the temperance campaign, prospered under the leadership of the nineteenth century's leading *relational* feminist.[20] In order to make the whole world "home-like," Frances E. Willard successfully encouraged masses of American women to develop what she—and they—believed to be woman's unique aptitude for good works. Women of the abolitionist movement had made similar claims for their unique mission to eradicate the sin of slavery. Even the woman suffrage movement, which Willard supported, achieved the status of a mass movement only by extolling woman's singular talent for "social housekeeping" beyond the absolute justice of equal voting rights. This faith continues to inspire contemporary cultural feminists, including the growing number who make the earthly environment or the divine cosmos their principal point of reference. In short, *difference* feminism has functioned across centuries of American history, although like neo-Freudianism it suffers from both scholarly neglect and political disparagement.

In this book I document a nearly continuous sliding between the two poles of *difference* and *equality*. It is this vacillation, I argue, that steadily shapes and reshapes the relationship between feminism and psychoanalysis.

As intellectual patterns take new shapes, and as new casts of players displace old ones, alignments as well as misalignments appear and then dissolve. Throughout, though, feminists and psychoanalysts repeatedly find themselves on the horns of a common dilemma. The odd couple of the century cannot either resolve or abandon the difficulty inherent in reconciling biological and social factors in their theories of causation. They also share a related near-impossibility of defining "woman" as distinct from "man" while making a claim for their common humanity. For these reasons, "biology *versus* culture" and "equality *versus* difference" play themselves out in a variety of often surprising ways. Yet, despite all possible combinations and permutations, psychoanalysts and feminists together advanced the modernist project of selfhood.

For the great philosophers of the nineteenth century, the struggle for self-recognition begins with procuring and creating the means of subsistence. As Marx and Engels put it, "men must be in a position to live in order to be able to 'make history.' But life involves before everything else eating and drinking, a habitation, clothing and many other things. The first historical act is thus the production of the means to satisfy these needs, the production of material life itself." Freud agreed, at least to a point. In *Civilization and Its Discontents* (1930) he explained that he took as his "starting-point a saying of the poet-philosopher, Schiller, that 'hunger and love are what moves the world.' " Freud acknowledged hunger as a basic instinct of self-preservation, along with the libidinal instinct, which, "favoured in every way by nature," functions ultimately in the preservation of the species. His earliest theories concern the relentless struggle between these two instincts—"the interest of self-preservation and the demands of the libido." In his later writings Freud presented a revised drive system, grouping self- and species-preservation under Eros, and naming the opposing instinct Thanatos, or death. This revision did not, however, fundamentally alter his understanding of work and sex as opposites. Freud viewed work as the means by which the species maintains itself while carrying out its ceaseless procreative mission and as an activity both unavoidable and disagreeable. He reminded those visionaries who held higher aspirations for the fate of humanity that "men are not spontaneously fond of work." It is clear that, unlike Marx and

Engels, the founder of psychoanalysis did not employ labor as an onto-logical category.[21]

If for Marx, "labour [is] the essence of Man," and this "transform-ing activity" the source of subjectivity, for Freud the fountainhead of psychic energy is Eros. Within the terms of the libido theory, all other activities, most especially work, stand in antagonism to sexuality, broadly defined as a drive toward pleasure through the release of ten-sion. Freud thus affirmed Hegel's dictum that labor is "desire restrained and checked, evanescence delayed and postponed" and built his entire system on this principle.[22] It is through repression and sublimation, that is, the inhibition or deflection of libidinal impulses, he reasoned, that the individual moves through several stages of psy-chosexual development—oral, anal, and genital—to become a happy member of society, capable of both production and reproduction. It is through repression and sublimation that civilization advances.

The libido, in sum, carries the species toward its reproductive goal, while the tortuous and unconscious processes of repression and sub-limation enable the individual to meet the more advanced require-ments of self-preservation that Marx and Engels examined so care-fully. "For what motive would induce man to put his sexual energy to other uses if by any disposal of it he could obtain fully satisfying plea-sure?" Freud asked. "He would never let go of this pleasure and would make no further progress." Thus, in Freud's metapsychology, there is no "instinct of workmanship"; to the contrary, the energy for work must be "withdrawn" from the primary instincts. And sublimation, according to Freud "one of the origins of artistic activity," occasionally actuates the finest creative impulses known to humanity.[23]

For Freud, the libido is the ontological category, Eros the source of subjectivity as well as civilization and its discontents. As Herbert Mar-cuse pointed out, it was Freud's genius to illuminate "the repressive content of the highest values and achievements of culture," that is, to track the psychic interplay between work and sex, broadly defined, between unhappiness and freedom.[24]

Freud's attempts to explicate the differences between the sexes hinge on the hidden meanings of this dialectic. In mapping the Oedipus com-plex, the cornerstone of classical psychoanalysis, Freud described the threat of castration as fundamentally different for boys and girls. Fear-ing the loss of his penis, the son abides by the father's law, renounces incestuous desire for his mother, and through the processes of repression and sublimation prepares himself psychically for the denials that civilization demands. Girls, in contrast, have less reason to fear, for they already lack the requisite anatomy. Daughters resolve the Oedipus complex by renouncing their mothers for sharing this "lack." Because they seek to make up for the deficiency by giving birth to a penis-laden baby, women remain forever psychically centered in the sphere of Eros. That is, according to Freud, women never develop the powers of sublimation that men acquire and therefore stand not only outside but against civilization. While Freud broke Victorian precedent to acknowledge the sexuality of not only women but children, he nevertheless continued the practice of assigning women to the libidinal realm. Women "represent the interests of family and of sexual life," he once wrote, men "the claims of culture."[25]

Historically speaking, feminism grew out of the same dialectic. As a major player in the modernist project advanced by both Marx and Freud, early feminists likewise addressed the relationship between work and sex, production and reproduction. The emergence of the so-called Woman Question in the bourgeois epoch was as much a consequence of as a reaction to structural shifts in the relationship between these two realms, that is, the division of society into "public" and "private" that accompanied the rise of capitalism and the liberal state. It might be better to say that feminists helped to define modernism against the rigors of these conventions and their detrimental impact on women and men alike. In any case, the so-called separation of spheres that prevailed in contemporary discourse, whether feminist or anti-feminist, found its origins here.

By the end of the nineteenth century the so-called Woman Question pivoted on this division. Social commentators reasoned that the Industrial Revolution, crystallized in the factory system, had divested the household of its productive functions and simultaneously catapulted men into the marketplace to be the family's chief breadwinner. The household meanwhile became a "home" where women reared children to adulthood and provided emotional rejuvenation to husbands worn thin by their "public" duties. This separation of spheres mirrored not so much the actual situations of men and women as the consolidating ideology of the sex/gender system as we still know it today. All modernist discourse, if only implicitly, concerns the significance of this division.[26]

Over the course of the twentieth century, feminists—as well as psychoanalysts (and Marxists)—struggled with the implications of this discursive arrangement. A large number demanded women's right to participate fully and equally in the realm of production, insisting on nothing less than the elimination of all constraints on access to the public sphere, including education, law, politics, as well as economics. Those following Marx believed that the inner logic of capitalism promised a solution, however painful the process. The mode of production, defining every relation according to its own needs, would eventually subvert the sexual division of labor by transforming women (as well as children) "into simple articles of commerce and instruments of labor."[27] Women would inevitably join the ranks of the proletariat to wage the grand campaign for human liberation. But there were also feminists, perhaps the numerical majority, who believed that women have a special relation to reproduction.

Freud presented his own reading of the situation. He not only assigned the "interests of the family" to women but declared that the "work of civilization has become increasingly the business of men." Moreover, this all-important work confronts men with "ever more difficult tasks and compels them to carry out instinctual sublimations of which women are little capable." Facing such pressure, men form even tighter associations with one another, he reasoned. "Thus the woman finds herself forced into the background by the claims of civilization," Freud determined, "and she adopts a hostile attitude towards it."[28]

Very few feminists have agreed with Freud's conclusion. They have often disagreed among themselves on where the emphasis should lie yet have generally allowed for both possibilities. Some feminists have demanded equality as a matter of simple justice, as a fulfillment of the principle of government by consent. They have also argued that women be allowed to contribute to public life on the basis of their distinctive capacity to reproduce. Quite a few have argued that men's exclusive claim on civilization has pushed humanity not toward some higher goal but to the brink of destruction. But if Freud's answer appeared too pat, feminists themselves across several generations observed a constantly shifting relationship between motherhood and citizenship, broadly defined. Are these categories mutually exclusive, coterminous, or simply irrelevant to women's self-definition in modern society?

My main narrative charts these various possibilities. Plainly, the "business of civilization" has not, as Freud among others anticipated, become increasingly the exclusive purview of men—however much the century's powerbrokers believe that it should. As a consequence, in seeking to establish the connections (as well as disconnections) between feminism and psychoanalysis, I do not focus on sexuality as such. One cannot begin a story with Freud without giving sex its due. Nevertheless, to a large extent my attention centers on a seemingly more prosaic rivalry in the annals of modern feminism, the conflict between motherhood and careers. What stands out is the increasing determination of Freud's successors to tighten the nexus between the spheres of production and reproduction. The alignment of psychoanalysis and feminism ultimately depends on the theoretical fluidity of these two realms as competing sources of subjectivity.

This book is by and large a standard history of ideas, although it covers far-flung intellectual tendencies rarely seen in intimate relation to one another. Only occasionally (and mostly for comic relief) do I succumb to the powerful lure of psychoanalytic reasoning so as to perpetuate a practice known as "psychoanalyzing psychoanalysis." And I inevitably always return to the book's initiating impulse, the problems and issues within feminist scholarship.

During the early 1970s, when women's studies took shape as an academic endeavor, teachers often introduced students to the new field in a standard course on feminist thought. They usually approached the subject historically, presenting excerpts from essays by Mary Wollstonecraft, Margaret Fuller, John Stuart Mill, Charlotte Perkins Gilman, Emma Goldman, Virginia Woolf, Simone de Beauvoir, and perhaps Angela Davis or Kate Millett.

By the 1980s courses on feminist "theory" had replaced those on feminist "thought." The new study focused on writings published since 1970, often organized around various strains of contemporary feminism, such as socialist, radical, cultural, or postmodern. In some cases teachers narrowed the field even further. Feminist theory soon became synonymous with the productions of writers influenced by poststructuralism or directly by psychoanalysis itself. At the same time the historical dimensions of feminism became the exclusive concern of specialists in the discipline of history. Alice Jardine has described this development in generational terms. She notes that academic feminists have been "brutally stylized" as "history-minded mothers and theory-minded daughters."[29] As the century draws to a close, one is tempted to speak of the granddaughters who face the exhaustion of one more paradigm and who will, it is hoped, find their own way forward.

Outside the academy Freud continues to rank among the century's great misogynists, just as in the university setting psychoanalytic theories and precepts set a standard of sophistication and elegance. Although now confronted with the gloomy prospect of fragmentation and waning credibility as cutting-edge methodology, psychoanalysis in some form has influenced nearly every discipline in the humanities if not the social sciences. At least one, literary criticism, emerged as an aesthetic arbiter and model for other fields. Major journals in the field—*Signs, Diacritics, Social Text,* and *Differences* in particular—have lionized this development, while a host of special conferences have highlighted its reign. As early as 1979 the sixth gathering of "The Scholar and the Feminist" at Barnard College previewed the role psychoanalysis would come to play in women's studies scholarship. Several academic publishers have moved into the front ranks by producing extensive lists in this area. The long-run effect of this development is more than ever uncertain, but as a piece of twentieth-century intellectual history, its importance is undeniable.

In this book I provide a historical context for the shift from feminist "thought" to "theory," precisely at the nexus between feminism and psychoanalysis. This approach has been unfashionable for some time, although fashions notoriously depend on new alterations and have perhaps begun to change rather drastically again. It has been common for feminist theorists to view history, in Joan Scott's words, as "a relic of Humanist thought."[30] Not too long ago, an anthropologist cum semiotician, upon learning my field of specialization, responded affably but as if she had met a time-traveler from a distant era: "Wow! I didn't think anyone wrote histories any more." Responding to the recent turns of intellectual events, I purposefully take the long view. In a way, then, my not-too-hidden agenda is the restoration of feminist "theory" to the realm of "thought."

1

Feminism, Freudianism, and Female Subjectivity

Like most other Americans, feminists viewed Freudianism, one popularist noted, as "somehow synonymous with 'sexual.'" According to his spirited interpreters, Freud's studies of anxiety neurosis and neurasthenia not only vividly document the baneful consequences of sexual repression but offer an irrefutable case for honesty in sexual relations. Emma Goldman described Freud's theories as the definitive argument against the "hypocrisy of puritanism" and its code of self-abnegation. Moreover, as Floyd Dell observed, psychoanalysis imparts an aura of "scientific propriety" to a topic that only a few years earlier would have been shunned by most Americans as too "horrific" to consider. The architect of the libido theory thus took his place as the leading expert on the dangers of prudery.[1]

Feminists, however, placed a distinctive spin on Freudianism by declaring it a handmaiden to women's sexual emancipation. With Freud's authority at their service, they exalted the pleasures of sexual encounters, condemned excessive self-restraint, and made it their business to position women at the forefront of this epochal transformation of both behavior and sensibility. In short, while feminists admired Freud for establishing the importance of sexuality, they exalted him for insisting that women and men share the instinct that makes the world go around.

Nevertheless, feminists circa 1910 wanted something more from the founder of psychoanalysis: a theory of *female* sexuality. Although Freud had made a magnificent case for sex as the primary link between the biological and psychic structures, he had not yet drawn out the implications of this proposition for women. Eventually he would issue some earthshaking pronouncements—but not until the 1920s and, then, only in response to critics who faulted him for this shortcoming. For the moment, Freud remained silent. Meanwhile writers in Europe and Great Britain filled the gap, producing scores of treatises on female sexuality.

American feminists did not let Freud's reticence slow them down. To the contrary, they blithely integrated psychoanalytic tenets into the reigning theories of the day to create a potpourri of competing idea-systems. Pushing forward their own concern with female sexuality, they also formulated new recipes for emancipation. Through their imaginative synthetic labors these first-wavers provided the inspiration for an all-out overhaul of Freudianism and feminism alike.

If Freud's American enthusiasts played fast and loose with his theories, they trampled just as recklessly on long-standing principles of women's emancipation. Many veterans of the century-old woman movement did not welcome the hoopla over female sexuality; the formidable Charlotte Perkins Gilman, for one, voiced her complaints quite clearly. Yet, in airing their differences the contestants began to define the principal terms of twentieth-century feminism.

But it was not simply the subject of female sexuality that proved politically pesky. The initial confrontation with psychoanalysis invigorated a debate that had pushed on, at varying degrees of intensity, since Mary Wollstonecraft issued her trailblazing treatise. Should women advance their claims by emphasizing their common humanity with men or by stressing their unique qualities as women? Should women aspire to gain equality in civil society or to profit from their special functions within the family? Throughout the nineteenth century, political activists grappled with these questions. However, first-wave feminists were the first to formulate them in distinctly modern terms, that is, as strategies grounded not simply in social utility or womanly duty but in self-realization. In sum, the fuss created by the quest for erotic pleasure tended to disguise a major facet of the feminist enterprise: the search for female subjectivity. In advancing this agenda, Freud's enthusiasts disrupted an older view of womanhood, thereby creating a rupture in the ranks that would not heal.

That such a small contingent could upset long-standing strategies for women's advancement makes their embrace of Freud all the more vital to the history of American feminism. Equally important, in their relentless refashioning of Freudianism, feminists were to play just as prominent a role in the history of psychoanalysis. True, these first-wavers boasted few original thinkers or strategists, achieving coherence only in the short-lived campaign for birth control. And, if Freud and his followers despaired over the distortion of psychoanalysis in the hands of American popularizers, they could point directly to feminists. In the space of a few years American feminists managed to push Freudianism to its limit and to pose a series of questions about female subjectivity that became increasingly hard to ignore.

The Sexual Emancipation of Women

Freud's admirers joined a long line of American reformers who had tagged sexuality as a key political issue. Nineteenth-century communitarians had made sex a principle of social organization. The Shaker leader "Mother" Ann Lee, along with many other pietists, sought to banish it entirely from communal society; "Father" John Humphrey Noyes of the famous Oneida colony sought to regulate its practice. In the 1820s Frances Wright advocated free unions in place of legal marriage; by the 1870s the "short haired women and long haired men" of Victoria Woodhull's entourage had endorsed her pledge to love anyone for as long or as short a time as she pleased; and two decades later the free-lover Lois Waisbrooker published *The Fountain of Life: or, The Threefold Power of Sex* (1893), proclaiming sex magnetism the foundation of all social relations. Less upbeat were the administrators of women's colleges who voiced their disapproval of the "special relationships" students and teachers enjoyed and the "Boston marriages" some adult women preferred. Similarly circumspect were Theodore Roosevelt and other prominent leaders who lamented the falling birth rate among white Protestants and predicted "race suicide" unless the "better stock" restored its procreative habits. Meanwhile campaigners against prostitution and for "social purity" gained strength in a succession of battles to form a sizable component of Progressive-era reform.

By the turn of the century hardly anyone could doubt that sex ranked next to war and the stock market as a matter of supreme importance. As one eminent physician put it: "I am beginning to think that the future will look back upon the present day and generation as having gone sex-mad."[2]

What was novel in this round was the element feminists found so appealing in Freud's theories—the recognition of passion in women. Not everyone entered the discussion so gingerly. Social workers bristled at the conversations they overheard among working women and noted the "smutty talk," off-color jokes, and casual exchange of sexual advice concerning both lovers and husbands. One shocked member of the gentility described this banter, always issued in the spirit of "good-natured comradeship" but punctuated by "the most vile epithets that [she] ever heard from the mouth of a human being." Off the job, working women appeared to social workers to spend their leisure hours solely in pursuit of men. They congregated in movie houses, amusement parks, and dance halls, where they expressed their intentions even more graphically. "Spieling," "pivoting," and "tough dancing" accented body contact and sensual, rhythmic movements. Those women on the sidelines, hardly wallflowers, openly hugged and kissed their partners for the evening. The rapid growth in the population of wage-earning women, up 60 percent since the 1870s, undoubtedly magnified this trend. But middle-class women evidently felt similar urges. One coed confided to her diary that she was always honest with men, telling them she was not bargaining for a promise of marriage; rather, "this intimacy was pleasant and I wanted it as much as they did." All in all, the novelist Gertrude Atherton reflected, young women seemed "determined to have their fling like men," and the tales they told made even her "sophisticated hair crackle at the roots."[3]

Female desire was finally emerging from the shadows, and this epochal event signified much more than what Michel Foucault later termed "a veritable discursive explosion."[4] The gynecologist Clelia Mosher had surveyed her clients born between 1850 and 1880 and found that while the majority usually enjoyed sexual intercourse with their husbands they preferred to engage in moderation. Women born closer to the turn of the century appeared considerably more enthusiastic and, at the same time, less willing to confine their ecstasy to marriage. Contemporary risqué humor confirmed this trend:

> A man enters a drugstore for a cure for his persistent erection. He is embarrassed to find only a woman attendant, but explains his trouble to her when she assures him he can speak freely. "Well," he says, "I've had this hardon for three days, and it won't go down. What can you give me for it?" She disappears into the back of the store, and returns a few minutes later, saying, "I've talked it over with my sister, who's my partner here and makes up the prescriptions, and the best we can give you is the store and two hundred dollars."[5]

Almost imperceptibly at first, woman was becoming an agent of her own passion rather than merely an object—or, worse, a victim—of man's.

Feminists defined themselves by celebrating this shift in attitude and behavior. Unlike their reforming forerunners a generation earlier, these women, mainly between the ages of twenty and forty, rallied against masculine privilege in the sexual arena mainly to demand more prerogatives for themselves. In the nation's major cities—Chicago, Boston, and especially New York—feminists launched the birth-control campaign, advocating smaller family size as well as women's right to nonprocreative sexual pleasure. As writers, they helped to forge literary modernism, recording female desire in numerous novels, memoirs, and plays. Evocative poems such as Annette Wynne's "Her Veins Are Lit with Strange Desire" and Gladys Oaks's "Climax" appeared in the radical magazine *The Masses* and its successor, *The Liberator*. In New York, where feminists had achieved a critical mass, they met to discuss these matters in clubs such as Heterodoxy, which sponsored biweekly luncheons followed by hours of conversation; or informally, with men, in coffeehouses and apartments. In their private lives, the most adventurous, such as Louise Bryant, Crystal Eastman, and Margaret Anderson, experimented with new forms of sexual liaisons, running a gamut from casual affairs, "semi-detached" marriages, to long-lasting same-sex relationships. The memoirs of Mabel Dodge Luhan, Emma Goldman, and Neith Boyce as well as Hutchins Hapgood, Max

Eastman, and Floyd Dell suggest that nearly everyone in their circle was striving to create satisfying alternatives to the sexual norms maintained so piously by their parents' generation.[6]

Exuberant as well as determined, feminists understood full well that sexual experimentation carried specific risks for women. They observed their Greenwich Village neighbors, mainly young Italian women, whose challenge to the rules set by their fathers too often resulted in tragedy. Working as a nurse in lower Manhattan, Margaret Sanger witnessed first hand the manifold dangers accompanying unwanted pregnancy and cheap abortions, the knowledge of which made her own "happy love life" seem "a reproach." But Sanger also knew that even her middle-class peers endured hardships in relationships inevitably weighted in men's favor. Her own marriage failed to survive the test of innovation. The novelist Neith Boyce confessed that the open marriage she and Hutchins Hapgood tried to maintain proved a far better deal for him than for her. He unwittingly provided the evidence for her claim in a memoir so graphic and self-centered that an anonymous byline could not disguise its authorship. Even Emma Goldman, whose autobiography exudes sexual self-confidence, found her own needs repeatedly subordinated to her partner's ego.[7]

Yet, for the most part, as mainly college-educated and professional women, feminists anticipated victory and sought to publicize their efforts. Uprooted from their families of origin, they took advantage of their privileges, which often included incomes large enough to pay for their own residences. With few kin around to monitor their behavior, and enough money to support their chosen lifestyles, feminists could not only experiment more freely but reflect more openly on the consequences than could their working-class contemporaries. Remarkable is the amount of contemplation their behavior inspired. In this regard, the introspective techniques of psychoanalysis served their purposes quite well.

These feminists acclaimed Freud as a leading authority on the "repeal of reticence" so central to their own lives. As the Heterodoxy member Elsie Clews Parsons put it, Freud's theories revealed that marriage is, above all, the institutional means by which "the natural sex life of the individual" is sacrificed to the demands of the group. Most of all, feminists appreciated Freud's distinctively modern assumption that one's sense of self is linked to sexuality, personality to its expression, and civilization to its management. Mabel Dodge Luhan (1879–1962), for example, stressed the importance of sexual encounters to her feeling of well-being. She described sexuality as self-defining, a principal means of affirming existence, and avidly promoted its virtues. Luhan could imagine no higher tribute to Sanger than to pronounce the famous birth-control advocate "an ardent propagandist for the joys of the flesh." In the same vein, Goldman acknowledged her gratitude to Freud. It was his work, she claimed, that allowed her to identify clearly her own sexual needs and to grasp "the full significance of sex repression." In sum, Freud's definition of sexuality charmed these feminists: a primary instinct *in both sexes*, distinct from procreative imperatives and driven by the singular aim of gaining pleasure.[8]

But Freud alone did not—indeed, could not—fully satisfy feminists' curiosity. His theories added new dimensions to their understanding of, for example, the role of the unconscious in obscuring psychic realities. His therapeutic methods of dealing directly with the personal ramifications of this process tickled their fancy, as did his equally innovative interpretation of dreams. Freud's insistence on the infantile origins of adult sexuality, especially his portrayal of the Oedipus complex, encouraged their penchant for retrospection. Even better was Freud's observation that "the great majority of severe neuroses in women have their origin in the marriage bed."[9] But despite his talent for depicting the malignant manifestations of sexual repression, Freud revealed very little about the matter so vital to feminists—the mysteries of *female* sexuality and femininity.

Despite their powers of perception, neither Freud nor his American devotees could fathom the full social implications of these changes. On the practical side, women could now demand rights in the bedroom that would have made their mothers blush and fathers steam. Although eager to claim these rights, feminists sensed that more was at stake than the birth of a new morality. But what did these new pleasures and dangers really mean? Although unprepared to provide a clear answer to this question, feminists, like Freud, were coming to understand sexuality as the leading indicator of selfhood or, as later generations would put it, subjectivity.

This historic milepost thus marked the debut of a new sexual morality and, equally important, a new and decidedly modern definition of femininity. Ironically in light of the approaching victory of woman suffrage, long considered the major symbol of equality in the public sphere, feminists turned to the ostensibly private arena of sexuality to discover women's true difference from men. The contemporary religious scholar George Burman Foster aptly summed up the "philosophy of feminism": "Woman is to be a free self but it is a *woman's* self that she is to be."[10]

Feminists did not turn to psychoanalysis only to justify their sexual rebellion or to ease the pain of transition. They hoped to gain from Freud a comprehensive theory of selfhood, one that would delineate the differences between the sexes and demarcate the special psychic parameters of femininity. For all its amazing and revelatory qualities, at this moment the Freudian canon could not satisfy their expectations.

What Freud Lacked

The "virtual author of sexual modernism" wrote surprisingly little on female sexuality or femininity, the very subjects that would bring him fame and, later, notoriety. Many of Freud's essays pertain to sexuality—over thirty directly address the topic—but only three brief essays and three case studies concern female psychosexual development. This oversight is especially perplexing in that female patients supplied the bulk of the data. The six major case studies completed before 1900, as well as the overwhelming majority—34 of 48—of Freud's minor studies, register extensive clinical experience with women. But, to Freud, female sexuality represented a "dark continent" not particularly worth exploring.[11]

Without comment, Freud forged his landmark "sexual thesis" investigating hysteria, an illness considered especially acute among women, its very name derived from the Greek word for womb. Rejecting the commonplace diagnosis as either neurological disease or willful malingering, he declared hysteria a sexual disturbance. This mysterious malady, Freud concluded, was merely the "dammed up libido" seeking an outlet in symptoms ranging from facial tics to debilitating neurosis. *Studies on Hysteria* (1895), written with Josef Breuer, follows this line of reasoning and culminates in a prescription for psychoanalysis, the "talking cure," whereby the patient comes to terms with the "primal experience" of early childhood that presumably sparked the fateful repression of sexual desire. But in terms of female psychology, this text offers little more than an incidental observation that men and women tend to present different symptoms.

Freud's most acclaimed study of a hysteric discloses such a huge blind spot that the celebrated case of "Dora" documents more clearly the author's own avoidance mechanisms. Here Freud claims to describe in minute detail the "human and social circumstances" producing his patient's hysterical coughing and aphonia, and he interprets Dora's bitter and "monotonous" complaints against her father as indicating thwarted incestuous desire. Considerably less significant to Freud is the fact that Dora's father has sexually bartered his sixteen-year-old daughter to a middle-aged businessman in order to secure for himself an illicit liaison with the businessman's wife. This case study, first published in 1905, elaborates important elements of Freud's larger theory, including transference, bisexuality, and dream analysis, but reveals minimal insight into the dynamics of a blatantly troubled relationship between father and daughter.[12]

One essay, however, came very close to making a special plea on behalf of women. " 'Civilized' Sexual Morality and Modern Nervous Illness" (1908), endorses the "repeal of reticence" sweeping Western Europe and argues forcefully for the sexual enlightenment of women in particular. As usual, Freud pitted the pleasure of the individual against the requirements of society, arguing that civilization had been built on "the suppression of instinct." A minority, mainly scholars and artists, survive this restriction, he noted, by sublimating their sexual desire for creative ends; a far larger number, disproportionately female, "become neurotic" and prove in their mental disability "hostile to civilization." The responsibility lies with parents who, in hoping to safeguard their daughters' chastity, keep them in the dark about sexuality. As a consequence, young women go to their wedding beds unprepared and, in their ignorance and fear, experience not the joys of sexual intimacy but psychic trauma. Women's intellectual inferiority, Freud added, could be traced to the "inhibition of thought necessitated by sexual suppression"—a notion that appealed enormously to Emma Goldman.

Yet, even here, at his most sympathetic, Freud remained preoccupied with men. After acknowledging that sexual repression fell heaviest on women, he suggested that it was their mates who suffered most from this "artificial retardation" of women's sexual instinct. Woman, "the actual vehicle of the sexual interests of mankind," he lamented, has "nothing but disappointments to offer the man who has saved up all his desire for her."[13]

As even his own closest colleagues noted, Freud appeared reluctant to delineate the differences between the sexes. His foundational *Three Essays on a Theory of Sexuality* (1905) offers little commentary on this subject. Published in translation in the United States in 1910, this monograph stirred considerable controversy in its bold depiction of sexual aberrations and infantile sexuality. But in terms of contemporary feminism, *Three Essays* offers a contrary thesis by raising a big question mark over the popular proposition that "a human being is either a man or a woman."

Freud actually argued against true psychological types defined by sex. He began by distinguishing between *sexual aim*, "the act towards which the instinct tends," and *sexual object*, "the person from whom sexual attraction proceeds"; and went on to illustrate just how shaky the connection is. So flimsy, according to Freud, "that the problem that needs elucidating" is adult heterosexuality, that is, "the exclusive sexual interest felt by men for women." Nor was he about to compartmentalize individuals according to sex. "Pure masculinity or femininity is not to be found," he insisted, "either in a psychological or a biological sense." To the contrary, Freud insisted that the psychic components of the opposite sex function to varying degrees in everyone.

If anything, Freud tended to minimalize the differences between the sexes. According to his theory of infantile bisexuality, introduced in *Three Essays*, everyone begins life without a mental or emotional awareness of sexual differentiation. In other words, the individual is not born with a specific sexual disposition but instead acquires a sense of masculinity or femininity only through highly complex and woefully precarious processes of psychosexual development. Moreover, as an individual painfully emerges from the pleasurable polymorphous perverse activities of infancy to an adult sexuality dominated by the genital zone, the potential for deviation is great. *Three Essays* thus makes a powerful argument for a continuing and relentless relationship between childhood and adult sexuality. It also casts the major distinctions between the sexes as products of thoroughly uncertain, and not particularly enjoyable, stages of psychic development.

In this essay Freud appeared to go out of his way to stress the symmetry of male and female psychosexual development. He noted anatomical discrepancies as well as subtle variations in the characters of adult men and women but nevertheless insisted upon the uniformity of sexuality, at least up to a certain point. "The autoerotic activity of the erogenous zones is . . . the same in both sexes," Freud contended, the clitoris being homologous to the penis. Nor is there a difference in sexual drive. The libido, he explained, is "invariably and necessarily of a masculine nature," using the descriptive adjective to convey "activity" rather than any conventional character trait attributed to men. Although Freud noted the existence of penis envy in young girls, he did not yet spell out how this "important wish" influences female development. Rather, he repeated the commonplace notion that the distinctions between the sexes become pronounced only during puberty, when the "sexual instinct is now subordinated to the reproductive function." Freud did not elucidate, however, beyond observing that while puberty represents "so great an accession of libido" for boys, it inaugurates "a fresh wave of *repression*" for girls. And he owned up to the inadequacy of these remarks. Men's erotic life "has become accessible to research," he absolved himself, while women's "is still veiled in impenetrable obscurity."[14]

Excuses aside, in his hesitation to comment on female sexuality Freud was unique among his peers. The majority of scientific investigators at the turn of the century were eager to discover fundamental tendencies and to map essential differences. A large number followed the intellectual tracks of Charles Darwin, whose *The Descent of Man and Selection in Relation to Sex* (1871) interprets woman's status in society as coterminous with her biology, that is, her reproductive function. Woman, according to the great evolutionist, remained closer to nature than did man, more conservative and truer to type than the agent of exploration and conquest, more primitive in sexual needs and desires than the pleasure-seeking and adventurous male.

Others closer to Freud such as the rampant Viennese misogynist Otto Weininger speculated with no apparent restraint on the distinctive qualities of female sexuality. Weininger's *Sex and Character: A Psychological Study* (1903), which was translated from the German and published in the United States in 1908, intricately correlates "male" and "female" physiognomy, sexuality, and character traits, in each instance to woman's disadvantage. Unlike Freud, Weininger did not hesitate to define the nature of woman. He claimed this prerogative for clear-thinking men like himself. Women are incapable of even this task because, he argued, they lack reason and objectivity. The fact that *Sex and Character* went through twenty-six printings by 1925 did not undermine Freud's judgment of it as a "shoddy piece of work" that could not possibly be taken seriously.[15] Weininger's treatise nevertheless made a big splash, and feminist reviewers in several nations reviled it.

Its excessive misogyny aside, *Sex and Character* was more typical of the growing number of books and essays on female sexuality than were Freud's early works. Marking out one place on a spectrum of opinions, Weininger correctly calculated the enormous energy his contemporaries would expend in analyzing and assessing the differences between the sexes. Freud thus shunned what his contemporaries avidly pursued.

Freud directed the psychoanalytic project along an independent course to emphasize not intrinsic distinctions but their psychic representation. In "The Sexual Theories of Children" (1908), he wrote: "If we could divest ourselves of our corporeal existence, and could view the things of this earth with a fresh eye as purely thinking beings, from another planet for instance, nothing perhaps would strike our attention more forcibly than the fact of the existence of two sexes among human beings, who, though so much alike in other respects, yet mark the differences between them with such obvious external signs."

What intrigued Freud was that children do not exhibit such power of discernment. Boys and girls, Freud noted, recognize only one sex and attribute *"to everyone, including females, the possession of a penis."* There is some logic to this proposition, he related, because the clitoris "behaves in fact during childhood like a real and genuine penis." In their curiosity about the origin of babies, children may come close to imagining the presence of the vagina in women but invariably stop short to remain "in helpless perplexity." They "refuse to grant women the painful prerogative of giving birth to children," preferring instead to imagine the anus as a sex-neutral reproductive site. Even teenagers, who often hear graphic stories about sexual intercourse, prefer to cling to their "false ideas." Only upon reaching maturity do men and women fully acknowledge the differences between the sexes, including woman's role in reproduction, and only at this stage does sexuality become understood as not only dualistic but biologically determined.

The significance of this "dogma" of sexual difference cannot be overestimated, according to Freud, and he was to devote much of his life to its exploration. But what stands out in this early essay is a singular focus on male psychosexual development. Freud justified this emphasis by claiming that his data were biased to such a degree that even these admittedly fragmentary hypotheses "apply chiefly to the sexual development of one sex only—that is, of males."

At this point Freud had not even taken up the subject that would become his signature for later generations of feminists: penis envy. He did note that a girl becomes a woman only at puberty when she abandons the unique pleasures of the clitoris for those of the vagina. And should she refuse to relinquish the "small penis," the consequences were dire, namely, frigidity or excessive repression leading to hysteria. But Freud went no further. He presented the concept of genital transference mainly to underscore the partial validity of the childhood proposition that women, like men, possess a penis. In short, he restated his belief in the undifferentiated quality of childhood sexuality and offered only the dimmest glimpse into the mysteries of female sexuality.[16]

Freud's reluctance to spell out the differences between the sexes did not seem to bother American feminists. With few psychoanalytic texts available in English and the number of interpretive studies still quite small, they viewed Freud as a great emancipator and generously credited him with the most astounding revelations about human sexuality. There was no question that Freud had certified female desire—even desire gone awry, as in the case of Dora, who had disclosed "*gynaecophilic* currents of feeling." Most important, Freud had demonstrated the centrality of the sexual instinct to the emotional well-being of both men and women. He issued a mandate for a sweeping denunciation of traditional sexual morality and provided a distinctive rhetoric to make the case. Whatever gaps remained in his doctrine could easily be filled in because scores of other scholars had produced an abundance of speculative literature. There was, feminists recognized, no shortage of ideas on female sexuality, however biased or ill-founded. In any case, as the Harvard-based promoter James J. Putnam noted in introducing the 1910 American edition of the *Three Essays,* Freud's genius lay in working out "the part which the instinct plays in every phase of human life and in the development of human character" and not in describing the many facets of human sexuality.[17]

In this first round, American feminists more than made up for Freud's shortcomings. Without thinking twice, they assimilated the agreeable and available parts of Freud's system into a stunning amalgam of theories concerning female sexuality. More often than not, his most enthusiastic fans attributed to the Viennese thinker ideas sharply at odds with his own predilections. Furthermore, they disguised ideas extraneous to Freud's system by cloaking them in the distinctive terminology of psychoanalysis. Such eclectic readings foreshadowed the impudent "Americanization" of Freud's theories in the 1920s and inaugurated the continuous interplay of experts and popularists that would shape the history of psychoanalysis in the United States. But by taking such liberties, feminists ultimately succeeded in making female sexuality and femininity central to the entire psychoanalytic project.

Toward a Feminist Theory of Female Sexuality

When it came to getting down to essentials, so to speak, American feminists by necessity combed the works of other experts on the subject. In fact, they profited intellectually from quite a few other writers, mainly men, who described female sexuality in rich and generous detail. Moving through and beyond the available writings of Freud to a circle of British sexologists and the most up-to-date theorists on the continent, feminists found what Freud's theories lacked: a seemingly timeless, thus irrepressible marker of sexual difference.

The most influential writers were the ones who, like Freud, promoted sexual enlightenment if not the emancipation of women in particular. Since the 1880s a movement had been gathering force across Europe, and by the time Americans embraced Freud and feminism, the New Morality (*Die Neue Ethik* in Germany) enjoyed a sizable following. The British Society for the Study of Sex Psychology and its continental counterpart, the Institut für Sexualwissenschaft, engaged physicians, philosophers, and proselytizers of various kinds to spread the word and to establish the new science of sexology. Belatedly, and in a sudden rush around 1910, these currents reached American shores. *The Masses* soon ran advertisements for the most notable titles in this genre, which included the few translated volumes by Freud. The radical magazine also conducted a book service to track down the more recondite sources, those ponderous tracts, the *scientia sexualis*, that had begun, in Foucault's words, "to keep an indefinite record of . . . people's pleasures," describing and classifying "their everyday deficiencies as well as their oddities or exasperations." Readers in the United States could savor the recently translated essays of the foremost European writers on sexuality such as Emil Lucka, Magnus Hirschfeld, Jean Finot, Auguste Forel, and Iwan Bloch. They reserved a special place for the most frequently cited Richard von Krafft-Ebing, whose massive *Psychopathia Sexualis* (1892) mapped "deviant" practices.[18]

For American feminists, the British New Moralists stood at the top of this list. Against the decorum of "polite society," the leading proponents Havelock Ellis (1859–1939) and Edward Carpenter (1844–1929) discussed sex as both "natural" and "healthy," a drive akin to hunger that demands satisfaction. Ellis's masterwork, the six-volume *Studies in the Psychology of Sex* (published in Philadelphia between 1897 and 1910), designates sex as "the chief and central function of life." Ellis amassed evidence ranging from historical and anthropological data to his own case studies to illustrate the wide range of sexual practices and an equally wide range of acceptance. He studied modesty, sexual periodicity (including menstrual determinants), autoeroticism and narcissism, and the erogenous zones. He wrote an entire volume on homosexuality entitled *Sexual Inversion* and argued against its commonplace classification as sickness or disease.

Ellis, in sum, had joined Freud in expanding the "normal" range of practices. He applauded Freud's propositions, especially his diagnosis of hysteria, and cited his works frequently. Ellis, however, surpassed Freud in condemning the current restraints upon passion and variety —especially the enforced monogamy of institutionalized marriage— as unnatural, harmful, and dangerous. And there was at least one monumental discrepancy. Whereas Freud underscored the problematical nature of sexuality in describing its complex, often incomplete processes, Ellis and his peers reversed the valence. A true visionary,

Edward Carpenter—with Oscar Wilde, arguably the only avowed homosexual writers to play a prominent role in socialist movements for generations—defined sex as "the allegory of love in the physical world" and assigned to this "fact" its "immense power." To Ellis, sex was, simply, "ever wonderful, ever lovely."[19]

The American appropriators of the New Morality proceeded blithely, squeezing Freud's theories into this more appealing framework. The admiring Floyd Dell later recalled that lustful men routinely quoted Carpenter and Ellis to convince women "that love without marriage was infinitely superior to the other kind, and that its immediate indulgence brought the world, night by night, a little nearer to freedom and Utopia." Contemporary feminists such as Margaret Sanger, who studied with Ellis, needed no convincing. Like her mentor, who described the sexual instinct as the primordial source of beauty, Sanger herself deemed sexuality "the strongest force in all living creatures . . . that inspires man to the highest and noblest thoughts; to all material endeavors and achievements, and to art and poetry." Even Freud's chief American translator, the psychoanalyst Abraham A. Brill, bore the imprint of this trend, treating the libido as a salutary source of creative energy.[20]

What pushed the New Morality over the top for American feminists, though, was a determination to take this blissful interpretation two steps further, first claiming for woman a capacity for sexual pleasure greater than man's and then extolling the significance of this wonder for the entire civilization. Ellis, who had been documenting the differences between the sexes for several years preceding the publication of his popular *Man and Woman: A Study in Human Secondary Sexual Characters* (1894), had come to a conclusion opposite to Freud's. It is less necessary to deal broadly with male sexuality, Ellis surmised, precisely because it is "predominantly open and aggressive" and encoded in social customs and civil law. Female sexuality, more "elusive," complex, and secreted by enclosed genitals, represented a more compelling and more weighty challenge. It was no small matter, for example, that men are more easily aroused, whereas women demand extensive courtship or foreplay; or that the sexual impulse in women "is at once larger and more diffused," involving a greater portion of body as well as mind, whereas male sexuality is "focused to a single point . . . the ejaculation of semen into the vagina." These biological differences, in Ellis's opinion, open a window to "those wider psychological characteristics by which women differ from men." They are, moreover, not acquired, as Freud reasoned, but intrinsic. Over the long evolutionary course of society, Ellis insisted, these "fundamental tendencies" may become obscured or suppressed, but in the final instance the differences between the sexes persist and serve as the motive force of existence.[21]

It was Ellis's compatriot Edward Carpenter, the first president of the British Sexological Society, who drew out the political significance of these observations. His major and very popular work, *Love's Coming of Age,* was published in Chicago by Stockham Publishing Company in 1900 and again in 1902 by the socialist house of Charles H. Kerr before making the list of a major New York firm in 1911. Here Carpenter greatly surpassed Freud. He described woman as sexual beyond previous imagination and, at the same time, remarkably suited for a task requiring dispassion—the advancement of civilization. Carpenter crisply formulated the seductive premise, claiming that women's instincts, "so clean, so direct, so well-rooted in the needs of the race," transform sex from "unorganized passion" into "constructive instinct." The sexually liberated woman, he opined, "will help us to undo the bands of death which encircle the present society, and open the doors to a new and wider life." Here, as sexual modernism and old-fashioned romanticism join hands to reinscribe the differences between the sexes, female sexuality gains both distinctive definition and titanic social purpose totally at odds with Freud's notions.[22]

What set the New Moralists apart from Freud was not their affirmation of female desire but their unbridled reverence for woman's capacity to bear children. Of course, Freud had also linked adult sexuality to the reproductive imperative. But whereas he defined this association as a developmental process, Ellis and Carpenter assumed that for woman the desire to bear children is nothing less than essential to her being. Thus Ellis asserted that "in a certain sense . . . [women's] brains are in their wombs." Freud might not have disagreed with this problematical proposition, but he was unwilling to explore the meaning of motherhood either for women themselves or for civilization at large. In contrast, the New Moralists enshrined the capacity for reproduction as women's special claim and thus the definitive marker of their difference from men. Unlike Freud, who envisioned no purpose for women beyond procreation and who attached little significance to this fact, the New Moralists endowed women with unique powers to advance civilization and for this reason welcomed both their sexual freedom and their advancement into civil society. This exaltation of motherhood became a vital element in contemporary European writings on women's emancipation.[23]

While Freud was relegating maternal factors to the margins of psychoanalytic theory, the prominent Swedish educator Ellen Key (1849–1926) was refashioning the basic tenets of the New Morality into a powerful political argument. Acclaimed throughout Central Europe well before her first books were translated into English, Key soon captured a sizable American audience. In the 1910s, while Freud's early essays were making their way across the Atlantic, Key's moved much more rapidly in the same direction. Along with Ellis, Key offered Americans an explicitly political statement.

At the center of Key's system was woman's reproductive capacity. Like Carpenter and Ellis, Key disregarded what was novel in Freud's theory, the untangling of the sexual drive from reproduction. Freud reasoned that only the attainment of pleasure sparks development; and that not until the arrival of puberty, that is, during the last phase of sexual organization, does the sexual life achieve "its final, normal shape" and give way to the reproductive function.[24] Key agreed to a point. She had no intention of confounding sexual impulse and maternal instinct. To the contrary, she denounced the Victorian practice of subordinating woman's sexual desire to her reproductive destiny. But Key struck out against the remnants of this repressive morality in a different direction, by sexualizing maternity. In her schema, it was the reproductive imperative that triggered sexual desire and, consequently, made that desire all the more critical to the psychological makeup of women.

It was on this basis that Key formulated a theory that heightened the differences between the sexes. Given their dissimilar roles in reproduction, men and women must diverge socially as well as sexually and psychologically, she concluded. According to her chief American publicist, Key heralded the emancipation of woman "both as a human-being and as a sex-being." In short, she acknowledged woman's common humanity with man but refused to sacrifice her special prerogatives as mother to an abstract ideal of equality.[25]

Key's major work, *Love and Marriage* (1904), published in the United States in 1911, actually added little to the etiology of female sexuality but made a forceful argument for its political significance. Key joined both Freud and the New Moralists in waging an assault on conventional morality, particularly the overvaluation of womanly purity. But she clearly sided with Ellis, who wrote an introduction to the American edition, in extolling the beauty of sexual passion and the joy and perfection of Eros; and she joined him in calling for a "new love" based solely on the "natural attraction of man and woman to each other for the continuance of the race" without regard to either civil or clerical law. For Key, the profound "difference of instinct" between men and women must serve as a basis of a new social order.

Key gained international renown espousing a singularly *feminine* feminism and encouraged numerous activists throughout Scandinavia, Germany, Austria, and Great Britain to organize under this banner. Economic and political rights remained important in her vision, but the demand for equality paled alongside the attainment of a uniquely female destiny. Speaking in Copenhagen in 1896, Key introduced a new slogan to mobilize women, *"Missbrauchte Frauenkraft,"* which was translated variously into English as "Misused Female Powers" and "The Abuse of Woman's Strength." Its meaning, however, was clear. Key criticized the historic woman movement for inappropriately raising masculine standards, encouraging women, for example, to adapt to men's model of success by seeking fulfillment in careers. Women must instead act on their difference from men, she insisted. Key was so committed to this faith that she regularly advised women "to preserve their possibilities of erotic attraction" by rejecting the unsavory model of "mannish emancipated ladies." Women must demand freedom on the ground of dissimilarity. This mandate overrode all others, according to Key, including the long-standing demands for equal wages and the vote. It also fired "that phase of the woman movement which," as her American promoter Katharine Anthony put it, "seeks to liberate and empower the mother in woman."[26]

On the continent, the Mutterschütz movement followed Key in claiming for women the special ecstasy of motherhood. Its leaders promoted sexual enlightenment in general and demanded woman's right to bear children under any circumstances she might choose. The legal designation "illegitimate" must be eradicated, its organizers insisted. They therefore sought to sanctify woman's "inward maternal imperative" through a series of campaigns to advance "volitional motherhood over sex slavery." The founding of the Bund für Mutter-schütz (Union for the Protection of Motherhood) in 1905, according to Anthony, rivaled in historical significance the meetings at Seneca Falls, New York, that launched the American woman's rights movement in 1848. Its program was, simply, revolutionary.[27]

To many of her contemporaries and future historians alike, Key proved difficult to classify along either radical or conservative lines. As a socialist, she endorsed women's right to labor and called upon the state to guarantee their financial independence. She quickly shaded into conservatism by qualifying this demand, advocating a restriction of their employment either directly to child care or to the helping professions. But even in rejecting what she labeled derisively as "amaternal feminism," Key offered radical alternatives to existing institutions. She rejected marriage outright as the foundation of patriarchy and questioned the merits of monogamy. Programmatically, she sought to abolish the stigma of illegitimacy and advocated the creation of a state-sponsored maternal welfare program, a "motherhood endowment" for all women regardless of marital status. Hers was a vision of what later generations of feminists would term radical separatism. Women must be able to live, love, and work free from the interference of men, she insisted. Thus, what appeared merely old-fashioned in Key's reverence for maternity was undercut by her demand for an entirely new context for sexuality and purpose for procreation.

Ellen Key took Americans by storm. One reviewer compared *Love and Marriage* favorably to John Stuart Mill's classic treatise and pronounced Key the distinguished liberal philosopher's worthy successor. The Heterodoxy notable Katharine Anthony produced a lengthy volume popularizing her ideas; *Feminism in Germany and Scandinavia* (1915) clarifies the disparities between Anglo-American and continental European feminism with the intention of preparing American women to forge ahead toward liberation once "released from the long struggle for political rights." Floyd Dell expectably applauded Key's ability to cherish "the spiritual magic of sex as the finest achievement of the race" and judged *Love and Marriage* a "revolutionary doctrine," the "Talmud of Sexual Morality." Key's renown filtered even into the realm of popular culture. H. L. Mencken celebrated the charming "Flapper of 1915," who, after reading Ellen Key, decided that "there must be something in this new doctrine of free motherhood" and took a strong stand against "the double standard of morality." Even the fictional bedside table of Fannie Hurst's flapper heroine in *Star-Dust* (1921) featured Key's writings beside Ibsen's and Freud's.[28]

The Swedish writer soon matched Freud in charismatic appeal, found her most impassioned audience among his fans, and supplied them with the elements they found lacking in Freudian theory. Key added a clear political dimension to this enterprise by specifying the parameters of the new path to women's emancipation. Hers was a strategy premised on the differences between the sexes and realized in free motherhood.

American feminists, with the help of Key, synthesized elements of the New Morality and Freudianism into a novel enterprise. Few proselytizers realized just how distant their aspiration to define a fixed psychology of sex was from Freud's effort to chart the complex processes of psychosexual differentiation. Fewer still noted the clash of fundamental assumptions. For example, William J. Robinson, a prominent physician and birth-control campaigner, ironed out all contradictions. In 1915 he published the first English translation of Freud's " 'Civilized' Sexual Morality and Modern Nervous Illness" in the *American Journal of Urology and Sexology*, which he edited. But despite his admiration for Freud, Robinson worked along different lines. His treatise *Woman: Her Sex and Love Life* (1917), one of the first popular sex manuals endorsed by feminists, outlined a bipolar model of human sexuality and psychology. It led off with the well-established dyad "aggressive *versus* nurturing" and displayed a host of equally familiar antonyms to cast "masculine" and "feminine" in stark opposition. Robinson captured the contemporary feminist mood by heralding the salutary power not merely of sexual emancipation but of the untethering of a specifically female sexuality that expressed itself most profoundly in maternity.[29] It was a highly imaginative act to pair these assumptions with Freud's, but Robinson, like other American feminists, worked wonders.

The Politics of Selfhood

In the decade after Freud's visit to the United States, American feminists found themselves embroiled in a major controversy. Deploying

European theories, they made a spirited case for sexual emancipation and argued just as energetically for the unbridled expression of woman's procreative power. This agenda shocked quite a few Americans, who would just as soon have reinstituted the "conspiracy of silence" that had served so nicely to keep women in their proper place. Feminists also antagonized many veterans of the woman movement, those stalwarts who had worked so assiduously to lower the profile of differences between the sexes. Thus, almost fortuitously, Freud's theories became enmeshed in the dispute over political strategy: should women advance their claims by emphasizing their unique attributes, or should they play down the differences between the sexes to achieve absolute equality? There was, however, an even bigger problem to resolve.

The famed birth-control agitator Margaret Sanger (1879–1966) mapped out one side of the divide. By 1912 she had decided to abandon her work as a visiting nurse among the poor women of New York City. These women were dying from pregnancies they could ill afford, perishing in great numbers from botched abortions and inadequate prenatal care. Something more drastic was needed than the ministrations of a trained nurse. Searching for solutions, Sanger devoured Ellis's mammoth *Psychology of Sex* "in one gulp," suffered "psychic indigestion for several months," and then joined radicals and rebels of various types to inaugurate the birth-control movement in the United States.

At the same time, Sanger became a convert not just to the New Morality but to its feminist variation. Threatened repeatedly with arrest, eventually exiled for her determination to wage a war for sexual enlightenment, the prominent radical activist steadfastly predicted that woman's self-realization "will come through a gradual assertion of her power in her own sphere rather than in that of men." Sanger saw nothing inconsistent in promoting sexual emancipation under the flamboyant banner of the *Woman Rebel,* the name of her short-lived newspaper, while warning women against trying "to follow in the footsteps of men" or even to think as men did. Society did not need woman to do man's work, she insisted. Woman's mission was not "to enhance the masculine spirit, but to express the feminine; hers is not to preserve a man-made world, but to create a human world by the infusion of the feminine element into all of its activities."[30]

Sanger's feminism closely resembled the philosophy of Ellen Key. She and her allies did not renege on the goal of political equality and continued to campaign for woman suffrage. Nor did they wish to limit women's participation in civil society. They nevertheless echoed Key in insisting, as George Burman Foster put it, that "woman's main significance and service is in her unlikeness to man."[31]

This perspective prevailed in the writings of the youthful literati who were the foremost publicists of Freud. The young journalist Walter Lippmann, for example, warned women against placing too much hope in their entry into the business world. In the first place, he declared, economic rewards were bound to be few. Although a handful of women might rise in the professions, a far larger number would find only menial, poor-paying jobs in factories and shops; far from ensuring their independence, wage labor promised further degradation. Woman, this devotee of Freud advised, should not expect to gain the satisfaction in work that comes so naturally to man: "She cannot do that, for the simple reason that she is a woman . . . She cannot taboo her own character in order to become suddenly an amateur male." A self-proclaimed admirer of Key similarly dismissed the New Woman, in her emulation of men's style and behavior, as "a very unpleasant product." Emma Goldman herself said as much. "Merely external emancipation," she observed, "has made of the modern woman an artificial being." Women's obsession with careers had turned them into "mere professional automatons." "Our highly praised independence is, after all," Goldman warned, "but a slow process of dulling and stifling woman's nature, her love instinct, and her mother instinct." Katharine Anthony summed up the new philosophy: the nettling but "final" problem of the woman movement is the woman who "wishes that she were a man."[32]

These sentiments were not, of course, totally alien to American activists. For nearly a century maternalists like Frances Willard had argued for greater civil rights on the basis of woman's unmatched ability to nurture; early twentieth-century suffragists similarly demanded the ballot to extend maternal influence into the public sphere. By the early twentieth century the popular slogan "social housekeeping" succeeded in bringing thousands of women into Progressive reform. But ideologues like Willard had differentiated sharply between social function and biological imperative. Willard quite comfortably attributed women's superior morality to their capacity for motherhood. At the same time, she insisted that women's grand contribution would come, not through the fulfillment of their biological destiny, but through the application of their special moral attributes to the work of civil society. With metaphorical flourish, Willard named the childless Susan B. Anthony the nation's greatest mother-figure.

In stark contrast, modern feminists celebrated maternity as a literal fulfillment of woman's potential. While they hoped that women as a group might reorganize society to mirror maternal sensibilities, they sought foremost their own self-realization, the accession of a "feminine spirit" that, according to Sanger, uniquely accompanied maternity. Goldman similarly acknowledged the importance of satisfying woman's "innate craving for motherhood." In rejecting the so-called Victorian notion of motherhood as woman's "crown and glory," Floyd Dell later recalled, the feminists he met regarded maternity as the "most interesting of [life's] adventures." Or, in the simplest terms: "They wanted babies."[33]

What distanced feminists from other activists, then, was not simply their unyielding emphasis on the differences between the sexes. Nor did they break entirely new ground by extolling woman's maternal virtues. They may even have acknowledged the brilliance of Eliza Gamble's *The Evolution of Woman* (1894), which inverts Darwin's conclusions to argue "that the maternal instinct is the root whence sympathy has sprung."[34] Feminists would readily affirm Gamble's well-liked assumption that womanly qualities were not only distinctive but necessary to the progress of civilization. But this was not their first concern. Unlike the majority of their peers, feminists advanced the needs of the individual over the claims of the community and raised the banner of self-realization.

Breaking with the formalist, positivist modes that had prevailed since the mid-nineteenth century, feminism and psychoanalysis arose in pursuit of the self. The precocious radical theorist Louis C. Fraina, who focused his interests simultaneously on mass strikes and jazz dancing, struggled to make sense of this wholesale departure. Noting dolefully that the average socialist still envisioned a simple correlation between material conditions (modes of production) and collective consciousness, he observed that "the study of psychology is revolutionizing modern thought, transforming the relative importance of various sciences," emphatically including socialist thought. Karl Marx had already insisted in *The Eighteenth Brumaire of Louis Bonaparte* that man makes his own history, and again in *Capital* that man makes his own nature. His mechanistic-minded followers, however, had subordinated individual volition to social forces. Now, the more complex truth had been virtually forced upon them. Psychology offered crucial insights into the "analysis of transformations in the nature of man," the changing relationship between man and woman high among them. Feminism represented a similar rupture in ranks and in epistemology. As Marie Jenney Howe put it, feminism meant more than "a changed world": it heralded a "changed psychology, the creation of a new consciousness in woman." Fraina, soon to emerge as the first communist theorist in the United States, fairly glowed in 1917 with his prediction of "sex as principle of life, femininity as poetic joy of life," the "beauty of the free personality," and above all "woman as a New Being."[35]

For these reasons neither feminism nor Freudianism advanced without stirring up a nest of angry critics. Indeed, the intensity of the reaction equaled the gravity of the shift. And it was not simply the sexual or maternal component that annoyed these detractors.

The formidable Charlotte Perkins Gilman (1860–1935) stepped forward to defend the old ways. Considered one of the few great American theorists on the Woman Question by her contemporaries and historians alike, Gilman had entered her prime as a writer and publicist. She lectured so often in the United States and throughout much of Europe and published so many books and articles that the suffrage leader Carrie Chapman Catt credited her with "utterly revolutionizing the attitude of mind in the entire country, indeed of other countries, as to woman's place."[36] Gilman reigned, in short, as a worthy antagonist to these new ideas.

Gilman wisely chose Ellen Key as her intellectual foil. At first she greeted the Swedish writer as an ally in the campaign to halt women's economic dependence on men. Writing in her own monthly magazine, *The Forerunner,* Gilman had favorably reviewed both *Love and Marriage* and Key's *The Century of the Child,* which appeared in English in 1909. She soon changed her mind, however. She heard that Key had described Gilman's writings as a "strong antithesis to hers."

Although initially puzzled by this judgment, Gilman finally understood following the publication of Key's *The Woman Movement* (1912). Here Key drew out the strategic lessons of her philosophy and excoriated Gilman—albeit only in a footnote—as a prime example of an undesirable "amaternal" feminism.[37]

Responding sharply, Gilman singled out Key's handling of motherhood. Although she believed wholeheartedly in its nobility, Gilman refused to narrow the meaning of motherhood to the efforts of the individual woman "to save her child from an evil world." She argued that only "the calm, strong determining force of woman united" could ensure a world of peace and security for all children. Speaking as if from the nineteenth century, Gilman adhered to the older convention of social motherhood promoted so effectively by temperance agitators and suffragists. "Any mother who is capable of giving all that a child needs, and keeps such unusual power exclusively for her own, is," she understandably charged, "a social traitor."[38]

Gilman followed a familiar trail to its logical conclusion. Not some special biological capacity but rather women's relationship to economic production—in short, to labor—determined their collective worth. "Doing human work," she insisted, "is what develops human character."[39]

Gilman thus rejected the premises of both Freud and Key, that is, their mutual consignment of women to the sphere of reproduction. If Freud had identified nothing remarkable in woman's capacity to procreate and had ruled her out of the affairs of civilization for this reason, Key and her compatriots attached an inordinately beneficial significance to this capacity. Gilman, in contrast, demanded a place for women in civilization on the same grounds as men. Her best-known treatise, *Women and Economics: A Study of the Economic Relation between Men and Women as a Factor in Social Evolution* (1898), argues that neither sex enjoys a monopoly on talent or temperament for any particular work but instead that both are equally capable. She therefore saw no reason to exalt women's maternal qualities, especially as prerequisites for the specific tasks associated with childrearing. She insisted that everyone would benefit, children as well as adults, if such jobs were integrated into the market economy and assigned regardless of sex to the best-qualified individuals. Women will achieve their potential, she specified, only after they gain the right to labor without restriction and thereby join men in advancing civilization.

Gilman's faith in collectivity led her, moreover, to reject the whole business of selfhood. A rigorous student of the older political economy and follower of protest movements against a self-indulgent ruling class, Gilman still measured civic virtue by the standards of the true producer-citizen—self-discipline, hard work, and sobriety. She could not abide the priority assigned to "the development of personality, of individuality, among modern women." The mainly youthful proponents of this new view had shifted the axis of the historic Woman Question, she reported with dismay, from the plane of society and social responsibility to that of the individual and self-fulfillment. Furthermore, Gilman grieved, they had subordinated the long-standing emphasis on material conditions to psychological processes and mental perceptions. Not that Gilman had joined the chorus of traditionalists who mourned the slackening of that "highest of womanly virtues," self-sacrifice. She made herself clear. No "self-sacrifice or self *anything*," she retorted, "but simply to find and hold our proper place in the Work in which and by which we all live."[40]

In the end, all Gilman's objections came together as one piece: "Now I hold that 'the universal human characteristics' have no sex connotation whatever." Against the grain, the esteemed theorist insisted that the womanly qualities celebrated by her Scandinavian adversary were merely a product of man's long-term domination, his success in exiling woman to a separate and inferior sphere of existence. Gilman refused to modify her opinion that the differences between the sexes had become, in fact, too extreme. If anything, society had become "oversexed" (meaning over-gendered) and consequently unable to function to its best advantage. Only when sex *lost* its power to define, Gilman insisted, would women advance.[41]

Well publicized, the controversy between Gilman and Key introduced many literate Americans to the basic tenets of modern feminism. An elder member of Heterodoxy, Gilman herself had sharpened her arguments by engaging with Key's ardent admirers, including Katharine Anthony; years later she may have freshened her memory by perusing the passages in her fellow Heterodite Rheta Childe Dorr's memoirs recalling Key as a "tremendous radical" and pointing out that "everybody who used to read Charlotte Perkins Gilman" had turned to Key. But even at the time, news of this controversy reached far beyond the rarified networks of New York intellectuals. Subscribers to such middle-brow magazines as *Current Opinion* could read a succinct summary of the disagreement: "Mrs. Gilman would minimize sex differences, placing emphasis on the human likeness between man and woman. Ellen Key, on the contrary, dwells on their 'ineradicable differences.' " In the wake of such commentary, scores of other writers began to distinguish between "*human* feminism" and "*female* feminism" and to position themselves accordingly. And Gilman, understanding the significance of this dispute, chose to declare herself "not primarily 'a feminist' but a humanist."[42]

These competing claims coalesced as the paradox of modern American feminism: the struggle to establish woman's *equality* with man requires a collective mobilization based on her *difference* from him.[43] The problematic had long been apparent, from the time of the early woman's rights movement through Frances Willard's temperance crusade onward to the eve of the mass suffrage mobilizations in the 1910s. But flirtation with Freudianism brought the paradox plainly to light.

Even Key's most avid American fans had perceived the inherent dilemma. Eager to emphasize woman's emancipation as a sex-being, they stoutly refused to withdraw from the century-old struggle for equal rights. Heterodoxy members, for instance, valiantly crusaded to allow New York City's female teachers to hold on to their jobs after they married and had children. Key, in contrast, would have preferred mothers to devote themselves exclusively to their children. American feminists wanted more. None of these prominent professional women would forsake her own career for a life of fecundity (any more than did Key herself). Likewise, mobilizations for the vote, which crescendoed in the decade following Freud's visit, garnered hearty support from nearly everyone, with the anarchist Emma Goldman the rare abstainer.

And yet members of this generation also determinedly pulled together the fragments of disparate doctrines, including Freudianism, so as to identify and to strive to secure the goal missing in the mighty campaigns for equal rights: the promise of a specifically feminine self-hood. They could not have done otherwise and remained faithful to some of the other grand crusades of the decade, especially the bold agitation for birth control. Most of all, they would have been untrue to themselves. They could appreciate Charlotte Perkins Gilman's contributions without endorsing her vision; so, too, they could admire Key while quietly ignoring the larger logic (or illogic) of her conclusions. Eventually this paradox would precipitate a fissure in the ranks of psychoanalysts as deep as that between Gilman and Key, and reminiscent of it in several odd ways. For the moment, though, Gilman seemed the lone worrier.

With the help of psychoanalysis as well as of the New Morality, feminists had put the distinctly female self at the forefront of their political agenda. Even Freud's chief American sponsor, G. Stanley Hall, had eagerly extolled the merits of a specifically feminine selfhood by incorporating aspects of Freud's theories into his own trailblazing work on adolescent psychology. Hall also trained several prominent women psychologists, such as Phyllis Blanchard, who called attention to their commitment to "true" feminism. Hall and his students thus welcomed the "new movement . . . based upon sexual differences, not identities." Even in the early 1920s, when Gilman was reviling flappers and Freudians alike, they held their ground. Whereas Gilman denounced the "selfish and fruitless indulgence" of young women and in large part blamed "the solemn philosophical sex-mania of Sigmund Freud, now poisoning the world," Hall hailed the sexually active flapper in terms that would have pleased prewar feminists. He greeted her as the "bud of a new and better womanhood, and the evolutionary progress of civilization toward maternal femininity."[44]

By this time it was clear that American psychoanalysts had already been infected with these ideas. For example, A. A. Brill, who after personally training with Freud in Vienna returned home to build a flourishing practice among the New York intelligentsia, unceremoniously proposed that woman's instincts were "finer" than man's.[45] Freud would never endorse such a proposition. The American popularists who misunderstood Freud proved so successful in transmitting their own interpretations that they actually helped to close the distance between their world and his.

And that was their greatest legacy. In ways that no one could have predicted, the sympathetic writers for *Munsey's*, the *Atlantic, Current History*, or *American Magazine*, almost as much as those for the *New Republic, The Masses, New Review*, and *The Liberator*, had made the dramatic shift in paradigm virtually synonymous with feminism, and feminism almost synonymous with Freudianism. If just a decade later, in the late 1920s, the books by Charlotte Perkins Gilman as well as those by Ellen Key gathered dust, and few could recall just what was so compelling about Mabel Dodge Luhan; if intellectuals like Louis Fraina had soured on sexual emancipation, yet a certain nostalgia for the 1910s remained. The decade symbolized the glory days of experimentation, of the playfully young and free-spirited, the years of optimism about the twentieth century and science in particular—before the Great Depression, the rise of fascism, and a second world war substituted dark ruminations about human nature and accelerated the destruction of the earlier faith in social progress and self-realization.

In some ways, this popular view of the 1910s was always facile, almost an excuse for moral cynicism. But it contained a kernel of truth, even if the diversity of voices tended to be condensed into a handful of briefly famous writers and a few vague impressions. The introductions of psychoanalysis and feminism had been part of a unitary process, and despite later attempts to disentangle them, the connection remained.

But first the scene shifted to Central Europe, where the issues that had fired the first generation of feminists became the property of psychoanalysts. Although Freud kept a close guard on his ranks, the impact of feminism on his practice was dramatic. By 1920 psychoanalysts, several trained by Freud himself, proved just as insistent as their American contemporaries. In the European centers—Vienna, Berlin, Berne, and London—Freud's colleagues forced the master himself to address matters marginal to his theoretical endeavor.

Finally, more than forty years into his scientific career, Freud began to make female sexuality and femininity part of his project. What he eventually did produce owed less to his own enthusiasm for the subject than to the transatlantic dialogue sparked by feminists. Although the highly technical quality of the psychoanalytic canon has obscured their impact, feminists in the United States and Europe had formulated many of the now-familiar questions. Between 1925 and 1933 Freud answered these queries in three major essays that set his colleagues spinning for decades. He himself turned back to his primary concerns as quickly as possible, but even the master could not subdue his vocal adversaries or shut down the discussion begun here. Disagreements—and not just among psychoanalysts—would flare up intermittently for the rest of the century.

2

Dissent in Freud's Ranks

Freud's reluctance to speculate on female sexuality or femininity did not preclude his taking a clear stand on the Woman Question. Even as a young man he held strong opinions. In a private letter dated November 15, 1883, and addressed to his fiancée, Martha Bernays, Freud noted that he had recently translated John Stuart Mill's *On the Subjection of Women*. This exercise, along with his impending marriage, prompted the youthful suitor to share his opinions with his wife-to-be:

It seems a complete unrealistic notion to send women into the struggle for existence in the same way as men. Am I to think of my delicate sweet girl as a competitor? After all, the encounter could only end by my telling her, as I did 17 months ago, that I love her, and I will make every effort to get her out of the competitive role into the quiet undisturbed activity of my home. It is possible that a different education could suppress all women's delicate qualities—which are so much in need of protection and yet so powerful—with the result that they could earn their living like men. It is also possible that in this case it would not be justifiable to deplore the disappearance of the most lovely thing the world has to offer us: our ideal of womanhood. But I believe that all reforming activity, legislation and education, will founder on the fact that long before the age at which a profession can be established in our society, Nature will have appointed woman by her beauty, charm and goodness, to do something else.

No, in this respect I adhere to the old ways, to my longing for my Martha as she is, and she herself will not want it different; legislation and custom have to grant to women many rights kept from them, but the position of woman cannot be other than what it is: to be an adored sweetheart in youth, and a beloved wife in maturity.[1]

Not yet thirty years old, Freud envisioned women almost solely as objects of men's affections and caretakers of the home.

Twenty-five years later the world-renowned theorist appeared to have changed very little. Speaking to a small circle of his colleagues in 1908, Freud reaffirmed his original assessment of Mill and once again discounted the liberal philosopher's idea that women could both work professionally and fulfill their domestic duties. "Women as a group profit nothing from the modern feminist movement," he argued, "at best a few individuals profit."[2]

By this time Freud had positioned himself well to grapple with the ever widening implications of women's advancement into civil society. He had just organized the Vienna Psychoanalytic Society from the small coterie of like-minded physicians who had been gathering weekly in his apartment since 1902. Meanwhile other groups had been forming in the European capitals, and they coalesced in 1910 as the International Psycho-Analytical Association. Although the actual number of trained analysts grew very slowly, Freud's self-assurance swelled at a rapid pace. He spelled out his disagreements with Alfred Adler and C. G. Jung and cleared his ranks of their influence. In 1912 the journal *Imago* debuted to set the theoretical tone for the era. By the time the European war began, Freud had endowed psychoanalysis with the status of a genuine movement and named himself its founder and leader.[3] Then, as the number of soldiers suffering from "war neurosis," or shell shock, grew, Freud saw his theories accorded the scientific recognition he had craved for decades. The opening of the Berlin Polyclinic in 1920, with a staff engaged in both research and therapy, established psychoanalysis as an unusual yet practically reputable profession. Now sixty-five years old, Freud was as ready as he ever would be to deal with the spirit of emancipation celebrated by a rapidly growing number of women who were choosing psychoanalysis as their vocation.

Despite his own prejudices, and against the wishes of several colleagues, Freud welcomed women to his ranks. At first very few women responded to his invitation, and Freud's circle remained the preserve of the licensed physician, an occupation for the most part closed to Austrian women until 1897, when the university medical school finally allowed them to enroll in a degree program. As late as 1910 only three women were practicing psychoanalysis professionally. But before the European war ended, more than forty women had become psychoanalysts. During the 1920s women entered the movement at a far faster rate than men, increasing their number by at least ninety. There is no question that these women excelled disproportionately as therapists and theorists. Karen Horney, Helene Deutsch, Melanie Klein, Lou Andreas-Salomé, Hermine Hug-Hellmuth, Joan Rivière, Jeanne Lampl-de Groot, Ruth Mack Brunswick, Marie Bonaparte, and Freud's own daughter Anna all forged brilliant careers within his trailblazing movement.[4]

Freud could not have predicted just how determined these pioneering women would be to shed light on the dim spots in psychoanalytic theory, specifically on female sexuality and femininity. The first woman elected at his behest to the Vienna Psychoanalytic Society, Margarethe Hilferding, proved very outspoken on the Woman Question. At one of the Wednesday evening soirees she castigated a fellow discussant for failing to take into account the social restrictions placed on women. The wife of a world-famous Marxist theorist and fellow physician, Hilferding soon exited Freud's ranks and later served as president of the Adlerian Vienna Society for Individual Psychology. Very few women defected, however. The majority not only stayed on but specialized their research on female sexuality. For example, Hermine Hug-Hellmuth (1871–1924), the society's first gentile member as well as the first child analyst, published several essays on the topic, including an especially courageous paper, "On Female Masturbation." Having reached a critical mass, and having benefited from their own clinical practices, women psychoanalysts began in the 1920s to raise serious questions about the adequacy of Freud's theories on female psychosexual development.[5]

Freud soon found himself, as Wilhelm Fliess's son Robert later remarked, "in a situation reminiscent of that of the mythical sculptor, when the female hewn by the chisel of his research came alive and responded with certain discoveries of her own."[6] Several of Freud's own protégées began to chip away at his hypotheses, forcing him and his allies to defend their basic principles. The controversy they generated spanned an entire decade and effectively served to mark off the parameters of orthodoxy.

Feminism entered these discussions in a new and complicated way. By the early 1920s both Europeans and Americans were witnessing the decline of the most vibrant phase of the historic woman movement. In the United States the ratification of the suffrage amendment coincided with the dissolution of the mass organizations that had secured its passage. Political discord reigned, while veteran activists struggled over the proposed Equal Rights Amendment. Meanwhile the vast majority of young women remained indifferent. Although the volatile political situation in central Europe kept alive a dissenting spirit led in Vienna by a sizable socialist movement, which included Helene Deutsch, the world war had drastically altered the tenor of reform. The underlying faith in progress fell away, and with that loss the vocabulary of liberation vanished. Even the clarion of sexual emancipation called out to surprisingly few adventurers.

As its political base disintegrated, *feminism* took on new meaning. In the United States the term no longer expressed an entitlement based on those qualities and capacities that marked woman's difference from man but instead gained generic properties. Feminism became an umbrella term encompassing an unwieldy assortment of ideas and actions directed at improving women's status. More important, feminism now stood for what its prewar originators had so adamantly rejected—masculinism. The object of frequent ridicule and mean caricature, feminists now represented those women who allegedly aspired to model themselves on men. As one American commentator put it, feminism now suggested "either the old school of fighting feminists who wore flat heels and had very little feminine charm, or the current species who antagonize men with their constant clamor about maiden names, equal rights, woman's place in the world, and many another cause . . . *ad infinitum.*"

This semantic declension was even more apparent across the Atlantic, where the term *feminism,* if used at all, had always stood primarily for equal rights. Ernest Jones registered this meaning, insisting that he did not see "a woman—in the way feminists do—as *un homme manqué.*" As feminism contracted to signify woman's desire to imitate man, it quickly became "a term of opprobrium" throughout the Western world. As the British chronicler Ray Strachey noted, after the war young women were typically showing "a strong hostility to the word 'feminism' and all which they imagine it to connote."[7]

Ironically, the term feminism began to appear more frequently in psychoanalytic discussions in the 1920s and eventually became a descriptive staple. Redefined as *masculinism,* feminism now served, along with homosexuality, as a handy signifier of deviancy. Not a few analysts routinely conflated *lesbian* and *feminist* to characterize a woman misaligned, sexually as well as socially. Furthermore, they rarely differentiated among several symptomatic desires: to *be* a man, to *be like* a man, or simply to *be equal to* a man. For most psychoanalysts the term *feminism* readily encompassed all three possibilities.

This stark transformation left Freud's critics without a convenient means to tag their arguments, but it did not in any way diminish their sense of urgency. Despite the political denouement of the 1920s, the majority of women analysts endorsed, if only tacitly, the tenets of the prewar woman movement. They aspired to be self-supporting, although they did not define themselves exclusively by work or career. Rather, they believed that all women possessed a fundamental right to achieve happiness in both public and private realms. They therefore valued marriage as well as motherhood and demanded a large degree of personal space within both institutions. As modern women, they claimed the right to selfhood and continued to place the primary emphasis on a sexual identity that included women's unique capacity to bear children. Very few, however, searched these familiar grounds under the banner of feminism.

Although the strong-minded women in Freud's ranks abjured the feminist label, they avidly pressed for a thorough discussion of the questions that had burned so brightly for prewar feminists. Some women managed to pique Freud's interest. Jeanne Lampl-de Groot and Lou Andreas Salomé, for example, tinkered with his basic categories but remained faithful to his intentions. Others moved in the opposite direction. His most intemperate critic accused him directly of phallocentrism. Freud, Karen Horney charged, framed all his theories from an exclusively male point of view; he had not only failed to consider female subjectivity but had stubbornly refused to acknowledge the significance of woman's reproductive capacity. Although Freud conceded that the first vital question a child asks is not about the differences between the sexes but about the origin of babies, the so-called Riddle of the Sphinx, he chose to put it aside. Like the child who preferred such fanciful explanations as the visiting stork over knowledge of his mother's vaginal canal, Freud sidestepped the very issue that feminists in both the United States and Europe had emphasized. But finally, in the 1920s, he could no longer hold back. Motherhood became the dark horse in the race for theory.

Toward a Freudian Theory of Female Sexuality

Before 1910—that is, before the influx of women—the psychoanalytic movement was remarkably impervious to feminist influences despite a confluence of interests. Fin-de-siècle Europe was in the throes of its own "repeal of reticence." Activists from various reformist quarters, including the house of Freud, were seeking to displace the "civilized" morality that Freud himself had found so injurious. Calls for a new sexual morality echoed from the neighborhood coffeehouses of Vienna to the hallowed halls of the Austrian parliament. Female sexuality in particular had become a prime political issue, the focal point of burgeoning modernist aesthetics as well as campaigns for legislative reform. But only belatedly did female sexuality move to the center of psychoanalytic inquiry.

While Freud was mapping his foundational theories, two major women's federations came into existence to promote sexual reform. The General Austrian Women's Association, founded in 1893, focused primarily on women's civil rights, while the League of Austrian Women's Associations, organized in 1902, presented a broad platform of social welfare. Like their American counterparts, Austrian activists divided roughly along generational and ideological lines, but they focused to a far greater extent on the sexual order and morality, questions at the center of Freud's own endeavors. By the 1890s Ellen Key's

Austrian publicist, Auguste Fickert, was already distinguishing between woman's rights, that is, the goal of civil equality, and "a great ethical mission" spearheaded by women. The women's movement encompasses both aspects, she declared, but it is foremost the vanguard of a new morality. As women played greater roles in civil society, she explained, they would wield their power to bring about a moral regeneration of society. The absence of legal means to dissolve marriage, Fickert and other activists reasoned, had produced an exceptionally high rate of illegitimate births and, in addition, turned far too many women into sexual slaves. For these reasons, the laws governing marriage, the rights of unmarried mothers, and the problem of prostitution stood far above suffrage on the political agenda. Austrian feminists focused, in short, on the realm of reproduction, and they found Key's philosophy especially attractive.[8]

Freud, the cosmopolitan clinician who drew his clients from ultrasophisticated Viennese society, inevitably came into contact with women engaged in campaigns for sexual reform. He was especially familiar with "Anna O," the real-life Berthe Pappenheim (1859–1936), allegedly the first psychoanalytic patient. Treated by Freud's collaborator Josef Breuer in 1882, Pappenheim later translated Mary Wollstonecraft's classic *Vindication of the Rights of Women* into German. Her own treatise, a play entitled *A Woman's Right,* cast light on the economic as well as sexual exploitation of women. Pappenheim founded the *Judischer Frauenbund* (Jewish Women's Union) in 1904 and served as its president until she stepped down twenty years later. Philosophically Pappenheim resembled Key, in that she too envisioned her political work along maternal lines, insisting that motherliness is "the primary feeling in women." Although she bore no children, Pappenheim worked productively as a surrogate, founding a home for unwed mothers and so-called illegitimate children. "Women who have to miss the happiness of real personal motherhood," she observed, could still avail themselves of the opportunities for "spiritual motherhood."[9]

Freud's own patient Emma Eckstein (1865–1924) was no less dedicated to the new sexual morality. She came to Freud in 1895 for help with her "dream psychosis" and ended up collaborating with him through her therapy to shape the important theory of wish-fulfillment. Freud remained close to the Eckstein family, which included several socialists. Emma's sister Therese Schlesinger, an activist in the women's movement, was one of the first women to serve in the Austrian parliament. Emma herself became a lay analyst and a specialist in childhood sexuality. At one point she even borrowed Freud's personal copy of Edward Carpenter's *Love's Coming of Age*.[10]

Pappenheim and Eckstein were exceptional women by any standard. But as a group Freud's patients represented a strikingly urbane middle class caught up in the vast social and political changes affecting women's lives in fin-de-siècle Europe. Their emotional lives encompassed—as Freud knew perhaps all too well—the hope for, and the fear of, this dramatic transformation. It is surprising, then, not that Freud acknowledged woman's sexual desires but that he did so little with this revelation.

Freud appeared unmoved even when several leaders of the Austrian women's movement applauded his pathbreaking work. Grete Meisel-Hess (1879–?), for example, boldly put forward "the clear demand of unsullied instincts." The current crisis in sexuality, particularly the repressive state of sexual desire, she insisted, had distanced her from those "women's righters" who focused solely on legal reform. Like so many other feminists in both Central Europe and the United States, Meisel-Hess found Nietzschean philosophy, with its advocacy of a new and freer morality, much more exciting than the campaign for suffrage. Embracing psychoanalysis as a scientific endorsement of women's right to a sexual life, she had nothing but unbridled praise for the great Doctor Freud.

Meisel-Hess supplied a distinctive political twist to Freud's theories. In 1909, just one year after the publication of " 'Civilized' Sexual Morality and Modern Nervous Illness," she issued the first in her trilogy on the Sexual Question. She followed Freud's line of thinking to attest that "the pathological condition we so often encounter today" arises not so much from the presence of "ardent desire" as from the "psychic inadequacy" of the discharge of sexual tension. Like Freud, she warned that the situation had become urgent because "sexual cripples" had come to outnumber the healthy.

Meisel-Hess paused here, however. In order to accommodate her own dual commitments to socialism and feminism, she reframed the problem. She insisted that all prospects for sexual emancipation depended entirely on women's economic freedom. It was far better for a woman "to provide for her own subsistence in a manner compatible with the preservation of human self-respect, than to give herself, in an unhappy marriage, as bond-slave to the first comer." Nevertheless, the goal of economic independence would do more than establish the grounds for social equality: it would serve foremost as a "means and pathway to sexual freedom" whereby women would finally be able to achieve their sovereign destiny in motherhood. To stave off neurosis, she clarified, women required not merely the release of sexual tension: they required "the stimulation furnished by the act of parturition" and relief from "the accumulation of tensions that should be discharged in lactation and in her love for her offspring." Nothing should encumber this primal experience. In was mainly for this reason that Meisel-Hess called for "the building of the new amatory civilization."[11]

Meisel-Hess excelled in synthesizing continental feminism and Freudian psychoanalysis and managed to broadcast her ideas quite widely. In Austria she proved a stalwart of the women's movement, taking leadership roles in the major campaigns for maternity insurance and marriage reform and writing major treatises as well as fiction highlighting sexual emancipation. She found receptive audiences in both Central Europe and the United States. The American birth-control advocate William J. Robinson put out a translated edition of her *The Sexual Crisis: A Critique of Our Sex Life* (1917). But whereas Meisel-Hess's psychoanalytic feminism appealed primarily to the radical fringe of the American woman's movement, those erudite intellectuals captivated by Key and Freud alike, her perspective meshed smoothly with mainstream continental activism.

Freud could not entirely evade the widening circles of the Austrian women's movement. Like the majority of liberals and socialists who filled his ranks, Freud endorsed the major campaigns to bring about a change in sexual morality. In 1905, for instance, he responded to a questionnaire issued to gauge public opinion on proposed legislation to reform the Austrian divorce law. Although he favored revisions in the laws governing marriage and even approved the plank to allow women to sit on divorce courts, he responded negatively when asked if "equality of the sexes" should be demanded as well. He thought such an idea "impossible" because of "their different role in the process of reproduction." Meisel-Hess, who testified during these legislative hearings, took the same premise to opposite ends, insisting that it was precisely woman's role in reproduction that made social equality imperative. Yet, despite their disagreement, Freud lent his name to one of Meisel-Hess's principal causes, the *Bund für Mutterschütz,* and signed its international declaration in 1911.[12]

It took one of Freud's most stunning students to prompt the reluctant theorist to sketch his first extended description of female sexuality. In 1912 Lou Andreas-Salomé, then fifty-one years old, moved to Vienna and began to study psychoanalysis. Freud judged Andreas-Salomé not only a sensitive interpreter of his theories but the "purest and truest" example of womanhood. Through the force of her personality and her own theoretical work, she inspired Freud to turn to the subject he had for so long avoided.

Lou Andreas-Salomé (1861–1937) might be described as Emma Goldman's alter ego. Born just eight years earlier than Goldman in St. Petersburg, she grew up in aristocratic circles. Her father was a high-ranking German officer in the tsar's army who maintained his family in an elegant apartment across from the Winter Palace. In contrast, Goldman's father, a struggling Jewish shopkeeper, saw his two daughters leave Lithuania for the United States, the "land of dollars." Seemingly worlds apart, Andreas-Salomé and Goldman were both swept up by the Russian revolutionary fervor of the late nineteenth century and embraced the lifestyle of the nihilist women celebrated in the popular novels of N. Chernyshevskii. They demanded for themselves not only sexual freedom but intellectual enlightenment.

Neither woman received much formal education, although Andreas-Salomé briefly studied philosophy and history at the university in Zurich. Undeterred in their intellectual pursuits, they feasted on the freshest modernist delicacies in literature and the arts. Both wrote extensively on the New Woman, and reigned in their respective domains as outstanding examples. But whereas Goldman threw her lot in with the revolutionary movement and emerged a world-renowned anarchist, Andreas-Salomé carried on from her privileged position to become the most notable *femme savante* of her era. Andreas-Salomé consorted intimately with such luminaries as Nietzsche and Rilke; Goldman, across the Atlantic, memorialized these writers in the pages of her anarchist magazine *Mother Earth*. Although their paths crossed only in the abstract realms of lifestyle and literary taste, Goldman and Andreas-Salomé shared a reverence for Freud and sought in psychoanalysis the kernel of a theory of female sexuality.[13]

On questions of female sexuality, Goldman and Andreas-Salomé stood on common ground. Both succumbed to the aesthetic idealization of woman so popular among the fin-de-siècle literati and feminists alike and portrayed female sexuality as equally passionate and spiritual. Andreas-Salomé was less taken with the contemporary focus on motherhood and criticized her friend Ellen Key for reducing woman to a primal and singular maternal drive. Yet, like Key and Goldman, Andreas-Salomé condemned all political efforts to make women into pale copies of men and thereby to desecrate their distinctive femininity. In *The Erotic* (1910), Andreas-Salomé described heterosexual love as a grand regenerative force pulling together the differentiating passions of man and woman, as a merger of oppositions or a crossing of psychic boundaries. Andreas-Salomé, like Goldman, valued the dissimilar functions of men and women in the contiguous realms of sensuality and morality.

Whereas Goldman tried to elicit a response from Freud when he visited the United States in 1909, Andreas-Salomé brought her mission to his doorstep. In 1911 she attended the Weimar Psychoanalytic Congress and told Freud that she wished to study psychoanalysis with him. One year later she approached him again and this time received a warm invitation. Between October 1912 and the following April, Andreas-Salomé frequented the Wednesday evening meetings. Having written ten novels and scores of essays and reviews on femininity and eroticism, she was quite ready to add psychoanalysis to her intellectual repertoire, especially as it applied to the female sexual instinct.[14]

Finally, Freud was ready to speak. Just two years after Andreas-Salomé entered his circle, he published "On Narcissism," a landmark essay that differentiated between the sexes. Freud and Andreas-Salomé shared a belief in the instinctual component of the libido, including its bodily origin, but they were principally interested in the psychic dimension of sexuality. Thus, like Andreas-Salomé, Freud approached the topic of female sexuality as an inquiry into love or desire rather than orgasm. Beginning at the customary point, infantile bisexuality, he reasoned that in infancy boys and girls alike love both themselves and the woman who nurses them. But whereas men eventually overcome self-love to experience "complete object-love of the attachment type," women do not. To the contrary, "the maturing of the female sexual organs . . . seems to bring about an intensification of the original narcissism," Freud wrote. This discrepancy manifests itself most clearly in maturity: men desire women, whereas women desire to be loved by men. In sum, women are able to maintain what men must inevitably lose, a certain "self-contentment and inaccessibility," qualities that Freud allegedly found especially enticing in Andreas-Salomé.

For her part, Andreas-Salomé offered a slightly different portrait of narcissism, one that would resurface in later feminist interpretations. Rather than emphasizing self-love, she postulated a state of primal undifferentiation that, while unconscious, remains a positive influence throughout an individual's life and, equally important, symbolizes Woman. All love begins here, she claimed. The desire to regress is a sign, therefore, not of neurosis but of well-being. "For a neurotic," she related, "the wish to become a woman would really mean the wish to become healthy. And it is always a wish to be happy." Freud hinted as much in his own essay, suggesting that the narcissistic woman stirs envy in man because she represents what he has lost. But, as Andreas-Salomé repeatedly complained, Freud chose to emphasize *self-love* rather than the bliss of primal union in his operative definition of narcissism.

Freud acknowledged that women might not be pleased by his treatment of narcissism and even offered an apology of sorts. If they found this scenario objectionable, it was not due, he insisted, "to any tendentious desire on my part to depreciate women." Moreover, he cautioned, not all women are true to type, and a sizable number are capable of "masculine" love. Clearly, Freud missed the point.

For Andreas-Salomé and the majority of her feminist peers, the prospect of "masculine" love was no compensation at all. Woman's love is superior to man's love, she insisted, and it enchants the opposite sex precisely because it unites the spiritual and sensual dimensions to achieve a wholeness unavailable to men. "Only in womankind is sexuality no surrender of the ego boundary, no schism," Andreas-Salomé stated. Sexuality abides in woman "as the homeland of personality, which can still include all of the sublimations of the spirit without losing itself."[15]

Despite her devotion to her mentor, Andreas-Salomé recognized how far apart they were; Freud, preoccupied with her charm, remained oblivious. Granting theoretical dispensations he characteristically refused his male colleagues, Freud once described Andreas-Salomé as the "poet of psychoanalysis" who "knits together the *disjecta membra* won through analysis and clothes them with living tissue." For her part, Andreas-Salomé might disagree with Freud, but she would never spurn him. Her essays on femininity and eroticism published in *Imago* were decidedly heterodox, but she acclaimed psychoanalysis with unreserved enthusiasm and lived the remainder of her life as a lay analyst. For over two decades, until her death, Andreas-Salomé maintained a correspondence with Freud and a special friendship with his daughter Anna.[16]

"On Narcissism" represents one of Freud's most forceful theoretical endeavors. Here Freud introduced the concept of the ego ideal, "the substitute for the lost narcissism" of childhood. Equally important, he reaffirmed the sanctity of the libido theory against Jung's attempts to desexualize it. Finally, the reluctant theorist measured "the feminine form of erotic life" against the masculine.

Although "On Narcissism" pinpoints "fundamental differences" in the object-choices of men and women, it does not account for this discrepancy very well. Freud speculated that "different lines of development correspond to the differentiation of functions in a highly complicated biological whole," but he did not cast this assumption in psychic terms. At best, he once again named puberty the dawn of sexual differentiation, in this case as the stimulus of women's tendency toward narcissism. Narcissism becomes especially acute for good-looking women, he added, and acts as a compensation "for the social restrictions that are imposed upon them in their choice of object." Both factors—the onset of puberty and the weight of social norms—had stood Freud well in his earlier speculations on the differences between the sexes.[17]

Despite the pressure of feminists, including the extraordinarily influential Lou Andreas-Salomé, Freud had not yet delivered a comprehensive theory of female sexuality. Only in the 1920s would the master provide a graphic map of female psychosexual development, compelled, it seems, by the growing number of women in his ranks who demanded a clear statement. Freud came late to a discussion that other psychoanalysts had begun shortly after the close of the war. By the time he presented his first essay on female sexuality in 1925, interpretive differences had already split his ranks into distinct factions. But despite his tardy response, Freud had set the terms of disagreement. His colleagues had already spotlighted two tenets—penis envy and genital transference—that marked psychoanalytic territory as distinctively Freudian.

Penis Envy and Its Critics

Given its subsequent celebrity, penis envy played a surprisingly small part in Freud's early theories. For a long time Freud had simply assumed that the "main distinction between the sexes" emerges at puberty, when boys fall under the sway of the libido and girls are "seized by a *non*neurotic *sexual* repugnance." He elucidated a little further in a letter written to his friend and colleague Wilhelm Fliess in 1897, pointing out that the "sexual zone" that persists in males is eventually "extinguished" in females. "I am thinking of the male genital zone," he clarified, "the region of the clitoris, in which during childhood sexual sensitivity is shown to be concentrated in girls as well." A little later, in *Three Essays on a Theory of Sexuality*, Freud stated decisively that a full understanding of "how a little girl turns into a woman" follows "the further vicissitudes of this excitability of the clitoris." Proceeding metaphorically, he described the mature function of the clitoris as secondary: "the task, namely, of transmitting the excitation to the adjacent female sexual parts, just as—to use a simile—pine shavings can be kindled in order to set a log of harder wood on fire." Freud did note that little girls, in observing the anatomical disparity between themselves and boys, naturally feel envy. He did not go on, however, to detail just how this crucial phenomenon shapes female psychosexual development.[18]

It was only with the publication of "On Narcissism" that penis envy figured more prominently in Freud's writings. In a brief essay, "On Transformations of Instinct as Exemplified in Anal Erotism" (1917), he noted that a girl's envy of a penis normally gives way to the wish for a baby. In "The Taboo of Virginity" (1918), he began to speculate on the neurotic consequences of a woman's failure to accomplish this psychic shift. He also unveiled what would become a characteristic reading, associating unresolved penis envy with a "hostile bitterness" against men that often manifests itself in "the strivings and in the literary productions of 'emancipated women.' " Finally, in "A Child Is Being Beaten" (1919), Freud reached a turning point and began to detail developmental differences between the sexes.[19]

Despite these advances, it was only in the 1920s that Freud singled out penis envy as key to female psychosexual development. Only then did he come up with a theory of causation, that is, an interpretation of the psychic processes by which the vagina ultimately replaces the clitoris. Overwriting his earlier, vague notions of pubertal vaginal awakening, Freud now provided a detailed outline of female psychosexual development, and penis envy and genital transference served as the conceptual building blocks.

But before Freud managed to develop these ideas into a full-blown theory, his colleagues began a serious debate. Several stepped forward to affirm the significance of penis envy and genital transference and, equally important, to secure an equally rigorous link between aberrant psychosexual development and feminism. Almost immediately a few women in the ranks registered their dissatisfaction. The atmosphere became so tense that Freud himself stepped in. Hoping to subdue the arguments, he succeeded in calling yet more attention to the two hypotheses, penis envy and genital transference, that his rising critics found beyond redemption.

Most prominent in Freud's corner was Karl Abraham (1877–1925), founder of the Berlin Psychoanalytic Society and Institute in 1910, Jung's successor as editor of the prestigious *Psychoanalytic Year Book,* and a prominent analyst in his own right. Known for pioneering work on libido development, psychosis, and alcohol and drug addiction, he had also trained a generation of stellar analysts, including Sándor Radó, Helene Deutsch, Theodore Reik, Karen Horney, and Melanie Klein. Freud regarded Abraham as Germany's first genuine psychoanalyst.[20]

Abraham broke new ground by tracing feminism to its source in penis envy. Speaking in 1920 at the Sixth International Psycho-Analytical Congress, he reported that a disproportionate share of his many female clients expressed a strong desire for sex equality. They resented the fact, he recounted, that "men are permitted to choose their profession and can extend their sphere of activity in many directions, and especially . . . are subjected to far fewer restrictions in their sexual life." Disregarding the political climate of Berlin, where the women's movement had been well organized and visible, Abraham attributed such complaints to an unresolved developmental problem. Many women "feel at a disadvantage as regards the male sex by their poverty in external genitals," and, he noted, they never entirely overcome this feeling.[21]

Penis envy manifests itself most commonly in two ways, Abraham asserted—directly in homosexuality and in its sublimated form as the woman who represses her wish to be male and instead takes up "masculine pursuits of an intellectual and professional character." Such a woman considers "it irrelevant to say that the performances of a human being, especially in the intellectual sphere, belong to one or the other sex." This genus of woman "is well represented in the woman's movement to-day." Abraham also delineated less familiar types: the woman who gets irritated at the analyst's prerogative to ask impertinent questions and the woman who obtains "great enjoyment . . . from using a hose for watering the garden." The most prevalent symptoms, however, are frigidity and a dread of marriage, the former defined as failure of genital transference, that is, a persistent desire for clitoral rather than the vaginal stimulation preferred by "normal" adult women.[22]

Abraham's presentation, "Manifestations of the Female Castration Complex," was the first full exegesis of the masculinity complex in women, its origins in penis envy, its unhappy resolution in unrealized genital transference, and its most common manifestation as feminism or lesbianism. What Abraham achieved through his authoritative stature, others managed through persistence. A few years earlier, at the 1917 meeting of the Dutch Psycho-Analytical Society, J. H. W. Van Ophuijsen had similarly noted an abundance of unsuppressed bitterness among his women patients, which he too had interpreted as a symptom of penis envy. These women, in his opinion, had failed to acquiesce psychically in the face of their anatomical inferiority and had therefore developed a masculinity complex. Van Ophuijsen proceeded to state boldly what was quickly becoming canonical: a fixation on clitoral eroticism in adult women most frequently accompanied "rivalry with men in the intellectual and artistic spheres." Even Hermine Hug-Hellmuth adhered to this line. She added to the concept of penis envy woman's disappointment in love to describe a dreadful emotional combination that prompts those women who "are well read and able to write a little bit" to produce tracts that "bitterly criticize men." The "masculinity complex" accounts more fully than does women's economic situation, she concluded, for "the cry . . . for equal rights in the social field."[23]

Freud himself tightened this connection. In "The Psychogenesis of a Case of Female Homosexuality" (1920), he described "a spirited girl, always ready for romping and fighting," who, after "inspecting" the genitals of her brother, developed a pronounced case of penis envy. "She was in fact a feminist," he clarified: "she felt it to be unjust that girls should not enjoy the same freedom as boys, and rebelled against the lot of women in general."[24]

Abraham's formulations won Freud's lasting admiration. In 1931, after refining his own theories of femininity in the face of sustained criticism, he continued to refer to Abraham's contribution as "still unsurpassed."[25] Other things being equal, Freud would have considered it a completely satisfactory answer to the problems at hand. But the debate was only beginning when Abraham issued his pronouncements. Others in the ranks were just as impressed as Freud but not so favorably.

Karen Horney (1886–1952) would have seemed, at first glance, a most unlikely candidate for chief challenger. One of Abraham's former analysands and his current colleague, she had become the secretary of the Berlin Psychoanalytic Society just two years after completing her training with Abraham. An intense scholar, she was thoroughly familiar with Freud's writings, including his recent remarks on penis envy. She believed there was some validity in the concept. What Horney abhorred was the way various male psychoanalysts construed its significance. The predominance of the masculine viewpoint had produced, she concluded, a warped interpretation of female psychology.[26]

The roots of Horney's criticism led back to the prewar woman movement. As a young woman she had been deeply impressed, and perhaps personally transformed, by the writings of Ellen Key. In 1904, while still in high school, she found the Swedish scholar's ideas especially invigorating. Determined to sort out her nascent feelings about sexuality, Horney found in Key's writings "a bright daylight." Reading them was "like a bath in the sea in autumn, when the cold is cutting and you have to battle with wind and waves," the adolescent recorded in her diary, "but once out you are refreshed and a new person." Horney imagined herself to be "pervaded by the same deep moral earnestness" that made Key such a "great person," and defined the core of their shared idealism as a faith in woman's unique capacity for love. Key had fired her youthful imagination. "If sometime in later years I ask myself who in these years lit the sacred flame of enthusiasm for me," Horney wrote, "who was the lustrous star toward which my soul directed its way, one name above all shines before me: Ellen Key."[27]

Horney undoubtedly had also noted the activities of the Bund für Mutterschütz, which promoted Key's program and attracted several psychoanalysts to its ranks. There was a sizable branch in Hamburg, her home town, and its principal office was in Berlin, where Horney settled after her marriage in 1909. Although the liberal-minded medical student avoided political entanglements, she undoubtedly crossed paths with the Mutterschütz leader Helene Stocker, incidentally a close friend of Lou Andreas-Salomé. Stocker, who had urged a "higher synthesis" for women, that is, a union of motherhood and career, became a member of the Berlin Psychoanalytical Society, where Horney trained and later practiced. By 1920 Horney found herself living out Stocker's philosophy, maintaining a successful clinical practice while mothering three young daughters. An occasional lecturer at women's meetings, she appeared a role model to women similarly set on combining career and motherhood.[28]

In some ways Horney merely expanded a role that had been defined so elegantly by Andreas-Salomé. She, too, aspired to imbue Freudian theory with a woman's perspective. However, she lacked her predecessor's refinement and, equally important, her accommodating demeanor. A generation younger, Horney approached psychoanalysis as a profession rather than an avocation. She was determined to have her say even if it meant offending her powerful male colleagues, including Freud himself. Yes, Horney was a different matter altogether.

Could one really believe, she insolently asked, that "one-half of the human race is discontented with the sex assigned to it?" At the Seventh International Psycho-Analytical Congress in 1922, at a session chaired by Freud, she rejected penis envy as the principal factor in the formation of femininity. She described penis envy as merely a transient jealousy of boys for their ease in urinating and exhibiting their wares. This envy, she added, soon passes and plays no further role in development. On rare occasions, a neurotic form may take hold, but only when a father encourages a perverse relationship with his daughter. No, penis envy is not the "axiomatic fact" of femininity, Horney concluded, merely a mistaken notion grounded in masculine narcissism. The idea that a little girl regards her lack of a penis as a sign of physical inferiority is, she insisted, simply untenable.[29]

The lines of disagreement were now clear, and in the wake of Horney's incisive objections, Freud finally decided to step in. At the time he was revising his basic paradigm to attend more fully to the object of sexual desire. "On Narcissism" (1914) had staked out this ground; *Beyond the Pleasure Principle* (1920) considered in more detail how sexual desire becomes directed toward a single person. As he turned to female object-choice, Freud modified his earlier views. He not only presented a new schema of development specifying an earlier, prepubertal origin of femininity but began to speculate that female inhibition appeared not necessarily as a symptom of neurosis but as a normal outcome of development. Whereas " 'Civilized' Sexual Morality and Modern Nervous Illness" (1908) attributes female inhibition to the excessive sexual restraints imposed by parents on daughters, the essays produced in the 1920s and 1930s fulfill the promise of *Three Essays*. With increasing fervor, Freud delineated a seemingly immutable and inescapable sequence of events culminating in a diminished sexual drive.[30] Rather than quieting Horney's objections, Freud's new speculations about female sexuality increased his distance from her.

The controversy heated up even more when Freud enhanced the significance of the Oedipus complex, making it not only the trigger of psychosexual development but the marker of sexual difference. It had not always been so. In his early clinical practice, Freud had heard numerous reports of sexual abuse or seduction by parents and had initially linked these childhood traumas to his patients' later neuroses. Eventually, however, he concluded that his patients were actually relating fantasies rather than memories. Abandoning the so-called seduction theory, Freud substituted the Oedipus complex, which he elaborated from the Greek legend of a son's incestuous relationship with his mother. Freud introduced the concept in *The Interpretation of*

Dreams (1900), insisting that all infants desire the parent of the opposite sex: "a girl's first affection is for her father and a boy's first childish desires are for his mother." He initially assumed, in other words, "a complete parallel between the sexes." Finally, in 1923, Freud admitted that the Oedipus complex differed in boys and girls.[31]

It was especially telling that Freud advanced the Oedipus complex by magnifying the factor singled out by Horney as both loathsome and absurd—penis envy. Freud located the onset of the oedipal conflict in the young boy at the moment when he begins to regard his father as a rival for his mother's love. But in observing the father's much larger penis and powerful figure, and noting the corresponding anatomical lack in girls, the boy begins to consider a terrifying possibility: perhaps the girl once possessed a penis but lost it as punishment for desiring her mother! This fear, castration anxiety, is so intense that it completely destroys the Oedipus complex. The boy represses all memory of his infantile desire, enters latency, and identifies with his powerful father. In this fashion, the dissolution of the Oedipus complex consolidates "the masculinity in a boy's character."

Freud then added that the Oedipus complex functions in "a precisely analogous way" in initiating in girls an identification with their mothers and thereby fixing their feminine character. But because girls already lack a penis, they cannot fear castration. Therefore their discovery, rather than destroying the Oedipus complex, gives rise to it: "Although initially, the little girl, like the little boy, disavows her discovery and believes her little organ will grow as big as a penis, she eventually renounces this wish and replaces it with a wish for a baby." To achieve this end, the girl transfers her object-love from her mother, who now becomes her rival, to her father. Freud concluded simply by remarking that the "two wishes—to possess a penis and a child—remain strongly cathected in the unconscious and help to prepare the female creature for her later sexual role." Considered by many Freud's last great theoretical work, *The Ego and the Id* (1923) thus squarely attributes the great psychic differences between men and women to dissimilar resolutions of the Oedipus complex.[32]

Although Freud claimed that his understanding of these processes was "unsatisfactory, incomplete, and vague," he had lent his authority to Abraham's contentions about the central function of penis envy in forming femininity. Insisting on the "primacy of the phallus," Freud specified that "only one genital, namely the male one, comes into account." "Here the feminist demand for equal rights for the sexes does not take us far," he added, "for the morphological distinction is bound to find expression in differences of psychical development." Freud then delivered what would become a much-quoted variation of Napoleon's aphorism: "Anatomy is Destiny."[33]

That "eager crowd of fellow workers" had finally forced him, Freud admitted, to supply a distinct outline of female psychosexual development. Suffering from cancer of the jaw, he asked his daughter Anna to deliver at the Ninth International Psycho-Analytical Congress at Bad Homburg in 1925 his long-awaited and provocative address. "Some Psychical Consequences of the Anatomical Distinction between the Sexes," the first of three essays on the subject, restates basic premises. But whereas Freud had phrased his earlier statements clinically and dispassionately, he now presented a narrative of female psychosexual development that bordered on melodrama. Girls are fated, he declared, to make a "momentous discovery" in noticing a boy's penis, described as "strikingly visible and of large proportions." Of course, they "at once recognize it as the superior counterpart of their own small and inconspicuous organ, and from that time forward fall a victim to envy for the penis." Moreover, the little girl makes "her decision in a flash": "She has seen it and knows that she is without it and wants to have it."

Freud, in describing several possible resolutions of penis envy, restated the familiar opposition, homosexuality and/or feminism versus femininity. Refusing to accept the fact of castration, a girl may behave as if she were a man; or if she does accept it, she may begin "to share the contempt felt by men for a sex which is the lesser in so important a respect" and similarly insist on acting like a man. More likely, a girl displaces her envy and simply exhibits jealousy toward men. Preferably, the girl directs her rage at her mother for bringing her into the world "so insufficiently equipped." Then, as she comes to accept her anatomical inferiority, the girl realizes she cannot compete with boys on this score and turns "violently against that pleasurable activity of masturbation." Now on track, the girl "gives up her wish for a penis and puts in place of it a wish for a child: and with that purpose in view she takes her father as love-object." At last, the girl "has turned into a little woman."

But even in this best case, according to Freud, femininity signals a lack. Because the fear of castration is so overwhelming, the boy thoroughly represses his desire for his mother, identifies strongly with his father, and becomes in the process psychologically prepared to take on the great work of civilization. Girls, in contrast, do not fear castration and consequently do not develop a strong superego. The feminine superego, Freud specified, "is never so inexorable, so impersonal, so independent of its emotional origins as we require it to be in men." Luckily, he suggested, civilization is spared this pernicious influence because genital transference—the rejection of the clitoris for the vagina—prepares the girl for her role in reproduction.

Hoping to close this discussion, Freud instead triggered a momentous feud. He certainly did not help his case by once again dismissing the "feminist" contention that the two sexes are "completely equal in position and worth."[34] His vocal adversaries did not target his patently gratuitous remarks about feminism, however, or even his increasingly sensational rendering of penis envy and genital transference. Rather, it was the assumption of female anatomical inferiority that bothered them.

True to a deeply rooted political tradition, several women who, like Horney, abjured the feminist label refused to regard woman's desire for motherhood, as Freud did, as mere compensation for genital deficiency. Nor would they consider femininity a quality incompatible with the work of civilization. Nevertheless, they were unwilling to forsake psychoanalysis to solve their problems with its chief male promulgators. They forged ahead, revising and revising until they achieved a satisfactory theory of female sexuality.

The Great Debate

For a decade Europe's leading psychoanalysts contested over the meaning of female sexuality. Karen Horney, in Berlin, led the dissenting ranks until the early 1930s. Although much more circumspect than Horney, Ernest Jones and Melanie Klein played important roles in Great Britain; Otto Fenichel and Sándor Radó carried on related discussions in Central Europe. Freud found his defenders in the faithful Jeanne Lampl-de Groot, Helene Deutsch, and Ruth Mack Brunswick.

At stake was nothing less than the basic doctrine of Freudian psycho-analysis.[35]

Horney started off on a high note, once again denouncing the masculine bias in psychoanalytic theory. Speaking to the Berlin Psycho-analytical Society in October 1925, she complained that Freud, who had admitted that female development held no interest for him, proved unwilling to limit his conclusions to the subjects he did study. Freud had a nasty habit, Horney charged, of conflating "human being" and "man" and then formulating all theory from the male point of view. Penis envy was, of course, the prime example. Only a male chauvinist, she brazenly added, could come up with such a preposterous idea.

Femininity did not depend on any male organ, Horney countered, or even on a homologous one like the "small and inconspicuous" clitoris. Nor did it develop in reaction to an ego-shattering confrontation with the phallus. A little girl might develop a transitory envy of a boy's ability to manipulate and display his genitals, Horney once again affirmed. Mainly, however, girls relate to the penis libidinally, as an object of potential pleasure, rather than narcissistically, as a possession they can never possess.

Horney was no longer willing merely to complain about the male bias in psychoanalysis: she was ready to propose an alternative model of female psychosexual development. But, having rejected the Freudian combo of penis envy and genital transference, she did not wish to reclaim the clitoris as a perpetual site of female sexuality. Instead, she recast tenets popularized by Ellen Key and given political urgency by the Bund für Mutterschütz into the distinctive language of psycho-analysis and posited a specifically female morphological site of femininity, the vagina.

Female sexuality does not originate in genital transference, Horney argued, but is a "primal, biological principle." She bolstered this contention with data collected by her friend the pediatrician and fellow analyst Josine Müller, who found that even very young girls experience pleasurable sensations in their vagina. Elaborating, Horney insisted that the vaginal zone, more strongly cathected than the clitoris, plays just as large a part "in incestuous fantasies in girls as the penis does in boys." She admitted that this hypothesis did not deal sufficiently with the origin of that "mysterious attraction" to the opposite sex.

Despite its shortcomings, Horney believed that her alternative to Freud's scenario was "more true to the facts of [woman's] nature—with its specific qualities and its differences from man." And, as if to settle a related argument, Müller added that the woman most likely to achieve full vaginal sexuality was one who succeeded in her career.[36]

Horney turned the tables and described masculinity as a reaction to female magnificence. Freud had formulated the concept of genital primacy, she charged, in order to evade "the other great biological difference, namely the different parts played by men and women in the function of reproduction":

At this point I, as a woman, ask in amazement, and what about motherhood? And the blissful consciousness of bearing a new life within oneself? And the ineffable happiness of the increasing expectation of the appearance of this new being? And the joy when it finally makes its appearance and one holds it for the first time in one's arms? And the deep pleasurable feeling of satisfaction in suckling it and the happiness of the whole period when the infant needs her care?

Horney refused to consider the desire for a baby a compensation for any lack, genital or otherwise. She designated motherhood a marker of woman's "quite indisputable and by no means negligible physiological superiority." Is it no wonder, then, that a boy's development hinges on envy of woman's power?

Everything added up to a conclusion opposite to Freud's. Horney judged men's masculine behavior and domineering attitude products of their need to overcompensate for their relatively insignificant role in the creation of living beings. Moreover—and here she appeared to strike directly at Freud—she argued that men responded intellectually to their feelings of inferiority by fabricating such implausible tenets as penis envy. Even more revealing was men's depiction of motherhood as "only a burden that makes the struggle for existence harder," a hardship they insist they are happy not to have to endure. The impulse to depreciate woman, Horney warned, "is a very powerful one."

Horney matched Freud point by point. Young boys, in confronting the reproductive capacity of their mothers, develop massive feelings of inferiority, a femininity complex. To offset this inadequacy, men not only aggressively pursue activities outside the sphere of reproduction but project, "brutally or delicately," their own shortcomings onto women. And because they are more physically powerful, men force women to internalize these derogatory attitudes. She went so far as to outline a primordial paternal rape fantasy.[37]

This reversal allowed Horney to reinterpret the genesis of the masculinity complex in women. She admitted that some women do become envious of men and seek to model themselves along masculine lines. But the source of this psychic malady is not a girl's envy of any protrusive part of male anatomy. To the contrary, women reject femininity because men, in reacting so spitefully to woman's procreative powers, enforce misogyny as a universal rule. Most women, however, resist this cultural dictate and delight in their femininity. Hardly a marker of normal psychosexual development, as Freud contended, the masculinity complex according to Horney is a sign of neurosis.

The bravado of Horney's formulations did not go unnoticed. At the Tenth International Psycho-Analytical Congress in Innsbruck in 1927, participants interrupted major debates over the merits of lay as opposed to medically trained analysts to reconsider Freud's theory of female psychosexual development. Breaking ranks, Melanie Klein unequivocally located early and distinct heterosexual desires in early infancy, "phallic impulses" to penetrate in boys and "vaginal receptivity" in girls. Ernest Jones implied that perhaps "unduly phallo-centric" male analysts had underestimated "the importance of the female organs"; a few years later he more boldly traced femininity to "the inner promptings of an instinctual constitution." Although always hesitant to criticize Freud, even the loyalist Helene Deutsch found it hard to ignore that "mysterious, heterosexual part of the little girl's libido."[38]

"It seems that this whole field of feminine psychology abounds in problems," one British observer concluded in 1932. While Horney, Klein, and Jones lined up on one side, Freud's defenders acted to shore up his major postulates, specifically penis envy and genital transference. At subsequent international congresses Otto Fenichel, Felix Boehm, Sándor Ferenczi, as well as Jeanne Lampl-de Groot affirmed the basic outline of Freud's interpretation. There remained, Jones admitted, "an unmistakable disharmony" in the ranks.[39]

By this time Freud had been pushed to the limit of his ability to respond reasonably to these criticisms. Experiencing considerable pain from his cancer of the jaw and fearing a serious division in his ranks, he sought to dampen dangerous controversy with a mixture of limited accommodation and chivalry (or feigned chivalry) toward his female colleagues. Mainly, however, he reasserted his own arguments and encouraged the ranks to move on to other subjects.

Freud underscored the importance of penis envy. Since 1924 he had been aware of rumblings about infantile vaginal sensations. Abraham, for one, had noted that the recent findings did not mesh well with the hypothesis of genital transference and advised Freud to follow up on this new research. At the time Freud had demurred, insisting as always that "the female side of the problem is extraordinarily obscure."[40] But now, embroiled in the controversy, Freud chose to restate his case. It is penis envy, he insisted, that gives "its special stamp to the character of females as social beings."

Freud held his ground. His essay "Female Sexuality," published in 1932, again traces the process by which a girl transfers affection from her mother to her father and moves from clitoral to vaginal sexuality, but with a new twist. Recent work by Lampl-de Groot had prompted Freud to reconsider the girl's pre-oedipal attachment to her mother. There is, he belatedly admitted, something significant in *very* early female development. But Freud used this new revelation to bolster rather than to modify his position. An "intense and passionate" pre-oedipal attachment to the mother lays the basis, he reasoned, for an equally strong attachment to the father. On the question of genital transference, Freud did not give an inch: "we are justified in assuming that for many years the vagina is virtually non-existent and possibly does not produce sensations until puberty." Horney's notion of "feminine impulses," he pointedly remarked, did not "tally" with his own. Freud added that he was not surprised that "women analysts" and "men analysts with feminist views" might disagree with him on this matter.[41]

By 1933 Freud had to concede that female sexuality was a subject of "interest second almost to no other." He also appeared especially eager to put it aside. He paused only long enough to characterize Horney's alternative hypothesis as "a solution of ideal simplicity." Then, after graciously acknowledging several "excellent women colleagues," he turned on the dissenters. Some "ladies," Freud complained, "whenever some comparison seemed to turn out unfavourable to their sex, were able to utter a suspicion that we, the male analysts, had been unable to overcome deeply-rooted prejudices against what was feminine, and that this was being paid for in the partiality of our researches." Of course, men "had no difficulty in avoiding impoliteness. We had only to say, 'This doesn't apply to *you*. You're the exception; on this point you're more masculine than feminine.' " This response corresponded with Freud's postulate that masculinity and femininity operate to various degrees in both sexes. Nevertheless, there is no doubt that in isolating his female critics from "real" women, Freud had cleverly personalized the dispute. He spitefully rehearsed the unpleasant mannish stereotypes of feminists that, ironically, Horney and others also abjured.

Once again, Freud reaffirmed the significance of penis envy. "If you reject this idea as fantastic and regard my belief in the influence of lack of a penis on the configuration of femininity as a *idée fixe*," he added, "I am of course defenceless." Freud meant not that he was without theoretical fortification but that he could not, or would not, continue to argue on behalf of this basic tenet. As a consolation, he reminded critics that he had only been "describing women insofar as their nature is determined by their sexual function." That influence "extends very far" but does not fully encompass all aspects of a woman's humanity. Yet, Freud persisted, there are "no other roots" of femininity than penis envy.

More to the point, Freud signaled his intention to close off discussion: "That is all I had to say to you about femininity." Once more he apologized for the "incomplete and fragmentary" character of his theories, and he repented that his remarks did not "always sound friendly." With that said, he fled the field. "If you want to know more about femininity," he advised, "enquire from your own experiences of life, or turn to the poets, or wait until science can give you deeper and more coherent information."[42]

The place of feminism in this dialogue remained conceptually vital although semantically confusing. So completely had its definition shifted after the war that even Freud's most furious adversaries accepted the new, narrowed meaning and commonly classified feminists as men-envying, or men-hating, women. This definitional metamorphosis necessarily blunted Horney's challenge. Horney might readily characterize Freud as a misogynist, but she lacked a means to position herself politically or even to identify her allies. On what basis could she respond to Freud's final word on this subject, issued long after he had formally withdrawn from discussion? In "Analysis Terminable and Interminable" (1937), one of his last essays, Freud contrasted the therapeutic goals for male and female patients. The therapist helps men to *develop* their capacities, sexual and otherwise, and assists women to *resign* themselves to their deficiencies. "Analysis cannot encourage in women new energies for success and achievement," he wrote, "but only and finally, teach them the lesson of a rational resignation to the demands of their natures." Horney, in contrast, saw nothing limiting in women's natures. To the contrary, she extolled not merely the compatibility but the mutual benefit of career and motherhood. But Horney lacked a language to fend off Freud's claim that women were intended for one specific role, a feminine role which "intellectual training" would only cause them to deprecate.[43]

There appears to be no question, though, that the tenets of prewar feminism continued to inform Horney's argument. The exaltation of female sexuality, especially the celebration of motherhood, not only persisted but served as the foundation of her critical judgment of Freud. On premises that would have been familiar to many prewar activists in Europe and the United States, Horney had no difficulty asserting that woman was essentially different from man but equal, if not superior, in her capacities. And the welfare of society, the progress of civilization, depended on woman's distinctive contribution.

Even Helene Deutsch (1884–1982), who considered herself Freud's implacable defender, could not help arriving at a similar conclusion. After training in psychiatry, she had joined Freud's weekly Wednesday evening sessions, become a member of the Vienna Psycho-analytic Society in 1918, and entered what proved to be a brief analysis with Freud himself. Founding president of the Training Institute of the Vienna Psycho-analytic Society, she became the first psychoanalyst to write a lengthy essay on female psychology, *Psychoanalysis of the Sexual Functions of Women,* which appeared in 1925 from Freud's publishing house in Vienna. Here, Deutsch opposed Horney on the penis-envy matter but agreed that procreation is the basic marker of sexual difference. Deutsch therefore could accept Freud's notion of genital transference but propose an entirely different trigger, not merely the trauma of anatomical deficiency but the psychic emergence of the vagina as the "maternal receptacle." "A woman who succeeds in establishing this maternal function of the vagina by giving up the claim of the clitoris to represent the penis," she expounded, "has reached the goal of feminine development, she *has become a woman*." Deutsch managed to surpass Horney in describing childbirth as "the acme of sexual pleasure."[44]

Although there was little correspondence between their formulations, Horney and Deutsch both remained intellectually within the maternal orbit. Female sexuality—as well as male sexuality, in Horney's opinion—derives from this essential difference from man and eventually shapes woman's subjectivity. Only woman, through pregnancy, childbirth, and lactation, according to Deutsch, can regain "the bliss of the primal state, the unity of subject and object" forever lost to man.[45] Woman enjoys, in other words, an autonomous source of, and sense of, self. In different ways, Deutsch and Horney rejected Freud's handling of motherhood, that is, his projection of woman's desire for a baby as a simple displacement of penis envy. Neither resolution, however, proved entirely satisfying.

The disagreement between the founder of psychoanalysis and the "ladies" and the "men analysts with feminist views"—mistakenly labeled the "Freud-Jones controversy"—did not conclude with Freud's pullout. It finally subsided in the mid-1930s but not before providing the context for the first major psychoanalytic revisionism carried out mainly in the United States. Questions of femininity would then follow the contours of an entirely different framework, where "culture" reigned clearly over "nature" to supersede both Freud and his "feminist" adversaries.

Meanwhile Freud and Horney struck at fundamentals, each accusing the other of the especially loathsome deviation known as *biologism*. In 1935, in a private letter to a colleague, Freud stated clearly that he objected "to all of you to the extent that you do not distinguish more clearly and cleanly between what is psychic and what is biological." Psychoanalysis, he insisted, must be maintained separate from biology. Yet Freud eventually became widely known, as one later critic put it, as a "biologist of the mind."[46] Horney repeatedly levied this very charge against Freud and went on to lead what became known as the "culturalist" school of American psychoanalysis.

During the 1920s, however, Freud and Horney appeared equally culpable of biologism. Freud generally sidestepped the issue by discounting the significance of such basic factors as the differing biochemistries of men and women. No one knew—and perhaps no one ever would know—how the production of semen or ova contributes to the shaping of masculinity or femininity, he argued, and to expect scientists one day to "disclose a substance to us whose presence produces a male excitation and another substance which produces a female one" struck him as decidedly "naive."[47] And even if such a biochemical substance did exist, he insisted, its psychological significance would still be a matter to be determined. Meanwhile Freud found "enough to study in those human individuals who, through the possession of female genitals, are characterized as manifestly or predominantly feminine." In any case, he did not define as his mission "to describe what a woman is—that would be a task [psychoanalysis] could scarcely perform—but . . . enquiring how she comes into being, how a woman develops out of a child with a bisexual disposition."[48]

But the gaps in Freud's arguments did not become smaller. Freud had regularly employed the term *bedrock* to refer to fields strictly beyond the reach of psychoanalytic investigation, such as the study of purely physiological origins of disease or the movement of blood through veins and arteries. At times it proved just too tempting to push annoying problems into the realm of the unknown and unknowable bedrock territory. One way out of the theoretical quagmire, then, was to define femininity, as Freud did on one occasion, as "nothing else than a biological fact, a part of the great riddle of sex."[49] In that light, femininity remained beyond analysis, its significance inexplicable.

Horney herself vacillated between two modes of argument. In describing vaginal sexuality as a "primal, biological principle," and in claiming "an instinct of procreation which is feminine," she had clearly succumbed to biologism.[50] Yet, while underscoring these constitutional differences, she also employed psychoanalytic reasoning, emphasizing the traumatic episodes of childhood that gave meaning to these phenomena. What set off Horney's paradigms from Freud's was not the means of argument as much as the relationship between figure and ground: she inverted the significance attached to "male" and "female." In "The Dread of Woman" (1932), for example, Horney again presented woman as the model human being and masculinity as a vengeful product of male envy of female reproductive power. It is the boy, not the girl, who suffers a major psychic wound in experiencing his mother's rejection of his tiny penis. This event, Horney alleged, compels men throughout life to compensate for feelings of inferiority. In attempting to redress their inadequacy, men develop a severe case of phallic narcissism and, moreover, seek to dominate and demean women in every possible way, materially, morally, and sexually. Horney's concept of "womb envy" thus structurally mirrored Freud's notion of "penis envy." By the time they finished sparring, however, Horney and Freud had certainly clarified the problem of, as Jones put it, "whether a woman is born or made." They had by no means resolved it.[51]

In addressing the question feminists had made so vital during the opening decades of the twentieth century, psychoanalysts of various stripes helped to overturn long-standing conventions. They all promoted a view of woman as a sexual as well as reproductive being and thereby broke definitively with whatever remnants of Victorian passionlessness still grabbed the public imagination. Their major antagonism stemmed from the meanings they attached to female sexuality, its origins and functions.

Freud had not intended to construct a psychology of sex differences. Until pushed by his colleagues, he preferred to discuss woman as object of man's desire and to avoid questions of female subjectivity. Feminists, for their part, had searched desperately for the emotional traits that distinguished woman from man and hoped, in addition, to correlate various qualities not only with a specifically feminine sexual desire but with a social imperative. Building on this foundation, Horney explicitly warned against the hazard "in accepting any ideas based on far-reaching parallelism between man and woman."[52] Instead, she and her allies intended to superimpose a psychology of difference on a sociology of equality. Freud, while generous to many aspiring professional women within his ranks, believed that only exceptional women could or should pursue life's adventures outside the domestic sphere.

If psychoanalysts disagreed on the origins as well as the meaning of the differences between the sexes, they found a common, although shaky, ground in vaginal sexuality. They might agree on the analogy basic to Freud's schema, that is, that the clitoris and penis are homologous organs. They also might commonly designate the vagina as the ultimate, although not necessarily original, site of mature female sexuality. But there was no accord on the processes governing this psychic reality. For Horney, Jones, and Klein, the vagina was primary, available to the woman since early childhood; for Freud and Deutsch, vaginal sexuality emerged through a complex sequence of psychosexual development. But whereas Deutsch clung to Freud's earlier description of pubertal awakening, Freud himself revised his chronology to emphasize the phallic stage, that is, oedipal trauma and penis envy. Thus even for the loyalist Deutsch, penis envy could not deliver the requisite explanatory power. Like Horney, she preferred to validate the vagina as intrinsic to femininity: the vagina symbolized woman's procreative power. But everyone, it seemed, was willing to give up the clitoris as the persistent site of female erotic pleasure. All the more remarkable was their timing: psychoanalysts promoted this argument just as researchers in the biological sciences had established the insensitivity of the vagina.

This profusion of irony escaped the major players, and for better or worse another transposition lay just ahead. In the United States, new oppositions were emerging: biology versus culture; Freudian versus neo-Freudian; and European versus American—all set against yet another permutation of feminism.

3

Culture and Feminine Personality

By 1932 Karen Horney had begun to move beyond the boundaries of Freudian psychoanalysis. Once merely faultfinding, she now rejected its fundamental premises. In an act of private protest she removed Freud's portrait from her home. Meanwhile her public statements sounded increasingly strident. The author of nine essays on female psychosexual development, Horney had prepared well to advance an alternative theory of psychoanalysis and to play a key role in the formation of a distinctly American school.[1]

Horney also broke with the tenets of prewar feminism. Within a few years she came up with an entirely new assessment of the causes and consequences of the differences between the sexes. This shift did not, however, constitute a retreat in her battle against the "masculinist" bias in psychoanalysis. If anything, she became even more determined to "fight against men's prejudices and fears."[2] But in the realm of theory, Horney moved in an entirely different direction.

These turns coincided with—and were facilitated by—Horney's newfound identity as an emigrée intellectual. In 1932, at age forty-seven, Horney moved with two of her daughters to Chicago, where she became associate director of one of the first American psychoanalytic institutes. Unlike many other (especially male) exiles from Hitler's Germany, she found the United States personally congenial, and she flourished. She arrived, according to her new friend Margaret Mead, a typical European intellectual with "a studiously neglected appearance, no makeup, a plain dress." At their next meeting Horney "looked elegant, with an expensive hat and dress." This eye-catching transformation went far beyond personal appearance. In attacking Freudian theory, Horney became so unyielding that she jeopardized her working relationship with the director of the Chicago Psychoanalytic Institute, Franz Alexander. Unintimidated, Horney persevered. "The greater freedom from dogmatic beliefs which I found in this country," she later observed, "alleviated the obligation of taking psychoanalytic theories for granted, and gave me the courage to proceed along lines which I considered right." Horney had, in short, exchanged the gray raiment of European theory for the green of the New World. In 1934 she moved to New York City, where she joined other distinguished emigrés—Wilhelm Reich, Erich Fromm, and Erik Erikson, to mention only the most famous—who would soon assist her in modifying the psychoanalytic canon and in placing its American practice on a solid footing.[3]

Horney immigrated at an opportune moment for her own career and for the development of psychoanalysis in the United States. Until 1930 Americans could not train in their own country. By necessity, they sojourned professionally in Europe before setting up a private practice in the United States or joining the faculty of an American university or medical college. Small in number, they enjoyed little status within the International Psycho-Analytic Association. As late as 1920 the American Psychoanalytic Society, which had formed in 1911, attracted only ten persons to its annual meeting. Within a decade the situation changed dramatically. Fleeing fascism in Central Europe, at least forty or fifty—some estimates run as high as two hundred— refugee analysts came to the United States and established the nation's first training institutes. In 1932 the *Psychoanalytic Quarterly* was founded, and the *Bulletin of the American Psychoanalytic Association* followed in 1937. Professional membership grew exponentially, and by 1938 Americans represented approximately one-third of the membership of the International Psycho-Analytic Association. The New York Psychoanalytic Association, with just under eighty members, had become the largest in the world.[4]

Contrary to Freud's earlier prediction, the United States proved very hospitable to the advancement of psychoanalysis and by 1940 served as its international center. Freudianism continued to stir controversy, especially among the clergy and religious leaders, but there was no denying its impact on the behavioral sciences. According to one estimate, over two hundred books on the subject appeared during the 1920s alone. Freudian ideas extended far beyond the bohemian circles and medical enclaves circa 1909 to reach nearly everyone and everywhere, occasionally with unanticipated results. In New York, where clinical practices flourished, one woman, according to the *New York Times*, "after reading 102 books on psychoanalysis and allied subjects, despaired of her life and turned on the gas" and killed herself. But even remote populations could sample books like James Oppenheim's *Your Hidden Powers* (1923) by ordering through the Sears, Roebuck catalog.[5]

At the same time, psychoanalysis in the United States expanded far beyond its own professional ranks to become an interdisciplinary endeavor. During the interwar period Freudian theory continued to engage left-wing intellectuals and attracted a growing number of historians, sociologists, economists, and literary critics, who soon outnumbered psychoanalysts in the production of books and essays on the subject. Anthropologists played a leading part by "testing" specific tenets of Freud's universal theory through field research among non-Western peoples, while literary scholars and dramatists found new, creative uses for them. Of course, European psychoanalysts were by no means narrow in their intellectual pursuits. Freud himself set a fine example in his avid pursuit of Western history and culture. The European training facilities all sponsored programs in the humanities. The Berlin Psychoanalytic Institute mandated, for example, courses in art, literature, and anthropology. In the United States, however, scholars of the humanities and social sciences increasingly cornered both academic and popular markets. When Horney arrived in the United States in 1932, professional consolidation still lay ahead, but this assortment of unaffiliated intellectuals, university-sponsored scholars, and psychoanalysts had already begun a major reworking of Freudian theory.

At the heart was a new emphasis on the external influences on psychic development. Unlike Freud, who stressed instincts and constitutional factors, the enterprising revisionists highlighted the social environment, including its historical dimension. Childhood experiences remained central, but the roles of parents and, indeed, of the entire society became much more prominent as determinants than the instinctual drives central to classical Freudian theory. What resulted was a novel interdisciplinary endeavor, inspired by psychoanalysis but tested by scholars in other disciplines, known as "Culture and Personality."

This perspective, also known as *culturalism,* became the hallmark of a unique (and later disparaged) brand of psychoanalysis that prevailed in the United States until well after World War II. Conditions in the United States such as the nation's democratic heritage and multiethnic population, Franz Alexander once proposed, favored this "exaggeration of environmental factors." Or perhaps merely the physical distance from Freud allowed his American successors to surpass their European peers in translating psychoanalysis into cultural theory.[6]

Freudian theory now seemed to beg for a major reassessment. As the American psychoanalyst Clara Thompson observed, so much had changed since Freud began his work, especially in the all-important realm of sexuality. Like the Victorian era which had inspired Freud, modern society fostered a multitude of problems, she admitted, but sexual repression was not the major one. Thompson joined other Americans who concluded that, in light of this major shift in sentiment, Freud's libido theory, including his prized Oedipus complex, no longer weighed in with its former prominence. They preferred to consider other, more social influences on psychic development, such as interpersonal relations. Moreover, they expanded the investigatory project to cover not only the familiar malady of neurosis but the whole of character, that is, the entire constellation of traits and behaviors that make up the individual personality.[7]

This sweeping, so-called Americanization process took a heavy toll on psychoanalytic orthodoxy. The energetic revisionists not only shunted aside the distinctively Freudian concept of penis envy but, in downgrading sexuality, broke away from the reproductive teleology that undergirded classical psychoanalysis. Within a decade American theorists had provided an entirely new basis for evaluating the differences between the sexes.

Karen Horney proved to be an exemplar of these changes. As a principal player, she helped to overhaul the reigning psychoanalytic theories of femininity, including her own. If she had previously challenged Freud's "masculine bias" by inverting his paradigm, substituting womb envy in boys for penis envy in girls, she and her new colleagues now escaped the entire logic of his system. Eventually she set aside all innate biological impulses for environmental influences. As a professed culturalist, Horney declared her new and decidedly modern faith: "Human nature [is] no longer unalterable but could change."[8] There is, in short, no causal relationship between anatomy and destiny.

Sexual Modernism

American intellectuals had begun to lay the foundation for these revisions well before Horney and other European analysts immigrated to the United States. Although World War I had fractured left political movements, and the Red Scare of the early 1920s had driven many prominent radicals such as Emma Goldman into exile, a resurgence was under way by the end of the decade. The cast of surviving players appeared eerily familiar. Charlotte Perkins Gilman, for example, complained about the renewed interest in Freud's theories, while Floyd Dell found fresh uses for them. These aging actors now met yet another generation of left and liberal intellectuals who shared the opinion of the bestselling French author André Siegfried, a modern-day Tocqueville, that the United States had "again become a new world."[9] They set themselves to meet the exigencies of the postwar era.

Feminism entered into these discussions in a new way. As Dell noted, "the extreme pre-war feminist theory" that had extolled the differences between the sexes had since narrowed in meaning to mere careerism now that women worked and voted alongside men. It had become for him, as for many Europeans, a negative point of reference, the banner of those obstinate women who advocated the unpopular Equal Rights Amendment. At best, feminism signaled a woman's desire to combine a career with marriage and motherhood; at worst, in its most "militant" form, feminism represented a sublimation of women's sex drive into careers. But to most Americans feminism seemed merely passé. The anthropologist Ruth Fulton Benedict resigned herself to this reality: "We can hardly drag back from oblivion the vital questions that were the life and death to us that early summer of 1914." Subsequent events, above all world war, had rendered feminism, in her opinion, "nonexistent."[10]

The issues that had given substance to prewar feminism—female sexuality and femininity—did not disappear. Nor did their political significance diminish. Yet in the 1920s American innovators advanced a reading strikingly unlike the one that had excited the prewar generation in the United States and continued to motivate Horney and her allies in Europe. If the earlier enthusiasts had forced psychoanalytic theory into a speculative mold that granted a distinct trajectory of female psychosexual development ending in motherhood, their successors now took an opposite tack. It was not only feminism that had become obsolete, it seemed, but the emphasis on sexual difference itself.

Both feminism and psychoanalysis had, in their own ways, entered the "Modern Age." Just as young women elected to label themselves "modern" rather than "feminist," so too did radical intellectuals aspire to revamp psychoanalysis. At the heart of this revision lay a new historicism. Modernism signified to this generation not merely an aesthetic sensibility but a discernible epoch of human history. The term *modern* referred to both the increasingly streamlined design of the built environment and the freer lifestyle and moral code emerging under the canopy of the new edifice. The Industrial Revolution, these intellectuals insisted, stood behind all these developments, reshaping the material basis of society and thus providing a foundation for new relationships—not just in the factory, the realm of production, but also in the bedroom, the site of reproduction. The revisionists of the 1920s placed sexuality in this new historical context and endowed Freud's famous theory with an equally updated function.

Nowhere is this shift more apparent than in the Jazz Age discussions of female sexuality. Whereas prewar radicals and feminists alike had embraced Freudianism to hasten the demise of Victorian morality, those who survived now believed that the carnage of world war had sealed its fate. Americans as well as Europeans emerged from the conflagration with a profound sense of realism about the human condition. It was, then, a *post*-emancipatory promise that fired their imaginations. As for modern women, their aspirations for sexual liberation had, it seemed, been more than realized.

If Freud had once singled out the excessive repression of female desire as the major source of neurosis in his women clients and frustration in the men, Americans in the 1920s fretted about a new problem—the wanton sexuality of flappers. Nearly half of all young women engaged in premarital intercourse, a proportion that would not change until the 1960s, while many others eagerly "explored the borderlands." Not inhibition but "sex starvation" dominated the complaints of these insatiable innovators. Having achieved widespread recognition, female desire now threatened to engulf the nation. Both popular culture and academic scholarship registered this risk. Magazine tabloids and Hollywood motion pictures, for example, played it up. The advertisement for *Flaming Youth,* a highly successful Hollywood film, guaranteed titillation from "neckers, petters, white kisses, red kisses, pleasure-mad daughters, sensation-craving mothers."[11] More middlebrow, a volume of essays edited by Freda Kirchwey, editor of *The Nation,* signaled the same message. *Our Changing Morality* (1930) provided a forum for leading scholars to discuss such burning issues as censorship of the media, "illicit sex," and especially premarital and female adolescent sexuality. The problem that had plagued the prewar generation—too little preparation for sex—had transmuted into a fear of far too much.

Not a few senior reformers expressed a sense of *Schadenfreude* over the current excesses and did not hesitate to blame Freud for this unsavory development. Before the war, the veteran reformer Lillian Wald reflected, sexuality had emerged as a liberating force, so much so that "only an inflexible watcher of the times could have failed to see the advantage of frankness over the hypocrisy and surreptitious experiment" of an earlier era. But the promise had been betrayed, psychoanalysis deserving much of the blame. Wald's colleague Jane Addams complained that "the Freudian theories as to dangers of repression were seized upon by agencies of publicity, by half-baked lecturers and by writers on the new psychology and finally interpreted by tackless youth as a warning against self-control." Not surprisingly, the "wild excitement over sex" alarmed Gilman, who feared that all the hard-won victories would be overturned as young women abandoned the pursuit of equality to chase their prospects for love and marriage.[12]

Those intellectuals determined to revivify psychoanalysis assessed the situation more calmly. Dell answered these complaints by insisting that excesses inevitably accompany any major transition. Phyllis Blanchard, the prominent psychologist who had trained with G. Stanley Hall, likewise mused that it was natural that, "in the first flush of delight in the discovery of sex as a source of pleasure," women were tempted "to exploit it." Just as careers fell short of providing women with "the universal gratification" once anticipated, Blanchard admitted, sex had not yet "fulfilled the promise of creating joy." Nevertheless, she joined Dell in holding out high expectations for the "modern girl."[13]

As for motherhood, this once hallowed goal had lost much of its former appeal and had become for the modern woman merely one of life's options. Fortified by Freud's wisdom and facilitated by "the most far-reaching invention of our age—effective contraceptives," the popular writer Beatrice Forbes-Robertson Hale announced, women were finally beginning to define their needs without regard to the biological imperative to bear children. Women now wanted to know "what proportion . . . of their activities must, or should be set aside for the sex life of love and reproduction, and what proportion can and will be deflected into more various human fields." They assumed, in short, that the spheres of production and reproduction held out similar, and not necessarily competing, rewards. Yet to address these monumental questions, and to ease anxiety in the meantime, psychoanalysis still appeared to be the best therapeutic mechanism.[14]

Psychoanalysis took on, then, a new function in the Modern Age. Men and women suffered less from old-fashioned sexual repression than from the confusion and stress of uncertainty, what the rising generation of theorists termed *anxiety.* "Instability rides the mind of modernity," one writer warned. Society had become so "agog with new creation," as another observer put it, that men and women "have not been able to adjust themselves to this incessantly changing and unstable scene." Drawing heavily on the observation of the famed sociologist William Fielding Ogburn that society suffered from severe "cultural lag," these critics boldly revised Freud's theories in order to calibrate the new, intensely heterosexual exigencies of post-emancipatory life. Dell went so far as to envision a trained corps of social workers—"a psychoanalytic Salvation Army"—combating malad-justment across the United States.[15]

Envisioning Freud less like Lenin than like Henry Ford, a notably left-leaning coalition swung into action. The erstwhile syndicalist André Tridon (1877–1922) had become an extraordinarily popular psychoanalytic performance artist, gilding his toenails and hosting salons until he died of cancer at an early age. Shortly before his death he addressed up to five hundred members of the National Opera Club gathered for a "psychic tea." His impassioned defense of psychoanal-ysis against the "horrid charges against it" prompted the woman chair-ing the session to implore the listeners to strip off their corsets, join the "unclad flapper," and "learn wonderful things." Tridon's writings, such as *Psychoanalysis and Love* (1922), sounded a similar note, insisting that young men and women needed above all to *adapt*. "Being old-fashioned in love, as in every other activity of life," he warned, "presents a great temptation to the lazy, the unintelligent, the neurotic." As to the "old-fashioned girl," she represented to Tridon "the absolutely sordid type."

Tridon's contemporary Floyd Dell, once a model radical playboy, had meanwhile grown into a more conventional middle age. No longer the free spirit, Dell insisted that Freud's theories could guide emotion-ally and sexually satisfying yet monogamous relationships. He put down his thoughts on this subject in *Love in the Machine Age: A Psychological Study of the Transition from Patriarchal Society* (1930), a massive volume intended "to make people modern-minded." By this time, though, a younger generation of writers had not only taken up the cause but began to lay a new foundation.[16]

An innovative magazine, the *Modern Quarterly,* proved vital to this enterprise. The team of Dell and his former partner Max Eastman, through their work on *The Masses* the editorial savants of the old gang, had in effect abdicated to a new editorial duo of V. F. Calverton and Samuel D. Schmalhausen. Calverton, the more famous of the two, was born George Goetz in Baltimore in 1900 and educated at Johns Hopkins University after a brief career as a semiprofessional baseball player. He came of age a little too late for the Lyrical Left yet embraced its cause. Perusing old copies of *The Masses* and current issues of its successor, *The Liberator,* he planned a new journal that would similarly combine literature, art, and radical politics. In 1923, under his pen name, Calverton dedicated *The Modern Quarterly* to the publication of essays and reviews "complete, scientific, and modern."

Schmalhausen, a decade older than Calverton and an occasional contributor on psychological questions to the pre-1920 socialist magazines, joined the editorial board in 1928. He aspired most of all to apply his doctoral training from Columbia University to a study of "the most meaningful and emotionally deranging transvaluation of habits and attitudes in the history of civilized life," that is, to sexual modernism. Although the *Modern Quarterly* never achieved the stature of *The Masses* or *The Liberator,* its editors managed to make their little magazine the principal forum for psychoanalysis in postwar left quarters.[17]

The popular press quickly labeled their work "the Americanization of Freud." Calverton and Schmalhausen, like their predecessors at *The Masses,* engaged many of the leading political writers and literary critics of the day. In the shifting intellectual climate, they also tapped the talent of outstanding academic scholars, adding an authoritative touch to the *Modern Quarterly* and to massive, very well received anthologies. *Sex in Civilization* (1929), *The New Generation* (1931), and *Woman's Coming of Age* (1931) featured a galaxy of notable writers spanning the generation gap from Havelock Ellis and Charlotte Perkins Gilman to Margaret Mead and reaching from political activism to academia. Margaret Sanger, Rebecca West, Judge Ben Lindsey, and Bronislaw Malinowski all contributed articles. Placing themselves at the center of discussions, and raising funds to cover the debts of the *Modern Quarterly,* the two "sex boys" (as the *New Republic* called them) also launched a series of public forums in Baltimore and New York. Here, Floyd Dell might controversially sing the praises of monogamy while other speakers promised (as advertisements read) to show, "Sex is Necessary! Or, Why You Don't Feel the Way You Should."[18]

The *Modern Quarterly* led the way in reformulating psychoanalysis as cultural theory suited to modern sex relations. If prewar radicals had hailed psychoanalysis as a corrective to economic-determinist Marxism, their successors now proposed a second revolution: they intended to give psychoanalysis a firm materialist foundation. The "Freudian topsy-turveydom" in thinking, argued Schmalhausen, had miscast "true causes" as effects and "by-products" as causes. Freud, the editors complained, had posited a human nature "divorced from social forces, psychology breaking loose from the historic process and floating off into metapsychological speculation without traceable roots in reality." Marx, in contrast, had keenly observed that history marked the continual transformation of human nature. In this era that was "achieving marvels in objective science and technology," Freudianism appeared static and sorely outdated while Marxism seemed surprisingly modern.

In short, Freud's instinct theory went the way of all nineteenth-century mechanistic or fatalistic reasoning, while Marx's open-ended historicism better suited the age of infinite possibility. It remained for the new generation, foremost among them Calverton and Schmalhausen themselves, to rebuild psychoanalysis as a theory "to link up the individual with society." Whereas Freud interpreted neurosis as a symptom of oedipal drama, they insisted on identifying "the hand behind the curtain, the factors that made the Oedipus complex." Whereas Freud envisioned civilization as the product of repressed and sublimated desires, the revisionists aimed to identify the sociohistorical forces that shaped personality. The "sex boys" thereby neatly inverted the causal relationship between the individual psyche and society en route to transforming psychoanalysis into a full-blown cultural theory.[19]

This same psychoanalytic historicism allowed Calverton and Schmalhausen to recast the logic of sexual difference. Befitting their Marxism, they began with the mode of production but focused not on the manufacture and distribution of goods but on its relationship to reproduction. Calverton and Schmalhausen thus appreciated the fit between Freud's own clinical methods and the psychic crisis at the dusk of the bourgeois epoch, a particular crisis that played itself out in the family rather than in the factory. It was Freud's genius to design a therapy suited to the "psychopathology of family life." But Freud's theory ultimately became stifled by its premises. He had provided a brilliant outline of female psychosexual development within the family of late nineteenth-century Europe but had fatally mistaken this thoroughly *bourgeois* and conspicuously *patriarchal* manifestation for a *universal* condition. In short, Freud lacked a historical perspective on sex relations. To wit: who could now believe that adult women experience a diminished sexual drive and desire babies merely as compensation for a feeling of genital insufficiency? This particular Freudian assumption routinely elicited, as one critic noted, "eloquent" smiles from modern women. The theorist who had identified humanity's "most vital urge" had failed to consider the historical factors governing its activation.[20]

Freud's notions of female sexuality simply did not hold up. Calverton, Schmalhausen, Dell, and a host of sociologists all agreed that the Industrial Revolution had successfully eroded the material basis for the patriarchal family. As women joined the paid labor force, they gained at least a modicum of financial independence and began to construct an identity for themselves outside the reproductive categories designated by either Freud or prewar feminists. "The great discovery of the ages," Schmalhausen insisted, is "the realization that woman wants sex love as men want it, desperately, preferring it, once they have tasted its compensations, to mother love." True, he admitted, the modern woman was going a bit overboard in indulging in the "petty, grand, and glorious 'vices' " that formerly only men enjoyed. "Our lascivious lassies in their Freudian hearts sing blithely," Schmalhausen mused, "Who loves to lie with me/Under the polymorphous tree,/Come hither, come hither, come hither!" Such "libidinous ladies" had found too much "delight and playfulness" in "recreational eroticism." But once she sowed her wild oats, the modern woman would, with the help of psychoanalysis, get her "bearings, in the perilous seas of modern experimentalism." She would never again, however, accept the restrictions placed on her by patriarchy. "The old family has decayed," Calverton cheerfully announced, and woman no longer lives—psychologically or materially—within its singular confines.[21]

This sociohistorical reading of female sexuality allowed the *Modern Quarterly* team to attack that sacred Freudian tenet, penis envy, from a new direction. Calverton and Schmalhausen summarily dismissed this concept as a vastly overrated mechanism invented by man to enhance his relative status. It had to be man who interpreted "every accidental difference of a biologic of psychologic or social nature, between the sexes, as meaning in actuality a difference in favor of himself," the esteemed British anthropologist Robert Briffault affirmed. Karen Horney had said as much in her denunciation of the masculine bias in Freudian theory; the *Modern Quarterly* writers went on to ground this argument within a specific historical context. The force of man's ideas had become so powerful in the patriarchal family that even trivial differences in constitution became symbols of his superiority. Moreover, as Briffault claimed, eventually even woman viewed herself as defined by anatomical differences, as "innately and inexorably feminine." The writers around the *Modern Quarterly* thus designated penis envy a reflection of Freud's not only masculine but decidedly patriarchal sensibility.[22]

Submitted to this critique, the entire edifice of sexual difference began to crumble. This expectation served as the main argument of one of the most popular and frequently cited books of the era, *The Dominant Sex* (1923), by Mathilde and Mathias Vaerting. The "peculiarities" known as masculinity and femininity are merely products of the domination of one sex over another, the German writers contended, a situation destined to end in the twentieth century as the movement toward equality of rights brings "the golden age of the highest possible development of individuality and the highest attainable sexual happiness." "Why should woman be," another writer agreed, "the eternal sphinx as if she inhabited a distant star or as if she were represented by only a rare specimen in some *terra incognita?*"

Contributors to Calverton and Schmalhausen's grand collection on this theme, *Woman's Coming of Age,* answered this question in a variety of ways. The majority rejected the notion of a distinctive or unfailing femininity and instead emphasized the social and economic factors restricting female development. Schmalhausen himself chose to cast his lot with "the blind brave attempt of the sexes to create together a humanized world in which sex differences will remain residually important and yet discontinue to be obsessive and neurotic." The anthropologist Alexander Goldenweiser posed the question yet more boldly, pushing the discussion almost into the realm of *post*modernism. He asked, "is there woman?" If femininity is nothing more than a "man-made illusion," Alice Beals Parson added, why should anyone, especially women, seek to track it down?[23]

The notion that femininity—even female sexuality—might be infinitely malleable marked a sharp departure from both Freudianism and prewar feminism and emerged as a keynote in the revisionist psychoanalytic theories of the 1930s. Neither innate as Horney had once assumed, nor anatomically determined as Freud appeared to argue, femininity had become what a much later generation would term a "cultural construction." Equally important, motherhood, previously the definitive marker of sexual difference, figured hardly at all into this schema. To modernists, motherhood signified a temporary condition requiring skillful management or a role to be avoided entirely by the miracle of effective contraception. More crucial were the dynamics of sexual relations within the family, that is, the sociohistorical context within which reproduction took place.

Calverton and Schmalhausen played no further part in recasting psychoanalytic theory. The famed editorial team described by the *New York Times* as "jointly the Karl Marx of the Sexual Revolution" soon broke up.[24] Schmalhausen resigned from the *Modern Quarterly* in 1932, while Calverton proceeded to revamp the journal in tune with the times. The Great Depression had reenergized the economistic tendencies of the political left, forcing to the back burner the questions of sexual modernism. Since Lenin's amply quoted "drink of water" metaphor, Communists regarded preoccupation with sex a sign of decadence; Stalin in turn banned Freudian psychoanalysis from the Soviet Union. In the United States the economic turmoil of the 1930s only strengthened this attitude, encouraging even Calverton to put aside the sex wars for the class struggle.

But the imprint of sexual modernism remained. The milieu around the *Modern Quarterly* had stretched far beyond the institutional left to include a cluster of left-leaning and liberal academics who would reshape their disciplines and simultaneously bring them into the era's monumental interdisciplinary project, Culture and Personality. Calverton had not failed, then, in specifying the "task of our new age" as creating "the technique of a new science" that will "integrate rather than separate the individual and society."[25] By the mid-1930s leading anthropologists and sociologists as well as psychoanalysts joined together to review sexual relations and behavior patterns throughout Western history and across cultures. This conceptual reformulation marked the revolution in thought, if not in deeds, that the sexual modernists had imagined.

The brilliant linguist Edward Sapir had predicted in the early 1920s that Freud's theories would make their most discernible mark in disciplines outside psychology and psychoanalysis. The anthropologist, he decreed, "needs only to trespass a little on the untilled acres of psychology, the psychiatrist to poach a few of the uneaten apples of anthropology's Golden Bough."[26] Refitted to the anthropologist's hand, the Freudian tool was destined to become a formidable weapon for the "psycho-sociology" that Calverton and his coterie advocated. For a variety of investigators, this new implement would unearth the necessary evidence to prove that femininity is incalculable. Ethnographic research might also reveal a multitude of sexual practices and thereby abet the modernist mission of promoting tolerance and broadmindedness. Everyone might then recognize the transient qualities of even such basic instincts as sexuality. From this point the door would open wide to a liberating cultural relativism outside both the house of Freud and the temple of prewar feminism.

Cultural Relativism

One of the earliest challenges to Freud's biologism originated with the century's greatest anthropologist and preeminent cultural relativist. At the 1909 conference at Clark University, Franz Boas (1858–1942) took over the podium from Sigmund Freud himself. Addressing the psychological dimension of anthropological inquiry, the leading antievolutionist discounted the biological factors in determining "composite" mental traits or characteristics. He attributed such distinctions to "the habitual reactions of the society to which the individual in question belongs."[27] Boas not only promoted a concept of culture that is "cumulative, historical, extra-individual" but presaged the sexual modernists' rejection of absolutes for a kind of "psycho-sociology." As early as 1888 he had insisted that emotions resulted from "the form of our social life and of the history of people to whom we belong." Forty years later *Anthropology and Modern Life* (1928), written for general readers, reaffirmed this principle, additionally arguing that a study of anthropology "illuminates the social processes of our own times and may show us, if we are ready to listen to its teachings, what to do and what to avoid."[28]

It was not so much Boas as his students who carried sexual modernism into the camp of academic anthropology. Boas directed his own research toward questions of race rather than sex, but he consistently accented social factors and thereby suggested to his students a means to modify the unfortunate biologism of Freud's theories. He did, however, greatly admire Freud's insight into family dynamics, especially the importance accorded childhood as the formative period in an individual's personality. For this reason, and despite his personal reservations, Boas heralded psychoanalysis as an "epoch-making discovery." Under his tutelage, a cohort studying at the New School for Social Research and at Columbia University (where Boas himself taught) began during the 1920s to make psychosexual development a focal point for ethnographic research. This teamwork strengthened the favored relationship between, as Alexander Goldenweiser specified, "anthropology, the science of man, and psychology, the science of the mind."[29]

Goldenweiser, who regarded Boas as a "culture-hero," provided a personal liaison between Calverton's circle and the academic anthropologists. A frequent contributor to the *Modern Quarterly*, he encouraged his students to excel academically while grooming themselves to become public intellectuals. His successes were major. Ruth Fulton Benedict studied with him at the New School after receiving her introduction to "Sex in Ethnography" from Elsie Clews Parsons, whose fascination with psychoanalysis dated to the 1910s. Both Parsons and Goldenweiser recommended their student to Boas, who in turn awarded her a teaching assistantship. In 1922 Benedict met Margaret Mead and soon thereafter became her mentor and, later, intimate friend.

Boas's students provided supplementary evidence to expose the patriarchal underpinnings of Freud's oedipal paradigm and its correspondingly restrictive theory of female psychosexual development. Whereas the *Modern Quarterly* editors examined primarily historical trends in Europe and the United States, the anthropologists marshaled ethnographic data on non-Western societies to certify the plasticity of "human nature," including the differences between the sexes. Not the rise and fall of the bourgeois family but the variability of kinship structure across cultures guided their research. In complementary fashion both techniques—historicist and ethnographic—facilitated a way out of the Freudian system.

It seemed only poetic justice that anthropologists should have figured prominently in this process. The Oedipus complex, as the linchpin of Freud's theory of origins, had been based on contemporary anthropological writings. *Totem and Taboo* (1912–1913), a set of four essays which Freud judged as among his best, synthesizes the scholarship of James Frazer, John McLennan, and Edward B. Tylor to form a Darwinist narrative of the rise of "civilization" from the primordial horde. In the beginning, Freud speculated, a single patriarch ruled over a small band and tyrannically reserved all sexual rights for himself. Eventually his lustful sons banded together and killed and devoured their father. Guilt and remorse soon set in, however, and the sons, having literally internalized their father, began to manifest his values and morality. They willingly renounced their incestuous desire and turned to sublimation. In Freud's schema, all the basic elements of civilization—morality, religion, art, and social life as well as the differences between the sexes—meet here in the primordial Oedipus complex.

This melodrama did more than trace the steps by which human culture comes into being: it served Freud as an analogy between social and individual development. The individual psyche, according to Freud, recapitulates the metahistory of civilization, progressing through the emotional savagery of infancy to the inhibited hence civilized state of adulthood, from polymorphous sexuality to a genital sexuality demarcated by the striking anatomical differences between male and female. Thus Freud utilized anthropological data on the symbolic mechanisms of "primitive" societies to probe both early infancy and adult neurosis. The mental life of the nonliterate peoples outside the West, Freud insisted, "must have a peculiar interest for us if we are right in seeing in it a well-preserved picture of an early stage of our own development."[30]

Anthropologists ridiculed this sweeping phylogenic hypothesis, as Freud anticipated they would. Boas immediately recognized the flaws in the oedipal paradigm. He rejected the famed psychoanalyst's shoddy and outdated evidence, objected to his grandiose evolutionism, and discounted the possibility of a universal application. Although Boas conceded that "suppressed desires" may account for some behavioral differences between adult men and women, he considered the Oedipus complex an insufficient explanation. His indictment boiled down to one prescient complaint: Freud had employed a "one-sided method," conflating large social patterns and individual psychology. Other anti-evolutionists such as Sapir and A. L. Kroeber criticized Freud's overlay of psychosexual development and stages of civilization, the latter already, in their relativist perspective, an outmoded concept. No anthropologist would logically claim, Sapir parried, to uncover "the archaic in the psychological sense." To the contrary, he insisted, anthropology is valuable precisely because it "constantly" rediscovers "the normal."[31]

In the 1920s, as sexual modernism conjoined with cultural relativism, anthropologists targeted the Oedipus complex and thereby undermined Freud's theory of female psychosexual development. At the forefront was Bronislaw Malinowski (1884–1942), the Polish-born anthropologist who led the British school of functionalism and helped to usher in the ethnographic method of participant observation. The title of his landmark study, *Sex and Repression in Savage Society* (1927), declares his indebtedness to Freud as well as to Havelock Ellis, whom he greatly admired. Like Boas, Malinowski stipulated several reservations. The data gathered during two years of fieldwork in the Trobriand Islands off the coast of New Guinea suggested to him the necessity of modifying psychoanalysis, at least "certain of its details." Like Calverton and Schmalhausen, Malinowski called into question Freud's assumptions about the family.

Malinowski found few traces of the Oedipus complex among the Trobriand Islanders. They neither associate sexual activity with conception—believing that pregnancy occurs when a deceased female relative implants a baby in a prospective mother's womb—nor exhibit the attitudes and behaviors outlined by Freud. More important, Trobrianders grow up without the restrictions common to Western societies and, therefore, as adults manifest none of the neurotic symptoms associated with sexual repression. Children routinely observe adult copulation and try it out for themselves at an early age. And although Trobriander males are likely to desire their sister and wish to kill their maternal uncle, they do not, Malinowski indicated, develop the classic version of the Oedipus complex.

It was the kinship system, Malinowski concluded, that predicated this outcome. The Trobriander family is not patriarchal, and consequently both men and women develop differently from Freud's clients. The matrilineal Trobrianders displace the father from the authoritative center not only of the family but of the entire household. Children reside with their mother and maternal uncles while their "father" stays with kin in a distant village. Trobriander children, Malinowski wrote, "never feel his heavy hand on themselves; he is not their kinsman, nor their owner, nor their benefactor."[32] Nor do they experience the weight of the paternal phallus over their sexual identities.

When published in the United States, *Sex and Repression in Savage Society* became a smashing success. Tantalized by the Trobrianders' sexual practices, the British anthropologist had expressed more than a hint of admiration. Their lovemaking, Malinowski suggested, outdid the West's. His readers readily accepted this conclusion and clamored, Sapir complained, for yet more reports on any "primitive community" that "indulges, or is said to indulge, in unrestricted sex behavior." Havelock Ellis, who returned Malinowski's admiration in full, judged Trobrianders' "art of love" as "in the best sense, more 'civilized' than ours." He recommended Polynesian sexual practices as a potential cure for the psychic illness that pervaded the West. Malinowski did not actually go quite so far but did note that these "savages" were, in contrast to contemporary Americans and Europeans, well-adjusted and generally free of neuroses.[33]

It was not just sexuality but *female* sexuality that stood out in Malinowski's reports. The relative lack of inhibition among women in the South Seas had fired the imagination of travelers, missionaries, and naturalists for well over a century. As early as 1795 the Reverend Thomas Haweis had described the Polynesian islands as uniquely safe for travelers except for the perils "as may arise from the fascination of beauty, and the seduction of appetite" caused by the "native" women readily available. Malinowski's private diary reveals that he too struggled with recurring "lecherous thoughts." But unlike the Protestants who carried an unambiguously Victorian mission to the South Seas, Malinowski had embraced the goals of the New Morality. He began his fieldwork in 1914, just five years after Freud published " 'Civilized' Sexual Morality and Modern Nervous Illness," and, like many other anthropologists, already regarded Freud as an ally in the campaign for sexual enlightenment. Far from aspiring to "uplift" Trobriander women, Malinowski bemoaned his own inhibitions, recording privately the troublesome vexation that he "was not a savage and could not possess" them. More dispassionately, he published uncritical descriptions of their erotic demeanor and sexual habits. Ellis also noted this aspect of Malinowski's report, concluding that Trobriander men play a major part in this appealing scenario. Unlike "civilized" men, Trobrianders are superb lovers: they "are considerate of the feelings of the woman and . . . recognize that in the art of love each sex has its part to play."[34]

More than a brief for sexual emancipation, *Sex and Repression in Savage Society* establishes the basis for female eroticism within a particular kinship system. Inspired by the "family drama" outlined by Freud, Malinowski set out to provide a comparative study and therefore chose a society unlike his own in terms of both family organization and sexual practice. The Trobriander kinship system, governed by matrilineal descent, projected a stark contrast to the patriarchal organization of Western society, not least in the realm of sexual arrangements. The anthropologist thus easily complemented Calverton and Schmalhausen's critique of the bourgeois family by describing female sexuality unrestrained by "civilization." If only implicitly, he also suggested what female sexuality in the West might become if unshackled by patriarchy. No wonder Floyd Dell spotted an uncanny similarity between the "savage" enjoyment of sex and post-emancipatory love among the Moderns, while Phyllis Blanchard drew from Malinowski's report decidedly "optimistic conclusions."[35]

For his part, Malinowski refused to play the part of heretic, despite the markedly polemical tone of *Sex and Repression in Savage Society*. Freud's theories continued to appeal to the anthropologist in him: the "open treatment of sex and of various shameful meannesses and vanities in man—the very thing for which psycho-analysis is most hated and reviled . . . should endear psycho-analysis above all to the student of man." And far from contradicting Freud, Malinowski insisted his data confirmed the overall validity of psychoanalytic theory, most especially Freud's contention that the experience of early childhood provides a key to adult personality. He did admit, however, to one major discrepancy. Freud failed to understand, Malinowski alleged, that "*the family* is not the same in all human societies." To correct for this lapse, the anthropologist advised his colleagues to contextualize the "family romance" within its specific kinship system. He speculated, for example, that the matrilineal Amphlett Islanders exhibit more patriarchal authority than the neighboring Trobrianders and, not surprisingly, more sexual repression; and that the patrilineal Mailu manifest the full-blown compulsive neurosis that Freud found in Western Europe. Redefining the "main task" of psychoanalysis as the exploration of the limits of variation, Malinowski thus joined other modernists in advocating an "elastic" application of Freud's theories.[36]

While sexual modernists welcomed Malinowski's interpretation, Freudians reacted defensively, giving no ground to either cultural relativism or sexual modernism. They immediately recognized the significance of his argument: the anthropologist had not merely refuted the universality of the Oedipus complex but had questioned its absolute worth as a sociopsychological regulator. Although initially optimistic about the fusion of psychoanalysis and anthropology, Ernest Jones became more circumspect in the wake of Malinowski's publications. Most of all, he resented the challenge to Freud's basic evolutionary paradigm. As soon as Malinowski began to preview his argument in the early 1920s, Jones staked out the Freudian position.

The Oedipus complex, as produced by the patriarchal family, undergirds Western civilization, Jones answered, and, moreover, determines its superiority: "The patriarchal system, as we know it, means the taming of man, the gradual assimilation of the Oedipus complex" that allows man to "face his real father and live with him." Freud had demonstrated clearly, Jones wrote, that this "recognition of the father's place in the family signified the most important progress in cultural development." The unrepressed sexuality of the Trobrianders impressed Jones only negatively: their lack of inhibition merely confirmed the primitive stage of their social development. Like Freud, Jones regarded the oedipally governed patriarchal family as problematic but as the institutional fulcrum for human advancement.

Although Jones sided with Horney in the controversy over female sexuality and acknowledged the masculine bias in Freudian theories, he absolutely refused to criticize patriarchy. He condemned the anthropologists' infatuation with societies that allowed an "extreme inversion of the relation between the sexes." Theirs was "a vision of a paradise out of which [woman] has been driven by the protesting male, but," Jones alleged, "to which she hopes one day to return." Matrilineal societies offer nothing appealing, he contended. Anthropologists manage to gain audiences for their dubious claims only because few subjects, he insisted, "arouse more emotional prejudice than the comparison of male and female." And Malinowski's ethnographic reports in particular read, Jones alleged, "like a feminist's wish-fulfillment dream."[37]

There was, of course, no ground to yield on the question of the Oedipus complex. Jones summarily dismissed Malinowski's argument by insisting that the Oedipus complex appeared in all societies regardless of kinship system. Freud's loyal analysand Marie Bonaparte also affirmed this faith, testifying a little later that her own son, Prince Peter of Greece, was finding plenty of oedipal manifestations among the polyandrous tribes of Tibet. As late as 1950 Geza Roheim claimed that his own research in the famous South Sea islands revealed a functioning Oedipus complex. Malinowski misread his data, Roheim belatedly complained, and overlooked evidence antagonistic to his purpose. The issue had not died even thirty years later: Melford E. Spiro's *Oedipus in the Trobriands* (1982) delivered a similar defense.[38]

Freud himself remained impervious to the entire modernist logic. *Civilization and Its Discontents,* published in full in 1930, reaffirms the principles outlined in *Totem and Taboo.* "We cannot get away from the assumption," Freud asserted, "that man's sense of guilt springs from the Oedipus complex and was acquired at the killing of the father by the brothers banded together." Even less sanguine about the prospects for human survival than when he wrote the earlier set of essays before World War I, Freud could not comprehend this "strange attitude of hostility toward civilization." Like his colleague Jones, he resisted the modernist preoccupation with "primitive" society as a source of sexual redemption, although he admitted that before the onset of civilization individuals undoubtedly possessed more liberty. Civilization encompasses, he insisted, "the whole sum of the achievements and the regulations which distinguish our lives from those of our animal ancestors and which serve two purposes—namely to protect men against nature and to adjust their mutual relations."[39]

Freud thus retained the evolutionary paradigm that undergirded his theory of female psychosexual development. Like the majority of fin-de-siècle social scientists and natural philosophers, he believed that a greater divergence in physiology, character, and function accompanies evolution. In short, he agreed with Darwin and Spencer that the degree of specialization by sex indicates a society's level of development. But Freud's emphasis was unique. The leading social and natural scientists imagined men's archaic past in hunting and fighting as the source of strong bodies, hardy intellects, and dynamic personalities suited to the masculine struggle for higher survival; and women's unchanging ties to home and family as the wellspring of nurturing, gentle temperaments suited to maintenance of the domestic realm. Freud produced a variation on this theme. Like other evolutionary thinkers, he reasoned phylogenetically, but he applied this schema not only to society but to individual psychology. According to his reasoning, woman never completely emerges from the "savagery" of early childhood and therefore stands in opposition to civilization. Woman's distinctively conservative disposition stems, in other words, from her failure to resolve completely the Oedipus complex. Moreover, in exalting the Oedipus complex, Freud scoffed at those modernists who in holding civilization "largely responsible for our misery" would forsake it for "primitive conditions." Freud thus refused to relinquish the notion that the differences between the sexes as established by the Oedipus complex were necessary not only to "civilization" but to emotional well-being. The impulse to regress to infantile "savagery," that is, to blur the differences between the sexes, remained for him a sign of neurosis.[40]

Freud's argument suffered a blow from yet another direction. If Malinowski pulled out a few props by examining various kinship systems, Margaret Mead (1901–1978) upset the entire evolutionary applecart. Pushing cultural relativism to its limits, she ultimately denied any direct correspondence between biological differences and sex-linked character traits. All fixed notions of female sexuality and femininity crumbled under her cross-cultural scrutiny and her extraordinary public acclaim.

Like Malinowski, Mead did not set out to overthrow Freud's theory of female psychosexual development. As an undergraduate at Barnard College, she had become acquainted with the writings of both Freud and Jung and developed an impassioned interest in psychoanalysis. According to her biographer, Mead "considered a night without a dream a total waste of time." Her curiosity about the determinants of women's status derived from her own childhood influences: both her grandmother, whom she adored, and her mother had been ardent suffragists. It was Boas, however, who pushed the young doctoral candidate to pursue her concerns in academia. Put off by his directive to study the "troubles" of teenaged girls as set forth by G. Stanley Hall, Mead consented only if she could conduct her research in Polynesia. Boas tried his best to discourage her. Fieldwork outside the North

American continent was still something of a rarity for American anthropologists, and the fatherly Boas feared for the safety of a relatively frail, twenty-three-year-old woman traveling alone to Polynesia. He advised her to conduct her research among American Indians. Mead eventually wore him down and, with Boas's grudging approval, set sail in 1925 to study female psychosexual development in a far distant setting.[41]

Persistence paid off. For nine months Mead lived in Samoa, a U.S. protectorate, and gathered data about sexuality directly from the island's young women. The study culminated in her first and best-selling book. *Coming of Age in Samoa* (1928) confirms many of Malinowski's impressions about female sexuality in the South Seas. Mead summed up the aspirations of Samoan girls: "To live as a girl with many lovers as long as possible and then to marry in one's own village near one's own relatives and to have many children." Mead found in Samoa little of the "stress and strain" typical of adolescents in Western societies and even less of the neurosis, frigidity, and impotence common among adults. *Growing Up in New Guinea* (1930), Mead's next book, reaffirms this conclusion, once again delivering a counterpoint to Freud's depiction of female sexuality.[42]

Spurred on by success, Mead now set out to demonstrate conclusively that "cultural conditions" rather than anatomical differences shape the distinctive characteristics of femininity and masculinity. In 1931, freed from the restrictions of her graduate advisor and encouraged by Ruth Benedict, Mead defined the central problem of her research as "the different ways in which cultures patterned the expected behavior of males and females." She decided to tackle this huge question because, she later reflected, questions about "biologically-given sex differences" could never be resolved until one understood "the effects of cultural stylization on feminine and masculine personalities."[43] Once she could demonstrate that woman's inferior status resulted not from biological dictates but from cultural norms, Mead believed, she would be able to make a clear and compelling case for specific changes in her own society.

Mead's third major book, *Sex and Temperament in Three Primitive Societies* (1935), deals directly with variations in normative concepts of masculinity and femininity. She analyzed ethnographic data from her observations of three very different New Guinea tribes, the mountain-dwelling Arapesh, the river-dwelling Mundugumor, and the lake-dwelling Tchambuli. Although living in close proximity, these groups show a wide variation in sexual differentiation. Mead found that Arapesh men and women are both mild and maternal in manner, whereas Mundugumor men and women are equally alike but very aggressive. The Tchambuli, in contrast, maintain clear-cut differences between the sexes but the opposite of those in Western societies.

Mead drew powerful conclusions from these observations. "If those temperamental attitudes which we have traditionally regarded as feminine—such as passivity, responsiveness, and a willingness to cherish children—can so easily be set up as the masculine pattern in one tribe, and in another be outlawed for the majority of women as well as for the majority of men," Mead reasoned, "we no longer have any basis for regarding such aspects of behaviour as sex-linked." This evidence made only one assumption credible: "human nature is almost unbelievably malleable."[44]

Mead aspired to enlarge and, if necessary, modify Freud's theories. Nevertheless, her conclusions about the temperamental differences between the sexes ran contrary to his principal tenets. Freud had described femininity as the sum of those "character-traits which critics of every epoch have brought up against women—that they show less sense of justice than men, that they are less ready to submit to the great necessities of life, that they are more influenced in their judgements by feelings of affection or hostility." Mead described societies that assigned these same traits to men. And not all societies, she further advised, differentiate personality types by sex. Her research demonstrated beyond doubt that variations in temperament had little to do with anatomy or instincts but instead illustrated what Benedict referred to as "the great arc" of possible human behavior.[45]

Sex and Temperament in Three Primitive Societies sparked a minor ruckus among the literati when it appeared. "Feminists," Mead later recalled, "hailed it as a demonstration that women did not 'naturally' like children, and recommended that little girls not be given dolls to play with." Others found her argument implausible. Mead dismissed her critics' objections as symptoms of their own "culturally acquired" prejudices, although in a new preface to the 1950 edition she finally admitted that her findings did seem "too good to be true." Still, the idea that personality traits varied without regard to sex remained attractive; and it was, in fact, what she had set out to prove.[46]

As Goldenweiser had advised, Mead planned to apply the lessons learned from ethnographic research to her own society. She joined other anthropologists and psychoanalysts who wrote for general audiences and who published essays and poetry in progressive magazines like *Modern Quarterly* and *The Dial*. "By exploring the different ways that separate lives had been shaped by common culture, they hoped to suggest," one historian has offered, "if not the possibility that lives might be shaped differently, then at least the need to be more 'chary of emphatic dogmas' in evaluating different 'visions of the human fate.'" Mead thus echoed Calverton and Schmalhausen in advising Americans to become "culture conscious" as a first step in reforming their society in a "sane and scientific direction." *Coming of Age in Samoa* reflects this evangelism in its telling subtitle, "A Psychological Study of Primitive Youth for Western Civilization."[47]

Mead hoped that her American readers would compare their institutions and values with those of other cultures: "Realising that our own ways are not humanly inevitable nor God-ordained, but are the fruit of a long and turbulent history, we may well examine in turn all of our institutions, thrown into strong relief against the history of other civilizations, and weighing them in the balance, be not afraid to find them wanting." How much better it would be, she pointed out, if "no Puritan self-accusations vexed [the] consciences" of our own young women in the throes of sexual experimentation. The problems resulting from sexual inequalities, however, did not bother her as much as the contemporary obsession with the personality differences between the sexes. Wherever sex serves to distinguish character traits, she argued, individuals find their options severely limited. This situation paves the way for "a kind of maladjustment of a worse order," impairing individuals and harming the entire society by squandering its precious human resources. "Such a system," Mead complained, wastes "the gifts of many women who could exercise other functions far better than their ability to bear children in an already overpopulated world." Such a system also fails to utilize the talents of those men who may be better suited for housework and childcare than for business or politics.[48]

Like Malinowski, Mead had produced her own, updated reading of "civilized" sexual morality as the source of modern nervous illness. Her formulation, moreover, contradicted both Freud and prewar feminists who, in opposing ways, viewed femininity as a fixed marker of womanhood. Differentiation of personality by sex, which Mead considered not only illogical but possibly pernicious, must go the way of sexual repression and be banished to the dark ages of human history. Mead joined Malinowski to cast into a cross-cultural framework what others in her milieu had derived by studying history. "We shall arrive then at a more realistic social faith, accepting as grounds of hope and as new bases for tolerance the coexisting and equally valid patterns of life which," Benedict affirmed, "mankind has created for itself from the raw materials of existence."[49] This aspiration, the foundation of Culture and Personality studies, found further expression among the revisionists who were refashioning psychoanalytic theory in the United States.

A Cultural Theory of Femininity

Karen Horney attributed her final renunciation of Freudianism to the cross-cultural perspective she gained by immigrating to the United States. The cause of neurosis lay primarily in "cultural conditions," she soon concluded, rather than the oedipal trauma that Freud deemed universal.[50] American scholars also encouraged her along this line of thinking. Working closely with anthropologists and sociologists engaged in Culture and Personality studies, Horney realized that throughout history and across cultures the traits and behaviors linked to masculinity and femininity varied tremendously.

This new understanding profoundly affected the way Horney mounted her campaign against the masculine bias in psychoanalysis. Initially she had tried to counter the Freudian concept of penis envy by postulating an equally resolute notion of instinctual femininity. She now disavowed her own essentialism. Not only female sexuality but motherhood itself, Horney ultimately resolved, exists primarily as a cultural formation.

Karen Horney helped to bring to theoretical fruition the ideas circulating since the mid-1920s. Working with associates in the new psychoanalytic institutes and training centers, she stood at the forefront of the revisionist movement, transposing into psychoanalytic terms the basic premises of the Culture and Personality enterprise. Moreover, Horney embraced their mission. She envisioned psychoanalysis as a cultural theory, as well as a clinical method, designed to assist men and women adjust to the new requirements of modern society. With this goal in mind, Horney issued major statements on female sexuality and femininity framed by a version of psychoanalysis extricated from Freud's Oedipus complex.

Horney revealed her new line of thinking in April 1933. At a meeting of the heterodox Baltimore-Washington Psychoanalytic Society, she attributed neurosis in women to the skepticism that greets their efforts "to achieve independence" and to work outside the home. "Accordingly, all efforts of this sort are said to be without any vital significance for woman, whose every thought in point of fact should center exclusively upon the male or upon motherhood," she complained, "in much the manner expressed in Marlene Dietrich's famous song, 'I know only love, and nothing else.' " Horney had reached this conclusion after reviewing the cases of thirteen women who all suffered "boy-craziness," a malady also running rampant, she poignantly added, in "our middle-class intellectual circles."

Why were most women obsessed with love and romance? To Freud the answer was elementary: by successfully resolving the Oedipus complex, women *normally* displace penis envy by desire for a (male) child. Only a few years earlier Horney, while refuting Freud's interpretation, had provided an equally determinist answer, identifying motherhood as a primary instinct. She now came back with a startlingly novel alternative. Citing Briffault, Horney argued that a centuries-old "inherited tradition" had compressed women's numerous possibilities into the "narrower sphere of eroticism and motherhood." In addition to the weight of tradition, shrinking opportunities for work outside the home cause in modern women "an excess of desire" for heterosexual intercourse, and romance becomes their only reasonable possibility for fulfillment. These women regard the pleasure they experience in sexual intercourse as "a kind of elixir of life that only men are able to provide and without which one must dry up and waste away." Far from normal, as Freud concluded, this aspiration is, Horney insisted, neurotic.

This essay, "The Overvaluation of Love: A Study of a Common Present-Day Feminine Type," marks a stunning departure from Horney's earlier views of femininity. And this, her first contribution to American theory, remains one of her most stimulating and forceful essays, an extraordinarily bold statement that, according to her daughter, "puts one in touch with the raw events." "The Overvaluation of Love" (1934) also previews the culturalism that would govern her future work. The psychoanalyst must take into account "sociological considerations," Horney now insisted, not because biology is unimportant but because such constitutional factors as those Freud specified never appear "in pure and undisguised form." They are "always . . . modified by tradition and environment."[51]

To distance herself even further from Freudianism, Horney chose the perfect foil, a recent essay by the loyalist Helene Deutsch that enshrines woman's " 'anatomical destiny,' marked out for her by biological and constitutional factors." At the December 1933 annual meeting of the American Psychoanalytic Association, Horney refuted Deutsch's arguments about feminine masochism, saying that she simply could not regard as perfectly normal the desire to be mutilated, raped, or humiliated. Could penis envy really cause all this, she asked rhetorically, and cause it universally? Although Horney conceded that some women derive pleasure from pain in intercourse or childbirth, she was unwilling to equate all feminine desire with masochism. To the contrary, she argued, masochism commonly appears in societies that restrict women's outlets for self-expression and sexuality, judge women as inferior beings, promote women's economic dependence on men, place women firmly in the home and make them singularly responsible for family life, and disallow women an autonomous emotional and social existence. In fact, Horney admitted, these conditions remained so prevalent in Western society that she found it "hard to see how any woman can escape becoming masochistic to some degree."[52]

Horney proceeded to outline her newly culturalist perspective on femininity. Her argument against Deutsch did not depend, she emphasized, on "any appeal to contributory factors in the anatomical–physiological characteristics of woman." All "sex-linked peculiarities," she insisted, are conditioned responses to the cultural environment. Rife among the contemporary white middle class, feminine masochism rarely occurs, for example, among Amerindians or Trobriand Islanders. Horney concluded by calling not for more conventional case histories but for cross-cultural research into the determinants of personality.[53]

At precisely the correct moment, in 1934, Horney left Chicago for the East Coast, where culturalism had been percolating since the mid-1920s. She joined the trailblazing faculty of the New School for Social Research, which routinely sponsored interdisciplinary seminars featuring prominent European psychoanalysts. Horney eventually affiliated with the New York Psychoanalytic Institute, where the Columbia University anthropologist Abram Kardiner instructed psychoanalysts in the latest in ethnographic scholarship. Horney also met members of the landmark seminar on Culture and Personality facilitated by Edward Sapir and the sociologist John Dollard at Yale University in 1932 and richly funded by the Rockefeller Foundation. She also came into contact with the esteemed group of scholars who met in Hanover, New Hampshire, in 1934 to chart what Margaret Mead described as a "multi-front operation." Horney rode the crest of this interdisciplinary movement and became by decade's end one of its most celebrated participants.[54]

Horney acknowledged her great debt to Harry Stack Sullivan (1892–1949), who provided both a conducive working environment and off-hours stimulation. In addition to directing the Washington-Baltimore Psychoanalytic Institute, where Horney taught, Sullivan oversaw his own salon, the Zodiac Club, where compliant guests indulged their host's fascination with symbols, a product of Sullivan's friendship with Sapir. Each person took on the identity of an animal suited to his or her personality—Horney's persona was a water buffalo—and, while in character, spent the evening discussing a range of aesthetic, political, and theoretical matters. Horney became friends with the anthropologist Hortense Powdermaker and the psychoanalyst Clara Thompson. She also deepened her relationship with her fellow emigré Erich Fromm. After Sullivan's club dissolved in the late 1930s, Horney continued to meet on a nearly weekly basis with social scientists, including Mead, Benedict, and Dollard. These social affairs, sometimes hosted by Horney herself in her stylish Manhattan apartment, served as a forum to explore variations in personality across cultures.[55]

It was Sullivan who encouraged Horney to think about the relationship of culture and personality in a new way. She had already turned away from Freudian premises but found herself theoretically mired by the vague and slippery formulation of "cultural conditioning." Sullivan, she found, not only had discarded Freud's libido theory but had provided an alternative model of development. He was, Clara Thompson agreed, the first psychoanalyst since Freud to outline a truly "systematic theory" of personality formation.[56]

Horney believed that Sullivan had advanced psychoanalysis to its full potential. He convincingly argued that an individual seeks from birth not merely pleasure or release from sexual tension, as Freud contended, but security and approval from others, and develops in tandem with this pursuit a self-image or personality. Moreover, it is not the child's own desires that determine the developmental course but the parents' timely intervention. And rather than stimulating infantile sexual drives, parents act instrumentally by purposefully transmitting their own culturally informed values. For Sullivan, then, the family serves less as an arena of sexual drama, as Freud imagined, and principally as an agent of acculturation.

Others shared Horney's assessment of Sullivan's contribution to American psychoanalysis. The most observant realized that Sullivan, in moving away from Freud's "id-psychology," had laid the foundation for "ego-psychology," the brand of psychoanalysis that would be pegged as distinctly American. This theoretical transposition, the eminent Harvard psychologist Gordon W. Allport later noted, made Sullivan a pioneer in "the fusion of psychiatry and social science."[57]

Like Sullivan, Horney did not repudiate all Freudian tenets but instead preserved what she considered the best of his doctrine. She continued to honor, for example, the causal relationship between unconscious motivations and emotions and behavior. The processes of repression and sublimation and the utility of dream analysis all figured centrally in her therapeutic techniques, and she maintained a focus on "inner conflicts." Psychoanalysis for Horney would always be a depth psychology.

Following Sullivan's lead, Horney rejected the "instinctivistic" underpinning of Freud's theories, including sexuality. She no longer envisioned the adult personality as "the ultimate outcome of instinctual drives." Furthermore, Horney realized full well that once the libido theory fell away the other troublesome components of Freud's system dissolved, not only her personal *bête noire*, penis envy, but the entire reproductive teleology. Freud's notion of the libido, she charged, seemed nothing more than a vague and mystical biological substance, and the Oedipus complex was no better. Why focus so exclusively on sexual formations, she asked, at the expense of "early relationships in their totality?" Her major books, *The Neurotic Personality of Our Time* (1937) and *New Ways of Psychoanalysis* (1939), expanded these insights into what would soon become a full-blown *neo*-Freudianism. What psychoanalysis seeks to explain, Horney summed, is the "way specific cultural conditions engender specific qualities and faculties, in women as in men."[58]

From this point Horney began to construct a cultural theory of femininity. She began by noting that all Americans suffer from neurotic anxiety and hostility and then rejecting Freud's hypothesis that oedipal disruptions cause such problems. She asked instead: "which special features in our culture" encourage this syndrome? The answer lay not in anatomy nor even in its psychic representation but in a social system driven by competition. The competition that propels the American economy also infests personal relationships, she argued. All relationships form in its image, including sibling rivalry, schoolyard rifts, the keeping-up-with-the-Joneses phenomenon that dominates community life, and, not least, love affairs. Our competitive social environment produces such profound insecurity, Horney alleged, that vast numbers of Americans desperately seek reassurance. Women, however, carry a special psychic burden. Upon marrying, they not only give up their work but develop "an attitude of dependency." But although women thereby comply with the norms of femininity, they necessarily harbor resentment because they have been unfairly robbed of their ambitions. It is no surprise that American women exhibit anxiety, nurture hostility toward their spouse, and at the same time crave approval.[59]

Working with Sullivan's schema of personality development, she could now pinpoint the processes by which women's neurotic traits, masochistic tendencies, or feelings of inferiority form. Unenlightened parents play the initial role, she specified, by transmitting a value system or moral structure that functionally limits a girl's aspirations to marriage and motherhood. Then, as American girls grow into women, they confront yet more obstacles. Repeatedly, they are forced to narrow their expectations and to suffer the feelings of inferiority experienced earlier in childhood. These circumstances produce adult women who, for very good reasons, lack self-esteem. Their resulting neurosis, then, has nothing to do with perceptions of anatomical deficiency and everything to do with the restrictions placed upon women in our culture. Unlike men, who have abundant excitements placed before them, women are "made" for love and nothing else.

There could now be no doubt, Horney insisted, about the cultural origins of femininity. Before the twentieth century, when knowledge of cultural variations was scant, scholars routinely ascribed the "peculiarities of one's own culture to human nature in general." Freud clearly followed this line of thinking. Such naive practices had passed away in the light of recent sociological and ethnographic research. The abundant new data now revealed that "The American woman is different from the German woman; both are different from certain Pueblo Indian women. The New York society woman is different from the farmer's wife in Idaho." Like Mead, Horney reasoned that femininity, like human nature, varies from place to place and from time to time.[60]

In reaching this conclusion, Horney crossed a major philosophical line. She decided that if most personality traits and behaviors customarily attributed to the differences between the sexes are, on closer examination, the products of culture, it follows that femininity as such does not exist. There is, in other words, no such biological or psychical entity that invariably structures the personality of women. If women commonly interpret their problems as specific to their sex, it is because society encourages everyone, men and women alike, to think in these dualistic categories. In actuality, Horney contended, men and women experience the same difficulties in establishing secure relationships and in realizing their potential. "Femininity" is thus merely a disguise.

Horney wrapped up her comments on femininity by referring to Freud's observation on the relationship between sexual function and personality. "The influence of this factor is, of course very far-reaching," he had insisted. But Freud had also advised his colleagues to "remember that an individual woman may be a human being apart from this." Horney chose to emphasize the latter advice, which she considered a "relief" in the entire Freudian canon. Having said this, she closed an entire chapter in her career. The phrase "the psychology of women" virtually disappeared from Horney's lexicon.[61]

Addressing the National Federation of Professional and Business Women's Clubs in 1935, the same year Mead published *Sex and Temperament*, Horney summed up the situation. It is not the differences between the sexes that are important but the peculiar fascination with these differences. She explained:

> Any sudden increase in interest over sex differences ... must be regarded as a danger signal for women, particularly in a patriarchal society where men find it advantageous to prove on biologic premises that women should not take part in shaping the economy and the political order. On these premises elaborate convictions serving the interests of masculine ideologies become strategical means of preserving masculine superiority in the economic and political world by convincing woman that innately she is glad to keep out of it.

She advised women to "stop bothering about what is feminine and what is not" and to work collectively to overcome their feelings of inferiority. That there are differences between the sexes, no one would deny. But a true understanding will come only after women develop their "potentialities as human beings." "Paradoxical as it may sound," Horney concluded, "we shall find out about these differences only if we forget about them."[62]

In dropping the nettlesome issue of femininity, Horney did not mellow her censure of Freud. *New Ways in Psychoanalysis* constituted an unrelieved critique of his work. After its publication the defenders of orthodoxy banded together. Fritz Wittels, who had voted against the admission of women to the Vienna Psychoanalytic Society in 1908, issued a missive accusing Horney of all kinds of psychoanalytic misdeeds. Soon thereafter the directors of the New York Psychoanalytic Institute rescinded her teaching privileges. In protest, Horney and several allies quit the institute in April 1941 and formed their own society and training institute.[63]

Horney had finally staked out her own territory. The new Association for the Advancement of Psychoanalysis soon began to publish the *American Journal of Psychoanalysis,* sponsor lectures by such luminaries as Franz Alexander and Margaret Mead, and provide its own course of instruction in psychoanalysis. Seemingly well established, the association nevertheless failed to gain recognition from the mainline American Psychoanalytic Association and by necessity took its place along the margins of the profession. But by this time Horney had put neo-Freudian psychoanalysis on a firm theoretical ground.[64]

For her part, Horney had evolved into an authentic culturalist, and she played out this role in her interpretations of both neurosis and femininity. And the significance of this departure from orthodoxy did not escape her colleagues. While friends Benedict and Mead praised her publications, Franz Alexander provided evaluations both critical and astute. He, too, had recognized the inadequacy of many of Freud's formulations, and he agreed with Horney that the introduction of cultural factors benefited psychoanalytic theory in general. Alexander nevertheless disapproved her excessively "antibiologic attitude." Horney had fabricated, he alleged, an artificial antithesis between sociological and biological approaches, which together are not only complementary but indispensable. Even worse, she had invented "an imaginary, exclusively biologically oriented Freud." Perhaps so, for compared to Horney, Freud appeared hopelessly mired in an outdated philosophical system. This was a web Horney believed she had finally escaped. She therefore flaunted her culturalism, almost with a vengeance.[65]

As early as 1930 Horney had expressed her regret that some of her colleagues believed she had attributed "all disaster" to "male supremacy" and had claimed that "relations between the sexes would improve if women were given the ascendancy." She offered a half-hearted apology but refused to back down. Women were once again daring "to fight for their equality," she declared. To her, it was only common sense that this "power struggle . . . between the sexes" would affect both clinical practice and ultimately the central tenets of psychoanalytic theory.[66]

Karen Horney's friend and ally Clara Mabel Thompson (1893–1958) illuminated another paradox inherent in the theoretical developments of the interwar period. Personally distant from the sources of animus, she judged Freud's theories more dispassionately than Horney, dismissing them as a necessary but transient stage in the history of psychoanalysis. She also sensed that neo-Freudianism itself had reached an impasse on precisely the matter that had inspired Horney's dissent.

Raised and educated in Providence, Rhode Island, Thompson had gathered excellent professional credentials. She received her medical degree from Johns Hopkins University and then, on Sullivan's advice, trained abroad for several years with Sándor Ferenczi. In the early 1930s Thompson returned to the United States and became the first president of the revisionist Washington-Baltimore Psychoanalytic Society. In 1935, at Horney's behest, Thompson also affiliated with the classical New York Psychoanalytic Institute. After 1941 the two heretical friends made their professional home together, although briefly, in the Association for the Advancement of Psychoanalysis. In addition to holding executive positions with the William Alanson White Institute and the Academy of Psychoanalysis, Thompson produced nearly sixty essays or reviews on various topics and one book, *Psychoanalysis: Its Evolution and Development* (1950), the first major assessment of neo-Freudianism. Described by Erich Fromm as a "thoroughly independent person," Thompson took up where Horney left off, publishing within one decade a series of six important essays on femininity.[67]

Thompson offered an excellent summary of the contributions of the Culture and Personality scholars to the field of psychoanalysis. It was now generally understood, she noted, that the Oedipus complex is "not universal but is a product of monogamous patriarchal society." This revelation toppled another fundamental tenet, penis envy. Thompson readily admitted that penis envy is "a symbolic representation of the attitude of women in this culture, a picturesque way of referring to the type of warfare which so often goes on between men and women." In other words, penis envy serves symbolically to express women's resentment of the power that men monopolize. Thompson assumed that our patriarchal culture, with "the restricted opportunities afforded woman, the limitations placed on her development and independence," provides a genuine basis for envy of the male. Thus, as the cross-cultural studies had clearly demonstrated, penis envy, contrary to Freud's proposition, has nothing to do with "a feeling of biological lack."[68]

But it was sexual modernism that fed Thompson's chief revisionist inclinations. Like other neo-Freudians, she understood the necessity of adapting psychoanalytic theory to the circumstances of men and women living, not in the bourgeois epoch that Freud knew, but in *modern* society. One of her finest essays, "The Role of Women in This Culture," published in 1941, replicated the central argument extending from Calverton and Schmalhausen, to Malinowski and Mead, and finally to Horney: women's submission to a sexually repressive moral code as well as their feelings of inferiority had been both integrally related and historically determined. Like the visionaries of the 1920s, Thompson had faith in the Machine Age. The removal of industry from the home, and increasing opportunities for employment outside it, presented women with new avenues for self-fulfillment and self-esteem. And with women's advancement, the foundations of the old moral order began to crumble. Thompson did not, however, advise women to measure their self-worth by masculine standards but instead to seek ways to lead productive lives without sacrificing their unique "biologic function." If only men and women could solve this problem, they might, with the help of psychoanalysis, achieve in their common humanity greater freedom and happiness.[69]

Thompson nevertheless appeared far less upbeat than her immediate predecessors. Writing shortly before World War II pulled the United States from the depths of the Great Depression, she could not help being more circumspect. She detected a dangerous drift backward. The Great Depression had taken its toll on the prospects for sexual equality. Single women found scant opportunity in the job-short economy, married women even less. Even stalwart women's organizations like the YWCA that had rallied behind the working girl for over half a century tempered their enthusiasm. Meanwhile trade unions, local school boards, and even the federal government enacted legislation narrowing women's options for self-support. In the realm of sexuality, young men and women did not necessarily abstain but appeared to find little joy in experimentation. The "wild excesses" of the "jazz-mad 20's," one survey of college students reported, had devolved into the "skepticism" of "the willful but soberer 30's."[70]

Thompson was swimming against the tide. An author in the mass-circulation *Saturday Evening Post* of 1937 similarly noted the back-sliding following the Great Depression but interpreted this data instead as a sign that "normal" sex relations were about to resume. Sigmund Freud had wisely insisted that women desire only marriage and motherhood, but feminists, "with their boast of being 'modern women,' " the author complained, "have always flown in the face of psychology." Luckily, hard times had dashed women's career ambitions, forcing them to accept their husbands as "natural allies in the dark days." And why shouldn't they? "Men give them many little privileges their brothers don't enjoy. Men pay their dinner checks and light their cigarettes; men defer to their preference in choosing curtains for the living room and send them roses on their birthdays. Men are merely fathers of their children, cut off forever from the experience of motherhood." Misbegotten as much as comical, the writer's argument does underscore a problem that had plagued theorists throughout this or, really, any period—woman's unique relation to reproduction, her singular capacity for motherhood. Without any doubts, however, the *Saturday Evening Post* writer resolved that "women are different" and insisted that most other women share this opinion. The women of 1937, she wrote, "have learned that women have no fundamental quarrel with the sex that is still in the saddle."[71]

Clara Thompson clearly did not share this writer's pleasure. As she reviewed current trends, Thompson felt only nostalgia for the "new freedom of the 1920s." As culture drifts "to the conservative side," she lamented, the prospect of sexual modernism fades from sight. Reversals had already set in, and not only in the United States: fascism threatened to turn back all advances.[72]

The rise of Hitler had a dramatic impact on American psychoanalysis. Not only did the number of practitioners swell with the rapid influx of refugee analysts, but psychoanalysts became increasingly urgent in addressing the threat of totalitarianism, immediately in Central Europe and potentially in their new nation. They joined a sizable sector of Culture and Personality scholars who now focused their research on class and race inequities within the United States. For example, Franz Boas, now near eighty years of age, retired from Columbia University to pursue research on race questions. Margaret Mead enlarged this project to include an analysis of sex inequities. She decried the Fascist plan to restrict women to the home as well as the Communist intent to obliterate as much as possible all sexual distinctions. In different ways, both Fascists and Communists sought to narrow the range of human possibilities. "If we are to achieve a richer culture, rich in contrasting values, we must recognize the whole gamut of human potentialities, and so weave," she advised, "a less arbitrary social fabric, one in which each diverse human gift will find a fitting place."[73] Others in Mead's milieu, however, acted on another impulse.

In response to the growing fear of fascism, psychoanalysts and other liberal commentators affirmed their faith in American institutions. "If what we have seen during the last four years in Italy, Spain, France, and Germany is a true expression of European civilization," the former Lyrical Leftist Harold Stearns concluded, "then I prefer to take my chances in backward and reactionary and hide-bound, capitalistic America, for all our abuses." The prospects for "a decent life," he added, were better in the United States than "anywhere else in a rather muddled and strife-torn world."[74] Many Americans, psychoanalysts included, abandoned cultural relativism to underscore the superiority of American democratic culture.

As any good culturalist could recognize, the times no longer inspired heuristic investigations and bold conclusions. The influx of refugee psychoanalysts also included a sizable component of classical Freudians, and the struggle between orthodoxy and revisionism became yet more intense. Writers like Thompson, as well as Horney and Mead, correctly saw themselves on the defensive while their colleagues moved more and more swiftly in the opposite direction. Cultural relativism became less appealing; it even seemed unpatriotic in an era crying out for moral absolutes. The Cold War, precipitating the collapse of liberal academia, including the scientific claims on woman's behalf, loomed on the horizon.

Psychoanalysts appeared unexceptional in this regard. A considerable number continued to doubt the validity of the libido theory and preferred to emphasize the importance of cultural factors. But Freud's death on September 23, 1939, after a brief period of exile in London, mellowed many erstwhile critics, and a major Freudian revival began. Eulogies and tributes flowed while, as in the world of art, the value of the master's own productions mounted. Freud's depth psychology, including his hotly contested theory of instincts or drives, regained its former prominence, and whole new fields such as dynamic psychiatry appeared to revive leading elements of classical psychoanalysis. According to Thompson, even neo-Freudians began to hew a "middle course." On questions of femininity and female sexuality, a new kind of theoretical rigidity appeared to be setting in.[75]

An almost certainly apocryphal story has Horney and Thompson sharing late moments of willful optimism. Following Horney's dismissal from the New York Psychoanalytic Institute in 1941, the heterodox allies gathered three of their friends, walked out of the hearing, headed for a bar. After a few drinks, they marched up Fifth Avenue, arms linked and singing "Go down, Moses, Way down in Egypt land. Tell old Pharaoh, to let my people go."[76] But there was no promised land, even for the resilient. What lay ahead was isolation, obscurity, and—worst of all—irrelevancy.

4

Momism and the Flight from Manhood

A few months after the United States entered World War II, Philip Wylie (1902–1971) wrote a biting critique of American society and, by extension, of a world that allowed so much human devastation. Americans had become complaisant about their democratic heritage, he charged, forsaking their civic responsibilities for the mad pursuit of material gain. "A dominant concern for goods," Wylie warned, "always blights goodness and leads the way back to despair." His bestselling *Generation of Vipers* (1942) beseeches Americans to "make a new appraisal" of themselves so that they may put aside their petty pleasures. Americans must pledge, first, to fight their enemies and win the war against fascism and, second, to plan intelligently for peace. Nothing less than the future of the world rests on the ability of American men to revitalize their historic passion for freedom.[1]

Having identified a problem of epochal proportions, Wylie proceeded to trace its root to women, in particular to the American mothers who had jeopardized the fate of civilization by precipitating (to paraphrase Karen Horney) a *flight from manhood*. Following the lead of another popular author, Wylie pronounced the United States "a woman's world." John Erskine, unlike many other Depression-era writers, had avoided the customary accusation that working women snatched jobs away from men. He focused instead on woman-as-parasite, that is, on the nonproductive wife and mother who wields her domestic authority to rob men of their virility. Erskine thus dedicated his timely missive *The Influence of Women and Its Cure* (1936) "To the Men of America (Those Who Remain)." Wylie made the same point by transforming the beloved tale of Cinderella into a modern horror story. In the original version, a dutiful young woman goes about her servile labors without complaint until a dashing prince comes along as a reward for her exemplary self-effacing feminine virtue. Not so in Wylie's updating. Now a guileless Prince Charming appears a mere mechanism for the willful, money-grubbing Cinderella to achieve her goal: a prominent place on the Social Register. Wylie hit the big numbers by diagnosing this sociopathology as *Momism*.[2]

Generation of Vipers stands out as an especially vivid prototype of a misogyny that blames mothers for nearly everything, from thumb sucking to premature ejaculation to world war. Having crushed the men of America, Wylie's Mom is a domestic powerhouse. She rules over her husband, a poor sap who works unremittingly to meet her voracious material desires and who receives nothing in return, not even the favors of a submissive, sexually appealing partner. Not only has Mom emasculated her husband. She has robbed her son of his manhood. In short, Mom has so thoroughly debased the nation's men—including its corporate executives, professors, clerics, and heads of state—that these would-be leaders no longer possess the (masculine) will to fight for democracy.

It is impossible to exaggerate the contempt for women expressed in this book. Although Wylie subsequently claimed he had been only joking, over a half-century later many readers were still reacting viscerally to his no-holds-barred description of Mom: "She is about twenty-five pounds over-weight, with no sprint, but sharp heels and a hard backhand which she does not regard as a foul but a womanly defense. In a thousand of her there is not sex appeal enough to budge a hermit ten paces off a rock ledge. She none the less spends several hundred dollars a year on permanents and transformations, pomades, cleansers, rouges, lipsticks, and the like—and fools nobody except herself." This often-quoted passage earned Wylie lasting distinction as "the all-out, all-time, high-scoring world champion misogynist." The provocative author disagreed with this assessment, insisting that he loved women, and loved them much more than he loved men. Nevertheless, the charge stuck. Nearly thirty years later the headline of his obituary in the *New York Times* read: "Philip Wylie, Author, Dies; Noted for 'Mom' Attack." His short chapter entitled "Common Women," touted by its author as "one of the most renowned (or notorious) passages in modern English letters," is emblematic of Wylie's whole enterprise.[3]

A highly readable volume, *Generation of Vipers* was a smashing success. Some reviewers found themselves amused by its acerbic tone; others judged its author a second-rate H. L. Mencken. The purchasing public responded unequivocally. The first printing soon sold out, and by the time the revised edition appeared in 1955 sales topped 180,000. This remarkable good fortune surprised even Wylie. He had not started out to produce a bestseller, he claimed. The project had begun as a form of "private catharsis" over the outbreak of global war. The unsuspecting author could not have predicted that *Generation of Vipers* would become required reading in college English and journalism classes; or that the American Library Association would select his treatise as one of the major nonfiction works of the century.[4]

Generation of Vipers undoubtedly derived at least part of its commercial energy from its ability to tap into the resurgence of psychoanalysis as a popular discourse. Although the prescient author's own "psychodynamic methods" had more in common with Jung than with Freud, his treatise played well with readers who helped Freud, posthumously, to realize his grandest expectations. A decade after the publication of *Civilization and Its Discontents* (1930), the American arbiters of social theory had accorded Freud a place in the reigning trinity of great thinkers, alongside if not above Darwin and Marx.

But, as Wylie revealed, the rise of psychoanalysis at midcentury coincided with its disaffiliation from modernism, serving its boosters less as a theory of emancipation than a prescription for restraint. *Generation of Vipers,* in addition to an increasingly rampant misogyny, documented a dramatic retrenchment from the heady days of Greenwich Village. It also reversed the aims and aspirations of the scholars who charted the relationship between culture and personality. Rather than following out the promises of cultural relativism, Wylie's treatise foreshadowed the reconfiguration of psychoanalysis in alignment with a liberalism that recognized far fewer possibilities for humanity.

By the time *Generation of Vipers* appeared, a new sobriety was setting in. Since Freud's visit in 1909, Americans had stubbornly resisted the joyless aspects of his doctrine. Feminists as well as other visionaries had preferred to emphasize the potential of psychoanalysis to free men and women from the most personally damaging and socially detrimental consequences of sexual repression. Well into the 1930s, even amid the Great Depression, psychoanalysts and their numerous allies in the social sciences tried to broaden the scope of inquiry to increase the prospect for human happiness within their own society. They compared "simple" and "complex" cultures, hoping that Americans would appreciate the diversity, expand their capacity for living, and enjoy the psychological fruits of modernity. The rise of fascism in Europe, followed by the outbreak of world war, inaugurated a new era, one far less sanguine about the prospects for human liberation. Disenchantment set in. Worried Americans now turned to psychoanalysis to help ward off the worst aspect of the Machine Age, namely, the mechanized slaughter of millions.

This is not to say, however, that the midcentury revival of psychoanalysis dispatched the interwar legacy to the outskirts of American intellectual life. To the contrary, it offered a new, larger, and more coherent context for Culture and Personality formulations. The literary critic Lionel Trilling, who himself had deserted Marx for Freud, summed up his new hero's chief insight: that man can achieve his full humanity "only if he is in accord with his cultural environment, and also if the cultural environment is in accord with the best tendencies in himself." This idea, the core of a centuries-old tradition of liberal thought, was not "specifically Freudian," the distinguished Columbia University English professor admitted, but psychoanalysis now provided its main conceptual framework. It was Freud, Trilling further insisted, who allowed us to understand culture "as a new sort of selfhood bestowed upon the whole of society."[5]

Wylie's generation merely altered the relationship between figure and ground, individual and society. Scholars and social commentators retained their interest in the way culture shapes character, but they became virtually obsessed with culture as a massive projection of individual personalities. Such standard Freudian concepts as repression, sublimation, and defense mechanisms now served to evaluate the affairs of state as readily as the psyches of individuals. For example, commentators might characterize a "bad" system of government as "pathological," its "errant" citizens as "neurotic," and its "evil" leaders as "psychotic." By midcentury the Freudian nosology prevailed, and not merely among psychoanalysts and their new allies, psychiatrists, but nearly everyone else. The "Age of Faith," according to the libertarian psychoanalyst Thomas S. Szasz, had been displaced by the "Age of Madness."[6]

Generation of Vipers, in its critique of Momism, promotes this new interpretive strategy. Central to its main argument is an extrapolation of the mentality of American society from a close reading of the individual citizen. Wylie reasoned that the public sphere based on civic responsibility incorporates traumas generated in the private sphere; or, as he put it, "the philosophy of the state is only a magnification of the philosophy of the person." It follows that even the most pressing problems plaguing the nation appear as symptoms of emotional malady writ large. Asking why Americans had become so lackadaisical about injustices both abroad and in their own country, he typically found his answer not in a ruinous nationalism or defective political economy but in an underlying psychic flaw. The majority had succumbed to apathy, indicating that America had become, in a phrase soon to resonate in liberal thought, a *sick society.*[7]

Generation of Vipers stood out, then, only for its lack of scholarly dispassion. Furiously criticizing the basic institutions of American society—politics, religion, education, business—Wylie appeared so crazed that many of his friends worried that he was, in fact, "nuts." Heeding their advice, the contentious author entered psychotherapy and discovered that the "perturbations of the American libido" had unduly distressed him. Yet in 1955, when his publisher asked for a new introduction to commemorate the twentieth printing of "the most explosive classic of our time," Wylie regretted mainly that he had rushed the book into print. Although he had written *Generation of Vipers* in less than two weeks, its major argument held up. If anything, the psychic threat to American democracy loomed even larger, Wylie cautioned, amid the Cold War.[8]

But it was only a matter of degree that separated Wylie from the more restrained psychoanalysts who provided the theoretical fortification for his main argument. They too evaluated large social problems according to the etiology of individual neurosis or personality flaws. They too worried about the flight from manhood, a concern intensified by the claims of world war. Like Wylie, they singled out mothers as the principal agents behind the greatest catastrophes of the twentieth century. Beginning during the Great Depression, consolidating during World War II, and flourishing throughout the 1950s, psychoanalysts mounted a direct attack on American womanhood—Momism.

The masculine bias of Freud's original theory of psychosexual development, which had driven an earlier generation to open dissent, paled alongside the raw misogyny of this new perspective on malevolent motherhood. From the rise of homosexuality to poverty among African Americans, Moms stood always in the foreground. Indeed, American Moms appeared only one small step away from their German counterparts who had reared the century's most malicious personality, Adolf Hitler. As one commentator summed it up, " 'Mom' is on the spot."[9]

As a preview of these major trends, *Generation of Vipers* served best to spotlight the flagrant rejection of the equalitarian principles of sexual modernism. If the generation before Wylie had welcomed the prospect of parity between the sexes, including the greater sexual freedom that would accompany such change, Wylie and his cohorts obviously believed that the balance of power within the family had shifted too far in women's direction. If descriptions of a sexually merry matriarchy had beguiled Malinowski's contemporaries, they now lost their credibility. Like Wylie, a generation of psychoanalysts chose to cast its lot with Freud in a determined effort to shore up the last remnants of patriarchy.

Generation of Vipers thus signaled a dramatic reconfiguration of the relationship between psychoanalysis and feminism. No longer aligned by their common modernist pledge to human liberation, psychoanalysis and feminism had become, finally, adversaries. Clara Thompson had hit the mark in her dour prediction. The search for moral absolutes which accompanied the war against fascism included a very dark side.

The Debut of Ego Psychology

The realignment of psychoanalysis and feminism depended on a major paradigm shift effected primarily by a second cohort of distinguished refugees. Several had worked closely with Freud or with members of his inner circle well into the 1930s. They had fled not so much his intellectual domination as political repression in Central Europe. Once in the United States loyalists such as Heinz Hartmann and Erik Erikson refurbished Freud's reputation and restored basic elements of his system, including the paramount function of drives or instincts. They imported the core of Freud's later work and elaborated it into a distinctive brand of American psychoanalysis, ego psychology.

By the 1940s American ego psychologists had opened the door to Momism by following the line of argument in Freud's own revised theories. They greatly relaxed the original emphasis on the relation of father and son in order to attend to the maternal influences on very early psychic development. Compared with Freud, who, if anything, underestimated the mother's role in personality formation, his loyal successors endowed the infant's first caretaker with extraordinary powers. But unlike the first feminists, who found Freud's theories lacking precisely for their inattention to motherhood, ego psychologists sought out not motherhood's beneficent but malignant potential. With the assistance of popularists like Wylie, psychoanalysts transformed mothers into the principal agents of children's disorders and the maladies that plagued the nation.

Ironically, in formulating the first premises of ego psychology, Freud frustrated his own ambition to expand psychoanalysis into a general theory or a true metapsychology. Believing that the potential of psychoanalysis extended far beyond the clinic, he had pledged early on to write a comprehensive history of civilization. He eventually published several major essays, including his renowned speculative studies of Moses and Michelangelo, but his production in this area remained fragmentary. Finally, when World War I halted meetings of the International Psycho-Analytic Association and interrupted even his private practice, Freud decided to carve out time to work on this long-delayed project. But once he began, he discovered significant gaps in his theoretical system and conducted instead a major overhaul. Three signal essays resulted. *Beyond the Pleasure Principle* (1920), *Group Psychology and the Analysis of the Ego* (1921), and *The Ego and the Id* (1923) all served as building blocks for what would become known as ego psychology.[10]

The first step Freud took toward ego psychology encompassed a dramatic revision of his theory of drives. The great war in Europe had prompted him to reflect on the "demonic" side of the psyche, so much so that he augmented his drive system to account for a second instinct equal to Eros. "The aim of all life," he now concluded, "is death." Freud then proceeded to alter the basic outline of psychological development to accommodate a continuous contest between these two primal drives. If " 'Civilized' Sexual Morality and Modern Nervous Illness" opened the first, almost optimistic chapter in the history of psychoanalysis, *Beyond the Pleasure Principle* marked a dour turn.[11]

At first the majority of Freud's peers rejected this revision and scoffed at the very idea of a death instinct. Eventually, though, a core group came around, if only partway. These psychoanalysts refused to concede the existence of a death instinct as such, that is, a primal longing for death. They nevertheless approved a modified hypothesis of dual instincts defined more narrowly as sex and aggression. But even this adaptation altered the thematic field. Less determined to work out the kinks in the pleasure principle, that is, in the realm of Eros, Freudians now became far more concerned with problems emanating from destructive impulses. Not simply guilt and anxiety but belligerence and hatred gradually reconfigured the etiology of neurosis and psychopathology.[12]

In the United States the approach of World War II encouraged psychoanalysts and social critics alike to name aggression, rather than sexuality, the instinct of the hour. Karl A. Menninger (1893–1990), founder in 1925 of the famous psychiatric clinic in Topeka, Kansas, actively promoted this idea. His bestselling *Man against Himself* (1938) popularized the dual instinct theory through case studies of suicidal patients who threw themselves into vats of boiling lead or ate crushed glass. Like other Freudians, Menninger argued that such self-destructive tendencies could also be directed outward, as in the deadly examples of murder and war.[13] Flowing with this gloomy current, many political observers, including Wylie, could not help wondering if the psychic forces of hate had overcome love.

In addition to his controversial hypothesis of dual instincts, Freud marked off new territory by paying greater attention to the ego. Equally heuristic, and far less bleak than his speculations on the death instinct, was Freud's companion piece to *Beyond the Pleasure Principle,* a slim volume entitled *The Ego and the Id.* This major essay outlines the tripartite structure of the psychic apparatus—id, ego, and superego—and likewise significantly broadens the scope of classical psychoanalysis. Although premonitory signs had appeared earlier, Freud had grown weary of exploring the id, the reservoir of instinctual impulses, and now preferred to ruminate on the operations of the ego, defined as "essentially the representative of the external world, of reality." The ego aims at self-preservation, according to Freud, and its success depends on its ability to delay and direct instinctual gratification. The ego thus attends to the reality that stands in the way of unrestrained expression of desire and provides organization and stability. "The ego is not only the helper of the id," Freud explained, "it is also a submissive slave who courts his master's love."[14]

Freud himself did relatively little to flesh out this framework. His genius continued to lie in his ability to illustrate the role of unconscious factors and instinctual impulses in shaping the psyche from early infancy, and he never managed to advance significantly beyond these, his most important discoveries. It remained for others to develop ego psychology into a full theory of personality formation.

Nevertheless, Freud had supplied ego psychologists with a key insight into the process. By defining the ego as that part of the id that changes in relation to perceptions of the external world, he had acknowledged, if only surreptitiously, the significance of factors that neo-Freudians themselves exalted: the social environment, including interpersonal relations, and learned behavior.[15]

Psychoanalysts close to Freud accomplished what some later observers judged, if not the "beginning of apostasy," a "decisive reorientation" of psychoanalysis. Erich Fromm, himself an ultra revisionist, considered the changes they brought about "drastic." In the United States, where ego psychology advanced rapidly, psychoanalysts readily affirmed the significance of not only dual instincts but the function of the ego. But in examining the context of instinct management, so to speak, they far exceeded Freud's intentions. Ego psychologists reversed the valence of Freud's original system and thereby paved the way for Momism.[16]

Emblematic of ego psychology is a focus on maternal influences. Instead of spotlighting the psychic events surrounding the Oedipus complex, especially the father's role in generating castration anxiety in his son, ego psychologists fix on the differentiation of the ego from the id *in very early infancy*. And who in the external world, they asked, could be more influential at this crucial moment than the infant's primary caretaker? Mothers were the first to respond to the infant's instinctual needs. By gratifying or frustrating these basic demands, mothers in effect furnished the rudimentary lessons in love and hate, security and fear.

Like Wylie, American ego psychologists attributed to mothers an inordinate psychic power. Specifically, in reformulating the etiology of neurosis, these psychoanalysts exchanged the libidinous impulses of the "bad" child for the inappropriate behavior or attitude of the "bad" mother. It is easy to see how their formulations suggested the theoretical gloss for *Generation of Vipers*: Moms, in mishandling their sons' instinctual strivings, routinely cause a multitude of developmental problems that show up in men and, equally important, in the society governed by these men.

For all his tinkering with drives and structures, Freud never approached this kind of reasoning. This emphasis on maternal factors represents a striking departure from the phallocentric premises of his basic outline of psychosexual development. Freud had reasoned logically that parents or other caretakers necessarily figure centrally in this process, but he rarely commented on maternal behavior or attitude beyond intermittent references to the mother's distinctive function during the oral stage. When he charted the tortuous path of psychic development, Freud focused on the child—in his own phrase, "the greed of a child's libido"—in passing through the three major stages of development. How the child manages the oral, anal, and phallic stages determines later patterns, especially the resolution of the all-important Oedipus complex. The child appears the active agent in constructing psychic reality, the mother much less so. More compelling is the father, the possessor of the phallus. It is the father who inspires castration anxiety in boys; and it is the father who diverts a girl's desire along a heterosexual path. The mother meanwhile stands rejected by the son because she becomes, according to the rule of the father, the forbidden object, and by the daughter because she, too, bears the stigma of mutilation.

Only in the early 1930s, in fending off the critics of phallocentrism, did Freud speculate on the special role of the first love-object, and then principally with regard to femininity. "Female Sexuality," published in 1932, acknowledges the importance of the girl's primary attachment to her mother in psychosexual development. "Our insight into this early, pre-Oedipus phase in girls comes to us as a surprise," he remarked, "like the discovery, in another field, of the Minoan-Mycenean civilization behind the civilization of Greece." But Freud found this pre-Oedipus phase "so grey with age and shadowy and almost impossible to revivify" that he readily handed over the work of exploration to women analysts, who he believed were psychologically better suited to the task.[17]

Psychoanalysts practicing in England led the initial forays into the mother-infant relationship. Melanie Klein (1882–1968), who readily incorporated the death instinct into her own theoretical work, focused principally on infantile fantasies provoked by the mother's power to grant or refuse her child's desires. The emotions of greed and rage, of fear and hate, directed at the seemingly omnipotent mother figured prominently in her theories of personality formation. Klein's erstwhile student Donald W. Winnicott helped to establish the competing school of psychoanalysis known as object-relations, which emphasized instead the benevolent mother's capacity to nurture her infant. Despite growing differences between them, Klein and Winnicott distinguished British psychoanalysis by exalting the interaction between mother and child. Both theorists would have a major impact on American psychoanalysis, including feminist derivations, but not until well after World War II.

American ego psychologists mined instead a growing body of psychoanalytic theory that complemented Freud's own later revisions but supplied a fuller elaboration than the founder himself was willing to provide. They turned to the work of two of Freud's most cherished pupils. His youngest child and devoted daughter and a prominent lay analyst in her own right, Anna Freud (1895–1982) charted the means by which the ego manages not only dangerous inner impulses emanating from the id but external threats as well. Her major work of theory, *The Ego and the Mechanisms of Defense* (1936), which she presented to her father on his eightieth birthday, cataloged for the first time such basic coping mechanisms as repression, regression, reaction-formation, and sublimation. The psychoanalyst whom Anna Freud regarded as a "slightly elder brother" because professionally they "shared the same father" complemented her work by emphasizing the ego's adaptive functions. Trained in Berlin in the 1920s, Heinz Hartmann (1894–1970) had taken a second training analysis with Freud in the mid-1930s in preparation for writing his landmark *Ego Psychology and the Problem of Adaptation,* which appeared in German in 1939.[18]

It was Hartmann's signature to endow the ego with a degree of autonomy—a "conflict-free sphere"—and to stress its ability to adjust to its environment through the functions of perception, memory, learning, and motility. Hartmann thus muted much of the pessimism associated with Freud's late-life perspective and greatly diminished his emphasis on conflict as the principle of development. "Victory," Freud brooded, "is always on the side of the big battalions," that is, the id. In contrast, Hartmann presumed, as did Anna Freud, the possibility of a strong, relatively autonomous ego.[19]

After the death of Sigmund Freud in 1939, Hartmann and Anna Freud made even greater strides in articulating the parameters of the mother-infant relationship. While running a British nursery during World War II, Anna Freud noticed how strongly children react to separation from their mothers. It was already clear to her that infants form their first emotional relationship with their mothers, but, in following her father, she had underestimated the full significance of this fact. She now acknowledged the magnitude of the mother's role in shaping the processes by which "unrestrained, greedy and cruel little savages" become "well-behaved, socially adapted, civilized beings."[20] Hartmann agreed, contending that the achievement of a relatively autonomous ego depends to a large degree on the mother's response to her infant's instinctual impulses. Theoretically, the mother displaces the father, the possessor of the mighty phallus: she plays the instrumental role in mediating between the dangers of the id and the promise of autonomy. If anything, Hartmann later affirmed, "the mother's personal attitude," as well as her attitude toward motherhood itself, had been heretofore "insufficiently taken into account."[21]

Under Hartmann's auspices, ego psychology became the hallmark of American psychoanalysis. While Anna Freud remained in England to found the famous Hampstead Child-Therapy Clinic and to defend psychoanalytic orthodoxy, Hartmann immigrated to the United States to take over as, according to Paul Roazen, the "American prime minister of psychoanalysis."[22] He dissuaded his new colleagues from conferring "emeritus status" on Freud's instinct theory and generated interest in the augmented drive system of sex and aggression. Hartmann also revived the use of basic Freudian nomenclature long discarded by neo-Freudians. Even Margaret Mead began to employ more Freudian concepts and granted a larger role to instincts overall. Hartmann provided theoretical coherence for several strains of psychoanalysis. He affirmed the importance of the environmental factors exalted by neo-Freudians and, at the same time, added luster to the formulations of those American Freudians who had been upholding the mantle all along.

Hartmann reaped the benefits of the efforts of several psychoanalysts who had been working independently in the United States to lay a foundation for ego psychology. The Hungarian-born René Arpad Spitz (1887–1974), for example, was on the brink of becoming one of the nation's leading scholars of the mother-infant relationship. He had earlier collaborated with Sándor Ferenczi, undergone didactic analysis with Freud in 1910–1911, and become a member of the Vienna Psychoanalytic Society. Moving from Vienna to Berlin and finally to Paris before immigrating to the United States in 1938, he became a pioneer in charting the earliest phases of ego development. Studying infants in private homes as well as nurseries and orphanages, Spitz established a strong link between emotional deprivation in early infancy and childhood illness, including a virulent emotional disorder, anaclitic depression, which not infrequently leads to death. Spitz observed that in a foundling home of high hygienic standards over one-third of a group of ninety infants pined away and died within a two-year period. This tragic phenomenon, known as hospitalism, firmed Spitz's conviction that maternal factors are at the forefront in determining an infant's well-being, physical as well as emotional. Mothers form the first and apparently the most meaningful partnership with infants, he insisted; furthermore, mothers mediate infants' every perception and behavior. The new, highly specialized annual founded in 1945, *Psychoanalytic Study of the Child*, provided a ready outlet for Spitz and a team of psychoanalysts similarly specializing in the events of early infancy.[23]

By the early 1940s several prominent American psychoanalysts not only had extolled the mother-infant relationship but had verged remarkably close to Momism. The New York psychoanalyst David Mordecai Levy (1892–1977) presented a truly remarkable postulate.

After conducting extensive psychological surveys of maternal behavior, he studied his 2,000 case records and found a positive correlation between a woman's propensity for nurturing and the duration of her menstrual flow. Levy compiled his research into a scholarly book, *Maternal Overprotection* (1943), that added a scientific patina to Wylie's charges. In the same year another New York analyst, Margaret A. Ribble (1890–1971), criticized modern women for an opposite failing, maternal deprivation. She even coined her own neologism, the acronym *TLC* (tender loving care), which neatly summed up her advice to American Moms. More precisely, Ribble recommended lengthy nursing and frequent cuddling. She even advised mothers to share their beds with babies.[24]

Published just a year earlier, *Generation of Vipers* fit in perfectly. By linking individual pathology to broader social failings, and by attributing both to Mom, Wylie helped to create an audience for this new wave of psychoanalytical speculation. He also proved especially adroit in intertwining these new hypotheses and raw misogyny. For example, Wylie echoed Freud in describing a woman's love as essentially narcissistic. But whereas Freud found this aspect of femininity somewhat alluring, Wylie emphasized its negative consequences. Overprotective of her infant, the narcissistic Mom stunts her son's masculine development, causing him to remain throughout his life in emotional "serfdom" to her. Wylie even improvised a bit on Freud's dual drive system. This doting Mom, he clarified, shields her young son from his aggressive impulses, so much so that as a man he must "spend most of his energy denying the barbarism that howls in his brain." When men can no longer contain this evil, Wylie warns, the results are catastrophic. Even World War II could be traced to Mom: because of her, "we are infants, still, with loaded guns for toys."[25]

Philip Wylie was scarcely alone, then, in exploring the perils of Momism. Psychoanalysts both in the United States and abroad had begun to probe ever more deeply into the childhood origins of emotional calamity only to discover a host of pernicious maternal influences. The horrors of World War II caused them to intensify their efforts. Equipped with the expanded theory of ego psychology, leading scholars thus shared Wylie's aspiration to identify the maternal factors responsible for such momentous human aggression.

If threatening to human survival, World War II proved beneficial to ego psychology. Because the dangers were so pressing, and because the latest revision muted some major differences between them, scholars began to cooperate not only across disciplinary but also factional lines. Hartmann himself proved a great facilitator. Although no proponent of Momism, he believed that if psychoanalysis was to advance beyond its origins as a theory of *inner* conflict to become a general psychology of *human* conflict, interdisciplinary teamwork was necessary. Hartmann looked to historians and sociologists and most of all to those anthropologists who had already identified a possible point of convergence in their prolific investigations of family organization and kinship structure. Ironically, the field of Culture and Personality, which had originated as a critique of the universalism inherent in Freud's Oedipus complex, gained renewed prominence as its leading scholars found much to admire in the latest emanation from the Freudian camp.

Propelled by the urgency of world war, notable Freudians and neo-Freudians found a common ground in ego psychology. The culturalists granted greater play to instincts or drives, particularly to aggression, and discussed Sullivan's concept of self-esteem in direct reference to the ego. For their part, Freudians allowed far more room for environmental factors, especially the interpersonal relations within the family. Even the arch-loyalist Helene Deutsch discussed the interplay between biology and sociology and generously cited such wayward scholars as Malinowski. As one psychoanalyst observed, the habit of grouping theorists as either "instinctual" or "cultural" became increasingly arbitrary and, really, now made "little sense." Freud's death also helped to abate the tide of revisionism. Only the most recalcitrant like Horney and Fromm held firm in their censure of the founder of their discipline. Helene Deutsch expressed the majority opinion. Freud was, she wrote, "the luminous star on the dark road of a new science." But it took the consummate crisis of global war to achieve a workable partnership.[26]

As the historian H. Stuart Hughes pointed out, the two major factions came together to address the major unanswered questions remaining in Freud's legacy: "the individual's relationship to society, and more particularly his vicissitudes in adapting to the circumstances of his group life."[27] Psychoanalysts and their allies restored several core concepts of Freud's dynamic system: the centrality of instincts or drives; the topography of the psychic apparatus (id, ego, and super-ego); and the disposition to restore equilibrium among conflicting psychic forces. They also fortified the neo-Freudian premise, the ability of the individual to adapt to the changing conditions of life. But what stands out is their *meta*psychology, that is, their fulfillment of Freud's aspiration to project psychoanalysis as a totalizing system. Not just the individual but the entire civilization moved within the psychoanalytic orbit. It is all the more ironic that these momentous developments coincided with—indeed, helped to propel—a snowballing misogyny.

National Character

It was commonplace for Americans influenced by psychoanalysis to discuss the global conflagration in Freudian terms, attributing the atrocities perpetrated by the Axis powers to a pervasive and formidable psychopathology. The Axis national leaders were clearly aggressive, their citizens passive to an extreme and dangerous degree. What, then, are the causes? What are the psychic factors behind such destructive temperaments? What kinds of personalities engage in such monstrous acts as the vindictive torture of prisoners of war and the Holocaust? What stimulates the perverse desire to rule the world? As the title of one timely book suggested, Americans wanted to know: *Is Germany Incurable?*[28] Inspired by recent turns in psychoanalytic theory, scholars searched for the origins of such emotional tendencies not, for example, in the harsh terms of the Versailles Treaty that had ensured Germany's economic stagnation. They looked instead to very early infancy and, not surprisingly, discovered the Axis Mom.

This enterprise, which advanced in the 1940s as the study of national character, had deep roots in the Culture and Personality movement. Ruth Benedict had suggested the rudiments of this argument in "Psychological Types in the Cultures of the Southwest," published in 1928, and in "Configurations of Culture in North America," published four years later. It was her bestselling *Patterns of Culture* that made these ideas common currency. Here she identified distinctive configurations of personality traits among various North American Indian tribes and supplied psychological labels such as megalomanic paranoid or, improvising upon Nietzsche, Apollonian or Dionysian. Benedict's work thus fleshed out Edward Sapir's musing that "the more fully one tries to understand a culture, the more it seems to take on the characteristics of a personality organization."[29]

The early Culture and Personality studies did not, however, highlight maternal factors. Benedict and Sapir were typical in attributing recurring manifestations of certain personality types to a common cultural and physical environment. Like the majority of their colleagues, they relied on the vague but gender-neutral concept "cultural conditioning." Childrearing practices were central to this process, they realized, but it was rare for anyone to single out mothers for excessive scrutiny.

By the 1940s the tide had turned, and leading scholars routinely credited the "basic personality structure" directly to mother's role in early infancy. Ralph Linton, Benedict's co-worker at Columbia University, offered a vivid example. Mothers, he reported, tend to subscribe to a common set of childrearing techniques and thereby reinforce in their offspring the personality traits prevailing in their culture:

> Let us suppose that it is the pattern in a society to feed infants whenever they cry and not to feed them unless they cry. Given the variations within such a culture pattern which must result from the exigencies of everyday life, we can be sure that not all members of this society were fed whenever they cried. However, all of them will have been fed on most of the occasions when they cried and not fed when they did not cry. As a result, all of them will have had abundant opportunity to develop crying as a first response leading to the satisfaction of their hunger needs. Their experience, in spite of all the variable factors involved in the operation of the culture pattern and in their individual differences will have much in common. All members of the particular society will resemble one another in this respect much more closely than they will resemble the members of some other society in which it is the culture pattern to feed children on a strict schedule in which crying is either ignored or punished.[30]

Mothers, then, in responding to their babies' instinctual impulses, shape not only their children's individual characters but collectively the personality structure of their entire society.

Linton was conservative in applying this rule. He cautioned that only small, relatively homogeneous cultures could be examined effectively through the refracting lens of maternal behavior. Any attempt to apply this formula to complex modern nations, he warned, was extraordinarily risky.

The outbreak of World War II overruled such reservations. "The conduct of the war," according to the anthropologist Geoffrey Gorer, added a new urgency to the "problems of national character, of understanding why certain nations were acting in the way they did, so as to understand and forestall them." The stakes appeared to be extraordinarily high—nothing less than the future of the free world.[31]

Especially after the federal government poured unprecedented funds into applied research, leading anthropologists, sociologists, and psychoanalysts responded to this patriotic appeal. Margaret Mead, for example, strongly encouraged her colleagues to put aside "the immunities of the ivory tower" and to direct their energies toward creating "the scientific basis for building an ever better world." The Office of Strategic Services and Office of War Information offered jobs to scores of scholars who were to study the personality structures of the nations at war. Assuming their astute assessments would help to refine military strategy and shape policies of postwar reconstruction, teams of researchers examined the national characters of Germany, Japan, Rumania, Burma, and Thailand, as well as Russia and the United States. This massive project would facilitate, Mead predicted, the most productive exchange yet between anthropology and psycho-analysis.[32]

The national character studies produced during wartime proved that Philip Wylie had no monopoly on Momism. Gorer, a wartime liaison officer between Britain and the United States, blamed Japanese mothers for their nation's belligerent personality. These mothers begin toilet training very early, he observed, when the infant is only four months old. "Any lapse from cleanliness is," moreover, "punished by severe scolding, the mother's voice expressing horror and disgust, and often also by shaking or other physical punishment." As a result, Gorer concluded, Japanese children grow up obsessed with order and ritual and as adults possess an "extremely strong desire to be aggressive." The American anthropologist Weston La Barre came up with similar findings. He described the Japanese as "probably the most compulsive people in the world ethnological museum." They are prone to "secretiveness, hiding of emotions and attitudes; preservation and persistency; conscientiousness; self-righteousness; a tendency to project attitudes; fanaticism; arrogance; 'touchiness'; precision and perfection; neatness and ritualistic cleanliness; ceremoniousness; conformity to rule; sadomasochistic behavior; hypochondrias; suspiciousness; jealousy and enviousness; pedantry; sentimentality; love of scatological obscenity and anal sexuality." La Barre summed up his findings on "character structure in the Orient" in this list of unsavory personality traits. Japan's propensity for aggression, both scholars affirmed, stems from a compulsive neurosis fostered by severe toilet training imposed by mothers.[33]

Some distinguished scholars bolstered this description of the Japanese national character by invoking Wylie's infamous neologism. Edward A. Strecker, president of the American Psychiatric Association, 1943–44, for example, discussed the psychopathology of "Nipponese momism." He portrayed Japan's emperor, the mythological "lineal descendant of the sun god," as "the repository of the eternal womb to which all loyal Japanese hoped to return." But fortunately, Strecker explained, Japanese Momism would ultimately work in Americans' favor, inspiring "a series of wildly enthusiastic banzai charges which were not only one-way tickets to death but were militarily futile." The "Nip soldier," in fighting ceremoniously to his death, endured the "logical penalty that must be paid for nationalist momism." Not even the atomic bomb, Strecker averred, possessed "sufficient explosive force to dis-womb the Japanese people."[34]

Nothing, however, surpassed the rhetorical Momism marking the studies of the national character of Nazi Germany. Strecker improvised upon his main argument to suggest that Hitler had ascended to power because Germans, hoping to regain the self-esteem they had lost during World War I, collectively indulged in the fantasy of an overprotective supermom: "Don't fret, children, Mom Fuehrer will fix it." And, of course, who would not obey a Mom who promised an end to dishonor?[35]

Not surprisingly, Hitler himself appeared as the prime example of Mom-induced psychopathology. Scholars employed a variety of psychoanalytic terms to characterize the imperialist Nazi leader as a "psychopathic paranoid," an "amoral sadistic infant," an "overcompensatory sissy," and a "neurotic laboring under the compulsion to murder." Equally revealing, they aligned themselves with Wylie, equating Hitler's emotional maladies with a flight from manhood.

One of the century's most renowned psychoanalysts, a pioneer of ego psychology, lent authority to the prevailing diagnosis: "mama's boy." Erik Homburger Erikson (1902–1972), an itinerant German artist whose formal education had ended at high school, found his way to Vienna in 1927, where he soon entered training with Anna Freud to become one of the first men to work in the field she cultivated, child analysis. By the early 1930s he had grown restless in Vienna and immigrated to the United States, where, after settling in Berkeley, California, he teamed up with Alfred L. Kroeber, the distinguished Boasian anthropologist and psychoanalyst. Erikson temporarily abandoned child analysis for field research among the South Dakota Sioux and the Yurok of northern California. Yet, as the war approached, he could not help ruminating on the cataclysmic events in Central Europe, and he set himself to prepare "a psychoanalytic book on the relation of ego to society."[36] The resulting *Childhood and Society* (1950) established Erikson as one of the foremost psychoanalytic writers in the United States.

Erikson's evidence against Hitler's mom came from the psychopathic dictator's own autobiography. *Mein Kampf*, Erikson noted, contains "an abundance of superhuman mother figures" indicating Hitler's deep-seated ambivalence about his own mother. The psychoanalyst surmised that because Hitler's father appeared to be both tyrannical and remote, bent on infantilizing wife and child alike, the young Adolf could appeal only to his mother for gratification. She in turn, rebuffed by her husband, responded by smothering her young son with excessive love and ceaseless attention. The first chapter of Hitler's autobiography reads, Erikson concluded, "as an involuntary confession" of his Oedipus complex. Hitler thus grew up as an overly indulged "mama's boy," replete with repressed homosexual leanings, to become the most notorious example of maternal behavior gone awry.[37]

Although both Strecker and Erikson lent their professional eminence to this particular rendition of Momism, they merely recapitulated the sentiments of the popular press. Writing in the *Ladies' Home*

Journal, the medical writer Amram Scheinfeld had blamed Hitler's overprotective mom for the entire global catastrophe. According to Scheinfeld, she had coddled young Adolf so excessively that he grew up emotionally ill-prepared for worldly rejection. She even indulged his baseless fantasies of becoming a great artist. When Hitler reached adulthood, he experienced unanticipated pain and rejection when his peers scoffed at his aspirations, and he proceeded to overcompensate on the greatest scale imaginable. "Had this one individual had a different mother," Scheinfeld opined, "history might have taken another course."[38]

Scholars hardly missed a beat as the Cold War followed on the heels of Allied victory. Between 1947 and 1953 Columbia University's Research in Contemporary Cultures, funded by the Office of Naval Research, engaged no fewer than 120 investigators from fourteen disciplines to analyze the basic personalities of sixteen different nationality groups. They targeted a different malady: Communist totalitarianism. Scholars pushed on, gathering data mainly from interviews with recent Russian immigrants and from textual analysis of Russian novels and films. Meanwhile the Harvard Project on the Soviet Social System sponsored an even more ambitious undertaking, interviewing and testing nearly 3,000 former Soviet citizens who chose not to return to the USSR after the war. Once again the mother's role in establishing childrearing patterns figured prominently in these timely studies of national character.

The "Bolshevik dilemma," it seemed, also originated in Momism. Gorer's *The People of Great Russia: A Psychological Study* (1949) fixed narrowly on swaddling as the source of Communism, while Erikson turned to the biography of Maxim Gorky for his illustrative case study of a pathologically compassionate grandmother. Whatever the maternal source, according to Erikson, stoic endurance marks the Russian people, so much so that they typically accede to fate, even to totalitarian rule. Much like the German variety, Russian Momism produces leaders plagued by megalomania and makes ordinary people unable to respond to inhumanity.

The study of national character could not sustain itself, despite the politically charged atmosphere of the early Cold War. Critics began to complain about the faulty methodology of the wartime studies. With on-site fieldwork impossible, anthropologists had utilized unconventional sources of information. They had gathered life histories from, and had administered Rorschach tests to, "displaced persons" and even second-generation immigrants. They had also reviewed folklore, art, and popular fiction as well as commercial films produced in Japan, Russia, and the United States. As many scholars suspected at the time, this research-at-a-distance was bound to yield unreliable data. Such was the case with Gorer and La Barre, neither of whom had ever visited Japan. Moreover, Gorer read only English-language books about Japan and depended on informants who were either foreign-born experts on Japan or part-Japanese at best. La Barre's insights into Japanese culture came from interviews with Japanese Americans at the War Relocation Authority's internment camp at Topaz, Utah. Critics now charged that the indignities of life in a prison camp could easily produce in any group the traits La Barre attributed to the national character of Japan. Researchers who could now travel abroad often discovered patterns wholly at odds with the wartime studies. Americans in Occupied Japan, for example, did not find unusually harsh toilet training; to the contrary, they judged the wide-ranging techniques similar to those in the United States. The overwhelming preoccupation with toilet training itself, a veritable fixation, prompted postwar evaluators to dismiss the entire body of scholarship as simple diaperology.[39]

By the early 1950s Heinz Hartmann had sounded a stern warning against drawing such large-scale conclusions from childrearing patterns alone, insisting quite reasonably that similar patterns actually produce a variety of results. With critics like Hartmann gaining speed, the entire enterprise soon fell into disrepute, and it remains to this day one of the dark spots in the history of the interdisciplinary movement.[40]

Momism proved more resilient. Even in disputing both the methodology and the conclusions of the highly stylized wartime studies of national character, scholars continued to affirm the primary importance of maternal factors. In line with Hartmann's advice, they turned away from examining childrearing techniques as such to focus more broadly on maternal behavior and especially the mother's personal attitude. Far from abandoning Momism, psychoanalysts judged it a particularly useful gauge of psychopathology at home.

Momism and Matriarchy in America

The specialized studies of American national character, also sparked by World War II, illustrate vividly just how far psychoanalysts and their allies had retreated from the high ground of sexual modernism. Where once they envisioned a greater equality in the institutions of marriage and family as well as the state, they now feared that women had gone too far in claiming traditional male prerogatives. As a consequence, American society stood on the brink of disaster. What were the clearest signs of this impending catastrophe? A flight from manhood, the authorities answered, manifested directly in the upswing in homosexuality and indirectly in racial conflict. Thus, in undermining masculinity, Momism had placed in jeopardy the future of the free world.

Geoffrey Gorer's highly acclaimed *The American People: A Study in National Character* (1948) documents this trend. Gorer, an affiliate of Yale University's prestigious Institute of Human Relations, had traveled extensively in this country during the 1940s and discovered a lassitude among American men that matched Wylie's assessment. American Momism, the eminent anthropologist similarly concluded, expresses a deeply rooted antipatriarchal sentiment. Its origins, moreover, were very old, dating at least to the American Revolution. Indeed, the colonists' rebellion against the British monarch bore an uncanny resemblance to Freud's own story of origination, Gorer surmised, although American mythology of primal patricide projected its own specific set of "major psychological truths." On the one hand, a healthy anti-authoritarianism bid fair for the future of democracy; on the other, the extreme disrespect of patriarchy foreshadowed the current drift toward matriarchy.[41]

Gorer found plenty of evidence to support his contention. Images of Momism were ubiquitous, James Thurber's *Men, Women and Dogs* (1943) an unsparing example. The acclaimed *New Yorker* writer captured repeatedly in his cartoons the typical middle-class couple: the outsized, menacing matriarch and her greatly diminished mate. The enormously popular comic strip "Li'l Abner" sketched, in the words of one admirer, an authentic image of "*the maternally overprotected boy*, the boy with an overpowering mother." Diminutive in size, corncob pipe set in crooked teeth, Mammy Yokum rules through supernatural strength. Not even castration anxiety can save the perpetually infantilized son, for his father is far too weak to pose any threat. Slighting the popular cartoon strip "Maggie and Jiggs," which provided similar images, Gorer chose to discuss "Blondie" as a reasonably accurate representation of American family life. Dagwood, the all-American husband and father, finds no haven in his home and instead seeks refuge from female tyranny, if only a fleeting moment alone in the bathtub. Soon dislodged from his unsure sanctuary, the defeated husband suffers yet more humiliation in the form of a stern rebuke from his domestic ruler. For Gorer, the slogan of the *Ladies' Home Journal*'s popular advertising campaign said it all: "Never underestimate the power of a woman." The domestic despotism of American women, he concluded, had precipitated a flight from manhood.[42]

Like Wylie, Gorer blamed clinging Moms for inhibiting their sons' bid for autonomy. But it was fathers—or, rather, their demise—that concerned him most. Their "patriarchal role" now merely "vestigial," fathers lacked the authority to generate castration anxiety and thereby spur the development of a genuinely masculine superego. Instead, the American boy matured carrying around, "as it were, encapsulated inside him, an ethical, admonitory, censorious mother." How, then, could these men conduct the world's work, take on those responsibilities "peculiarly masculine," if they functioned emotionally in "the realm of feminine morality?" Gorer even targeted the New Deal, specifically the enactment of social legislation that, in effect, introduced "into the domain of masculine privilege the meddling female morality."[43]

A sizable number of social commentators, influenced by psychoanalysis, reported that the maternal pathology described by Gorer had already spread far enough to pose a genuine danger to national security. Like Wylie, they judged American men to be poor specimens of their sex, emotionally ill-equipped to protect their home and country against the increasing perils. Moms had produced two of the most troubling symptoms, they contended: the growing incidence of homosexuality and the pervasive low self-esteem that plagued African American men. These two "maladies" became the target of research and speculation that supplied ego psychologists with evidence of a massive psychopathology affecting not only unfortunate individuals but the nation at large.

Inquiries into homosexuality had soared in number during the war. The government's new policy of screening prospective recruits for personality or emotional disorders, along with physical disabilities, engaged nearly 2,400 medical doctors, the great majority lacking prior experience in psychodynamic techniques. But once under the direction of prestigious psychoanalysts—Harry Stack Sullivan worked for the Selective Service System; William C. Menninger of Topeka, the first psychiatrist to hold the rank of brigadier general, headed the army's Neuropsychiatric Division; and John M. Murray of the Boston Psychoanalytic Society served the Army Air Force—many physicians quickly learned the basic principles of psychoanalysis. More than 1,000 psychiatrists, who had formerly worked in mental institutions with acutely ill patients, acclimated themselves to treating psychosomatic symptoms and various kinds of "combat neurosis." They also helped to reject for service, and to weed out those who slipped through the screening, all "anti-social personalities," "asocial personalities," and "sexual deviates."[44]

Medical personnel trained in psychoanalysis measured the amount of homosexuality in the American population and established the link to Momism. Especially well positioned to make such a sweeping diagnosis was Edward A. Strecker, who reported so expressively on Momism in Japan and Germany. Strecker had joined the first group of specialists—social workers, psychologists, psychiatrists, physicians with training in neuropsychiatry, as well as psychoanalysts—employed by the armed services to screen military personnel for mental disturbances and personality defects. As a wartime military advisor he examined the case histories of 1,825,000 men who were rejected for military service (12 percent of 15 million examined) and another 600,000 who were subsequently dismissed because they were "psychoneurotic." The magnitude of these figures alarmed him as well as most other experts. Far, far too many men, Strecker railed, had proved insufficiently masculine to fight this war. The cause was obvious. Although "biological deviations" undoubtedly played some part, he reasoned, in the vast majority of cases the fault lay with "mom and her wiles."[45]

The practice of blaming possessive mothers for "feminizing" their sons was, of course, nothing new. Eugene O'Neill, for one, found it a highly marketable dramatic subject, as did Sidney Howard in one of the most popular plays of the 1920s, *The Silver Cord* (1926), which portrayed an adult son too infantilized to marry. Howard's contemporary Floyd Dell agreed. Dell believed that it was not uncommon for a mother to turn to her son for emotional satisfaction, thereby "homosexualizing" him. Even if a boy fought against this situation, according to Dell, growing up as "a pet or 'mama's lover' " he had only a poor chance of achieving "psychic manhood." Childrearing advice in the 1920s had delivered the same message. The behaviorist John B. Watson carved out a rewarding career for himself warning against the dangers of mother's love. Strecker merely added the combined authority of psychoanalysis and psychiatry to these clichéd stereotypes, claiming that Moms encourage their sons' homosexual tendencies by keeping them "paddling about in a kind of psychological amniotic fluid."[46]

This perspective had little in common with Freud's. Freud had assumed that homosexuality emerges invariably in psychosexual development as a stage through which all children pass. Although he labeled adult homosexuality a "perversion," he stressed that the term was not one of "reproach." Nor did it imply degeneracy. Freud treated homosexuality mainly as "an inhibition" of normal development, a problem in object choice rather than a distinct pathology. Although he did not consider homosexuals necessarily feminine in character, he did suggest that a boy tending toward homosexuality prizes his penis too much. On the question of mother's influence, Freud was characteristically circumspect. He acknowledged the boy's attachment to his mother as central but placed far more emphasis on excessive fear of the father's retaliatory rage, a terror forcing the boy to flee women altogether. True to form, Freud fixed on the Oedipus complex and the son's struggle with his father.[47]

In the mid-1920s a few psychoanalysts had begun to associate homosexuality with pre-oedipal factors and thereby to spotlight the relationship between mother and child. Such was the case with Melanie Klein, who had recently settled in England, and Edmund Bergler in Germany, who considered homosexuality a severe regression to the oral stage of psychosexual development. By the next decade Bergler was renowned for his work on the "breast complex," which he introduced as *Der Mammakomplex*. Of course, few Americans outside the psychoanalytic community were familiar with these early writings on homosexuality. Only in the 1940s, with the rise of ego psychology, did it become routine to label homosexuality a deep personality disturbance caused by an overly solicitous mother.[48]

In the United States the medical personnel employed by the armed forces promoted this new classification of homosexuality as a serious mental illness. As early as 1942 policies adopted by local draft boards and branches of the military service designated homosexuality a "perversion." The inflection was decidedly unlike Freud's, for this term now covered not only a set of "deviant" sexual behaviors but a configuration of personality traits that together made a person unfit for combat. Although relatively few men were rejected specifically for this reason—4,000 to 5,000 of nearly 18 million examined—the U.S. government had now officially defined homosexuals as "sex psychopaths."

Not all psychoanalysts and psychiatrists went along with this policy. Harry Stack Sullivan, who was himself gay, remained determinedly tolerant in his views. The outspoken majority, however, accepted and helped to elaborate this new designation of homosexuality. Even after Alfred Kinsey's well-publicized *Sexual Behavior in the American Male* (1948) established homosexual behavior as common and widespread, they would not budge. The most extreme, such as Bergler, who now lived in the United States, dismissed Kinsey's findings as fantastic. Published in 1952, the first edition of the *Diagnostic and Statistical Manual of Mental Disorders (DSM-1)* incorporated nomenclature directly from the War Department's *Technical Bulletin 203* issued in 1943: homosexuality is a sociopathic personality disorder. Meanwhile the military's campaign against homosexuals in its ranks advanced; by the early 1950s discharges for homosexuality averaged 2,000 per year.[49]

The causal relationship between Momism and homosexuality not only outlasted the war but became even more firmly rooted in psychoanalytic and popular discourse alike. The readjustment to peacetime signaled a second round of alarms. Psychoanalysts warned that the fatal combination of a mother with enhanced prerogatives and a father absent from the home had guaranteed a rise in the incidence of homosexuality. Gorer found that American men endured lives "bounded . . . by [the] constant necessity to prove to their fellows, and to themselves, that they are not sissies, not homosexuals." In the mass-circulation *Parents' Magazine,* one of scores of postwar writers "verified" this hypothesis, reporting on "a thought a mother can hardly face"—that there was something "sissy," even downright "girlish," in the behavior of her young son. Seven-year-old "Donnie" liked to try on his mother's earrings and admitted unashamedly that he enjoyed sleeping with dolls. Fearing the worst, his mother sought professional advice. The caseworker calmed her by explaining that Donnie, born during the war, had passed the crucial first three years of life with only his mother at home and now suffered from her overly solicitous care. However, the solution to his problem lay close at hand: Donnie's father had returned home from the war. Let his father take over, the therapist advised, and Donnie would—so to speak—set himself straight.[50]

The commentaries on homosexuality, which became more vicious in the postwar decade, continued to provide ammunition for the case against Momism. American psychoanalysts played down the intrapsychic processes so central to Freud's early theories to emphasize instead the dangers of impaired development. They scrutinized the psychological environment of interpersonal relations with a keen eye on maternal influences. As a distinguished veteran of Culture and Personality studies put it, the "flight from masculinity" originates not in constitutional variations but in the earliest stages of development. It is the dominant mother—"what is popularly known as 'momism' "—who easily produces a "character type whose hold on masculinity is very tenuous." The problems with American men—fear of combat, tendency toward homosexuality, indeed, their very flight from manhood—could all be traced to American Moms. And the problem stemmed not simply from faulty childrearing practices but from the defective personalities of American women themselves. Modern women, according to popularists and behavioral scientists alike, transmitted their own psychopathology to their sons.[51]

After a decade of research, a group led by Irving Bieber published the results of the first long-term investigation of homosexuality conducted by psychoanalysts. This "systematic study of 106 male homosexuals," which appeared in 1962, rejected Freud's assumption of bisexuality, proclaimed exclusive heterosexuality as the "biologic norm," and, moreover, insisted that "every homosexual is a latent heterosexual." Psychoanalysts thus defined their mission as restoring "normal" masculinity through analysis. This study appropriately culminated in an indictment of the "demasculinizing and feminizing attitudes" of mothers. The authors also blamed fathers, but only for being too "detached" to protect their sons from "destructive maternal influences." In short, two decades after Strecker fired the initial warning, the psychoanalytic profession had lined up on his side. Mom was still at fault.[52]

Momism cast yet another, equally malevolent shadow on American democracy, according to psychoanalysts, by bolstering racial inequality. This theme emerged in the mid-1930s when Culture and Personality scholars, partly in response to the rise of fascism in Europe, began to pursue the causes and consequences of bigotry and intolerance in their own society. Influenced by the interpersonal psychology of Sullivan, they pinpointed for examination low self-esteem among African American men. The legacy of slavery and its perpetuation in the modern caste structure as well as the racist attitudes of whites appeared to be the major causal factors. But the leading investigators, such as the sociologist E. Franklin Frazier, targeted the African American family structure only to discover what later scholars would judge a true pathology—the Black Matriarchy.[53]

The flight from manhood appeared nowhere more prominently, these scholars concluded, than among African Americans. They drew up a composite portrait of the "Negro Personality" that accentuated femininity. The African American man was, accordingly, likely to be expressive rather than active, manipulative rather than direct, and artistic rather than rational. Like women, he remained childlike, so infantilized that he could not control his impulses, either sexual or aggressive. "He is, so to speak," according to the sociologist Robert E. Park, "the lady among the races."[54]

John Dollard's *Caste and Class in a Southern Town* (1937), which was considered a classic for decades, enriches the psychodynamic aspect of this portrait by highlighting African American Momism. The Yale University social psychologist tested the hypothesis that this configuration of feminine traits signified self-hatred or low self-esteem and, finding a positive correlation, traced the psychopathology to the "mother-led" family. African American women possessed an unusual degree of economic independence, Dollard observed, which tipped the balance of power in the family in their favor. Moreover, he added, African American women enhanced their authority through their highly charged sexuality. Thus Dollard interwove several common stereotypes to "explain" the low self-esteem he observed among southern black men.[55]

The Black Matriarchy underwent further psychoanalytic refinement in the writings of Abram Kardiner (1891–1981), who had also linked Momism and homosexuality. Kardiner was renowned by this time, according to Reuben Fine, as "the first to offer a comprehensive integration of psychoanalysis and anthropology in the terms of ego psychology."[56] Trained initially by Boas, Kardiner abandoned anthropology early on for medical training in psychiatry but gradually came full circle. Shortly after World War I he traveled to Vienna to become one of Freud's last analysands and there met the Hungarian psychoanalyst Geza Roheim, who reintroduced him to anthropology. Kardiner returned to the United States, began to offer courses in psychoanalytic anthropology at the newly formed New York Psychoanalytic Institute, and built an enrollment of illustrious students including Benedict, Sapir, and Dollard himself. In September 1939 Kardiner joined the anthropology faculty at Columbia University and designed several of the most esteemed Culture and Personality projects.[57]

Kardiner had highlighted the flight from manhood in several of his earlier publications. *The Psychological Frontiers of Society* (1945), a comparative study of three cultures, identifies a crisis in masculinity among mainly white Americans. The mothers of Plainville, U.S.A. (a small town in Missouri but supposedly a microcosm of American society), Kardiner discovered, coddled their infants, nursed them on demand, and slept in the same beds with their young sons. Such forbearance produced sons who remained excessively attached to their mothers throughout their adult lives and, he concluded, unable to take up their manly responsibilities.[58] But African American families, according to the distinguished scholar, harbored an even greater degree of pathology created by a different form of maternal abuse. Not overindulgence but neglect proved the mechanism of the matriarchal black mother.

In *The Mark of Oppression: A Psychosocial Study of the American Negro* (1951), Kardiner and his coauthor Lionel Ovesey provided clinical data to substantiate the basic argument of Dollard and Frazier. Like many historians who wrote in their wake, the two psychoanalysts insisted that African American men had emerged from slavery without their manhood intact. Slavery, they reasoned, had divested black men of their rightful authority over wives and children; and economic discrimination continuing into the twentieth century only perpetuated this situation. The result was the noxious "uterine" family structure that prevailed in African American communities. As long as African American men were unable to fulfill the "masculine" role of breadwinner and thereby achieve dominance within their families, Kardiner and Ovesey warned, all African Americans would suffer psychologically.

Although sociohistoric conditions laid the basis for psychopathology among African Americans, according to Kardiner and Ovesey, it was the working mother who actuated the "disease." On the basis of data culled from a mere twenty-five interviews, including Rorschach and TAT tests, they reasoned:

> If the mother now has to work, she cannot be the mother she ought to be. By her mere absence from the home for the greater part of the day, she imposes restrictions and frustrations on the child. She takes the psychological position of the father, in which case she automatically elevates the female role as provider and derogates the established role of the male. Her idealization is, however, mixed with a great deal of ambivalence; she inspires fear as well . . . The result of all this is that the affectivity potential of the child is undermined. The child has no one to trust and idealize. He is obliged to take his ideals from the street, where he forms new types of values; but these are likely to be asocial if not antisocial.

This interpretation, centered on "loveless tyrants" who "hold the purse strings," pushes the long history and current impact of white racism into the distant background. Rather, African American women are said to jeopardize the masculinity of their sons and husbands by dominating the family, their current status as wage-earners abetting matriarchal tendencies rooted in slavery or even earlier, in the African matrifocal family structure.[59]

Most of the arguments revisited in Daniel P. Moynihan's *The Negro Family: The Case for National Action* (1965) as well as later neoconservative commentary originated here. Moynihan's report referred directly to the "fundamental insight of psychoanalytic theory" that made early childhood experiences central to all further development.

Moynihan further bemoaned all the factors that "worked against the emergence of a strong father figure," for, in his opinion, it was the "very essence of the male animal, from the bantam rooster to the four-star general . . . to strut." For many other postwar liberals, this "tangle of pathology" stood as decisive proof of the pernicious influence of Momism, not only on African Americans but on American society in general.[60]

Taken together, the alleged rise in homosexuality and persistence of low self-esteem among African American men represented to these scholars only the most pronounced examples of the baneful consequences of Momism. No group of Americans, as Strecker, Gorer, Kardiner, and others pointed out, was immune to this dreadful influence. As the data indicated, the flight from manhood was reaching near-catastrophic proportions. Even such mainstream media as *Better Homes and Gardens* were running articles with titles like "Are We Staking Our Future on a Crop of Sissies?" Other magazines asked the same question in different words: "Family Man or Mouse?" and "Are Husbands Slaves to Women?" The editors of *Look* pulled together several typical essays and published a short book with the timely title *The Decline of the American Male* (1958). Even the historian Arthur Schlesinger Jr. admitted that "something has gone badly with American men" and gave his own distinguished stamp to "The Crisis of American Masculinity."[61]

Stripped of sexual modernism, matriarchy no longer signified the prospect of pleasures known to the Samoans and Trobrianders but, reconfigured as Momism, now loomed as the nation's chief peril. Wylie admitted that he had originally intended to entitle his notorious chapter in *Generation of Vipers* "a treatise on Matriarchy" until someone at a cocktail party suggested a less pedantic alternative. Immediately he recognized the popular appeal of "Momism" over the old-fashioned term "matriarchy." Psychoanalysts and social scientists, more comfortable with academic language, proved they could swing either way. Strecker did not hesitate to adopt Wylie's terminology. In April 1945 he previewed his bestselling *Their Mothers' Sons* (1946) in an address—his "Mom" lecture—delivered to medical students. Although he insisted that he found Wylie's presentation "too vindictive," Strecker nevertheless employed "Mom" or "Momism" in the title of twelve of nineteen chapters of his book. And when Momism proved too mild an epithet, he invented his own neologism, "Mom-archy." It made little difference, for Momism, matriarchy, and even Momarchy conveyed the same danger to American manhood, and both popular and scholarly writers latched on to the terms with a vengeance.[62]

These sweeping indictments of Momism flagged more than a festering misogyny: they marked the denouement of sexual modernism as well as the cultural relativism that had shaped American psychoanalytic theory between the wars. Psychoanalysts among others had emerged from the catastrophe of World War I with their faith in progress badly shaken and had hoped to locate the prerequisites for an emotionally healthy society by gazing through the prism of "primitive" cultures. Civilization, it seemed, had less to offer than the sexually uninhibited and relatively placid peoples of the South Seas. The spread of fascism across Europe, however, ultimately undermined such generosity. Not the problems of sexual repression but the very real terrors accompanying mass aggression moved to center stage. As new fears of barbarism intensified, not a few erstwhile relativists evinced a growing respect for the mechanisms of both social and psychic control. In this light, Western civilization began to look pretty good.

Even Erich Fromm (1900–1980), an ardent critic of capitalism, fell under the sway of this sensibility. In *Escape from Freedom* (1941), he had already diverted psychoanalysis, according to the historian H. Stuart Hughes, "toward a celebration of the humane, libertarian values of the civilized West." But by the mid-1950s Fromm feared that even his closest colleagues had gone too far. He readily observed that it had become increasingly fashionable, even among intellectuals, to celebrate "the American way of life." Psychoanalysis was becoming, Fromm declared, "the apologist for the status quo."[63]

Compared to the belligerent Axis powers and totalitarian regimes, the United States emerged in the interdisciplinary literature as a slightly flawed but nevertheless model democracy. The many psychoanalysts who had fled fascism in Central Europe and now feared the spread of Communism over their homelands promoted this view and helped to shape a new hierarchy, not the evolutionary schema of pre-Boasian anthropology but the dualism of modern liberalism, "free" versus "unfree." American society stood for democracy against totalitarianism, for psychological well-being against mass neurosis, for toleration against hostility and aggression, and, not least, for male dominance against the equality of women.

There was a trickle of dissent. Even under wartime duress, Benedict offered her study of the Japanese national character, *The Chrysanthemum and the Sword* (1946), as a means to understand, rather than to condemn, a distant culture. She went so far as to caution self-assured Americans that even a democratic political system did not guarantee freedom.

More often than not, Benedict's colleagues disavowed their relativist beliefs. Gone was the expectation that knowledge of the tremendous range in personality across cultures would promote a more tolerant and nurturing attitude toward variations in American society. To the contrary, these liberal scholars now sought to preserve—or to restore—the "best" aspects of American culture and envisioned their task as encouraging adaptation to normative values.

In this context, Wylie's hyperbolic treatment of Momism appeared decidedly mainstream. The temper of the times encouraged many psychoanalysts in a direction they were already willing to travel. The studies of homosexuality and low self-esteem among African American men provided the most compelling evidence. As Edward Strecker put it, American mothers, by keeping their children "enwombed psychologically," were threatening the democratic heritage: "Here is our gravest menace." Or, as Wylie affirmed, "the winds of destiny are blowing hard now and we must decide to grow up or perish."[64]

Between the wars, upbeat scholars had celebrated the expanding opportunities for women's work outside the home as the harbinger of greater parity between men and women in both public and *very* private realms. Freed from the restraints of the domestic sphere, they reasoned, women would become more worldly in the full meaning of the word. Their successors, now embroiled in Momism, concluded that the Machine Age had changed sexual relations for the worse. American women equipped with paychecks, they charged, upset the "normal" balance of power within the family. The situation was most acute in African American families but also widespread among the white middle class. Even the mere possibility of wage earning had enhanced their status so much that women were now constantly testing testing the limits of their power. Modern women fell far short of being the sexual playmates such optimists as Floyd Dell had envisioned. To the contrary, they had become "ball-breakers." In sum, women had placed American manhood at risk.

This interpretive shift dated, as Clara Thompson noted, to the closing years of the Great Depression, when social scientists investigating the impact of unemployment on the family documented a sharp decline in self-esteem even among white American men. Many husbands, it appeared, interpreted their economic losses as personal failure, all the more so when their wives managed to find jobs.[65] The war should have reversed this trend, because mortal combat allegedly affords men the supreme opportunity to prove their manhood. When a surprising number proved unfit for service or succumbed to combat fatigue, psychoanalysts decided that the Machine Age, by emancipating women, had derailed masculinity. Women had exercised far too much authority in the Depression household; and the exigencies of wartime further enhanced female power in a family devoid of men and a workforce in short supply. A psychoanalyst writing in the journal *Psychiatry* discussed several cases of neurotic women who, because of the war, had to "assume masculine traits that they do not ordinarily develop or customarily hide."[66] Less generous commentators identified malicious intent in women's desire to displace men. Complaints against American women swelled in number, ironically, just at the time both government and industry were actively encouraging women to subordinate their customary domestic responsibilities, including full-time child care, to the patriotic expediency of high production quotas—to get a job.

Psychoanalysts were not alone in seeing a solution to this problem in the restoration of the "traditional" family. In the aftermath of the Great Depression and throughout World War II, many Americans expressed their desire for a return to "normal" family life, that is, to men as breadwinners and women as homemakers. A Gallup poll conducted in 1936 revealed that 82 percent of respondents believed that wives whose husbands held jobs should not work outside the home; by 1939 nearly 90 percent of those surveyed had reached the same conclusion. Although crucial to Allied victory, the prospect of women's wartime service provoked yet more nostalgia for the "traditional" family.[67]

Psychoanalysts gave a special gloss to these sentiments. Convinced that humanity's darkest dangers always lurk within the private realm, they scrutinized the psychosexual dynamics of the American family all the more closely. The sexual modernists had placed their faith in the Machine Age to turn the home into a veritable sexual playground, thus relieving men and women of the deleterious necessity of repressing their most basic impulse. In contrast, psychoanalysts writing during and after World War II worried more that the home no longer provided emotional sustenance to any of its occupants. Despite all the new household appliances introduced since the 1920s, modern women had clearly failed to become sexually free spirits and had perversely redirected their emotional longings toward their sons. American Moms now constituted such a major problem, Wylie concluded, because they had been stripped of their once vital and highly valued domestic role:

> Nowadays, with nothing to do, and all the tens of thousands of men . . . to maintain her, every clattering prickamette in the republic survives . . . to stamp and jibber in the midst of man, a noisy neuter by natural default or a scientific gelding sustained by science, all tongue and teat and razzmatazz. The machine has deprived her of social usefulness; time has stripped away her biological possibilities and poured her hide full of liquid soap; and man has sealed his own soul beneath the clamorous cordillera by handing her the checkbook and going to work in the service of her caprices.

Most scholarly writers did not enjoy Wylie's rhetorical flair, even if they shared his opinions. Erikson came close, however. He described the American Mom as "a woman in whose life cycle remnants of infantility joined advanced senility to crowd out the middle range of mature womanhood, which thus becomes self-absorbed and stagnant" in her boredom. These experts, giving a new spin to the meaning of the Machine Age, had begun to obsess on what one commentator described as the "dark side of modernity."[68]

The resolution to this crisis, most experts agreed, depended on the restoration of women to psychosexual equilibrium. Psychoanalysts advised working women to give up their paychecks and to return home. Put aside your aspiration to compete with men, they admonished, and embrace motherhood fully. Only then would American women be able to offer the requisite emotional security to the developing child and thereby protect the entire society from the lethal effects of Momism.

Even while World War II still raged, psychoanalysts began to issue stern warnings about the detrimental consequences of women's labor-force participation. René Spitz, for example, extrapolated from his studies of infants in orphanages and foundling homes to pinpoint "the social consequences of the progressive disruption of home life caused by the increase of female labor and the demands of war." While acknowledging the expediency of women's wartime contribution, he nevertheless predicted "a corresponding increase in asociality, in the number of problem and delinquent children, of mental defectives, and of psychotics." Even the return to peacetime promised no guarantee. National security amid the Cold War did not depend on women's engagement in industry but most certainly required their special domestic talents. Thus J. Edgar Hoover, who headed the Federal Bureau of Investigation, envisioned full-time mothers as important weapons against crime and communism.[69]

As Hoover suggested, the restoration of motherhood was not simply a matter of men's mental well-being, or even a precondition for the psychological welfare of the coming generation, but a question of national survival. The Cold War had readily supplanted World War II as the context for alarm. As one psychiatrist put it: "I personally cannot think of anything more essential during these wild and disturbed times, than the fulfillment of the truly feminine role in society. At this period in history, when even the most solid foundations of our established laws and policies seem to be trembling beneath us, women, by a true appreciation, understanding and acceptance of their feminine role, can be a source of security, safety, warmth, tenderness, and happiness."[70] Building on the tenets of ego psychology, psychoanalytic advisers thus assigned to women a singular, maternal role, and demanded from them not only total absorption in its functions but profound satisfaction. American women showed signs of concurring with this recommendation, helping to set off the baby boom even before the end of World War II and thus reversing a downward trend in fertility rates nearly two centuries old.

Dr. Benjamin Spock (1903–) could not have happened upon a better moment to publish *The Common Sense Book of Baby and Child Care* (1946), which sold over a half-million copies within a year of publication. Described by one critic as "a Freudian missionary on the pediatric frontier," Spock found psychoanalytic theory useful in guiding his private medical practice. Since the early 1930s he had cared for children of mainly psychoanalysts or other professionals who, like himself, had undergone analysis. Spock eventually trained at the New York Psychoanalytic Institute, tried his hand at therapy, and soon came to appreciate his far greater talent for pediatrics. Renowned for his permissive attitude toward infants and children, Spock urged mothers to follow their own intuitions. "Trust yourself," he advised in his bestselling advice manual; "You know more than you think you do." The nation's most famous "baby doctor" also introduced an entire generation of mothers to basic concepts of psychoanalysis, such as infantile sexuality, but spared them the cumbersome technical jargon. And although he once publicly described his own mother as a "tyrant," Spock advised all others to address themselves full-time to the needs of their developing children.[71]

Spock's advice was surpassed only by John Bowlby's *Maternal Care and Mental Health* (1951), which according to Reuben Fine established psychoanalysis as the "official doctrine for the world at large." Bowlby was one of a generation of British psychoanalysts who worked primarily in child guidance clinics. Bowlby himself first practiced at the London Child Guidance Clinic in the late 1930s and, after World War II, became director of the Children's Department at Tavistock Institute and Clinic, which had served as a model since its founding in 1920. Delegated by the World Health Organization to study the needs of orphans and children separated from their families, the prominent British scholar concluded that all children deprived of "a warm, intimate, and continuous" maternal relationship are "a source of social infection as real or serious as are the carriers of diphtheria and typhoid." To stave off this dangerous trend, Bowlby advocated a "constant attention day and night, seven days a week and 365 in the year," which, he recognized, "is possible only for a woman who derives profound satisfaction from seeing her child grow from babyhood, through the many phases of childhood, to become an independent man or woman, and know that it is her care which has made this possible." Bowlby's report became a bestseller in Great Britain and soon found its way into a popular version, *Child Care and the Growth of Love* (1951), which not only sold well but restated in simple terms the author's thesis that children require their mothers' uninterrupted attention.[72]

It was no surprise that Margaret Mead, who had conducted much of the pioneering comparative research on early childhood development, identified an ominous pattern in this literature. Because her own studies had suggested that an exclusive maternal role benefited neither women nor children, she could only suspect the motivations of the new generation. "Under the guise of exalting the importance of maternity," she charged, men "are tying women more tightly to their children than has been thought necessary since the invention of bottle feeding and baby carriages." Here we had, she charged, "a new and subtle form of antifeminism."[73]

Mead was correct. This was not the motherhood that Ellen Key's followers had acclaimed. Feminists in the 1910s had predicated their maternal utopia on women's economic independence from men. It was impossible for women to achieve self-realization, they insisted, as long as patriarchy persisted. The psychoanalytic writers at midcentury were worlds apart from their forerunners. For them, motherhood flourished only under patriarchy.

A few years before the outbreak of World War II, the campaign for the Equal Rights Amendment enjoyed a revival. In July 1937 the National Federation of Business and Professional Women's Clubs made the ERA its prime legislative issue. A few years into the war, in May 1943, the Senate Judiciary Committee reported the amendment favorably and requested approval from the entire Senate. With prospects so bright, luminaries like Margaret Sanger, Georgia O'Keeffe, Pearl Buck, Clare Boothe Luce, and Katharine Hepburn added their public endorsement—as did Margaret Mead. By 1944 the platforms of both the Democratic and Republican parties included planks recommending passage. But when the Senate finally voted on July 19, 1946, the vote split, thirty-eight to thirty-five, far short of the two-thirds majority required for passage. The *New York Times* captured the sentiments of the opposition: "motherhood cannot be amended, and we are glad the Senate didn't try." As the historian Cynthia Harrison notes, in the aftermath of war "equal treatment for women in the public sphere seemed beside the point. Women were needed at home."[74]

The incurably outspoken Abram Kardiner summed up the conclusions of this first generation of ego psychologists. He concluded that recent history had witnessed the "fruition of two powerful influences," feminism and psychoanalysis. He admitted that psychoanalysis was not an "unmitigated blessing," but considered feminism, because it altered women's position in both the family and society, not only more important but decidedly more detrimental. By confusing children about their proper sexual roles, feminism provoked troubling symptoms of "failure of development" that emerged full-blown in adult men as a flight from manhood. Moreover, by competing with men in the marketplace, women had enhanced this crisis. "By stepping up the requirements of masculinity," he explained, these assertive women had "made the most vulnerable flee from it more precipitously." In addition to endangering men, feminism derailed women from their central mission and therefore jeopardized their own psychological well-being. The evidence bore this out, he insisted. His research indicated that a woman's mental health correlated inversely with her inclination toward feminism.[75]

5

Ladies in the Dark

Soon after the appearance of *Generation of Vipers,* Hollywood produced one of the most antifeminist films of all times. Paramount's *Lady in the Dark,* based on a hit Broadway musical, opened in 1944 to rave reviews. The *New York Times* film critic Bosley Crowther could not recall another movie with "such a display of overpowering splash and glitter." Audiences agreed and made the first Freudian musical a box-office smash. Directed by Moss Hart, with a musical score by Kurt Weill and Ira Gershwin, *Lady in the Dark* starred the recent Academy Award winner Ginger Rogers in the role of a vaguely disturbed career woman.[1]

The movie opens with a portrait of fashion magazine editor Liza Elliot, hair pulled back and dressed in a severe business suit. The high-powered executive is complaining to her physician: "There must be something wrong. Why do I have this horrible depression, this panic? Why am I frightened all the time? The nicest man in the world is in love with me. I'm doing the work I adore. The magazine's a huge success." When her doctor advises her to seek help from a psychoanalyst, Liza responds incredulously: "You're not serious. You don't really believe in *that?*" Liza's skepticism soon vanishes once she begins dream therapy with psychoanalyst Alexander Brooks.

Relationships with men provide the first clue to Liza's predicament. Charlie Johnson, played by Ray Milland, is a staff writer for the magazine who covets Liza's editorial position and constantly berates her. He makes fun of Liza's masculine attire by suggesting that they patronize the same tailor, and he hints broadly that she should quit her job and let a real man take over. In the wings is Kendall Nesbitt, an older, wealthy milquetoast who would marry Liza if only he could summon the courage to demand a divorce from his wife. Finally, Randy Curtis, a movie star hunk, aggressively pursues the attractive editor for romantic ends. Consciously, Liza is clear about her feelings for the various men in her life. She despises Johnson, loves Nesbitt, and remains indifferent to Curtis. Her dreams, however, tell another story.

Illustrated through elaborate dance sequences choreographed by the surrealist Raoul Pene du Bois, Liza's nocturnal fantasies disclose Repressed Desire. In her first dream, Nesbitt has finally secured the long-awaited divorce and is about to take Liza's hand in marriage. But when Liza reaches the wedding altar, she finds herself in the arms of, not the kindly gentleman, but the physically alluring Randy Curtis. Doctor Brooks, played by Barry Sullivan, has no trouble interpreting this dream. He tells Liza that she unconsciously resists marrying the older Nesbitt because he reminds her of her father, a situation just too oedipal to tolerate. When Liza scoffs at this reading, the psychoanalyst asks her directly why she resists the obvious sexual appeal of Curtis. "Aren't you rejecting his invitation because," he presses, "you're afraid of competing with other women?" Dr. Brooks interprets Liza's resistance as symptomatic of a severe masculinity complex.

At this point, as Liza enters depth analysis to uncover early developmental mishaps, the spotlight turns away from Liza to illuminate her parents. Her mother, a strikingly beautiful but vain and callous woman, made Liza feel dowdy and unfeminine by comparison. As a little girl, Liza once tried to perform a special song for her father, while her mother, oblivious as ever to her daughter's strivings, flirted openly with another man. Her mother not only impugned Liza's femininity but figuratively castrated her father, thus robbing him of the phallic power to propel Liza's development. After her mother's untimely death, Liza tried to cheer her mournful father by putting on one of her mother's favorite dresses. Rather than affirming Liza's innocent effort to fill the vacant feminine role in the family, her father flew into a rage. Both parents made it clear to Liza that for her femininity could be only a parody.

To repair the psychic damage, Liza Elliot needs, in Dr. Brooks's words, "some man to dominate her." Readily eliminated is the weak-willed Kendall Nesbitt. The sexually potent Randy Curtis appears a better candidate, but he proves insufficiently masculine: in proposing marriage, he promises Liza that she can keep on working. Indeed, he wants her to run the production company that the studio is giving him. "Don't worry," Curtis fatally adds, "you're still going to be the boss." In the film's final scene, bully Charlie Johnson, in a rare moment of contrition, apologizes for his boorish behavior by saying that he didn't mean to hurt Liza's feelings: he simply wanted her job. Suddenly Liza realizes that the cure to her anxiety is at hand. As the movie fades to a close, Johnson sits in the boss's chair, and Liza stands behind him. The proper order of the sexes has been achieved as the domineering man embraces the blissfully obeisant woman. And the voiceover announces, "This is the end, this is really the end."

Lady in the Dark is so one-dimensional that today's audiences often view it as a satire of psychoanalysis rather than a light comedy about contemporary sex roles. Its censure of career women, its "rabid anti-feminism," according to one film historian, makes it almost too perfect an example of psychoanalytic misogyny. Still, women participated in its production, one as co-writer, another as editor. It starred Ginger Rogers, who would eventually play more analysands than any other Hollywood actor. And it presumably appealed to the disproportion-ately female audiences of wartime. *Lady in the Dark,* with its simple resolution of Liza's problem, may have eased these viewers' feelings of ambivalence about their own achievements outside the home. Or perhaps the movie dispelled fantasies of even greater opportunities in the postwar marketplace.[2]

Whatever the case, *Lady in the Dark* made a fitting companion to *Generation of Vipers.* Both texts score a striking misogyny, but *Lady in the Dark* bypasses the impact of women's domestic disruptions on American men to illuminate the downside of their growing presence in the labor force, most especially the heavy price paid by women themselves for the abandonment of their reproductive role. Holly-wood thus made top-notch entertainment in depicting a woman whose successful career jeopardizes her emotional well-being. In complementary ways, then, Wylie's polemic and the Hollywood musical played upon two interrelated themes. If the former focused on the causes and consequences of the alleged flight from manhood, *Lady in the Dark* spotlighted an equally pressing concern—a crisis in femininity.

As media triumphs, *Generation of Vipers* and *Lady in the Dark* also illustrate the incomparable popularity of psychoanalysis. Not only the esteemed liberal thinkers of midcentury, such as Lionel Trilling and Arthur Schlesinger Jr., or dynamic psychiatrists like Edward Strecker, but masses of Americans jumped on the Freudian bandwagon. Hollywood excelled in unlocking the "secrets" of psychoanalysis, but no medium was excluded. A growing number of poets, novelists, and playwrights, such as Eugene O'Neill, Lillian Hellman, and Tennessee Williams, cast their characters into psychoanalytic molds. *Time* and *Life* magazines both ran substantial features on this phenomenon, owing in part to the personal encounters with analysis of publishers Henry and Clare Boothe Luce and much of their editorial staff. The number of such articles in magazines like *Good Housekeeping* and *Cosmopolitan* climbed in the 1950s. Even the comic book publisher widely condemned for its *Crypt of Terror* and *Tales from the Crypt* produced three issues of *Psychoanalysis Comics,* en route to creating *Mad Magazine.* By 1960 at least three children's books made Freud the subject of heroic biography. Meanwhile newspapers, radio, and eventually television provided forums for advice and instruction.[3]

Psychoanalysts themselves contributed to the processes of popularization. Several prominent analysts, such New York's A. A. Brill and Gregory Zilboorg, literally served the entertainment industry by building their clientele from its stars. Beverly Hills began to rival Manhattan as a therapeutic center, its "headshrinkers' row" home to a lucrative profession. The founding of the Los Angeles Psychoanalytic Institute in 1946 added academic luster to this enterprise and tightened the relationship between analysts and entertainers. For example, the distinguished psychoanalyst Lawrence S. Kubie, who "cured" the director Moss Hart of his homosexuality, published in the *Hollywood Quarterly,* the first scholarly journal on film. Others participated in the production of films. *Spellbound* (1946), directed by Alfred Hitchcock and starring Ingrid Bergman as a psychoanalyst, credited producer David Selznick's own analyst as "psychiatric advisor." This gem of the genre also illustrates the authenticity Hollywood attempted to impart to its products. Its prologue read: "Our story deals with psychoanalysis, the method by which modern science treats the emotional problems of the sane. The analyst seeks only to induce the patient to talk about his hidden problems, to open the locked doors of his mind. Once the complexes that have been disturbing the patient are uncovered and interpreted, the illness and confusion disappear . . . and the *evils of unreason are driven from the human soul*."

Objecting to this depiction of psychotherapy as "too quick and easy," Kubie advised the film industry to endow an independent research foundation to improve the quality of its productions. He further recommended the establishment of a national board of psychoanalysts that would certify accuracy and give its official stamp of approval. Heedlessly, Hollywood writers and producers rushed ahead, refashioning psychoanalysis for their own purposes in a variety of films ranging from light comedies like *Oh Men! Oh Women!* (1957) to melodramas like the extraordinarily misogynist *The Shrike* (1955).[4]

Although some psychoanalysts were unhappy with the representation of their profession in the mass media, quite a few continued to rely on the popular form to circulate their ideas among nonspecialists. Karl Menninger published articles critical of mothers in the *Atlantic Monthly* and reached an even wider audience with his "Mental Hygiene in the Home" column for the *Ladies' Home Journal,* begun in 1930. The educated classes made bestsellers of books by Erich Fromm, Karen Horney, and Rollo May and read their articles in *Atlantic Monthly* and *Scientific American*. Less sophisticated readers undoubtedly chose Louis Bisch's *Be Glad You're Neurotic* (1955), E. Oakley's *Self-Confidence through Self-Analysis* (1957), or Lucy Freeman's *Hope for the Troubled* (1953). For those who preferred the confessional form, John Knight's *The Story of My Psychoanalysis* (1950) or Harold Greenwald's *Great Cases in Psychoanalysis* (1959) provided semi-sensationalist packaging. The front cover of the Bantam paper edition of Dr. Robert Linder's *The Fifty Minute Hour* (1956) featured a sketch of the posterior of a naked woman, and its back cover described the contents as "stories of a sadist, of a woman driven by incestuous guilt, of a teen-aged rapist and murderer."

Psychoanalysis walked hand in hand with mass culture through its Golden Age. Its celebrity among intellectuals not only accompanied but nourished the rapid expansion of commercialized mass media.

Psychoanalysts in turn made greater use of the mass media for their own purposes. It became increasingly routine, for example, for theorists to supplement clinical studies with examinations of film, popular fiction, and music. More than Freud could have imagined, or would have liked, psychoanalysis had become common currency among Americans as an all-inclusive theory of personality as well as a medium of diverse social commentary. As early as 1946 one scholarly commentator spoke for many, claiming that "no other single scientific theory has so much affected the outlook of the present generation as psycho-analysis." On October 4, 1953, Walter Cronkite closed the popular television program *You Are There*, which aired a teleplay on Sigmund Freud scripted by the blacklisted writer Abraham Polonsky, by saying that psychoanalysis "had penetrated the intellectual life of western civilization. Its words and ideas had become a commonplace in education, literature, law and medicine, and everybody was psychoanalyzing everybody else."5

Much of the glory of psychoanalysis arose from its enhanced professional standing. Before World War II, although the vast majority of American-born psychoanalysts had trained first in medicine, usually in psychiatry, they had received a less than cordial welcome from the American Psychiatric Association. Not until 1932 did the association create a section on psychoanalysis; only in 1934 did the eminent psychoanalyst A. A. Brill, addressing a joint session of the American Psychiatric Association and the American Psychoanalytic Association, make a compelling case for their common interests. Two years later the American Psychiatric Association commemorated Freud's eightieth birthday by naming him an honorary fellow.

By this time not a few psychiatrists were recognizing the appeal of psychotherapy as an alternative career to low-paying institutional medicine, which had been their lot since the nineteenth century. Then, during World War II, large numbers of psychiatrists, as well as psychologists and social workers, converted to the principles of "dynamic" personality theory. When they returned to civilian life, a sizable number set up private or community-based clinical practices for psychotherapy. In 1945 the Menninger School of Psychiatry opened; it soon became the chief training school for psychoanalytically inclined psychiatrists. Within two years of the war's end, the American Psychiatric Association reported that more than half of its members were working in private practice. For their part, psychoanalysts found more hospital-based positions, especially as the Veterans' Administration greatly extended its psychiatric services after the war, and well over two-thirds of the members of the American Psychoanalytic Association held teaching positions in hospitals or clinics.

As the lines blurred between the various "helping" professions, membership in all professional organizations skyrocketed. Before the decade closed, six new psychoanalytic societies had come into being, and the nation's finest medical students were choosing to specialize in psychiatry, the overwhelming majority undergoing a lengthy analytic training. The passage of the National Mental Health Act of 1946, which provided federal funds to create the National Institute of Mental Health in 1949, indicated that psychoanalysis had become central to public policy, and not merely for wartime.[6]

It is no small matter, then, that as psychoanalysis reached the peak of its popularity and its professional prestige an overt antifeminism emerged as a central theme. Nothing in its early history presaged the ferocity of this development, not even the rancorous yet erudite debates between Freud and his adversaries in the 1920s. Freud himself, of course, occasionally belittled feminism, but he lacked sufficient interest to offer more than casual commentary. During the interwar period Freud's adversaries in the United States scrupulously avoided the term "feminism" but embraced both sexual modernism and equal rights. Not until the Freudian revival of the 1940s and the rise of ego psychology did a rampant misogyny and a virulent antifeminism overtake the scholarly discipline and root themselves firmly in its popular emendation.

By 1953 Clarence P. Oberndorf, one of the first Americans to train in psychoanalysis, could look back at nearly a half-century of practice and take pride that psychoanalysis had "finally become legitimate and respectable." There was, however, another factor to consider. Psychoanalysis seemed to be paying a price for its success, the movement's leading house historian continued, "in becoming sluggish and smug, hence attractive to an increasing number of minds which find security in conformity and propriety."[7] On questions of femininity, Oberndorf's judgment hit the mark. Psychoanalysts had definitively cast aside their avant-garde reputation to align with the American mainstream.

The degree of mutation is stunning, as a comparison between the antifeminist perspective of *Lady in the Dark* and a similar case study by Freud's unyielding critic might suggest. In her highly popular third book, *Self-Analysis* (1942), Karen Horney introduced an analysand who bears an uncanny resemblance to the film's protagonist. Horney's "Clare" is a successful magazine editor who enters analysis to alleviate feelings of fatigue and anxiety. She, too, discovers the childhood origins of her problems in the inappropriate behavior and attitude of her parents. Like Liza, Clare grew up the unwanted child of unhappy and inattentive parents. Clare's father similarly neglected his daughter to dote shamelessly on his wife, who in turn openly despised him. Growing up in the shadow of this beautiful and adored mother, Clare, too, came to think of herself as "unlikable." No wonder, Horney concludes, the adult Clare lacks self-esteem, appears anxious and insecure, and craves affirmation from an "all encompassing partner."

From a technical standpoint, *Lady in the Dark* and Horney's case study stand together outside the Freudian paradigm. Interpersonal rather than intrapsychic factors figure prominently in both. Neither Clare nor Liza suffers the consequences of infantile libido problems, as an orthodox Freudian might contend. Rather, their anxiety traces back to their parents, to fathers who fail to encourage a budding femininity and to mothers who prove insufficiently maternal.

The similarity between the two presentations ends here. Although *Lady and the Dark* and Horney's case study find common ground in ego psychology, the two reflect opposing views of femininity. Unlike her fictional counterpart, Dr. Brooks, Horney does not encourage her client to seek a domineering male. To the contrary, she helps the "ever-tired editor" to combat an unhealthy desire for dependence on "a great and masterful man." Horney counsels Clare to cultivate instead her professional ambition and to apply herself completely to her work. The therapist "cures" her female client, in short, by encouraging her to advance her career.[8]

Although Horney's case study also reached many nonspecialists as a chapter in *Great Cases in Psychoanalysis* (1959), a mass-marketed paperback, the Hollywood musical proved a more accurate bellwether of both professional and public opinion. In 1947 *Life* magazine ran a feature touting psychoanalysis as a timely antidote to the "sense of futility" plaguing many Americans and then a few months later narrowed the focus to spotlight the disproportionate number of beset women. The perspective of the Luce publication was not unusual. As the historian William H. Chafe has noted, American women could pick up nearly any magazine and find themselves "castigated, praised, worried over and analyzed." Or they could turn directly to psychoanalysts. Regardless, consensus ruled that women's emotional stability had been undermined by the competing attractions of domesticity and expanding opportunities outside the home. Experts and publicists now agreed that the Machine Age had failed to liberate women and instead had actuated, as *Life* put it, the "American Woman's Dilemma."[9] And there was no easy solution. Women might choose domesticity only to become Moms; or, opting for careers, women risked jeopardizing their femininity.

Psychoanalysts like Horney were a dying breed. Gregory Zilboorg, coeditor of the *Psychoanalytic Quarterly*, conceded that psychoanalysis "seems to have stumbled and even failed" to offer a satisfying solution to women's dilemma, "problems peculiarly its own, specifically psychoanalytic." Few of his colleagues, however, shared his humility.[10] To the contrary, by 1952, the year of Horney's death, a significant number were more than ready to offer expert advice. Perfectly aware of the pitfalls of domesticity, especially women's proclivity toward Momism, psychoanalysts imagined only greater adversity in careers. Like Dr. Brooks, they encouraged women to give up their fantasies of competing with men and to turn instead to the private sphere of the home for a more "natural" kind of fulfillment.

Feminism, because it reputedly encouraged women along the misguided path to professional employment, quickly became the psychoanalyst's archenemy. Even without the provocation of an organized political movement—or even much public discussion of women's rights—psychoanalysts ranged wide and far to strike at feminism as symbol of the Machine Age and all its baneful consequences. That women suffered as much as men only strengthened the psychoanalysts' determination to restore, as in *Lady in the Dark*, the supposedly normal sexual order.

At a time when white middle-class wives and mothers constituted the fastest-growing sector of the labor market, thereby speeding the long trend toward the "two-income family," psychoanalysts were advising women to return home and to occupy their important but subordinate position in the patriarchal family. Rather than struggle for equality in the marketplace, women should seek their emotional salvation by following out their reproductive destinies. Motherhood, that indisputable and well-defined marker of femininity, again reigned supreme. But unlike the early twentieth-century feminists who saw in maternity the possibility of female self-realization, midcentury psychoanalysts looked upon motherhood as a functional role, that is, a clear demarcation of the division of labor by sex, the assignment of men to breadwinning and women to homemaking and childrearing. As Betty Friedan later pointed out, psychoanalysts were far from unique in staking out this prescriptive territory, but they took ample advantage of their extraordinary authority to help shape the Feminine Mystique.

Feminism versus Motherhood

The year 1947 was a propitious one in the popular history of American psychoanalysis. It heralded not only the appearance of illustrious features in *Life* and *Time* magazines but the publication of *Modern Woman: The Lost Sex,* soon to be a bestseller and a classic in the genre of antifeminist psychoanalytic literature. Ferdinand Lundberg (1902–1995), a well-known, politically progressive journalist, biographer, and sometime historian, provided the lucid style. Marynia Foot Farnham (1900–1979), a prominent psychiatrist—and, as noted on the book's flyleaf, a mother of two children—supplied an extensive collection of case studies compiled from her own private practice and the outpatient service at the New York State Psychiatric Institute and Hospital. The two authors combined their talents to fashion a full-length psychoanalytic assessment of the dilemma of the modern woman. The substance of Lundberg and Farnham's achievement can be readily appreciated: Philip Wylie pronounced *Modern Woman: The Lost Sex* "the best book yet to be written about women."[11]

Much like the many articles appearing in popular magazines, and precisely like the Hollywood film *Lady in the Dark, Modern Woman: The Lost Sex* focuses on the "conflicting demands" of career and marriage that had supposedly reduced American women to "a bundle of anxieties." Lundberg and Farnham restated the increasingly common complaint against the Machine Age for stripping the home of its productivity and propelling its natural caretakers into the marketplace to compete with men. They did, however, add a unique twist to this cliché by pinpointing this aberrant competition as the source of emotional dislocation. It was not work as such that had ruined American women but the pursuit of careers: "The more importance outside work assumes, the more are the masculine components of woman's nature enhanced and encouraged." Lundberg and Farnham thus recapitulated the main thesis of *Lady in the Dark* in writing that any work "that entices women out of their homes . . . provides them with prestige only at the price of feminine relinquishment."[12]

This "masculinization" of women exacted an enormous cost, and not just from women. Like so many of their contemporaries, Lundberg and Farnham believed that American society was poised on the brink of emotional disaster, with only one-third of its citizens lacking neurotic symptoms. Women represented the vast majority of neurotics and served, moreover, as "the principal transmitting media of the disordered emotions." Whether the problem was juvenile delinquency or alcoholism, the skyrocketing divorce rate, or even the threat of thermonuclear war, the trail led invariably to women. Lundberg and Farnham readily agreed with the wartime scholars who had singled out mothers for their pernicious influence. They also shared the expectation that someday psychopaths like Hitler or Mussolini, "standing before the bar of historical judgment, might often well begin their defense with the words: 'I had a mother. . . .' "[13] The crisis in femininity, in their opinion, both caused and complemented the flight from manhood.

Modern Woman: The Lost Sex stood out among the customary attacks on mothers because its authors traced all maladies to a single source, feminism. The claim to political rights did not bother them; woman suffrage (although not the Equal Rights Amendment) met with their approval. Feminism, standing mainly for careers and more generally "for objective female achievement," was another matter altogether: feminism had caused women's "psychic disorder."[14]

Lundberg and Farnham proposed a unique tautological relationship between Momism and feminism. It was the feminist agitation beginning in the nineteenth century that had diverted women from their natural source of fulfillment in marriage and motherhood. And once so denied, women became seriously disturbed. Even if they did marry and bear children, these women sowed only disorder within their families. And, elaborating on Wylie's insight, these Moms produced similarly malcontented daughters who, when grown, gauged their status not by a domestic yardstick but by success in careers. Thus the feminism-Momism cycle perpetuated itself ad nauseam in all subsequent generations of women.[15]

To illustrate this process, Lundberg and Farnham chose a timeworn example of feminine psychopathology. For over a century antifeminists had been castigating the British author of the *Vindication of the Rights of Women* (1792), Mary Wollstonecraft, for having fomented discontent among otherwise unruffled women. Lundberg and Farnham gave a new twist to this now-familiar assault on the man-hating Flaming Amazon. Wollstonecraft's life "reads like a psychiatric case history," they claimed, and the "shadow of the phallus lay darkly, threateningly, over every move she made, as it lay over the minds of the latter-day feminists." Mary Wollstonecraft suffered from a "severe case" of penis envy.[16]

It should be noted that Lundberg and Farnham did not present a Freudian interpretation of penis envy. According to Abraham and Freud, the development of femininity depends on penis envy to spark the rejection of clitoral sexuality and, equally important, of the mother as object of affection. Penis envy "normally" sets the girl along the preferred track toward heterosexuality. Neo-Freudians had come to regard the concept as a relic of phallocentric prejudice. Penis envy, Horney explained, does not trigger feminine development but instead indicates neurosis. Lundberg and Farnham actually agreed with this hypothesis: penis envy is "a phenomenon, like much that Freud encountered, peculiar only to an extremely neurotic culture and period."[17] Nevertheless, in taking this revisionist stance, the two authors did not in any way mitigate their attack on modern women.

Modern Woman: The Lost Sex appeared as the first popular application of selected—and bowdlerized—tenets of ego psychology to a refutation of feminism. In discussing penis envy, the authors invariably focused on the parents' misdeeds. And, in the especially disturbing case of Mary Wollstonecraft, they found ample data to trace the cause to maternal dysfunction.

At first glance, one might conclude that Momism was not the major factor in the etiology of Wollstonecraft's neurosis. Rather, her abusive father, described as "an habitual drunkard, rough and uncouth," appears a more likely candidate. But, as it turns out, according to Lundberg and Farnham, the chronic wife-beater played only a minor part. Mary's dysfunctional mother must shoulder the blame for her daughter's psychological problems. While worshipping her son, Mrs. Wollstonecraft remained indifferent to Mary, despite the little girl's heroic if futile efforts to shield her beloved mother from her hated father's blows. From this situation Mary Wollstonecraft allegedly developed her perverse ideas about sexual relationships: "To Mary, all men were oppressors of women. All women were long-suffering, all the cards in the deck stacked against them." "Out of her illness arose the ideology of feminism," which, Lundberg and Farnham concluded, "was to express the feelings of so many women in years to come."[18]

Lundberg and Farnham stretched the principles of ego psychology even further to describe Wollstonecraft's part in laying the foundation for the crisis in femininity of the mid-twentieth century. Just as Mary herself had let down her daughter by dying during childbirth, modern women fail to prepare their daughters for adulthood. Made neurotic by the feminism inaugurated by Wollstonecraft, these Moms pass on their own "deep disturbances" to their babies in a variety of ways: rejection, overprotection or oversolicitousness; dominating or domineering behavior; overaffectionate behavior; or subtle "nuances in her approach," such as muscular tension in handling the susceptible infant. Any one of these aberrant behaviors is guaranteed to produce the complement of the wimpish son, that is, the feminist daughter. Then, too, relentless agitators for equality step in to lure anxious young girls away from the domestic vocation. "Propaganda of the feminists and stories about famous career women," Farnham wrote, "have convinced most of the public that motherhood is an untidy and bothersome breeding process that carries no prestige whatever." Given the weight of feminist arguments, how could American women be happy in their homes? How could they demonstrate to their daughters the true qualities of the "feminine mother"—deference to men and joy in homemaking?[19]

Modern Woman: The Lost Sex advanced specific remedies, which, appearing just one year after the passage of the National Mental Health Act, seemed almost feasible. Government subsidies for a program of mass psychotherapy for American women, along with the immediate establishment of community mental health clinics to meet the current epidemic, were surely its boldest suggestions. The politically liberal authors implored President Harry Truman to fulfill his predecessor's promise by enacting comprehensive welfare legislation comprising cash payments to needy mothers and a series of other ameliorative economic policies to reduce the pressure on women to work outside the home.

Like *Generation of Vipers, Modern Woman: The Lost Sex* whipped up a storm of controversy. Lundberg and Farnham's text went through several printings, including a cheap paper edition, and made the non-fiction bestseller list. Despite its commercial success, not everyone applauded. The readers of *Coronet,* which published spinoff articles by Farnham, deluged the magazine's editorial office with complaints. The reviewer for the liberal *New Republic* charged the authors with "using psychoanalysis as a child uses a knife," while the Marxist journal *Science & Society* scored the book's "surly contempt for women" and the "offensively vulgar quality never found in Freud in whose tradition [Lundberg and Farnham] claim to be speaking." The wry commentator Dorothy Parker mused: "There is something curiously flattering in being described by the adjective 'lost' . . . I find myself digging my toe into the sand and simpering, 'Oh Dr. Farnham and Mr. Lundberg, come on now—you say that to every sex!' "[20]

But *Modern Woman*'s antifeminism did appeal to some well-positioned reviewers. Not surprisingly, Wylie found the book's arguments persuasive in dispelling "certain feministic myths current in America." Even those scholars who judged Lundberg and Farnham's grasp of sociology somewhat tenuous admired their depiction of "the neurotic character of the feminist movement." The well-publicized controversy undoubtedly helped *Modern Woman: The Lost Sex* sell well over 30,000 copies within a few years of publication.[21]

The basic thesis of *Modern Woman: The Lost Sex* outlived the book's celebrity and gained further elaboration in the popular writings of its principal architect. Farnham's subsequent book, *Married Neuters* (1949), failed to achieve much acclaim, despite its intriguing title. But Farnham herself did well as a journalist, publishing a string of articles in mass-circulation magazines including *Ladies' Home Journal, McCall's, Coronet,* and *Cosmopolitan.* Her "Let's Talk about Modern Woman" column undoubtedly served as a perfect vehicle for her antifeminist message, appearing in *Glamour* (1947–1948), a magazine designed for teenage and young adult women.

Although at least one historian has delimited the significance of *Modern Woman: The Lost Sex* to the conservative fringe of public opinion, in neither form nor content did the bestselling text deviate from standard practices within the psychoanalytic community. One reviewer went so far as to allege that the book "tempers extreme views" of modern sex literature. Even the leading neo-Freudian journal, *Psychiatry*, praised the authors' attention to cultural factors without commenting on their disparaging attitude toward women. The venerable Bostonian Abraham Myerson, reviewing the book for the *American Journal of Psychiatry*, was one of the few to consign its alarmist attack on women to "the long line of scapegoat seekers." But even this longtime supporter of woman's rights admitted that he had come to represent the minority opinion. *Modern Woman: The Lost Sex* gave witness, Myerson sighed, to the current "little epidemic of psychiatric antifeminism."[22]

A sizable number of American psychoanalysts and psychiatrists stood alongside Lundberg and Farnham to examine in tandem the flight from manhood and the crisis in femininity. Neurotic men, they charged, often exhibit "feminine" traits, making them inadequate to the manly demands of breadwinning, weapon bearing, and miscellaneous civic responsibilities; and neurotic women signify their accommodation to feminism by preferring careers to homemaking. Distinguishing between the popular journalism of Wylie or Lundberg and Farnham and the scientific scholarship of leading psychoanalysts became ambiguous.

Helene Deutsch, for example, not only preceded Lundberg and Farnham but established the basic contours of their powerful argument. One of the first women to be trained by Freud, Deutsch had become internationally renowned as a specialist on female psychology. Since the early 1920s she had regarded maternity, including childbirth itself, as the primary source of femininity. Deutsch now found an opportunity to reaffirm her faith. She also sharpened her perspective, making motherhood and careers mutually exclusive in the emotional well-being of women.

In 1934 the *New York Herald* had welcomed Deutsch to the United States, designating her "the first accredited ambassador of her sex to come here from the king of Psycho-Analysis." A decade later another reviewer claimed that she "still follows the strict Freudian line." By this time she stood, along with her erstwhile rival Horney, as the most eminent female psychoanalysts in the United States. Although she considered herself ever faithful to Freud's legacy, Deutsch's own scholarly writings and clinical practice told a different story.[23]

Her magnum opus, *The Psychology of Women* (1944, 1945), moved close to ego psychology. Although she later retracted some of her praise, Deutsch approved the recent turn in psychoanalytic theory, its broadening beyond the Freudian foundation. Her new, two-volume text fit right in. In both subject and format, *The Psychology of Women* resembles her earlier essay *Psychoanalysis and the Sexual Functions of Woman* (1924). The new volumes incorporate the original outline, tracing female development from infancy to old age. *The Psychology of Women,* however, in a patently non-Freudian fashion, gives equal weight to childhood and adult experiences, and one entire volume is devoted to motherhood. Deutsch cited the work of her longtime friend and colleague Heinz Hartmann and generally applauded those researchers who were now "turning with increasing interest to the psychology of the ego." Required reading for many training analysts, and selected for special acknowledgment by Lundberg and Farnham, *The Psychology of Women* exudes a specific kind of antifeminism not found in Deutsch's earlier work.[24]

Like her admirers, the prominent psychoanalyst now coupled feminism qua careerism to the alleged crisis of femininity. To make her argument Deutsch chose yet another example, the unhappy life of Aurore Dupin, the nineteenth-century French novelist who wrote under the pen name George Sand. In 1928 Deutsch had presented a paper on Sand, but she now sought to direct her comments to an audience of similarly troubled women. In her opinion Sand rivaled Wollstonecraft for the honor of being "the first feminist" and appeared "the classic type of man-woman, the strange being who seems to carry a masculine soul in a feminine body." The question of preeminence aside, Wollstonecraft and Sand both suffered the consequences of maternal dysfunction. For Sand, the problem was extraordinarily deeply rooted in her family's history.

George Sand, it seems, was caught between two Moms. First, there was her paternal grandmother, Madame Dupin, whose possessive love had emotionally destroyed her son, Maurice. If only to free himself from her tyranny, Maurice Dupin chose for his wife a woman temperamentally unlike his mother. What ensued was "a life and death struggle" between the two women for Maurice's affection, with little Aurore caught in the middle. "Upon which of the two models was she to create her mother-woman ideal? Which would she take as a model to guide her in her relations with men?" Permanently confused, Sand "set herself against all things feminine, dressed in mannish garb, and in every way tried to ruin her good reputation as a woman." When she fell in love, she responded sadistically. George Sand not only chose "so-called feminine men" like Frédéric Chopin but ruined them. The sins of the mother—and, in this striking case, of the grandmother—passed on to the daughter. Even Sand's considerable literary talent did not compensate for the damage done to her femininity. A woman's intellectuality is, Deutsch explained, "to a large extent paid for by the loss of valuable feminine qualities: it feeds on the sap of the affective life and results in impoverishment of this life either as a whole or in specific emotional qualities."[25]

Apparently both Deutsch and Farnham could readily put aside their own personal experiences of combining highly successful careers and childrearing, as well as the combined joys of femininity and a rich scholarly life. Farnham managed a fast-paced workweek while reportedly enjoying two children from her husband's previous marriage and her own two offspring. For her part, in the 1920s Deutsch had commonly put in twelve-hour days at the Vienna Psychoanalytic Society's training institute, which she had helped to found, while raising her young son, Martin. Both women not only maintained lucrative clinical practices but produced a wealth of essays and several well-received books.

In their publications, however, Deutsch and Farnham advised women to focus their emotional energies narrowly on motherhood. Freud had designated motherhood as compensation for women's anatomical deficiency and reasoned that women therefore attain fulfillment primarily from the birth of a baby who possesses the superior organ. He had described the relationship between mother and son as "altogether the most perfect, the most free from ambivalence of all human relationships" because the mother "can transfer to her son the ambition which she has been obliged to suppress in herself, and she can expect from him the satisfaction of all that has been left over in her of her masculinity complex."[26] Freud's most forceful critics resoundingly rejected this idea that motherhood serves primarily as a means to redress women's sense of injustice. Motherhood signified to them an emotional epiphany as manifested in the unique and precious empathy that develops between mother and child.

Yet, while venerating motherhood, these early feminists did not bar the possibility of satisfaction through other means. Nor did they conflate motherhood and domesticity. The most radical, like Ellen Key, insisted that the joys of motherhood could best be realized outside marriage and apart from all men. The American apostles of motherhood, ranging from Emma Goldman in the 1910s to the emigrée Karen Horney in the 1930s, had advocated motherhood only if premised on equality of opportunity in all realms of public affairs. They therefore encouraged women to nourish intellectual and career ambitions along with their maternal desires. Then, in the 1930s, having abandoned all prescriptions for femininity, neo-Freudian modernists like Horney and Margaret Mead refused to overvalue women's reproductive capacity. But the authors of *The Psychology of Women* and *Modern Woman: The Lost Sex* did not simply restore old arguments in embracing motherhood as the exclusive source of women's emotional well-being. They now cautioned specifically against careers or other forms of intellectual achievement and, moreover, advised women to accept their subordinate place within the family.

Their advice boiled down to an edict for the restoration of patriarchy. Thus the exemplar of the truly "feminine mother" finds ultimate satisfaction in giving birth to and nurturing *her husband's* children. *Modern Woman: The Lost Sex* describes such a mother as one who demonstrates her acceptance of herself "fully as a woman" by recoiling from anything smacking of feminism:

> She does not understand when she hears other women speak bitterly of the privileges of men. She does not see things that way. Men, to her, are useful objects and if, being useful, they extract enjoyment from various of the strange things they are up to it is quite all right with her. She knows, at any rate, that she is dependent on a man. There is no fantasy in her mind about being an "independent woman," a contradiction in terms . . . Having children is to her the

most natural thing possible, and it would never occur to her to have any doubts about it.[27]

The opposition between motherhood and careers, between femininity and feminism, was so stark as to destroy all possibility for compromise.

This stand was by no means exceptional. In condemning feminism as the renunciation of motherhood, psychoanalysts supplied the unique theoretical underpinnings of their trade to a polemic widespread in the decade following World War II. But in the history of their own profession, this attack represented more than a minor deviation from long-standing practices, and not only with regard to the perennially thorny questions surrounding the differences between the sexes. This particular denunciation of feminism exposed the new, decidedly heterodox direction in which ego psychologists were traveling at midcentury.

Femininity as Identity

The clamor over the crisis in femininity echoed a major nosological shift within psychoanalytic theory: an abating emphasis on neurosis in favor of the quintessentially modern concern with *alienation*. Since the 1930s psychoanalysts had observed that patients rarely presented the symptoms cataloged by Freud—hysteria, compulsion, obsession, sexual inhibition—but complained instead about indeterminate feelings of anxiety or hostility. Men and women today sought help mainly to ease an underlying uncertainty about who they were or might be, Erik H. Erikson affirmed, whereas Freud's clients had hoped to dispel the inhibitions preventing them from being what and who they thought they were. Lundberg and Farnham, as well as Philip Wylie, shared this assessment. Lundberg and Farnham astutely noted that many American men and most women suffer from "feelings of vague malaise or uneasiness, of not being 'all there,' of being mysteriously out of kilter, of some nameless lack within oneself or sense of 'halfness,' of living with unreal people in a world that is 'empty.' "[28] And it was precisely this malady that plagued the protagonists of *Lady in the Dark* and Horney's case study of "Clare."

The neo-Freudians had noted this trend as early as the 1930s and, without singling out women, had looked for causes external to the individual psyche. Karen Horney's *The Neurotic Personality of Our Times* (1937), for example, blames the nation's competitive socioeconomic system for the veritable epidemic of anxiety. Published just a few years later, Erich Fromm's *Escape from Freedom* (1941) traces in tandem the rise of industrial society and the emergence of the personality who "feels powerless and alone, anxious and insecure." A decade later Fromm had honed his argument to a sharp critique of capitalist society in particular and, improvising on the Marxian concept of alienated labor, described the dehumanizing effects of large-scale production and corporate society in general. In *The Sane Society* (1955), alienation achieved conceptual clarity. Originally, Fromm noted, the French word "alien" denoted an insane or psychotic person, but in the last century, specifically in the wake of Hegel and Marx, alienation had come to mean a less severe yet nearly universal form of self-estrangement. "The alienated person," Fromm wrote, "is out of touch with himself as he is out of touch with any other person."[29]

This emphasis on alienation and anxiety within psychoanalytic practice punctuated the critique of the Machine Age that had been growing since World War II. Wylie's *Generation of Vipers* (1942) had presaged the almost obsessive concern with alienation that surfaced less than a decade later in the bestselling works of David Reisman and Jules Henry, splashed across the silver screen in films noir, and permeated the middlebrow commentary in the *New Yorker, Atlantic Monthly,* and *Partisan Review.* By 1949 the Cold War historian Arthur M. Schlesinger Jr. characterized the era as both a "time of troubles" and an "age of anxiety." Many psychoanalysts agreed with this assessment. A general "state of turbulence" prevailed, one expert announced. "With a tense and sickening kind of apprehension," another prominent analyst fussed, Americans "await their doom."[30]

This preoccupation manifested itself as a literary boomlet in the late 1950s. J. Ortega y Gassett's *Man and Crisis* (1958) and Franz Pappenheim's *The Alienation of Modern Man* (1959) appeared as outstanding contributions to an imposing series of books and essays dealing with the relationship between advanced capitalist society and psychic dislocation. "Modern man, alienated from nature, from his goods, and from society, in an increasingly mechanized, atomized and depersonalized world," one author typically lamented, "too often is unable to achieve an identity and relatedness to others." This prognosis, the coda for a popular anthology of essays entitled *Man Alone* (1962), meshed well with Lundberg and Farnham's own observations fifteen years earlier: "The further one penetrates behind the brave facade of modernity," they had written in a timely sullen fashion, "the less impressive do surface values become and the more impressive the psychic disorder."[31]

Laments about the crisis in femininity fit precisely into this mold. Propelled by the Machine Age into a disabling conflict between career and home, the modern woman appeared to many psychoanalysts the prime victim of estrangement. In 1950 the iconoclast Philip Wylie rallied to warn women against the lure of feminism. Do not try to rob "the Machine Age of its fruits" by trying to be like men, he advised, and instead fulfill your destiny by protecting "the first human purpose," the care of children. As late as 1964, even the century's most important historian of American foreign policy would connect "increasing misery" to widespread disturbances in femininity. To William Appleman Williams, American women offered "the most striking example of alienation in advanced capitalism" because they had forsaken "the central human community," the family, "for the impersonal marketplace." By "defining emancipation in precisely the terms that describe the condition of males in a capitalist political economy," he further explained, women best express the dangerous trend toward, in Erikson's pithy phrase, "identity diffusion."[32]

It was Erikson who reconfigured femininity as identity—similar in meaning to what later scholars call "gender"—by recasting in psychoanalytic language the familiar sociology of sex roles. Indeed, the term "identity"—an antonym of "alienation"—has been "indissolubly linked" with Erikson. Warren I. Susman, the most astute scholar of twentieth-century American culture, singled out "identity" as the coda for the 1950s and went so far as to declare the entire decade "the age of Erik Erikson."[33] It was Erikson who refined the new psychoanalytic nosology by elaborating the concept of identity, making it both the rhetorical signature of ego psychology and the chief marker of sexual difference. In sum, he provided yet another way to fashion a reproductive teleology for woman and a productive teleology for man.

The basic premises of Erikson's argument appeared in his first, loosely organized book, which the reviewer in *Psychoanalytic Quarterly* nevertheless judged a "masterpiece of scientific writing." *Childhood and Society* (1950) was soon translated into seven languages, making its author, at age forty-eight, one of the most widely read psychoanalysts of the era. Scholars in several disciplines and lay readers as well as psychoanalysts and analysts-in-training kept the first edition in print until 1963, when an expanded version appeared. It was here that Erikson popularized his ideas on Hitler's childhood and Gorky's youth in spirited chapters bearing the vivid stamp of the wartime infatuation with national character and Momism. Even more memorable was Erikson's own claim. *Childhood and Society,* he proudly noted, was the first book-length examination of "the relation of the ego to society."[34]

Childhood and Society showcases Erikson's daring prediction that the study of identity would become "as strategic in our time as the study of sexuality was in Freud's time." As Erikson pointed out, the term appears only once in Freud's hefty canon. Discussing neither masculinity nor femininity, Freud briefly referenced his sense of "personal identity" as a Jew. For Erikson, though, the concept of identity encompassed much more than ethnicity or religious conviction. It signified "the ability to experience one's self as something that has continuity and sameness, and to act accordingly."[35]

Working within the framework of ego psychology, Erikson outlined a new model of sexual differentiation with identity formation its apex. Trained by Anna Freud, he surprised no one in mapping a vastly complex, ongoing process starting with the relationship between mother and infant. Identity begins to form very early, he reasoned, as early as the very first months of infancy. By four months of age, a rudimentary ego identity has come into being, when the infant demonstrates a "basic trust" by calmly accepting the mother's disappearance from sight. Maternal behavior and attitude either expedite or impede the crucial processes by which the child attains an autonomous and stable identity.[36]

For Erikson, the differences between the sexes arise from these processes, originating in early infancy but becoming expressive only in the post-oedipal years. He appreciated Freud's emphasis on the anatomical differences between the sexes and even stressed the significance of disparity in not merely genitalia but musculature. Moreover, he continued to utilize Freud's sequence of stages, from oral, to anal, to phallic, and acknowledged the importance of the sexually differentiating events of the Oedipus complex itself. Despite these similarities, Erikson's model departed from Freud's by making the achievement of either masculine or feminine *identity*, rather than male or female object choice, the teleological heart of the whole adventure.

In the long history of psychoanalysis, and despite Erikson's own disclaimers, this revision was nothing less than momentous. Psychoanalysis had become less a theory of sexuality than one of sex roles.

Specifically, Erikson gave theoretical substance to the assumption shared by so many commentators at midcentury, that masculinity and femininity were grounded in decidedly different social roles reflecting the "polarized" relationship of men and women to production and reproduction. Freud's theory of infantile sexuality, Erikson concluded, fell short in this area. He admired its elegance in sketching the early stages of development leading to "a rudimentary genitality" but found it lacking in the capacity to track development beyond the Oedipus complex. Freud had defined the libido too narrowly, Erikson complained, bypassing reproductive objectives for the singular pursuit of pleasure. In other words, Freud failed to consider "a rudimentary generative mode, representing the dim anticipation of the fact that genitality has a procreative function." Erikson corrected this error by locating the primary differences between the sexes, not in their disparate relationship to the pleasure principle but in "a uniqueness which is founded on the performed functions of the future inseminator and the future child-bearer."

Research into the play patterns of children bore out this hypothesis. Erikson noted that girls consistently configure scenes consonant with their future reproductive roles, that is, scenes of interior harmony. They prefer closed spaces, such as domestic settings, and conduct their fantasy life within these confines. Boys, on the other hand, psychologically anticipate their activities in the competitive marketplace and build high towers and imagine scenes of peril and danger. Although "anchored in the ground plan of the body," he wrote, these differences gain cultural and psychological specificity as girls and boys grow into adults.[37]

While Erikson went on to map development as the "eight stages of man," other scholars firmed up the sociological dimension. The sociologist Talcott Parsons (1902–1979), founder and director of Harvard's prestigious Department of Social Relations, provided not only the clearest but the most authoritative emendations. Having launched his career within the Culture and Personality milieu, Parsons emerged in the 1940s even more well-versed in the principles of ego psychology. The "internalization of the socio-cultural environment," he typically reasoned, provides the "central core" of personality. It is, he added, the chief means by which the individual becomes integrated into the social system and achieves a stable and suitable identity.

Like Erikson, Parsons interpreted psychosexual development principally as the achievement of sex roles. He, too, conceded that anatomical differences serve as "fundamental points of reference" but nevertheless insisted that children still must learn the meaning of these differences in relation to behavior and attitude. Like other ego psychologists, Parsons stressed the importance of parents. Unlike the national character analysts, however, he did not consider in any great detail toilet training or weaning. Rather, everything rested on how well fathers and mothers served their children as proper "role models." Both parents must position themselves to reflect the different parts men and women play in the systems of production and reproduction, Parsons argued. Thus situated, parents set into motion the processes of identification. Then, through such elementary routines as imitation and mimicry, their children acquire their proper sex-linked identities.

"Differentiation" was a key concept for Parsons, the Cold War liberal. An abundance of institutions—government, industry, schools, churches, and hospitals, for example—keep American society strong and secure, he noted, by each carrying out a specialized function. They mirror the perfect symmetry of the system's foundational institution, the "isolated nuclear family." The American family, in Parsons's view, is the "major point of departure for . . . further differentiation": the father serves as breadwinner and liaison with all other institutions; the mother meanwhile cares for the home and acts as the family's "emotional hub." By maintaining this rigid division of function based on sex, the family thus serves as the symbolic representation of the entire social system and therefore provides the best possible environment for the psychological development of young children. Boys and girls not only internalize the differentiation personified by their parents but simultaneously prepare to perpetuate the arrangement in the subsequent generations. Sexual differentiation, in short, is the bulwark of the free world.[38]

If Freud wrote little on identity, he did describe the intricate processes of identification, but not along the lines suggested by Erikson and Parsons. For Freud, identification with the father is a process central to the formation of the superego in boys. Following the normal dissolution of the Oedipus complex, the son relinquishes the mother as object of desire and intensifies his identification with his father by internalizing his father's authority, thereby forming the nucleus of his own ego ideal or superego. "In this way," according to Freud, "the dissolution of the Oedipus complex would consolidate the masculinity in the boy's character." The process is, of course, different for girls. Lacking a penis, girls cannot succumb to castration anxiety; and therefore, because their Oedipus complex never entirely dissipates, girls fail to achieve the inexorable, hence masculine, superego.

This disparity was, for Freud, an important marker of sexual difference in the social realm. Late in his life, Freud considered the significance of a girl's identification with her mother, a process which begins as a pre-oedipal "affectionate attachment" but ends with the Oedipus complex, to be resumed only when the daughter becomes a mother herself. Freud noted, "the phase of the affectionate pre-Oedipus attachment is the decisive one for a woman's future: during it preparations are made for the acquisition of the characteristics with which she will later fulfill her role in the sexual function and perform her invaluable social tasks."[39]

Freud's commentary on both the mother "as a model" and woman's "invaluable social tasks" stopped here. Truly extraneous to his system is the notion of imitation or mimicry common among ego psychologists like Parsons and Erikson. For Freud identification is an unconscious process. Nothing in his canon comes close to specifying the disparate processes of identification by sex in the following way:

The little girl plays at keeping house, cooking, handling dolls, and being a miniature mother. The little boy is interested more in physical activity, which is nearly always associated with manliness. He wants to do the things his father does—drive a car, play golf, go to baseball games, work with tools. In this way children also come to accept their parents' attitudes, principles, and ideals.

The author of this description, a professor of psychiatry, did not exclude Freud's concern with the formation of the superego, that is, with the means by which the child "gradually acquires standards of conduct, a conscience." But more integral is the understanding of identification as "what it means to belong to one sex or the other" according to disparate sex roles as determined by the functional link between men and production, women and reproduction.[40]

While Erikson and Parsons bridged the disciplines of psychoanalysis and sociology, popular writers like Farnham brought these new formulations to the attention of the reading public mainly, as might be expected, in the form of childrearing advice. So prolific were their efforts that they virtually transformed a well-established genre into a set of rules concerning the behavior not so much of children as of parents. The most enthusiastic writers discussed the basic principles of health and hygiene, the staple of earlier prescriptions, but they excelled in codifying guidelines for maintaining clear distinctions between the sexes. They advised parents to concentrate their efforts on this, their chief responsibility, by establishing themselves as appropriate role models.

In childrearing advice, ego psychologists found a perfect forum to air their concerns about anxiety and alienation. To alleviate these maladies, they instructed parents to maintain sharp distinctions between sex roles within their own families. Thereby parents could provide, according to one popularist, "the most important conditions" for their child's entire development, that is, "to feel safe, secure, and satisfied in his emerging sexual *identity*." Parents couldn't start too early. It was their duty to establish the proper atmosphere immediately following the birth of their baby. If, for example, parents felt disappointed by the sex of their newborn, the baby would "sense this attitude" and would "be torn by conflicts about his role as a boy or a girl." But more than attitude, it was the parents' own status as "role model" that shaped the feminine or masculine identity of their offspring.[41]

Mothers, as primary caretakers, bore a special responsibility. *Modern Woman: The Lost Sex* supplied popular writers with a precise formula for being a good mother: one who attends to her child's physical needs and also understands the importance of her own sex-marked attitude and behavior. If a daughter is to develop properly, it is absolutely necessary for a mother to achieve "complete satisfaction, without conflict or anxiety, in living out her role as wife and mother." If the mother is "beset by distaste for her role, strives for accomplishment outside her home and can only grudgingly give attention to her children, has regrets for whatever reason at being a woman, then, no matter how much or little of it she betrays, the child cannot escape the confused impression that the mother is without love, is not a satisfactory model."[42] To Farnham as well as to dozens of other popularists, there was no question that a woman's acceptance of her feminine role provided the only satisfactory environment for her developing children.

Well into the 1960s, childrearing advice stressed the responsibility of parents to guide their children along the path to an unambiguous sex-linked identity. One of the most popular manuals, *Between Parent and Child: New Solutions to Old Problems* (1968) by Haim Ginott, develops this line of argument to the fullest. "The importance of rearing sons and daughters who are individuals," Ginott insisted, "should not obscure the need to bring up sons who are male and daughters who are female." Or, as another essayist opined, "It is up to his parents to see that he [their son] becomes the sort of man, some twenty years later, who will be a mature, responsible, tender and understanding carrier of the torch of life which they have handed on to him and which he, in turn, will hand on to their grandchildren." The import of this advice could not be more explicit: "To raise a man, a husband, a father is the obligation laid on two parents by the birth cry of every newborn male."[43]

It was this reasoning that allowed ego psychologists, as well as a multitude of social commentators influenced by them, to treat the alleged crisis of femininity as a byproduct of the Machine Age, namely, disruption of the "normal" sexual division of labor. Newspapers and magazines published scores of articles on this theme. Although opinions varied, the problem itself achieved succinct definition in the *New York Times Magazine* feature, "Trousered Mothers and Dishwashing Dads."[44]

Writing in the mass-circulation *Parents' Magazine*, Marynia Farnham summed up the situation. "Little boys and girls are brought up very similarly and in many ways this makes things more difficult for them when it comes to understanding and accepting their sex roles in life." Because "Daddy makes the living but Mother may give music lessons and make money, too," or even because "Mother does most of the housework but Daddy often washes dishes or does other household chores to help," both boys and girls grow up hopelessly confused about the differences between them. Farnham advised parents to put a stop to this dangerous trend. They should serve as appropriate role models themselves and then reinforce the lesson by praising their children's attempts at mimicry. Even fathers could help by encouraging their daughter's "budding femininity." Fathers could "praise the things she does to be like mother, such as setting the table or helping to make the muffins." Such rigorous defense was absolutely necessary, according to Farnham, lest children grow up without achieving firm sex identities.[45]

Here was the kernel of an argument that held far-reaching implications, and not only for psychoanalytic theory. Should anyone not quite get the point, Abram Kardiner put it bluntly: "The woman is the one who cares for the household and rears the children; the male is the authority in the family and the one who procures the economic means of subsistence." There was, of course, nothing new in this idea except its psychoanalytic rhetorical trappings. Much more significant was the utter, adamant renunciation of the Machine Age. If psychoanalysts had once aspired to lead the modernist vanguard, they now joined other Cold War liberals in signaling a conspicuous retreat. Fearful that society had advanced to the precipice of its own dissolution, psychoanalysts looked inward to the family. But instead of discovering the eternal triangulated conflict of early childhood as documented by Freud, they determined to find the source of psychological rejuvenation—if only women would cooperate. The best advice Kardiner could offer those stubborn young women who nurtured career ambitions was: "Marry young, have your children between eighteen and twenty-four, spend the next fourteen years giving them effective care, and then enter on a career."[46]

Kardiner's suggestion came at a peculiar moment. For the vast majority of American women, an exclusively domestic vocation was beyond reach. Often without completing college, middle-class white women were marrying at unprecedentedly young ages and, on the average, were completing their baby-boom families by age twenty-six. The only hitch was that many of these young mothers could not follow Kardiner's advice and wait fourteen years before finding a job, if only part-time, in the high-inflation times of the Cold War era. By 1952 the number of wives at work was triple the number in 1940; and women with children under eighteen represented one-quarter of the female workforce. As a report from the U.S. Women's Bureau noted, the United States was "approaching a period when for women to work is an act of conformism."[47]

But there really was no need to worry about careers, for professional employment had become an increasingly scarce commodity. The proportion of women in professions continued to decline from the peak reached in the 1920s, a downward trend abetted by quotas imposed, for example, by the nation's medical colleges and law schools. So, too, for the profession of psychoanalysis itself. Whereas women represented a high proportion of refugee analysts, approximately 30 percent, by the late 1950s women accounted for under 10 percent of all students enrolled in training institutes in the United States.

The 60 percent of women who dropped out of college to marry and start a family would find only "feminine" jobs available to them. Instead of entering careers, these women were quickly filling the ranks of the growing clerical, retail, and service sectors, where pay was low and advancement rare. Given their options, it was little wonder that the majority of American women agreed with their expert contemporaries: when polled they too expressed a preference for highly conventional sex roles, with men the chief breadwinners and women responsible for the home. Psychoanalysts should have granted these women at least some credit, for polls indicated that only 20 percent sought employment to fill "a need for accomplishment." But would they really be happier at home? Polls also revealed that more women than men described marriage as a source of distress and, moreover, reported feelings of inadequacy as a parent.[48]

Clara Thompson now appeared to be caught between two generations. On the one hand, like her former associate and close friend Karen Horney, Thompson had always admired woman's unmatched capacity for reproduction and never sought to deny its claim on her identity. She conceded that women, in following men into the marketplace, had perhaps "lost touch with the unique value of being women." Nevertheless, Thompson did not believe motherhood and domesticity were equivalent and underscored her main disagreement with "Dr. Farnham": she adamantly refused to overlook the significance of women's subordination to men. "Women must learn to find importance and dignity in their own functions," Thompson wrote. "They must struggle against leading empty and unreproductive lives without feeling they must necessarily become a part of the competitive system of our culture, a system created by males in which males have a distinct advantage." If the "militant fighters for women's rights" had mistakenly tried to show that women were equal to men by mimicking them, there was no doubt in her mind where the responsibility lay. In postwar American society, men maintained a firm grip on the reins of power.[49] By the time she died in 1958, Thompson had found little support for her views.

Most psychoanalysts endorsed the patriarchal family as the American ideal. Feminists, they charged, aimed to blur the very roles that the patriarchal family kept so cleanly defined. What made feminists so dangerous, then, was not their aspiration to extend women's civil rights or even their unrelenting criticism of men. Feminists posed the worst threat by endorsing careers for women. If women worked outside the home on a par with men, the reasoning went, they would disrupt the crucial processes of identification that allegedly ensured differentiation by sex. These ambitious women would bring about further social disorder by fostering children who were alienated from their proper sexual identities. In short, they would upset the "natural" order. The argument had come full circle, the sociology of sex roles redeeming the biology of sex differences.

Feminism – The Rejection of Biology

In 1954 Edward A. Strecker, with his coauthor Vincent T. Lathbury, published a sequel to his infamous wartime sermon on the manifold dangers of Momism. A timely update, *Their Mothers' Daughters* exalts the opposition between femininity and feminism to the extent that the authors regret even the common prefix of the two words. Strecker and Lathbury hoped to clear up any confusion by crafting a precise definition of feminism. Like their contemporaries, they skipped past all issues of women's civil rights to center exclusively on careers. Feminism, they charged, embodied women's "deep wish to compete with men" and expressed simultaneously their "dissatisfaction with being a woman." *Their Mothers' Daughters* also records an equally timely definition of femininity: "the biological motivation and psychological art of being a woman."[50]

The key conjunction here links "biology" and "psychology." For Strecker, as well as for the majority of leading psychoanalysts, it took only a simple twist of logic to reason that, if societies operate more smoothly and more humanely when sex roles are highly differentiated, this beneficent social division just might mirror a natural order. Indeed, functionalist social theory appears even more elegant when premised on biology and all the more so when framed within psychoanalysis.

The discussions of alienation, particularly the "American Woman's Dilemma," deployed both sociological and biological arguments. For example, in his popular book *Sex and Morality* (1954), Abram Kardiner distinguished between these two factors but insisted that they operated simultaneously and with equal force. He therefore complained against feminists because they encouraged women to abrogate their domestic responsibilities by seeking work outside the home to enter the realm of "male pursuits." Kardiner defended the "normal" division of labor between the sexes by suggesting that it mirrored "natural" differences. The idea of parity was "preposterous," he insisted, precisely because it *socially* blurred *biological* disparities, that is, the relationship between "two biologically differentiated creatures whose social functions were so diverse." Like Farnham, Kardiner advocated the enactment of social legislation to fortify women's position within the home as part of a larger program to reinstate "the value of the male and female biological role."[51]

Psychoanalysts proceeded to reverse the causal relationship between nature and culture that had been in vogue throughout the interwar period. If culture had then served as the foundation for systems of sexual difference, by midcentury biology promised to establish the limits of variation. Not only psychoanalysts but theorists in several disciplines now searched for important clues in the unlike bodies of men and women.

Even the era's premier culturalist drifted in this direction. Margaret Mead had always acknowledged that all societies, in one way or another, "seize upon the conspicuous facts" of sex and force men and women "to conform to the role assigned to it." But rather than celebrating this practice, she presented abundant comparative evidence in

Sex and Temperament in Three Primitive Societies (1935) to suggest that the very richest cultures allow the greatest degree of variation and thereby encourage all members, women as well as men, to fulfill their innate capacities. "We must recognize," she implored in true modernist fashion, "that beneath the superficial classifications of sex and race the same potentialities exist, recurring generation after generation, only to perish because society has no place for them."[52]

As the midcentury mark approached, Mead modified her position. She complained that "this whole question of the relationship between men and women" was taking the form of "raucous and angry" arguments, and she cited *Modern Woman: The Lost Sex* as a glaring example. She found the habit of heaping blame on women equally annoying. And describing the United States as a matriarchy was not only ludicrous, she charged, but injurious to sound anthropological constructs. But even while Mead begged fellow Americans to recognize men and women as "human beings first," she herself opened a biological can of worms. In *Male and Female: A Study of the Sexes in a Changing World* (1949), Mead explored various causal relationships between biology and culture, including the different "reproductive strategies" of the sexes. She went so far as to refer to maternity as woman's "biological role."[53]

Mead's retreat from the unyielding culturalism of her youth reflected a sweeping turnaround in the behavioral sciences at large. As the historian Carl N. Degler has pointed out, just as anthropologists were boasting of their exploits in refining "the concept of culture," distinguished scholars such as Harvard University's Clyde Kluckhohn were seeking a comparably sophisticated understanding of biology. "Some patterns of every culture," Kluckhohn argued, "crystallize around focuses provided by the inevitables of biology," including the differences between the sexes.[54]

By the late 1940s a sizable group of social scientists, including sociologists, anthropologists, psychologists as well as psychoanalysts, were mining reports from the rapidly advancing biological sciences—biophysics, biochemistry, physiology—and the new theories of genetically based social evolution. The World Health Organization played a major role by sponsoring conferences and promoting new kinds of interdisciplinary research. In 1953, for example, the WHO invited leading scholars like Mead, Erikson, and Bowlby to Geneva, Switzerland, and asked them to pool their opinions on "the influences of biological, psychological and cultural factors in the development through childhood of the adult personality" with experimentalists like Konrad Lorenz and Julian Huxley. It was just a matter of time before scholars in several disciplines would agree that an understanding of either psychology or biology demanded "an appreciation of the unifying closed circle of events which encompasses both."[55]

Even the notion of instinct, which had been bolstered by ego psychologists, gained yet more popularity. Psychoanalysts began to dabble in ethology, the study of animal behavior, to derive a better understanding of the interplay between instinct and learning as one moved up the phylogenetic ladder. Psychoanalysts welcomed the recent publications of the European pioneers of this new field, especially works by Lorenz, Nikolaas Tinbergen, and William Thorpe. The timing was right. The year 1959 marked the centenary of Darwin's *Origin of the Species,* and psychoanalysts found special reason to celebrate in tandem the contributions of Freud and his esteemed predecessor. Both the American Psychoanalytic Association and the International Psycho-Analytic Association featured panels on ethology and psychoanalysis at their annual meetings. The most optimistic participants interpreted this revival as a major step in restoring to psychoanalysis Freud's primary concern, basic human nature.

This increasing attention to the operation of instincts in both animals and humans enriched many aspects of psychoanalytic theory, including the cornerstone of ego psychology, the mother-infant relationship. The British psychoanalyst John Bowlby in the 1950s defined "attachment" as an innate drive to establish a loving, ongoing relationship with an empathic mother, an instinct primary not only among humans but throughout the animal kingdom. The imprinting process of birds, studied in depth by Lorenz, had underscored for him the primacy of the events of early infancy for emotional development, and not merely for goslings, ducklings, and baby jackdaws.

Bowlby made his case on behalf of ethology in his pathbreaking "The Nature of the Child's Tie to the Mother," which he delivered at the London Psychoanalytic Society's meeting in 1957. Although both Melanie Klein and Anna Freud dismissed this essay as reductionist, others readily endorsed not only Bowlby's conclusions but his research methods.[56] In the United States, for example, the work of the experimental psychologist Harry Harlow found a receptive audience among psychoanalysts. Studying the mother-infant relationship among rhesus monkeys, Harlow had concluded that the drive for physical contact outstripped the need even for food. Baby monkeys, he observed, routinely reject cold, wire-constructed but milk-laden "mothers" for soft, terry-cloth versions which offer no nutritional rewards. Harlow's findings on "The Nature of Love" complemented Bowlby's, affirming the overall importance of the mother-infant bond and specifying its origins in the infant's instinctual need for attachment or love.[57]

Several other psychoanalysts explored the other half of this equation, hoping to establish the dynamics of a maternal instinct. Anathema to Freud, the notion of motherhood as a biological imperative had achieved its clearest expression in Deutsch's *Psychology of Woman*. Deutsch in essence savaged her mentor's libido theory to describe a maternal instinct, a "biologic-chemical source . . . beyond the psychologic sphere." It was gestation, Deutsch reasoned, the lengthy period of physiologic symbiosis between the woman and the developing fetus, that roused the maternal instinct. Writing in the early 1940s, she judged the state of scientific research insufficient to explicate this process more fully or to define precisely the relationship between the "complex emotional attribute" called "motherliness" and a specific "biologic condition." Deutsch nevertheless had observed sufficient similarity between animal and human behavior to insist that the "natural and primitive phenomenon of motherhood" obeyed both biologic and psychic laws, both subject to clarification by psychoanalysis.[58]

It was Therese F. Benedek (1892–1964) who discovered the missing clues in the female reproductive system itself. Benedek specialized in the primary unit of mother and child and had similarly pursued the "psychodynamics of the symbiosis" that directs and motivates the interaction between the two. It is the mother, she explained, who patterns the infant's behavior and emotions, her own tenderness serving as the model for expressions of love and being loved through life. Benedek also placed the mother at the center of the crucial processes of identification, for boys as well as girls. The confidence provided by the mother gives the boy "permission for self-assertion and a sense of courage in using his growing muscular power," she reasoned, and thereby allows him to "free himself from his dependence on the mother in order to start a development in which identification with the father becomes a leading motive." In daughters, emotional security sparks the process so that she "easily imitates her mother and learns from her."[59]

As Erikson observed, Benedek was among the first psychoanalysts to sketch the formative moments of identification. Benedek herself found the principles of ego psychology, including the emphasis on learned behavior, entirely consistent with her own imaginative search for the biological substratum. Shortly after emigrating from Hungary she had teamed up with an endocrinologist, Boris B. Rubenstein, and together they had conducted a landmark investigation into the "propagative, biologic meaning of sexuality."[60]

Benedek soon appeared at the forefront of a growing movement within American psychoanalysis, psychosomatic medicine. Since the publication of Flanders Dunbar's trailblazing *Emotions and Bodily Changes* (1935), several psychoanalysts had been studying such mysterious phenomena as "organ neurosis," which, unlike hysteria, produces both somatic symptoms and actual changes in body structure. A group of New York psychoanalysts formed the Association for Psychoanalytic and Psychosomatic Medicine in 1942, but the most important impetus came from Franz Alexander and his colleagues at the Chicago Institute for Psychoanalysis, who pioneered clinical studies of various physiological diseases, such as asthma, hypertension, arthritis, colitis, and ulcers. They not only produced numerous essays on the theoretical aspects of the brain-body-mind relationship but offered psychoanalytic treatment to affected patients.

Alexander, who defined personality "as the expression of the unity of the organism," made fields such as neurology and endocrinology logical companions to psychoanalysis. He followed developments in even such novel specialties as psychoneuroimmunology to speculate, for example, about the impact of endorphins on psychological processes. Neither Alexander nor his associate Benedek found a conflict between biological research and the culturalism emblematic of their emigré generation. Personality development depends, Alexander insisted, on two factors: "the inherited equipment and molding influence of the environment."[61]

This range of methodology, extraordinary in the history of psychoanalysis, undergirded Benedek's studies of female sexuality. Benedek believed that the menstrual cycle, particularly the pattern of hormonal fluctuation, played a crucial part in determining a congruent emotional cycle in women. Although she did not expect to find a situation approximating the changes in behavior determined by estrus in lower animals, Benedek believed that female sexual desire and receptivity to motherhood varied in relation to ovulation and menstrual flow. To get at the heart of this matter, she used conventional techniques of dream analysis but also asked her patients to record basal temperature and to provide a daily vaginal smear. Based on a study of 152 cycles of fifteen women of childbearing age, she specified a direct interplay between somatic and psychic processes, namely, a significant correlation between gonad function and female personality. These findings, Benedek insisted, did not by any means undermine Freud's theories, but, methodologically, did shift the emphasis from anatomy to physiology.[62]

The turning away from anatomy and toward physiology, despite Benedek's disclaimer, did represent a major philosophical as well as methodological reorientation. Many psychoanalysts resisted this trend. Staunch culturalists such as Erich Fromm held firm against any restoration of instinct theory. A lay analyst himself, Fromm had little reason to accede to the authority of biological science. Yet the majority of neo-Freudians fell quickly into line. Since Horney's dramatic exodus from the New York Psychoanalytic Institute in 1941, culturalists themselves continued to hive yet more splinter groups until 1956, when several coalesced as the American Academy of Psychoanalysis, headquartered in Chicago. Early on, the American Academy registered the new intellectual mood and inaugurated an annual publication entitled *Science and Psychoanalysis*. Its tenth-anniversary issue proudly marked the transformation of psychoanalysis from "an increasingly isolated, doctrinal cult to a modern scientific organon." Biology, even for the legatees of neo-Freudianism, now served as the baseline for cultural variations. And, as if to mark the distance traveled since the heady culturalist days of the interwar period, a leading member of the American Academy drew out the lesson. Always remember, he insisted, to take into account "both the biological differences between the sexes and the variations in cultural reactions to these differences."[63]

The biological turn thus fired the well-entrenched notions of femininity and provided yet more ammunition for the battle against feminism. Psychoanalysts could now draw comfortably on a host of evidence from the biological sciences to enumerate the detrimental consequences of women's desire to find fulfillment in careers. Seemingly programmed by nature to depend on men and bear their children, women who followed an antagonistic course not only jeopardized the emotional well-being of their offspring but impaired their own mental health. Thus Abram Kardiner advised feminists to seek redemption in "the restoration of the dignity that goes with the female's biological function." His colleague Lionel Ovesey was a bit more generous, allowing women some latitude as long as they did not "seriously interfere with the acceptance of womanhood and of woman's sociobiological role." Although psychoanalysts like Ovesey and Kardiner might condemn the feminist movement for the psychological disruptions that allegedly followed in its wake, they managed to find solace in the "scientific" assurance that its "real essence" was "a blind alley." As Kardiner boasted, feminism was "doomed to defeat not by society but by biology, for it seems that sex differentiation is here to stay, as well as differentiation by social function."[64]

The psychoanalytic fusion of biologism and functionalism reached its apex of pure misogyny in one of the decade's most renowned popularizers, Theodor Reik (1888–1969). The founder in 1948 of the National Psychological Association for Psychoanalysis, an organization of lay analysts, and editor of its journal, *Psychoanalysis,* Reik was a successful author and an extraordinarily loyal Freudian. Described by the historian Paul Roazen as "the heel-clicking admirer of every word the Professor uttered," Reik reputedly suffered great separation anxieties after his immigration to the United States. By way of compensation, he affected Freud's habits, styles of writing and talking, and even the distinctive clipped beard. Reik adorned his office with photographs of Freud, a sight suggesting to Roazen nothing so much as "the adoration of a schoolboy."[65]

To the obviously insecure Reik fell the self-chosen task of integrating these sociobiological notions of sexual difference into the Freudian canon. He began by emphatically denying the importance of culture as a determining factor. While feigning remorse for exhibiting such pessimism, he dismissed the culturalist hypothesis about the plasticity of human nature. True, he admitted, there were a few inconsistencies in sex-linked behaviors. But such seemingly minor deviations could not undermine his faith that "certain characteristic emotional features of the two sexes reveal themselves everywhere and under the most variable culture patterns." The reason was simple: men and women had different sexual functions. The phrase "biological determination" flowed easily from Reik's pen.

This was orthodox Freudianism, Reik insisted. To make his case, he quoted a passage from one of Freud's unfinished and not yet translated papers written in 1938: "the biological fact of the duality of the sexes emerges before us as a great enigma, something lost to our knowledge, defying any attempt of tracing it back to something else. Psychoanalysis did not contribute anything to the clarification of this problem. It belongs obviously as a whole to biology." Discounting Freud's own reservations, Reik insisted that his hero had in fact grasped the "unchangeable" nature of masculinity and femininity. Freud knew from the beginning that, in his immortal phrase, "Anatomy is destiny."[66] Reik nevertheless admitted that another comment by Freud puzzled him. If Freud understood the role of biology, why did he later ask—in another enduring phrase—"What does a woman want?" Perhaps this question was merely rhetorical, Reik mused, a sign that Freud had recognized that woman's needs are so voracious as to defy enumeration. Reik himself had found a proper response in the writings of Nietzsche: "All in woman is an enigma, and all in woman has a single solution. It is called pregnancy."[67]

Reik received a warm reception for these comments delivered to a gathering of lay analysts celebrating his sixty-fifth birthday. The medical writer who made Momism a household word in the 1940s, Amram Scheinfeld, expressed his delight on this occasion because he, too, had been deeply troubled by the Culture and Personality scholars who treated "sex" as if it were a social construction like class, race, or ethnicity. The latter were, of course, historical formations, but "women and men remain," Scheinfeld insisted, "perpetually distinct as both biological and social groups." Yes, yes, he echoed Reik, anatomy is destiny. Scheinfeld ended his commentary by taking pleasure in joining Reik "in our school yell, the fine old traditional, 'Vive le difference!' "[68]

On this matter, it is only fitting to allow Marynia Farnham the last word. Like Reik, she and her coauthor Lundberg had disputed the culturalist presumption of a common humanity embracing both man and woman. Such an idea meant, she countered,

> that society was being asked to accept as identical two similar but decidedly different and complementary organisms, one endowed with ovaries, uterus, Fallopian tubes, cervix, vagina, vulva, clitoris and mammary glands and the other with testicles, seminal vesicle, prostate gland and penis but none of these other organs. It meant, also, that society was to accept as identical the functions of these different sets of organs along with their functional effects and emotional accompaniments, and was to act as though the social consequences of their functioning or nonfunctioning were identical.

Armed with scholarly and public opinion on her side, Farnham put aside the culturalists' concerns for her own. Poorly differentiated sex roles, Farnham argued, had fostered "individuals who are seriously handicapped because they don't have sex identities." What were the prospects, she worried, for well-being in a society that tended to regard men and women "not primarily as male and female, but as people?"[69]

The place of biology in Freud's system remains ambiguous to this day. Numerous detractors allege that Freud never overcame his grounding in the reductionist principles of Victorian science. Others make the opposite claim, underscoring Freud's own emphasis on the influence of unconscious mental factors on personality formation as well as on traumatic bodily events such as hysterical paralysis. There is some truth in both perspectives. Freud took great pride in establishing "abundant points of contact" with unconscious mental processes as the factors propelling his grand theory of psychoanalysis. He had overcome many of the limits imposed by his training as a neurologist and, above all, had rejected biology as the unmediated source of mental life. As he pointed out in confronting Karen Horney in the late 1920s, his was a "pure psychology" advanced by purely psychological methods. Nevertheless, even in his later writings Freud supplied ample evidence indicating that he never totally discounted the importance of "physical or somatic processes."

If not a crypto-biologist, as one iconoclast has alleged, Freud simply judged the state of knowledge about neurophysiological processes insufficient for his purposes. "Biology is truly a land of unlimited possibilities," he once admitted. "We may expect it to give us the most surprising information and we cannot guess what answers it will return in a few dozen years to the questions we have put to it."[70] Yet, at the peak of the debates on female sexuality that burned into the 1930s, Freud roundly denounced all forms of biological determinism. He did not live long enough to see its triumph in the 1950s—or to see American psychoanalysts prompt a biological rereading of his theories, especially his late-life work on ego psychology.

For American feminism, this convoluted history of psychoanalysis contains a multitude of ironies. The original enthusiasm circa 1910 for Freud's ideas as a lever for female sexual emancipation depended largely upon ignorance (and perhaps evasion) of his larger theoretical framework. Decades later the wellsprings of neo-Freudian heresy, most notably in Horney's ripened polemics, centered in the determination to deny biology as the singular determinant of womanhood. And yet, by almost any standard, Freud's position on the biological determinants of sexual difference compares favorably with psychoanalytic theory at midcentury. Equally astounding is the evocation of Freud as the source of these reductionist ideas. Unlike the pioneering culturalists who emphasized their distance from Freud, the fashionable postwar ego psychologists went out of their way to claim his mantle. Now squarely in the domains of both popular and academic culture, Freud, the icon of psychoanalysis, consequently carried the weight of both a crude biologism and a rampant misogyny that had never been his.[71]

Apparently the circle had not only closed but spiraled in upon itself. After years and years of intense dialogue about the differences between the sexes, the origins of masculinity and femininity as well as their various manifestations, the great minds of psychoanalytic theory had seemingly advanced very little beyond their nineteenth-century ancestors. The sexual modernism celebrated by interwar scholars represented in the long history only a brief and decidedly fleeting interlude, and feminism again appeared as chief antagonist. Passages written by such distinguished psychoanalysts as Abram Kardiner or Helene Deutsch could be readily exchanged with the following statement published in the inaugural issue of the *Quarterly Journal of Psychological Medicine* of July 1867:

> We affirm, then, that there is a great need for raising women in position and education and multiplying lucrative employment for them within the sphere of their own sex; but we think they make a mistake in undertaking duties which are better fulfilled by men. It is an aberration of the sexual instinct in any girl to aim at occupations which are incompatible with the duties of maternity and an equal aberration to smother those maidenly instincts which should lead her not to intrude into occupations which custom has associated with the male sex . . . For, after all, women cannot get rid of their sex. What is their real glory, their very life-purpose? To be mothers.[72]

When second-wave feminists searched for their ideological enemies, they not surprisingly found in contemporary psychoanalysis a Freud deserving their unleashed rage. But not even the most angry feminist could escape entirely the logic of a system by this time deeply imprinted on American culture.

6

Feminists versus Freud

Very few writers, professionals or popularists, protested the antifeminist bias of American psychoanalysis at midcentury. The Cold War climate did little to encourage a dissenting spirit. Margaret Mead complained occasionally but never went head-to-head with the likes of Kardiner or Erikson. Clara Thompson maintained a lonely vigil until her death in 1958. Meanwhile liberals such as Wylie, Lundberg and Farnham, and Parsons staged a crushing polemical victory over the residual cultural relativism of the interwar generation. In the name of American democracy and world peace, they locked arms, closed ranks, and froze out intellectual competition. Psychoanalytic misogyny reigned proudly, even haughtily, evidently secure—if only for the time being.

A few rumblings interrupted what proved to be a lull before the storm. One year before the publication of *Modern Woman: The Lost Sex,* an outsider to psychoanalysis decried the immeasurable harm done by Freud. Mary Ritter Beard (1876–1958), with her husband Charles Beard the century's most popular American historians, had planted the seeds for what later would become a blossoming field, women's history. In 1946, in *Woman as Force in History: A Study in*

Traditions and Realities, her magnum opus, she offered a succinct and astute indictment of psychoanalysis.

The pernicious idea that woman exists merely as "a servant to man's biological propensities," Beard wrote, was directly attributable to the "cult" of Freud. Nothing in her vast researches conducted over a half-century supported this mistaken and mischievous conclusion. Turning the "psychological assumptions" that she despised on their head, Beard surveyed the course of Western history to document the paramount importance of women's contribution. As mothers and as caretakers of the domestic sphere, women possess, she countered Freud, an unsurpassed capacity to advance civilization.[1]

On one level, Beard's perspective could be seen as a throwback to the Progressive era, her book the kind that a scholar of seventy could produce as if unaffected by the intervening eras and fashions. But Beard was arguing against the weight of contemporary psychoanalytic theory, including the recent popular renditions aimed at containing women's advancement. *Woman as Force in History* also expressed a forceful critique of the claustrophobic liberalism that had emerged in the wake of World War II.

Beard's complaint went unnoticed until the 1960s, when a new edition of *Woman as Force in History* inspired a much younger generation to deliver a more forceful blow. Second-wave feminists proved especially eager to rebut Freud and ferociously attacked the misogynist underpinnings of psychoanalysis. But the vast majority could not find an adequate counterweight in either woman's sphere or motherhood. Too much had happened in the interim, in terms of women's relation to both the marketplace and civil society, and in terms of the punishing ideology that had accompanied these changes. Coming of age in the wake of Momism, they measured their own personal aspirations against the experiences of their mothers, who by and large had sought to realize the roles that the experts had defined for them. These daughters saw nothing positive in domesticity and very little in maternity. "She has stayed at home for twenty-three years and raised four children," one woman wrote dishearteningly about her mother. Whereas psychoanalysts would have applauded such domestic devotion, this writer found the "emptiness of her [mother's] life" appalling.[2] Many young women could therefore appreciate Beard's animosity toward psychoanalysis, but they built on different premises. Indeed, they were positioning themselves to open a new chapter in the history of American feminism.

The opening salvo came from an atypical woman of their mother's generation. A hard-working journalist for a left-wing labor weekly (albeit under a pen name), Betty Friedan (1921–) began to question the ideal of wife and mother mandated by postwar psychoanalysts. In 1957 she surveyed 200 Smith College alumnae fifteen years after their graduation to discover that her hunch was correct. The data revealed a pervasive ennui, specifically a growing aversion to an existence defined exclusively by the sex roles prescribed by midcentury psychoanalysts.

The pathbreaking *The Feminine Mystique* (1963) thus spoke across generations, appealing to both the author's middle-class contemporaries and the young women determined to avoid their mothers' fate. Eventually selling well over a million copies, Friedan's manifesto brought feminism once again into public light and this time with widespread approval.

Friedan denounced Freud, claiming that his theories had become an "all-embracing American ideology . . . [settling] everywhere, like fine volcanic ash." Moreover, that ideology's authoritative stature inhibited women from questioning what was in essence merely long-standing prejudice hardened into dogma. "The feminine mystique, elevated by Freudian theory into a scientific religion," Friedan wrote, "sounded a single, overprotective, life-restricting, future-denying note for women."[3]

Friedan's acerbic critique of Freud's "sexual solipsism" proved the harbinger of a full-scale assault on the psychoanalytic legacy. The National Organization for Women, which Friedan had helped to found in 1966, explicitly rejected marriage and motherhood as an exclusive vocation and campaigned vigorously to expand women's employment opportunities and civil rights. Equality became the watchword. The very idea of highly differentiated sex roles, the prescriptions and proscriptions of authors ranging from Wylie and Farnham to Erikson and Parsons, went out the window. Meanwhile the mushrooming women's liberation movement spread the message among millions of college-age women. By 1967 consciousness-raising (CR) groups had begun to form across the country. The year 1968,

Freud & Spurred women's movement

which marked social upheaval around the globe, saw hundreds of clamorous protesters at the nationally televised Miss America beauty pageant in Atlantic City. This action vividly illustrated women's determination to break, as one radical agitator put it, "the bond of woman as a biologically and sexually defined creature."[4]

Second-wave activists revived and soon eclipsed the feminism of their distant predecessors. Rising from the social movements and counterculture of the 1960s, youthful activists often summoned images of the great campaigns for the vote but more spectacularly recalled the latent memories of the old avant-garde: Emma Goldman's impassioned oratory, Margaret Sanger's militancy, and even Louise Bryant's nude sunbathing, all conducted with the prospect of Revolution in sight. Like their charismatic forerunners, second-wavers pushed politics directly and dramatically into the realm of personal experience. From the education and jobs they pursued to the makeup and fashions they rejected, this generation protested the dogma of sex roles. But unlike the earlier experimenters, second-wave feminists inspired a mass movement.

Women's Liberation quickly took off. The media, which only years before had doted on the poor beset husband and maladjusted son, placing blame squarely upon the frivolous Mom, discovered a new angle. As the press and television simultaneously explored and exploited the excitement, rebellious daughters stood at the center. An inch thin but a mile wide, women's liberation, as one sympathetic observer put it, "moved across the land leaving encouragement and trembling in its path."[5]

All the more significant, then, was the daughters' point of departure. Unlike the feminists of yore who had touted Freud as a supreme liberator, the so-called Sixties generation joined Beard and Friedan to make him an arch-enemy. Potshots at Freud began to appear in scores of polemics, from the burgeoning feminist and radical presses to the avant-garde slick magazines and even the liberal pulpits. By the opening of the next decade, thoughtful commentaries marked feminist writing on the subject. Four major texts appeared in 1970–1971 alone, each indicting Freud for the crime of misogyny. Kate Millett in *Sexual Politics* names Freud "the strongest individual counterrevolutionary force in the ideology of sexual politics"; Shulamith Firestone in *The Dialectic of Sex* refers contemptuously to Freudianism as "our modern

Church"; Eva Figes in *Patriarchal Attitudes* describes Freudian psychoanalysis as "a magic formula more powerful than any fence"; and Germaine Greer in *The Female Eunuch* dismisses it cavalierly as "nonsense."[6] After reviewing this literature, one scholar concluded that Freud surpassed all other theorists as a target of feminist criticism. The repudiation of Freud, another affirmed, was a basic principle in second-wave feminism.[7]

The most prominent critics were, like Friedan, neither psychoanalysts nor interdisciplinary allies. Firestone held a Bachelor of Fine Arts from the Art Institute of Chicago; Figes had graduated from London University with a degree in English; Millett and Greer earned advanced degrees in the liberal arts. These writers put aside academic decorum to craft hard-hitting polemics. It was not so much the scholarship of psychoanalysis that engaged them but the popular renditions in Hollywood films, middlebrow commentary, childrearing and marriage manuals, and the bestselling trade books. For this reason second-wave feminists issued their complaints within the realm of public rather than learned discourse. Detouring around theoretical complexities to catch the unmistakable iconography of Freud, these critics also proved far more resolute in protesting psychoanalytic misogyny than did Freud's first adversaries. Whereas Horney had quietly removed Freud's portrait from her home, one member of a Boston-Cambridge women's group recalled that at every meeting members used a photograph of Freud as a target for darts.[8]

Building on Friedan's success, these critics were the first to fault Freud explicitly in the name of feminism. Although Horney and her colleagues had objected to Freud's masculine bias or phallocentrism, they had disclaimed any association with feminism. To the interwar generation, which included Mary Beard, feminism implied masculinism, that is, an androcentric valuation of men's roles and personality as well as anatomy. Horney, like Beard, initially reversed the valence, making woman's reproductive capacity the measure. But even after she relinquished all notions of a distinctly feminine psychology, Horney found the contemporary understanding of feminism too narrow for her tastes. While certainly approving careers for women and justifiably proud of her own accomplishments, she preferred to keep all prescriptions at a minimum. Second-wave proponents knew little of this history and felt few constraints. They proudly embraced the label and, at the same time, refused to settle on a single definition. It was clear, though, that feminism would no longer be exclusively associated with careers. But neither would it be linked, at least initially, to woman's reproductive destiny.

Does this make a good woman?

The feminists who came of age in the 1960s could therefore appreciate the objection that Horney, Beard, and Friedan held in common: to Freud's biological determinism. All parties appeared unaware that Freud himself had hesitated to fashion a psychology of sexual difference and had done so only when prompted by the women in his ranks. But Freud's legacy had become so entangled with reductionist ego psychology that he served as a convenient target of arrant attack. Second-wavers therefore assailed Freud for making the biological disparities between man and woman the basis of an elaborate rationale for sexual inequality. Freud's theories constituted, feminists charged, a grand argument for confining women to the home and ensuring men's monopoly of all positions of authority. Almost everyone shared Friedan's wrath at Freud for fostering the Feminine Mystique and, by extension, curtailing women's advancement in civil society. As Friedan had aptly documented, the ascent of Freud's theories paralleled a decline in women's status in the professions as well as a simultaneous surge in the birth rate. American women were now better schooled than their foremothers, but, thanks to Freud, they made far less use of their education. What Freud had done, as Beard had likewise recognized, was to guarantee that any dissatisfaction with this situation would be interpreted as a symptom of psychopathology. Psychoanalysis now stood at right angles to feminism.

Going to college to get your MRS.

Ironically, in order to prove this point, second-wavers chose the very topic that had initiated the alliance between feminism and psychoanalysis in the first place: female sexuality. Like their distant predecessors, they were coming of age amid—and giving a special political spin to—a sexual revolution. Heralded by *Playboy* since its appearance in 1953 and later by Helen Gurley Brown's bestselling *Sex and the Single Girl* (1962), the so-called Second Sexual Revolution, like the first, promoted the idea of recreational sex detached from the obligations of matrimony and maternity. Spreading rapidly within a growing singles culture, sexual defiance had once again become the red flag of rebellious youth. The feminist writer Alix Kates Shulman might have been paraphrasing Floyd Dell in declaring, "skirts were up, prudery was down."[9]

For second-wave feminists, however, the much-touted sexual revolution was about sex roles as much as sexuality, about men's power as much as women's pleasure. This argument found its clearest expression in Kate Millett's *Sexual Politics,* which in its critique of patriarchy set the standards of anti-Freudianism for an entire generation. Coitus, Millett contended, "serves as a charged microcosm of the variety of attitudes and values to which culture subscribes." One group, The Feminists, issued a paper in 1969 that presaged Millett's complaint against Freud and all other ideologues of sex roles: "if sexual relations were not programmed to support political ends—that is, male oppression of the female—then the way would be clear for individuals to enter into physical relations not defined by roles, nor involving exploitation." The famed slogan of the era—the personal is political—encapsulated this perspective. It was from this vantage point that feminists like Millett aimed direct fire at psychoanalytic theories of female sexuality.[10]

The attack on Freud nevertheless came as a surprise. Many commentators interpreted the second sexual revolution as a revival of the grand movement toward the sexual liberalism that had been inaugurated by the founder of psychoanalysis. After all, they asked, who surpasses Freud in delineating the dangers of sexual repression? "Now, to think of Freud as any sort of counterrevolutionary," one cultivated writer opined in the *New York Times Magazine,* "requires a difficult mental adjustment for a man who, like myself, has been accustomed to thinking of him as a great insurrectionary."[11] Feminists knew better.

The Great Orgasm Debate

There was considerable grist for the feminist mill. In the psychoanalytic literature published at midcentury, descriptions linked female sexuality to exclusively reproductive goals and additionally offered unfavorable comparisons to male prowess. Recently reprinted as trade paperbacks, works by both Helene Deutsch and Marie Bonaparte compared man's active search for pleasure to woman's passive service to the species. Bonaparte's *Female Sexuality* (1953), reprinted in 1973, describes "normal" female sexuality as passive resignation, a legacy of the initial dependence on her inferior sexual organ, the clitoris. *Psychology of Women* (1942), reprinted in 1967, meanwhile, restates Deutsch's long-standing opinion that the orgasm women achieve through heterosexual genital encounter is decidedly inferior to the ecstasy they experience in childbirth.

Lundberg and Farnham had presented these ideas in a lighter mode. Like Deutsch and Bonaparte, the popularists set masculine activity against feminine passivity and vividly described coitus from the female perspective: "it is not as easy as rolling off a log. It is easier. It is as easy as being the log itself." They also correlated a woman's orgasmic potential with her desire to bear children and postulated a negative relationship between sexual satisfaction and level of education. College-educated women, especially those who chose careers over motherhood, they reasoned against fact, were unusually prone to frigidity. Second-wave feminists, who could find excerpts of the notorious *Modern Woman: The Lost Sex* in new scholarly anthologies, understandably found these notions repugnant.[12]

New to this round of discussion was one tenet that feminists designated as especially odious: vaginal orgasm. A cluster of popular psychoanalytic texts defined "normal" female sexuality as the ability to experience orgasm exclusively through vaginal stimulation during coitus and, in turn, labeled any preference for clitoral stimulation as a symptom of frigidity, hence neurosis. Kate Millett spoke for many in pronouncing this notion not only "groundless" but one of the best examples of Freud's "rather gross male-supremacist bias." Indeed, it was the Freudian prescription of vaginal orgasm, two critics later noted, that "sparked the contemporary feminist examination of all psychological thought . . . [and drew] the greatest public attention."[13]

Freud himself had never used the objectionable phrase, although feminists concluded that his description of genital transference implied as much. As late as 1933, after nearly a decade of fending off Horney, Freud insisted once again that with "the change to femininity the clitoris should wholly or in part hand over its sensitivity, and at the same time its importance, to the vagina."[14] But on the specific nature of orgasm, Freud wrote virtually nothing.

His followers, however, embroidered freely on the original hypothesis. The distinguished Hungarian analyst Sándor Lorand, publishing in 1939 in the authoritative *International Journal of Psycho-analysis,* outlined a therapeutic procedure to help women overcome vaginal anesthesia. The chief credit, nonetheless, belongs to two refugee analysts who made "vaginal orgasm" a household word in the United States. In a monograph published in 1936, Edward E. Hitschmann, a Vienna-trained analyst loyal to Freud, and Edmund Bergler, who, like Hitschmann, became an expert on homosexuality, defined the "sole criterion" of frigidity in women as "the absence of the vaginal orgasm." Not surprisingly, he estimated that between 70 and 80 percent of all women were frigid. Highly influential within his profession, Bergler restated his thesis in a book designed for a wider audience, *Neurotic Counterfeit-Sex* (1951).[15]

The popularists ran wild with this idea. Lundberg and Farnham specified the primary symptom of derailed femininity as vaginal anesthesia, that is, the preference for orgasm achieved "only from the stimulation of . . . external genitalia" rather than from "the male organ with its pleasure-giving and impregnating capacities." Several mass-marketed "marriage manuals" carried the same message. One such advice book devotes an entire chapter to the "normal orgasm." *The Power of Sexual Surrender* (1959), which sold over a million copies within three years of publication, insists that all sexually mature women gladly relinquish the clitoris to focus their pleasure in "the most important part" of their "sexual equipment." The "clitoridal woman," in contrast, suffers from a pathological form of orgasm as well as identification with men. *The Sexually Adequate Female* (1953, 1966), by Frank S. Caprio, M.D., prescribes "psychiatric assistance" for this malady. Well into the 1960s psychotherapists and authors of advice literature sought to help women to overcome their unhealthy preference for clitoral stimulation. Mass-circulation women's magazines such as the *Ladies' Home Journal* spread this advice via regular columns on "marital problems" and special articles by notable authorities.[16]

That these popularizers succeeded in making vaginal sexuality the norm was testimony, feminists reasoned, to their ability to shape medical as well as public opinion contrary to fact. This contention had considerable merit. Since the turn of the century, leading biologists, psychologists, and physicians had acknowledged the sensitivity of the clitoris and its function in orgasm and, furthermore, had routinely

instructed men to be more attentive to this special part of female anat-   HA !
omy. Realizing that "it takes two persons to make one frigid woman,"
one early advisor developed a set of instructions that became commonplace in many marriage manuals published during the interwar
period. Stressing mutual satisfaction as key to happy marriage, this
writer advised men specifically to refine their techniques in foreplay
involving the manipulation of the clitoris.[17] But, at the very moment
when the readership for books on sexuality began to grow at a fast
rate, psychoanalysts overwrote these interpretations of female sexuality and made the vaginal orgasm, like the "simultaneous orgasm," a
veritable icon.

Nevertheless, despite its prominence in the popular media, the vaginal orgasm enjoyed only an unstable lead. Alfred C. Kinsey stepped
forward to demonstrate that psychoanalysts neither monopolized the
field nor provided the most astute analysis of human sexuality. Kinsey,
who had carved out a profession from the sexology pioneered by
Havelock Ellis, had secured funds to compile sexual histories of a large
sample of white, middle-class Americans. His conclusions were shock-
ing. Kinsey documented the actual frequency of such tabooed behaviors as premarital and extramarital sexual intercourse and homosexual acts. His well-publicized reports, published in paper for mass
consumption, became bestsellers and the literary flagship of the second
sexual revolution.

Kinsey presented evidence that undermined the reigning psychoanalytic theories of female sexuality. After reviewing extensive sexual
histories gathered in standardized interviews with nearly 6,000 white
women, he concluded that these women enjoyed sex as much as men
did, that they responded just as quickly to stimulation if their partner's
technique was adequate, and that their level of desire equaled that of
men. In addition, *Sexual Behavior in the Human Female* (1953) established the insensitivity of the vagina and identified the clitoris as the
site of physical satisfaction in women. "There is considerable evidence," Kinsey concluded, "that most females respond erotically, often
with considerable intensity and immediacy, whenever the clitoris is
tactilely stimulated." The psychoanalytic notion that the ability to
experience a vaginal orgasm marked female sexual maturity, he stated
emphatically, lacked credibility. "It is difficult," he added, "to understand what can be meant by a 'vaginal orgasm.' "[18]

If Kinsey knocked down one pillar in the theory of vaginal orgasm, William H. Masters and Virginia E. Johnson destroyed the remaining structure. Following Kinsey's suggestive leads, the two sex researchers at Washington University in St. Louis planned a comprehensive study of physiological responses to erotic stimulation in both masturbation and coitus. They managed to gather a group of men and women of various ages who under laboratory conditions provided over 10,000 orgasms. The summary of their findings, *The Human Sexual Response* (1966), offers seemingly irrefutable evidence that women experience only one kind of orgasm, regardless of the way it is induced. Masters and Johnson judged the rhythmic muscular contractions in the outer third of the vagina, which they carefully measured, secondary to the response of the clitoris. But women reach this orgasmic plateau, they concluded, through clitoral friction either during masturbation or foreplay or by indirect penile stimulation during coitus. Masters and Johnson, who became veritable media stars in the aftermath of publication, did more than merely confirm Kinsey's findings about the function of the clitoris: they discovered that women, unlike men, enjoy a virtually unlimited capacity for orgasm. So much for the diminished response of the sexually mature woman.[19]

The popular psychoanalytic assumptions about female sexuality, including genital transference, had suffered irreparable damage by the time feminists organized their attack on Freud. Kinsey's refutation of vaginal orgasm temporarily got lost in the totality of his sensational revelations about the range of sexual behavior, but the conclusions drawn a decade later by Masters and Johnson escaped no one. Feminists, then, were far from the cutting edge and added nothing to the well-publicized evidence provided by the famous sexologists. Nevertheless, they compensated for their lack of originality by mercilessly targeting Freud.

Although somewhat misguided and definitely belated, the feminist attack on the vaginal orgasm did not lack for enthusiasm. Susan Lyon, writing in *Ramparts* magazine in 1968, accused Freud of nurturing a "demoniac determination" to "complete the Victorians' repression of feminine eroticism." The Berkeley activist blamed the "enshrined Freudian myth" for the bulk of women's sexual problems.[20] The most incisive critics, while sharing Lyon's anger at Freud, went one step further. They took the compelling evidence provided by the sexologists and showed how it shored up the entire system of sex roles. In sum, unlike Kinsey or Masters and Johnson, these feminists were not satisfied with debunking the myth of the vaginal orgasm. They set themselves to demolish the underlying structure, the contemptible liberal ideology that kept women down.

A short essay by Anne Koedt became the premier polemic on the subject. "The Myth of the Vaginal Orgasm" appeared originally in a small-circulation journal and was soon reprinted in several popular anthologies of feminist writings. Dog-eared copies of the pamphlet edition circulated widely among friends. Feminist writers cited it frequently.[21]

The heart of Koedt's argument, based on the research by Kinsey and Masters and Johnson, constituted a flat denial and virtual condemnation of vaginal orgasm. Sexual arousal might involve any part of the body—or might depend entirely on fantasy—but orgasm occurred only in the clitoris. Although women might experience various degrees of intensity or diffusion of sexual climax, she added, everything centered in the clitoris. How could the vagina, which needs no anesthesia during routine surgery, be the site of erotogenic release? The answer, to her, was obvious. The vaginal orgasm was a myth invented by Freud and perpetuated by other men to ensure the "best physical stimulant for the penis."

Koedt thus supplied the political framework for the discussion. Men purposefully try to keep women ignorant of their sexuality, she asserted, and for good reason. If women knew the truth about the clitoris, they might realize that men were sexually expendable. "The recognition of clitoral orgasm as fact," Koedt suggested gleefully, "would threaten the heterosexual *institution*."[22]

In undermining the myth of the vaginal orgasm, feminists like Koedt envisioned themselves one step closer to liberation. "Knowledge about the clitoris . . . along with increasing acceptability and openness of discussion around masturbation, lesbianism, and other critical issues," the neurophysiologist and long-time political activist Ruth Bleier averred, "have greatly advanced the liberation of women's sexual pleasure from mere service to men's sexuality, from male standards and values in sexual practices, and from phallocentrism." As another writer put it, sexual liberation marked "a beginning."[23]

The attack on the vaginal organism began, then, as a spirited campaign for female sexual autonomy. The Boston Women's Health Book Collective endorsed masturbation as "the first, easiest, and most convenient way to experiment with your body." Even the politically moderate Alice Rossi criticized those aspects of Freudian theory that projected women as sexually reliant on men. The prominent sociologist likewise recommended masturbation as an alternative to heterosexual intercourse, describing the practice as "different" but "not necessarily less gratifying." Breaking with total dependence on men also went hand-in-hand, she added, with finding fulfillment even in nursing, through the genital stimulation afforded by the baby's sucking. Alix Kates Shulman claimed that these arguments collectively exposed the lie behind the popular idea that the penis and vagina are the primary sex organs. The combination of these organs serves in the reproduction of the species and in producing orgasmic pleasure for men, she explained, but "very rarely do the two together make female orgasms." Shulman advised: "Think clitoris."[24]

However, in attacking the vaginal orgasm, feminists raised questions that extended far beyond the erotic realm. They affirmed woman's absolute right to sexual pleasure. But they also charted the tenets of a *radical feminism* that sought to overturn—in a phrase by Koedt that clearly echoes Talcott Parsons—the entire "male-female role system." Millett, in *Sexual Politics,* eloquently elaborates this argument, insisting that women's oppression originates in men's sexual power over women, takes institutional form through the political economy of patriarchy, and spawns an ideology that inflates the differences between men and women. In defending clitoral sexuality, these feminists were affirming a woman's right to live free of male domination and to control all aspects of her life. Or, as the popular radical feminist slogan blasted from numerous posters, t-shirts, and greeting cards: "A woman needs a man like a fish needs a bicycle."[25]

These two purposes, literal and metaphorical, came together in the radical feminist celebration of lesbian sexuality. Lesbians not only embrace the clitoris as the primary site of female sexuality, Koedt stated, but they lead the way by staking out a relationship independent of men. Lesbianism, she insisted, chips away at the foundation of sexism and as such is a central component of the quest for women's liberation. Following out this symbolic logic, Jill Johnson declared that "a true political revolution" would not occur until "all women are lesbians." Or, as the timely slogan put it: "Feminism is the theory; lesbianism is the practice."[26]

In attacking the vaginal orgasm, radical feminists were actually confronting the entire legacy of American ego psychology, particularly its sociobiological advocacy of highly differentiated sex roles. They envisioned themselves "all crawling out of femininity," as Koedt put it, "into a new sense of *personhood*." Indeed, radical feminists located the primary obstacle to social equality precisely in the reproductive biology that indelibly marked woman as different from man. They therefore determined to snap the link between woman's unique capacity for maternity and the prevailing prescription for the domestic role. Lucy Komisar thus asked, *contra* Farnham, why "a uterus uniquely qualifies a woman to wield dust mops and wash dishes." But radical feminists also proposed dramatic solutions. In one of the most provocative treatises of the era, Firestone took a giant step further, arguing for the transformation of reproduction itself. *The Dialectic of Sex: The Case of Feminist Revolution* (1971) names the debilitating state of pregnancy and childbirth as the source of women's subjection to men and, consequently, the foundation for the entire sex-role system. Placing her faith in the promise of technology, Firestone proposed a dramatic alternative: a method of artificial reproduction to eradicate both childbearing and the biological family. A considerable number of feminists shared her determination, if not her strategy, to burst apart the connection between "woman" and "motherhood."[27]

Radical feminists spoke directly against the principles of ego psychology that had reigned since midcentury. Thus one writer explained that radical feminism begins "with the assumption of the absolute equality of men and women notwithstanding biological differences. Humanness and not anatomy is the irreducible component that both men and women share." Firestone, a founder of New York Radical Women and a close associate of co-members Millett and Koedt, shared this assumption. She projected an androgynous future, a time when the differences between the sexes would play no role in human consciousness. Radical feminists advocated, in short, the eradication of all markers of sexual difference: as Firestone put it, an equalitarian future when "genital differences between human beings no longer matter culturally."[28]

Contemporary psychoanalysts could not enjoy the simple luxury of this resolution. Nor could they ignore the challenge presented by these critics. If Freud had once fended off criticism by claiming that the "sexual life of the adult woman is a 'dark continent' for psychology," his successors stood before a mountain of new evidence and, equally important, compelling counter-arguments.[29]

Psychoanalysts Return to the "Dark Continent"

Feminists struck at a portentous moment, just as the psychoanalytic profession was undergoing, as one analyst put it, its own "identity crisis." The therapeutic side flourished, although mainly as a subfield of psychiatry. The number of trained analysts, approximately 1,000 at the end of World War II, had increased nearly tenfold by the onset of the women's liberation movement. As a provider of well-paying vocations, psychoanalysis prospered; as an endeavor to understand and interpret the human condition, American theory faltered. At the same time, adjacent professions such as clinical psychology and psychiatric social work were expanding at an even faster combined rate. "It comes as a distinct surprise that psychoanalysts, despite years of endeavor," Reuben Fine noted in 1979, "have been unable to define their own field with precision." A highly variegated field, contemporary psychoanalysis had begun to fall from the grace it enjoyed at midcentury and, according to many observers, it lacked vitality.[30]

Feminists actually dovetailed with the experts in providing an inventory of shortcomings. In the mass-marketed *Uses and Abuses of Psychology* (1953), H. J. Eysenck had disparaged the therapeutic claims of psychoanalysis; and in 1958 the philosopher Sidney Hook had organized a major symposium to assess its scientific status. One scholar reviewed the voluminous faultfinding literature produced during this period and estimated that Freudian theory outdistanced every other branch of psychology in terms of the number of times appraised and found wanting as a legitimate science. This ruinous evidence beguiled feminists: it proved that Freud had been both "vicious towards women" and, the psychologist Naomi Weisstein declared, "*wrong*, not just about women, but about humans in general."[31]

These complaints against psychoanalysis coincided with a major antipsychiatric revolt that peaked in the late 1960s. Inspired by the biting commentary of Thomas Szasz, David Cooper, and R. D. Laing, an anti-establishment movement formed to challenge the political assumptions underlying concepts of mental health and illness. In the United States psychotherapists centered in Berkeley, Cambridge, Chicago, New York, and New Haven pledged themselves to experiment with new forms of clinical practice. The movement also encompassed organizations devoted to mental patients' rights, such as the Insane Liberation Front of Portland, Oregon, which challenged involuntary commitment practices and the use of restraints, drugs, and surgical procedures, and waged legal battles to restore patients' civil rights. In 1970 the magazine *Radical Therapist* began a ten-year publication run, its slogan expressing the dissenting notion that "therapy means change not adjustment." The *Radical Therapist* also endorsed the radical feminist slogan coined by Carol Hanisch, "The Personal Is Political." As Hanisch so aptly summed up, "Women are messed over, not messed up!"[32]

These discordant currents soon flowed into even the most orthodox psychoanalytic preserves. The number of women psychoanalysts had begun to grow in the 1960s, mirroring the overall increase in the number of women working outside the home. By 1970 not just antipsychiatry activists but feminists themselves were making their cases within the ranks of the major professional associations. A sizable number were now ready to break with the principles of ego psychology and to advocate greater opportunities for women across the board. In response, several leading psychoanalysts publicly endorsed the Equal Rights Amendment and called for an end to the double standard in sexual morality. Others reacted to the pressure of events by rallying their defenses.

A small movement advanced to salvage Freud's reputation from the feminist assault. Counter-arguments included the anemic rebuttal that, after all, Freud himself had never claimed to know the whole score; to the contrary, he had repeatedly qualified his conclusions, insisting always that he "was working on a theory, not sharing a revealed truth." At the other extreme was the stubborn insistence that Freud's formulations, minor shortcomings aside, were nothing less than "revolutionary." The most condescending respondents chastised feminists for failing to appreciate Freud's insight into female desire, including the ill consequences of sexual repression. One writer went so far as to describe Freud's "gifts to women" as "greater than women yet know how to use."[33]

In general, though, psychoanalysts responded conscientiously to the feminist challenge. The vast majority had already come to terms with new scientific evidence provided by Kinsey and Masters and Johnson and were therefore mainly perplexed by the misconstrued assault on their professional integrity. They were eager to put themselves in good standing. Not a few psychoanalysts matched feminists in their enthusiasm to return to the original problem. Given Freud's place in history, it was only proper, they believed, that his successors preserve the intimate association between psychoanalysis and sexuality and refine their theories in the face of new evidence.

Nevertheless, psychoanalysts soon confronted the politics just below the surface of discussions. It was soon clear to everyone that there was far more at stake than merely a difference of opinion about the nature of the female sexual response. Psychoanalysts were willing to grapple with the larger implications. But what was truly surprising was the way the ranks divided.

The orthodox American Psychoanalytic Association (APA) had replied defiantly to the reports by Kinsey and Masters and Johnson by initiating a major review of Freud's theories of female sexuality. A few members denounced Kinsey's *Sexual Behavior in the Human Female* when it appeared in 1953. Not surprisingly, Edmund Bergler, who had promoted the concept of vaginal orgasm, rushed ahead with a full rebuttal. Enlisting the aid of a prominent gynecologist, he quickly produced *Kinsey's Myth of Female Sexuality: The Medical Facts* (1954) and refused to budge from his original position. A decade later the tide had clearly turned. So much appeared to be changing in both the scientific and social realms that no practicing analyst could afford to be so theoretically rigid. Henrik M. Ruitenbeek, a prolific writer and practicing analyst, signaled this major shift in tenor. He collected from his colleagues a handful of essays on female sexuality, attributing the timeliness of his project to the contemporary rebellion of women against male domination. At the same time, several professional societies arranged symposia on the topic, and the major journals published scores of articles incorporating the new scientific research. After a hiatus of nearly three decades, American psychoanalysts had begun to reexamine Freud's original formulations on female psychosexual development.[34]

Well in advance of the women's liberation movement, leading members of the APA had already reconsidered Freud's theory of genital transference. At the 1960 annual meeting Helene Deutsch opened the session on frigidity by unexpectedly asking whether the vagina had been designed for sexual pleasure. She noted its function in reproduction but went on to speculate that perhaps, after all, it was the "biological destiny" of the clitoris to serve as the principal sexual organ in woman. This dramatic recantation by a major architect of the reigning theory guaranteed a rejoinder. Burness E. Moore, future president of the APA, met Deutsch halfway. "What is probably important," he conceded, "is not the presence or absence of sensitivity but the cathexis of the organ as the site of erotic satisfaction." The female orgasmic experience depended, in other words, on the *psychic* representation of the vagina.[35]

In 1966 this equivocation came to an abrupt end when Mary Jane Sherfey (1933–1983) published an article that not only prefigured the radical feminist critique but came to an astounding conclusion. "The Nature and Evolution of Female Sexuality in Relation to Psychoanalytic Theory," which appeared in the *Journal of the American Psychoanalytic Association,* certified the findings of Kinsey and Masters and Johnson by designating the clitoris the central factor in the female sexual response. The New York psychiatrist went a giant step further. Utilizing embryological and primatological data, she speculated that what had once been a cyclical sexual response in both primates and women had evolved "to the paradoxical state of sexual insatiation in the presence of utmost sexual satiation." Simply put, contrary to the accepted Freudian emphasis on passivity, female desire is not only extraordinarily powerful but limitless.

Although Sherfey cautioned that she did not intend to "blow away" but merely to "transform" Freud's hypotheses, she in fact virtually set them on their head: it is not male lust but female desire that demands control. Like Freud, she located the origins of civilization in sexual repression, but with a major distinction. Whereas Freud focused on the taboo against maternal incest, the original Oedipus complex, Sherfey concerned herself with containment of female passion. "The rise of modern civilization . . . was," she wrote, "contingent on the suppression of the inordinate cyclic sexual drive of women." The epochal shift from matriarchy to patriarchy was certainly detrimental to female erotic pleasure, she affirmed, but unfortunately for women it was necessary for social evolution.[36]

Sherfey concluded on a boldly feminist note. She predicted a major change in social organization that would allow female sexuality to regain some—by no means all!—of its original power. Noting that each baby girl still carries a capacity for as many as perhaps fifty orgasms per hour, she encouraged women to anticipate a sexually rosier future. "Theoretically," she averred, "a woman could go on having orgasms indefinitely if physical exhaustion did not intervene."[37]

The publication of Sherfey's provocative essay encouraged members of the APA to take a stand. When the *Journal of the American Psychoanalytic Association* devoted an entire subsequent issue to replies, few writers endorsed all her conclusions. The majority, however, praised her contribution. Even the most intractable could no longer hold out against the primacy of the clitoris. The consensus seemed to be, as the Londoner W. H. Gillespie, a long-standing member of the International Psycho-analytic Association, put it: "we must agree that an orgasm is an orgasm."[38]

Even the most orthodox practitioners defied probability and yielded surprisingly easily. Few would go as far as Sherfey. She not only popularized her ideas in the *New York Times* but allowed excerpts of her tantalizing essay to be reprinted in Robin Morgan's landmark radical feminist anthology, *Sisterhood Is Powerful* (1970). Although more circumspect, the majority willingly conceded the identity of the sexual responses of men and women.[39]

Members of the American Academy of Psychoanalysis could not agree with this conclusion. The legatees of Horney, Thompson, and Sullivan not only had survived many factional squabbles but now appeared eager to resume their roles as social critics and to address the questions stemming from the social ferment of the late 1960s. Indeed, the American Academy of Psychoanalysis, which claimed 600 members, had its finger on the pulse of American politics. While the annual meetings of the APA featured papers on such technical subjects as "Xerostomia: The Dry Mouth Syndrome," the revisionist society sponsored sessions on "Psychoanalysis and Dissent," including papers on the psychodynamics of the long-time socialist Norman Thomas and civil rights workers.[40] On the question of vaginal orgasm, however, the ties of tradition proved stronger than the appeal of modern science.

The resistance of the American Academy is all the more poignant when measured against its bold endorsement of women's liberation. The organization had determinedly overcome the misogyny that plagued its ranks during the 1950s and now extended a warm welcome to feminists. Several prominent members even endorsed consciousness-raising techniques over conventional forms of psychotherapy. Writing in *Psychiatry,* the journal founded by Sullivan, one analyst suggested that self-esteem accrued more rapidly through participation in the women's liberation movement than through conventional psychotherapy. Others echoed Friedan to encourage women to think of their own emotional needs apart from childbearing and domesticity. No one challenged the "femininity" of feminists, as Freud had done, or as Irving Howe did at the appearance of Millett's *Sexual Politics.* To the contrary, a noted scholar rushed into print an essay denouncing the popular image of the feminist as "a sexually frustrated, physically and verbally aggressive, socially unsuccessful person whose choice of participation in the Women's Movement reflects her frustrations and neurotic ambitions." A self-described "middle-aged white male professional" went so far as to thank the women's liberation movement for teaching him "much later in life what should have been completely evident right from the beginning."[41] *What most think of*

As long-time critics of Freud, these psychoanalysts easily located points of convergence with feminists. The concept of penis envy infuriated everyone. What could be more familiar to descendants of Horney than the charge levied anew by Kate Millett, that Freud confused "biology and culture, anatomy and status"? Several analysts readily affirmed feminists' impression that Freud's theories better served to oppress than to liberate women. Others, more reserved, merely acknowledged "blind spots" in his works.[42] *Was his intent to suppress women?*

On the question of vaginal orgasm, though, there was no easy resolution. Judd Marmor, who presided over the American Academy in the 1960s, had been one of the first psychoanalysts to define clitoral sexuality as "normal" in adult women. As early as 1952 he drew on the new scientific research to question the validity of genital transference. He decided that clitoral sensitivity continued throughout a woman's active sexual life. In light of Sherfey's "definitive" argument, Marmor could only reaffirm his earlier opinion. His colleague Leon Salzman similarly acknowledged the importance of Sherfey's "highly informative" study underscoring woman's capacity for multiple orgasms as well as the functional role of the clitoris in this remarkable phenomenon. He summed up the American Academy's line: "Orgasm in the male and the female is identical biologically."[43]

Others in the ranks strongly disagreed with this assessment. The most resistant to this line were women analysts who treasured the legacy of Horney and Thompson. Like their colleagues, they hailed the women's liberation movement and applauded the new tenor within the American Academy. Although they shared feminists' reservations about Freud, they could not view the vaginal orgasm as a myth that oppressed women.

A good deal of their reluctance could be traced to scholarly tradition. The original case against Freud's phallocentrism had concentrated, they knew, on his notion of penis envy as well as the genital transference it allegedly triggered. Jones, Klein, and Müller had come back at Freud not by asserting the persistence of clitoral sexuality but instead by presenting ample evidence to argue for the primacy of vaginal sensations from infancy. Horney had made vaginal sexuality the centerpiece of her case against Freud's depiction of femininity as a secondary formation.

Horney never waged a war for the clitoris. She resented both Abraham's infelicitous remarks about woman's deficiency in external genitals and Deutsch's equally demeaning caricature of the clitoris as a poor substitute for a penis. She objected even more forcefully to Freud's notion of genital transference, arguing that female sexuality originated in, and remained cathected to, the vagina. Female sexuality, in her estimation, required no external conditioning factor, least of all penis envy. This is not to say that Horney failed to recognize the function of the clitoris in enhancing female desire and in providing pleasure. But reverence for woman's reproductive capacity, as symbolized by the vagina, encouraged her to prize the anatomical structures that marked woman as different from man. In the 1930s, at the peak of her culturalism, she dramatically cast off all these notions and, like other neo-Freudians, also abandoned the whole discussion of sexuality. Unfortunately for her successors, she neither repudiated nor even revised her early statements on female sexuality.

Those psychoanalysts loyal to Horney's legacy were left in a quandary. While they shared her enduring dedication to female self-esteem, they could not find in her scholarly corpus the means to overthrow the myth of the vaginal orgasm. Instead, they revived her earliest formulations on female sexuality, written in the 1920s, and proceeded to interpret clitoral sexuality as an insult to womanhood, a devaluation of femininity. They therefore found themselves, uncharacteristically and despite their own feminist intentions, in the political backwater in an untimely defense of the vagina.

Ruth Moulton (1915–), an affiliate of the William Alanson White Institute, offers a case in point. Even after reviewing the works by Masters and Johnson and Sherfey, she still could not give up the vagina as a principal site of female sexuality. She had to admit, given the new evidence, that it was unlikely that the clitoris faded out of the sexual picture at adulthood. Nevertheless, she insisted that the continuing role of the clitoris did not preclude vaginal or even uterine sensations. The best she could do was to define the clitoris and vagina as complementary structures, both responsible for producing female orgasm. Intensity might vary, Moulton added, but discrepancies resulted from the situation as a whole rather than the superior function of one or the other genital organ.[44]

Natalie Shainess (1915–), who had trained with Clara Thompson at the William Alanson White Institute and later joined its teaching faculty, proved even more recalcitrant. In 1966 she contributed to the American Academy's decennial edition of *Science and Psychoanalysis,* a timely anthology on the sexuality of women. Like her colleagues, she saw no reason to be content with Freudian theory and welcomed the novel data supplied by disciplines outside psychoanalysis. This new evidence, she hoped, would finally demolish the Freudian depiction of female sexuality as deficient and functional only as a preparatory step to reproduction. The recent scientific research demonstrated beyond a doubt, Shainess said enthusiastically, women's capacity for orgasm for its own sake.

Yet Shainess, who believed Freud's metapsychology impeded women from realizing their potential, did not rush into the camp of the so-called militant clitorists. Clitoral orgasms occurred, she admitted, but they were not only different from but grossly inferior to those involving the entire introital area. Shainess sketched a hierarchy of responses, ranging from frigidity to "authentic orgasmic response," a label which she preferred to "vaginal." The clitoral orgasm stood just above frigidity but below "missed." Even the much-touted "multiple" orgasm fell short of Shainess's "authentic."[45]

Several years later, at a meeting of the Society of Medical Psychoanalysts, Shainess updated her argument in light of the now voluminous literature on "the great orgasm debate." This time the sex researchers Masters and Johnson as well as "militant feminists" like Anne Koedt served as foils. Noting, too, that men outnumbered women in this debate, Shainess insinuated that the concept of multiple orgasm might serve mainly to "feed male fantasy of endless indulgent acceptance by women." All these factors led her to believe that the clitoral orgasm represented "a questionable honor and capacity in women, of unproven validity." Shainess further disparaged "manual clitoral fiddling" as "push-button sex, and sex fixated upon passivity, sex deprived of spontaneity."

Once again Shainess extolled the allegedly superior "authentic orgasmic response," although her description proved neither clear nor compelling. She resorted to poetic imagery, ironically, turning to men for inspiration. D. H. Lawrence and Robert Browning, according to Shainess, shared with Freud "great insight into feminine response" and fostered her own understanding of the sexually fulfilled woman:

> The woman who experiences authentic orgasmic response needs no reassurance, has no doubts. Actively participant, involved in the "sexual dialogue," but not apart and intellectualizing, nor obsessively ruminating, nor fantasying special conditions, nor anxiety-ridden, nor narcissistically "on stage," nor competing with her partner—she feels her passion grow, dares to respond in a way that increasingly heightens her sensations, becomes aware of a time when an almost automatic rhythmic movement takes over, and experiences the full flood of release, with its various central nervous system changes; and then the stillness, with its backwash of gratitude and appreciation of the partner—the tenderness in the wake of the storm. She needs no reassurance about whether her orgasm is real, superior, or anything else. She knows, because in this sexual area she is completely auton-omous.[46]

The final phrase is especially salient: it retains Horney's original con-tention that femininity carries its own value and requires no confirmation—even sexual—from man.

Shainess was not alone in her professed loyalty to Horney. To the contrary, the rise of the women's liberation movement had sparked a Horney mini-revival. In 1967 the Association for the Advancement of Psychoanalysis, the organization founded by Horney, sponsored the publication of a collection of her early essays on femininity and female sexuality. Previously locked away in small-circulation professional journals, the early Horney canon now became readily available in English and in an inexpensive paper edition. A whole new generation gained access to a psychoanalytic view of female sexuality that emphasizes its unique character and reproductive function.

Psychoanalysts like Shainess clearly appreciated the larger meanings embedded in sexual metaphors. Unlike radical feminists, they celebrated a view of female sexuality that expresses woman's difference from man. As the analyst Ann Ruth Turkel complained, the "push of women's liberation has been to make women more like men" when the true goal should be to encourage women "to become more like themselves." Horney, perennial symbol of resistance to Freudian phallocentrism, now inspired allegiance to what she herself had ultimately rejected.[47]

Nevertheless, and despite the irony of this turn of events, the profession had begun to disavow the misogyny that had prevailed at mid-century. Psychoanalysts of various persuasions had successfully cut the nexus between sexuality and sex roles. Although they might disagree on the kind of orgasm that typified the "normal" female sexual response, no one tried to establish a basis in biology to limit woman's destiny to domesticity. The women who defended Horney's legacy might resist the pull of the androgynous future promised by radical feminists, but they just as adamantly refused to equate a vagina with a dishmop.

The great orgasm debate, despite its initial intensity, quickly subsided. Unlike Sherfey's prognosis, its capacity proved surprisingly limited, an outcome that spared the reputations of Horney's descendants. Like Horney herself, they preferred to move on to other matters. Shainess indicated that she had all along considered the emphasis on orgasm a liability, a diversion from more important questions concerning feminine identity. Jean Baker Miller, a member of the American Academy, pulled together an anthology of writings to "dispel myths and explore realities." Reprinting essays by Horney as well as Sherfey, Marmor, and Moulton, Miller actually apologized for the "undue emphasis" on sexuality. Sounding a lot like her predecessor, she hoped such discussions would not deflect the reader's attention away from women "as total people."[48]

Psychoanalysts of various affiliations apparently agreed with Miller and soon put aside the whole matter of female sexuality. A few researchers persisted. One psychiatrist surveyed a small number of women college students and nonstudents, and interpreted the former's slightly greater preference for clitoral stimulation as a sign of their greater "masculinity," that is, as moderate support for Freud's hypothesis. A mini-revival in the 1980s accompanied revelations concerning the Grafenberg stimulation spot, that infamous "G" spot allegedly located on the anterior vaginal wall which, upon tactile stimulation, may lead to not only orgasm but female ejaculation.[49] For the most part, psychoanalysts preferred to target problems more central to current issues in theory and therapy. No prestigious professional really cared (or still believed) deeply enough to defend precepts so dear to the master and central to his view of civilization at large.

Just as Horney had let the matter drop in the late 1930s, psychoanalysts forty years later quickly moved on. Psychoanalysis was finally becoming, the scholar Roy Schafer dramatically announced, "the study of the whole person developing and living in a complex world." The implications of this tribute were clear. As Robert J. Stoller, a Los Angeles psychoanalyst and professor of psychiatry at UCLA, warned his colleagues, orgasmic response offers no measure of the total personality. He advised his colleagues to turn to more fruitful topics.[50]

Across the ocean the British feminist Juliet Mitchell was making a compatible plea. In *Woman's Estate*, published in the United States in 1973, she intended to demonstrate that feminism and psychoanalysis actually share a common purpose, that is, to map the "land where sexual distinction originates" in order to explain "how women become women." Even in criticizing Freud, Firestone had offered a similar observation. "Freudianism and Feminism are made of the same stuff," she had written, in that both are concerned with the dynamics of power within the family. It would be some time before a sizable number of Mitchell's American peers would appreciate this insight and affirm her contention that "psychoanalysis is not a recommendation *for* a patriarchal society, but an analysis *of* one."[51] But it was truly just a matter of time.

Freud, Reviled and Revived

Freud as icon, his personality the source of psychoanalytic misogyny, remained a tantalizing subject. But despite their hostility, even his most severe critics revealed just how comfortable they were with the very logic they reviled. Feminists were no exception. Like most educated Americans, they had yielded to the sweeping influence of psychoanalysis as an explanatory philosophy. Even as they debunked Freudian notions of female sexuality, feminists moved gradually toward a new partnership.

It was none other than the venerable Margaret Mead who by the early 1970s had recognized the futility of the obsession with Freud's theory of female sexuality. Initially irritated by what she took to be feminist hyperbole, she had set herself to reread Freud's three major essays on female psychosexual development. She was shocked. "It is only too true that the militant feminists have a case against Freud," she observed, "but not the case they thought they had: that it is only his ideas about penis envy and the normality of the vaginal orgasm that have permeated and contaminated our society." Far more troubling, Mead insisted, was the totality of Freud's derogatory attitude toward women.[52]

Actually, most feminists would have agreed with Mead. The majority viewed Freud's theory of female sexuality as merely the most expressive component of a bounding misogyny. Indeed, many psychoanalysts also endorsed this proposition.

For their part, psychoanalysts wanted feminists to understand that all that is psychoanalytic is not Freudian. Not only did feminists have "an incomplete grasp" of Freud's theories, one psychoanalyst complained, but they disclosed "an almost total ignorance and disinterest" in contemporary psychoanalysis.[53] Very much like the popular media that had for generations reduced psychoanalytic complexity to the accents of the bearded Viennese analyst, feminists regularly credited Freud even for concepts alien to his system. If contemporary psychoanalysts preferred to consign Freudian misogyny to ancient history, feminists had closed their eyes to the entire development of American psychoanalysis from its neo-Freudian roots to its more recent efflorescence as ego psychology. Psychoanalysts therefore flaunted their astonishment that anyone would waste time complaining about penis envy. As one impatient observer commented, in this respect feminists were only "beating a dead horse."[54]

Feminists, however, were not so far out of step with the march of psychoanalysis. In making their complaint against Freud, they replayed the doctrinal history of psychoanalysis in the United States. Much like contemporary psychoanalysts themselves, they moved effortlessly between Culture and Personality theory and ego psychology to arrive at a credible explanation of Freud's personal misogyny. Psychoanalysts and feminists proved equally relentless in "psychoanalyzing" Freud and, along the way, turning up malicious maternal influences.

Why was Freud such a sexist? Like their predecessors who searched for the origins of the personality flaws of their Japanese and German enemies, feminists looked for cultural clues, first, in Freud's Victorian background. In 1950 Clara Thompson had produced a signal essay describing Freud as "a male quite ready to subscribe to the theory of male superiority prevalent in the culture," an overview that appealed to the feminist editor who chose to republish it twenty years later in a new anthology. Both Friedan and Figes revived this popular argument, dismissing Freud as a mere "child of his own times." Even the psychoanalyst Ruth Moulton attributed Freud's "phallocentric point of view" to his "highly patriarchal Victorian culture."[55]

Other critics were unwilling to cede this much ground. Millett noted that the bulk of Freud's essays on femininity appeared in the early twentieth century amid a sexual revolution and the rise of feminism. Freud shaped his arguments directly in response to these challenges and, she emphasized, "conceded nothing." Firestone agreed, identifying Freudianism as an ideological backlash to the first stirring of women's emancipation. These critics refused to depict Freud's misogyny as a blind spot attributable to the fading Victorian culture. As Erich Fromm had observed as early as 1959, Freud was not "an average man" but a rebel "against some of the most deeply ingrained prejudices."[56]

If Freud should have known better, perhaps his patients—neurotic but in other ways ordinary middle-class women—communicated the conventional attitudes that marked his theories. Thompson had offered this argument in 1941, writing that Freud's *Studies on Hysteria*, which dated from the 1890s, was based on descriptions of women "with ambitions and prospects very different from those found in the average psychoanalytic patient of today." These women did present neurotic symptoms, Thompson explained, including sexual inhibition, and Freud based his theories of femininity on these cases, conflating the "normal" and the psychopathic. "The real tragedy of Freudian psychology," Millett later affirmed, "is that its fallacious interpretations of feminine character were based upon clinical observations of great validity." Most feminist writers placed the onus squarely on Freud. His descriptions of hysteria or neurosis reflected, they insisted, his own personality and prejudices. Hannah Lerman, cofounder of the Feminist Therapy Institute, dismissed the possibility of patient responsibility. Freud's theories, she concluded, incorporated "his unanalyzed and unresolved view about sex and women." Freud, Lerman added, "seems to have indeed been his primary patient."[57]

Scrutiny of Freud's clinical practice yielded the most damaging evidence for his personal culpability. In 1977 Florence Rush published a lengthy exposé accusing Freud of altering his theories to cover up actual instances of child abuse. Rush noted that early in his career Freud heard so many reports of sexual molestation from his hysterical female patients that he identified a direct connection between childhood sexual abuse and adult neurosis; by 1896 Freud had reversed his interpretation, claiming that this "memory" of being seduced by the father was, after all, a fantasy typical of the Oedipus complex in women. Freud, Rush further contended, intentionally altered his later case studies to rid them of evidence of paternal sexual abuse. Freud "cautioned the world never to overestimate the importance of seduction," Rush wrote, "and the world listened to Freud and paid little heed to the sexual abuse of children." Although Rush concluded by exonerating Freud of personal responsibility, she insisted that his "theories, surrounded by scientific aura, allowed for the suppression and concealment of the sexual exploitation of the female child."[58]

If not shaped directly by the dominant culture of his time or indirectly by his patients, where did Freud's retrograde notion of femininity originate? Feminists constructed a credible answer via the technique of psychoanalysis itself or, more precisely, by the analytical procedures developed by his successors. Unwittingly, they had absorbed aspects of the interpersonal psychology advanced by the neo-Freudians and developed further by ego psychologists. Freud was, Ellen Frankfort contended in *Vaginal Politics* (1972), "the product of a repressed Victorian upbringing and an authoritarian education."[59] And the primary responsibility lay, a surprising number of feminists concluded, with Amalie Freud, Sigmund's own mother.

The psychodynamics of Freud's childhood proved the centerpiece of commentary. Friedan profiled his parents' personalities and reasoned that Freud developed the concept of the Oedipus complex from his own childhood experiences. Of course, Freud admitted as much. But unlike Freud, who dwelt on his own reactions, Friedan flagged the behavior of Amalie Freud. She described Freud's mother as overindulgent, his father as a source of jealousy, and interpreted Freud's theories as a reflection of his "extraordinary" attachment to his mother and the guilt and hostility it provoked.[60]

Feminists had to dig deep to re-create Freud's relationship with his mother but eventually struck gold. Freud himself had supplied only a few hints, mainly fragments reported in the analysis of his own dreams. But such evidence was far from trivial; it constituted one of the basic building blocks of his theories. "I always find it uncanny," he noted in 1882, "when I can't understand someone in terms of myself." Freud therefore attached considerable significance to one revelation in particular, his very early childhood memory of glimpsing his naked mother in the close sleeping quarters of an overnight train from Leipzig to Vienna. Self-analysis disclosed, Freud later wrote to his colleague Wilhelm Fleiss, that his "libido toward *matrem* was awakened."[61]

As early as 1935 Freud's official biographer, Ernest Jones, had underscored Freud's libidinous desire for his mother, claiming that his reticence in discussing his personal life with even his closest confidants stemmed from his strong motive "for concealing some important phase of his development . . . his deep love for his mother." Despite the significance of this insight, Freud fixated on his feelings toward his father, a logical course given his stress on the Oedipus complex and castration anxiety. It was his father's death in 1896 and the emotional turmoil it caused that facilitated, Freud claimed, the "return of the repressed," allowing him to recognize and understand his hostility in oedipal terms. Freud did not, however, attach much meaning to his parents' behavior toward him, their childrearing practices or attitudes. Consistent with his theoretical framework, he centered on his own libidinal drives.[62]

It was the neo-Freudians who first focused on Amalie Freud's behavior toward her son. In *Sigmund Freud's Mission* (1959), Fromm had proposed that an understanding of the determinants of "any man's character must begin with his relatedness to his mother." Unfortunately, he continued, Freud left very little information about his mother, only accounts of two dreams about her. Still, this fact itself, Fromm speculated, indicated a suppressed yet intense attachment. Sigmund was Amalie's firstborn son, her lifelong favorite; she spoiled and imbued him with self-confidence and at the same time encouraged a fateful dependency. Here, in Amalie's maternal possessiveness, Fromm explained, is the root of Freud's own neurosis and authoritarian personality. Judith Bernays Heller, Freud's niece, confirmed this reading, recalling her grandmother as a woman with "a volatile temperament," selfish, very demanding toward her children, and always insistent on getting her own way.[63]

Finally, analysis of Freud

Lucy Freeman and Herbert S. Strean, in *Freud and Women* (1981), enshrined this characterization of Freud's mother as a vain and self-centered woman and the dominating influence in Freud's early life. A young mother still in her early twenties, Amalie doted on her "golden Sigi." She apparently believed a peasant woman's prophecy that her son was destined for greatness, and she determined to secure this fate. A German writer similarly contended that "Amalie was not a giving mother figure but one who loved her son demandingly and selfishly." She appeared to Freud, this writer added, "a 'masculine' woman in that sense, i.e., one who wanted to have her unfulfilled ambitions achieved by her son." Despite her exceptional devotion, Freeman and Strean alleged, Amalie aroused jealousy by giving birth so frequently during Freud's formative years. Made insecure by the arrival of siblings, Freud raged at his mother and came to resent his five younger sisters. Although unconscious of these feelings, Freud displaced his grievances onto other women. "Unconsciously," they concluded, "Freud was, in all likelihood, alluding to the major tyrant in his life —his mother. She was a beloved tyrant, but a tyrant nevertheless."[64]

This particular study of Momism expanded as another cultural factor came into play. Friedan situated Freud squarely in "that Jewish culture in which men said the daily prayer: 'I thank Thee, Lord, that Thou hast not created me a woman,' and women prayed in submission: 'I thank Thee, Lord, that Thou has created me according to Thy Will.'" Friedan and others also described Freud's mother in stereotypical terms, as a possessive woman who, believing in the special destiny of her firstborn son, pushed him excessively to succeed and at the same time spoiled him. Amalie Freud was, according to Paul Roazen, a "classic Jewish matriarch." As a consequence Freud grew to maturity with an inflated sense of his own importance and in turn expected all women to acknowledge masculine preeminence. Not the quintessential Victorian, Freud appears here like Portnoy or the thousand other Jewish boys of satirical literature and film, overwhelmed and subsequently haunted by his mother's smothering affections.[65]

Freud himself, and later Ernest Jones, had commented on the relationship between Judaism and psychoanalysis, although not in terms of its impact on his theories of femininity. Other analysts easily made the connection. Maryse Choisy, president of the Association for Applied Psychoanalysis, not only analyzed the "castrating and important personality" of Freud's mother but his "gentle," middle-class Jewish father. Writing in the early 1960s, Choisy reasoned that Freud resented his father for his weakness and easily usurped the role as family patriarch. Feminist writers played out this theme. As late as 1987 the British analyst Estelle Roith produced a major critical study of Freud's personality and sexual theories from the perspective of Jewish influences.[66]

Freud's relationship with his domineering Jewish mother, feminists contended, established the pattern for his adult attitudes toward women, including his wife, Martha Bernays. Freud provided ample evidence in the nine hundred letters written during the four years of his engagement (1882–1886), and in later life he discussed with his closest colleagues some intimate details of his marriage. Freud revealed himself, feminists pointed out, to be very conventional, indeed backward and even sexually repressed. In reading Freud's letters to Bernays, Friedan found the "patronizing sound of Torvald in A Doll's House, scolding Nora for her pretenses at being human."[67]

Freud's wife, according to many writers, reinforced his mother's negative influence. In most biographies Freud's courtship and marriage appeared quintessentially Victorian. Martha Bernays emerged an efficient housewife who, in Paul Roazen's account, "fully appreciated who her husband was, and enjoyed his fame. To her, as to Freud's mother, he was a great man and she glorified him." Ernest Jones shared this generous assessment while admitting that Freud's views on women were "rather old-fashioned": "It would certainly be going too far to say that he regarded the male sex as the Lords of Creation, for there was no tinge of arrogance or superiority in his nature, but it might perhaps be fair to describe his view of the female sex as having as their main function to be ministering angels to the needs and comforts of men. His letters and his love choice make it plain that he had only one type of sexual object in his mind, a gentle feminine one."[68]

Feminists read this evidence quite differently. They portrayed Freud as a possessive suitor, subject to fits of jealousy and vulnerable to his own restrained passions. As a husband he appeared both complacent and authoritarian, demanding obedience, loyalty, and service but returning little save a platonic affection for the mother of his six children. He never involved his wife in his work, regarding her solely as the manager of his household, and he evinced no sexual passion. His attitude toward women, as documented in his relationship with Martha Bernays Freud, thus complemented his theoretical writings on femininity. Simply put, Freud believed women existed to be dominated by men and, once subdued by marriage, belonged in the home and nowhere else.[69]

A corollary to this analysis of Freud's relationship with his wife was an assessment of his personal sexual history. "Since Freud's theories rested, admittedly, on his own penetrating, unending analysis of himself, and since sexuality was the focus of his theory," Friedan explained, "certain paradoxes about his own sexuality seem pertinent." His earlier biographers had already noted this probability. Jones concluded his lengthy biographical study by puzzling over the "quite peculiarly monogamous" side to the architect of modern sexual theory. He had no ready explanation, but speculated that "Freud's deviation from the average in this respect, as well as his pronounced mental bisexuality, may have influenced his theoretical views to some extent, a possibility to be borne in mind when assessing them."[70]

Later writers, commenting more directly on Freud's prudery, focused on tantalizing tidbits, such as his abstention from sexual activity after the age of forty and his repressed desire for his sister-in-law Minna Bernays, who lived in the Freud household and served as his principal confidante. Fromm stated directly that Freud's emphasis on sexuality, as well as his pessimism about its place in civilization, stemmed from his own, severe sexual inhibitions. Feminists readily conceded that Freud's theories reflected a fundamental uneasiness with women. Hannah Lerman concluded that "Freud's own sexuality was repressed . . . even for the time."[71] Freud's theories of femininity thus reflected Freud's own inability to relate sexually to adult women.

Feminists had thereby joined their erstwhile adversaries in constructing a hostile psychobiography of Freud. Not content with merely documenting incidences of sexist assumptions in his texts, feminists outstripped their peers in locating the genesis of Freud's misogyny in his early childhood. Their argument bore an uncanny and certainly unintentional resemblance to Lundberg and Farnham's openly misogynistic attribution of mass neurosis to mothers, and even to Erikson's association of Hitler's warped personality with a weak father and a powerful mother. The logic of psychoanalytic formulations, even their substance, invaded the camp of declared enemies.

This intellectual engagement capped a series of developments from the turn of the century onward. Feminists and psychoanalysts found each other first as unlikely bed partners of Modernism, then as fretful opponents who reached a high point of bad temper at midcentury. The revenge of feminists, long in the making, seemed for a moment to be a search-and-destroy mission against the spawn of Vienna. Soon, however, it began to assume other dimensions.

In only a few years after the publication of the fierce tirades, leading feminists would emerge as hyper-psychoanalytic theorists, veritable high priestesses of the Freud cult reborn. Cutting a wide swath across methods and philosophies, they embraced along the way the likes of heterodox analysts Melanie Klein, Heinz Kohut, and Jacques Lacan. Dissimilar as these various thinkers appeared, they all promoted means to reconcile major points of contention between psychoanalysis and feminism, and sought to establish a new realm of inquiry and politics vastly larger than feminism proper. In a stunning development, self-styled avant-gardists turned with enthusiasm, as they had not since the 1910s, to Europe for intellectual inspiration. Large themes of American thought, running parallel and often crisscrossing since 1909, converged, and fresh patterns formed.

Psychoanalytic feminism, in several varieties, took to the field. Characteristically, all began as if utterly unencumbered by the weight of history. The familiar dilemma of sexual difference refashioned itself in the spectrum of contemporary theory. Unbeknownst to feminists, the "return of the repressed" forced theorists and practitioners to rehearse old problems without obvious solutions.

7

Feminine Self-in-Relation

While Betty Friedan and Kate Millett busied themselves lambasting Freud, a small coterie of feminists were preparing the way for a reunion with psychoanalysis. Even the uproar over the vaginal orgasm could not derail these scholars. If psychoanalysis failed to offer genuine insight into the minute details of female sexuality, it nevertheless held promise as an assessment of the broader, all-encompassing concept of femininity. Granted, Freud himself had fallen short. Yet, despite this major failing, he had formulated the relevant questions. On this score, these particular second-wave feminists resembled the French philosopher Simone de Beauvoir, who, two decades earlier, contended that "woman is a female to the extent that she feels herself as such." Although Beauvoir adamantly rejected Freud's explanation, she heartily sanctioned his undertaking and praised psychoanalysis for its insights into the psychic life of femininity. Several of her American successors went further, claiming that "a feminist current" had flowed with psychoanalysis since its debut. A larger, more cautious number merely acknowledged the compatibility of the two endeavors.[1]

Prospects for a new alliance depended on the willingness of feminists to abandon their assault on Freud and to take stock of psychoanalytic theories as currently constituted. As many well-meaning psychoanalysts tried to tell them, Freud did not prevail over either American theory or therapy. Since the early 1950s, when Freudian iconography reached its apex in the United States, the founder's image had been receding steadily into the shadows. This reality impinged on the operations of even the arbiter of orthodoxy, the International Psycho-Analytic Association. As late as 1967 delegates to its annual congress adopted statutes defining psychoanalysis as "a theory of personality structure and function . . . derived from the fundamental psychological discoveries of Sigmund Freud." A few years later, in 1971, the IPA hoped to refine this denotation but let the matter drop after its American delegates balked. American psychoanalysts, the most numerous in the world, would not be pinned down. Most feminists were unaware of these events. Nor did they seem to notice that statutes of the American Psychoanalytic Association did not even mention Freud.[2]

If feminists could put aside misplaced hostility, they might discover a field rich for exploration. Since the advent of ego psychology at midcentury, psychoanalysis in the United States had grown more and more variegated. Americans had embraced several additional imports from Europe, including existential psychoanalysis from France, Gestalt psychology from Germany, and object relations theory from Great Britain. Meanwhile practitioners like Erich Fromm promoted their own versions of radical humanism. All these tendencies came together under the broad rhetorical umbrella of "contemporary psychoanalysis" and collectively decentered Freudian authority. It also helped that several leading psychoanalysts had conceded the misogynist underpinnings of Freudian theories and endorsed women's liberation.

The feminist retrieval of psychoanalysis depended most of all, however, on recognition of its distinctively *post*-Freudian character. The majority of American psychoanalysts had followed the path charted earlier by ego psychologists and, in emphasizing the relationship between mother and infant, had resisted the phallocentric pull of Freudian theory. But the most up-to-date theorists further distinguished themselves by modifying, either implicitly or explicitly, Freud's drive theory, particularly his dedication to the organizing power of the libido. They no longer viewed the individual as driven primarily by physically based urges such as sex and aggression. Rather, relationships with others, or, in psychoanalytic parlance, attachment to "objects," became the principal motivating factor. What emerged was an entirely new narrative of psychological development, a relational model that continued to spotlight the first three years of life. All in all, this move beyond ego psychology signified nothing less than, as one commentator put it, a "revolution" in psychoanalytic theory.[3]

By exploring Freud's early childhood for clues to his misogyny, feminists indicated that they were already intellectually primed to make this leap. But there is a big difference between unwittingly replicating popular interpretive practices and enjoying insight into their significance. If feminists were to follow Beauvoir's lead and reclaim psychoanalysis for their own purposes, they first had to realize that Freud's oedipal paradigm, including penis envy, no longer stood as an obstacle. Second, feminists had to come to terms with post-Freudian theory and, most important, apprehend for themselves the meaning of the mother-infant relationship.

The key players turned out to be two maverick scholars, Dorothy Dinnerstein and Nancy Julia Chodorow. Their vastly influential books—Dinnerstein's *The Mermaid and the Minotaur: Sexual Arrangements and the Human Malaise* (1976) and Chodorow's *The Reproduction of Mothering: Psychoanalysis and the Sociology of Gender* (1978)—set in motion a dialogue across several academic disciplines and throughout the women's liberation movement.

Dinnerstein (1923–1992), a psychology professor affiliated with the Institute for Cognitive Studies at Rutgers University, had considered the early feminist charges against psychoanalysis "aridly polemical," at best "a waste of energy." Despite his "sexual bigotry," she reported, Freud had "deeply affected" her own understanding of the psychological differences between men and women. She set out to show that "the conceptual tool that he put into women's hands" was "a revolutionary one."

A generation younger, the sociologist Chodorow (1944–) shared Dinnerstein's assessment. While a graduate student at Brandeis University and a member of the Cambridge-based Bread and Roses feminist collective, Chodorow had broken step with the women's liberation movement and had begun to assimilate psychoanalysis into her investigations of women's oppression. Freud and his successors had demonstrated, she boldly pronounced, how boys appropriated their "masculine prerogatives" and girls their "feminine subordination and passivity."[4] Albeit in different ways, both Dinnerstein and Chodorow took it upon themselves to work out the links between post-Freudian psychoanalysis and women's liberation.

Although professionally outside all psychoanalytic camps, Dinnerstein and Chodorow were much better informed about the intricacies of contemporary theory than most of their feminist peers. Dinnerstein blended Kleinian and Gestalt perspectives, adding smatterings of existentialism into the theoretical stew-pot. As a result, *The Mermaid and the Minotaur* exhibits a fluid quality bordering on conceptual breakdown. Sidebars and advanced notes stuck between chapters suggest the impossibility of integration. Also eclectic, Chodorow wrote with considerably more precision and control but no more orthodoxy than Dinnerstein. Neither author espoused "feminist Freudianism," the label supplied by the library journal *Choice*.[5] In *The Mermaid and the Minotaur* and *The Reproduction of Mothering* they imaginatively synthesized, popularized, and reformulated post-Freudian psychoanalysis.

The publication of these two books also marked a shift from the realm of polemics energized by a political movement to the smaller domain of learned texts produced for students, scholars, and well-read intellectuals. Their success was, nevertheless, stunning. After swimming upstream intellectually for years, Dinnerstein and Chodorow suddenly found themselves leading authorities, acclaimed paradigm-smashers, and feminist celebrities. Both authors demonstrated that post-Freudian theory, with its focus on the relationship between mother and infant, could open a window not merely into the processes of sexual differentiation but into the structures of inequality itself. Indeed, not since the first decades of the century had anyone sought so avidly in psychoanalysis a resolution to the perpetual paradox: the claim to equality on the basis of woman's difference from man.

The feminist rehabilitation of psychoanalysis did not, then, answer the original complaints. By the late 1970s tirades against penis envy and vaginal orgasm had subsided. Meanwhile feminist scholars situated mainly in the academy revitalized the question posed decades earlier by Simone de Beauvoir: Why is woman the Other? By emphasizing femininity rather than female sexuality as such, feminists returned to the subject pursued by Freud, the origin of sexual difference and its psychic significance. They now added a new political twist.

These second-wavers determined to find in post-Freudian theory what their distant forerunners had tried so hard, and failed, to gain from Freud—a theory of empowerment configured around mothering. This is not to say that theorists like Dinnerstein and Chodorow backed away from the historic mission of gaining for women equal status with men in civil society; both writers were firmly wedded to this goal. Nevertheless, they succeeded best in revivifying the realm of reproduction. For many feminists, it was a victory too long in coming.

From Sex to Gender

While Dinnerstein and Chodorow were exploring new territory, American psychoanalysts themselves were seeking absolution from the sins of their distinguished forerunner. The problem had never been, they surmised, solely Freud's personal misogyny or adherence to Victorian beliefs about womanhood. Rather, his devaluation of femininity flowed logically from the assumptions undergirding his entire theory. The biological basis of Freud's metapsychology, Roy Schafer pointed out, predetermined a reliance on drives or instincts, which in turn produced a narrative of psychological development with little room for either cultural factors or, equally important, interpersonal relationships. Putting it yet another way, Schafer insisted that Freud could not fully understand female development for the simple reason that his "biological, evolutionary model" demanded "a teleological view of the propagation of the species." Where Freud unfailingly subordinated woman to procreation, he allowed man—and man only—to play a dynamic part in civilization. Post-Freudians were determined to project an entirely different schema of development.[6]

Post-Freudians once again tilted the theoretical balance to favor culture over biology. The early revisionists had repudiated Freud's biologism, going so far as to discard the libido theory altogether. But, in emphasizing cultural factors, they had never successfully generated an alternative theory clarifying the complex processes by which an individual internalizes external reality. Horney and Sullivan came close in their theories of interpersonal relations, and Erikson and Parsons formulated compelling descriptions of the processes of identification. Although post-Freudians were just as concerned with the intra-psychic dynamics and unconscious formations emblematic of classical psychoanalytic theory, they rekindled the faith that everything is, in sum, "socially negotiated."[7]

As a step along the way, post-Freudians began to distinguish more precisely between "sex" and "gender." The term gender was, in fact, as new to the canons of feminism as to psychoanalysis. A recent out-growth of the Parsonian sociology of sex roles as well as Erikson's formulations on identity, gender signifies a cultural or social construc-tion distinct from either morphological or genetic markers. Unlike the midcentury originators, post-Freudians distinguished among biologi-cal sex, sexual orientation, and sexual behavior. They defined gender simply, as the consciousness of being male or female, that is, as a sense of masculine or feminine identity acquired through the processes of socialization or internalization.

The development of gender, psychoanalysts now insisted, depends most on experiential rather than innate or instinctual factors. As the psychoanalyst Joel Kovel summed it up, a "biological fact—like any other fact—is of no value in itself; it is given value only by our wishes."[8] What clearly distinguished the post-Freudian viewpoint, however, was the recognition that gender emerges *within a relation-ship,* specifically a relationship central to the infant during the first moments of life.

This new perspective on gender broke step with classical psycho-analysis in more ways than one. The term if not the concept was alien to Freud. So were the heterodox methods used to formulate the new theories. Two areas were proving increasingly important: laboratory research into the origins of sexual differentiation, and direct obser-vation of mothers and infants. Both procedures degraded the Freudian practice of gathering data within the context of analysis itself through a continuing dialogue between primarily adult clients and therapists. Post-Freudians did not disregard data derived from the clinical setting, but they eagerly sought supplementary information from the bur-geoning field of infancy research, which was conducted mainly by developmental psychologists. But unlike their professional colleagues who recorded only behavior, psychoanalysts made huge inferential leaps to speculate furiously about the nature of the psyche of preverbal infants. Despite vast room for interpretive error, this innovative research made it possible, according to post-Freudians, to challenge both Freud's biological premises and his developmental paradigm.[9]

The new case for gender gained authority from the extraordinarily heuristic investigations of John Money. Money (1921–) and his co-workers at the Johns Hopkins University program in psychohormonal research had examined the rare condition of hermaphroditism. They looked closely at *in utero* hyperadrenalism, a condition which produces in genetically sexed girls "androgenized" or "masculinized" genitals, that is, external organs resembling a penis and scrotum. The researchers found that if the attending physician names this baby a girl, and if parents unequivocally accept this designation and rear the child according to conventional gender norms, a firm feminine identity establishes itself, complete with expected sexual object choice. The variable "that holds the balance of power would seem to be," they concluded, "the consistency of experiences of being reared as feminine, especially in the early years."[10]

Robert J. Stoller (1925–1991), prominent within the American Psychoanalytic Association, found in Money's reports ample evidence to support the contention that, although humans are "prenatally primed" to be either male or female, postnatal events—particularly the assignment of sex—actually determine gender identity. In his own clinical practice Stoller had compiled cases of women who deviated from the norm in terms of chromosomes or genitalia but nevertheless had strong feminine identities. Women born without vaginas but raised to consider themselves female might at adulthood feel "defective" but feminine in every other respect. They had no doubts about their womanhood and exhibited no longing to be male. Stoller concluded that anatomy, even biology, played a far less important role in the construction of femininity and masculinity than psychoanalysts had once supposed.[11]

Stoller and his associates at the UCLA Gender Identity Research Clinic pinpointed the formation of "core gender identity" in early infancy. They established the age when children first recognize the differences between the sexes to be between one and two years, in some cases as early as ten months, and certainly well before the onset of the Oedipus complex. Although infants must reach a certain stage of cognitive development before they are able to conceptualize their perceptions of sexual difference, the processes leading to the achievement of the core gender identity, which Stoller considered "overpowering," begin very early. The infant's "perception of herself as 'a girl' . . . begins to form," another psychoanalyst attested, "as soon as her parents recognize her as female."[12]

Although this new research indicated that Freud's view was "incorrect," Stoller advanced little beyond the earlier heretics who had also discounted the influence of the Oedipus complex and penis envy. In sum, he, Money, and their colleagues merely ratified the formulations advanced by earlier culturalists and ego psychologists. "If one wants the appearance of femininity in a baby," Stoller concluded, "all one need do is encourage and encourage and encourage and encourage."[13]

Other psychoanalysts reasoned that if gender identity establishes itself as early as Stoller claimed, something more than parental encouragement has to be at work. Infants are not simply responding to verbal cues or learning their gender through a simple conditioning process. Discounting the importance of the imitation or mimicry central to ego psychology, post-Freudians located sexual differentiation in the very earliest, unconscious and preverbal stages of development.[14]

The second field of research, observational studies of mothers and infants, supplied the theoretical underpinnings. Since the pioneering work of René Spitz, David Levy, Margaret Ribble, and Therese Benedek, other psychoanalysts had transformed the investigation of mother-child pairs during the first three years of life into a major enterprise. Working independently, Sylvia Brody, Phyllis Greenacre, Edith Jacobson, and Judith S. Kestenberg had all contributed to the growing scholarship. Eleanor Galenson and Herman Roiphe, who monitored the interaction between seventy babies and their mothers over nine years, also confirmed that boys and girls confront sexual differences much earlier than Freud imagined. Collectively, these psychoanalysts insisted that it is during the first year of life that a child, in achieving a sense of self distinct from its mother, also gains a sense of gender.[15]

At the helm of this research was Margaret Schoenberger Mahler (1897–1985). While still in high school in Budapest, Mahler had become interested in psychoanalysis through a "deep adolescent friendship" with her classmate Alice Balint, who also became a principal theorist of the mother-infant relationship. After completing medical school and training in psychoanalysis, Mahler entered the profession as a pediatrician and director of a well-baby clinic in Vienna. Driven from her practice by the Nazis in 1938, she immigrated to the United States, settled in New York City, and soon became fast friends with colleagues who were about to make Momism a household word. Dr. Benjamin Spock referred patients to her. David Levy's seminar at the New York Psychoanalytic Institute passed into her hands. Margaret Ribble invited Mahler to her summer home on Cape Cod, and the two enjoyed frequent conversations on the importance of mothering to a baby. Mahler even affiliated with the New York State Psychiatric Institute and Hospital, where Marynia Farnham worked in the out-patient clinic.

Although continuing her research into the mother-infant dyad at the Masters Children's Center and publishing scores of papers over the next two decades, Mahler passed relatively unnoticed through the era of psychoanalytic misogyny. Only in 1955 did her imaginative formulation of the separation-individuation phase begin to attract considerable attention. She continued her research through the 1960s and collected her findings in her magnum opus, *The Psychological Birth of the Human Infant* (1975). In the end, Mahler had produced a new narrative of psychological development, one which emphasizes the infant's struggle not to conquer libidinous impulses but to attain autonomy from the mother.[16]

"I have maintained a rather personal interest in one specific aspect of the rich heritage that Freud bestowed upon us," Mahler reported, "—namely, his emphasis on the fact that a lifelong, albeit diminishing, emotional dependence on the mother is a universal truth of human existence." Bows to Freud aside, she continued to reorient psychoanalytic theory away from its original phallocentric principles. Mahler further magnified the mother-infant dyad, describing in minute detail the tangled processes of an infant's emergence from an original state of symbiosis with its mother. Over the course of several years, she reasoned, an individual achieves self-integrity, a sense of self or identity, by differentiating from its primary caretaker. This "psychological birth of the human infant," triggered by an innate drive toward separation or individuation, determines emotional stability.[17]

Mahler's projection of human growth, from infantile attachment to mature individuation, soon replaced Freud's original conception of psychosexual development. Mahler retained Freud's demarcation of stages—oral, anal, and phallic—and likewise described the Oedipus complex as a significant event. But in reducing sexuality to a dependent variable, she disputed Freud's estimation of its "exemplary function" in psychological development. A person gains a sense of identity, and most emphatically gender identity, she countered, through the complex processes of differentiation from the mother during the years *preceding* the Oedipus complex.

This new paradigm, stressing the child's emergence from the symbiotic relationship of early infancy, represents more than a simple modification of Freudian theory. This so-called relational model dramatically alters the teleology or story line of psychological development. One psychoanalyst judged it nothing less than "a reevaluation of the existential structure of human reality."[18]

There is no doubt that this new relational paradigm facilitated an alliance with feminism. By 1973 Jean Baker Miller's anthology *Psychoanalysis and Women* offered documentary evidence that her up-to-date colleagues were already working along congenial lines. They understood, she declared, that biology "poses no inherent limitations to women's development." Jean Strouse, a student of Erikson's at Harvard University, produced a collection of essays for the same purpose. *Women and Analysis: Dialogues on Psychoanalytic Views of Femininity* (1974), likewise affirms that psychoanalysts now realized that the weight given to biology said more about the "cultural climate" than about the "facts themselves." Like Miller, Strouse was optimistic. She too insisted that the project begun by Freud, if not the substance of his contribution, continued to be relevant "for any profound political or psychological understanding of women."[19]

Still, even the most prescient post-Freudian analysts had not yet explored the developmental dynamic of self-and-other in terms useful to feminists, as a source of not just gender identity but woman's subordination to man. Nor did they highlight the disparities in the process for boys and girls or account for the formation of the specific character traits designated masculine or feminine. It remained for Dinnerstein and Chodorow to transpose these post-Freudian theories into feminist terms.

The Good Mother/The Bad Mother

It is an axiom of post-Freudian psychoanalysis that the pre-oedipal stage comprises a high degree of ambivalence. While mothers supply nourishment and comfort, they do so intermittently and not always at the moment of the child's greatest need. Mothers also leave their babies alone for long periods and thereby provoke "separation anxiety." The mother (or the mother's breast) is to the infant, then, the source of both pleasure and pain. The child cannot act on momentary feelings, even the most intense rage, lest he or she risk destroying the one object that ordinarily fills all desire. The infant manages this crisis through fantasy, by "splitting" the offending object into different parts, "good" and "bad." The "good mother" represents the infant's initial fusion of self and object and serves to encourage a primary identification supported by love. The "bad mother" stands for the frustrating or intrusive object who stimulates separation. Eventually the child matures cognitively to the point of making sense of the mother's repeated disappearances and begins not only to anticipate her departure but to wait confidently for her return. Thus the ability to control ambivalence and to maintain object constancy along with a unified self-image becomes the mark of healthy development. No one, however, passes emotionally unscathed through this period of early infancy.[20]

The degree of emphasis placed on the "good" and "bad" mother nevertheless varies, depending on the theorist's perspective. This distinction is especially pronounced within the British School of psychoanalysis, object relations, that influenced both Dinnerstein and Chodorow. Melanie Klein, for example, underscored the mother's power to grant or to refuse an infant's desire and her baby's inevitable encounter with a world both gratifying and aggravating. The baby thus forms a symbolic representation of the mother as an object of fear and hate, comfort and love. Klein focused primarily on the baby's aggressive feelings, its rage toward its mother and her breast and the sadistic fantasies it produced, and made the resulting anxiety the centerpiece of therapy.

Whereas Klein emphasized the infant's bundle of projections, or the subjective object, other British analysts allowed equal room for external reality, including the mother's actual behavior, especially her nurturing qualities, and the baby's own beneficent symbolic imagery. Donald Woods Winnicott (1896–1971), who had studied with Klein, leaned so far in this direction that his one-time mentor accused him of sentimentalizing the mother-child relationship. Winnicott emphasized the infant's ability to pull through by appropriating a "transitional object"—a thumb, teddy bear, or blanket—that mediates desire and frustration. Equally important, the distinguished pediatrician emphasized the mother's emotional disposition. He suggested a stage of "projective identification," a period during late pregnancy when the mother develops a keen empathy with her infant and a desire to satisfy its longings. The resulting "good enough mothering," in Winnicott's famous phrase, encourages the infant to be dependent at first, then gradually to accept the strains inflicted by the reality of separation, and ultimately to develop a secure sense of self-in-relation to others.[21]

Dinnerstein and Chodorow positioned themselves squarely on this theoretical divide. Both began from the premise that it is women who universally mother, and they judged this reality extraordinarily significant in the development of not only a differentiated self but a gendered identity. But, in utilizing disparate branches of object relations theory, Dinnerstein and Chodorow headed in opposite directions. "Dinnerstein saw female mothering as a source of rage," the scholar Hester Eisenstein observed, "while Chodorow saw it as a seductive locus of connectedness and intimacy." And it was precisely this divergence that determined their places in the annals of contemporary feminism.[22]

Dorothy Dinnerstein followed Melanie Klein's *Envy and Gratitude* (1957) and emphasized the pre-oedipal image of the imperious mother—"the ultimate source of good and evil." All infants vacillate between the extremes of love and hate and grow anxious about their conflicting emotions, she noted, but boys and girls handle them differently. Girls, facing the awesome prospect of becoming mothers themselves, seek to harness their own potentially omnipotent power and find security in a subordinate relationship with a man. Boys, in contrast, never psychologically outgrow the original ambivalence: they enter adulthood with an overwhelming need to control women.

This disparity shows itself in many ways, Dinnerstein reasoned, not least in sexual desire. Permanently ambivalent about love relationships, adult men want to control both women and female sexuality while avoiding commitment. Once a boy separates from the object of primary love and hate, his mother, the prospect of dependence on any woman looms as the paramount threat to his painfully won autonomy. As adults, men simultaneously demand absolute fidelity from their wives and avoid emotional entanglement themselves; they also more easily achieve sexual gratification without intimacy. Women, who never entirely overcome their guilt for separating from their mother, seek to re-create the all-encompassing love of the primary relationship; they readily conjoin emotional intimacy and sexual gratification, and they treasure fidelity. These diverging developmental tracks thus produce, according to Dinnerstein, polygamous men and monogamous women, jealous husbands and tolerant wives.

Dinnerstein concerned herself primarily with the significance of this disparity for the future of civilization, and for this reason she focused on the functional relationship between maternal omnipotence and masculinity. Whereas women remain fixed in the pre-oedipal psychological realm and continue to seek a nurturing relationship, men expand their capacities for destruction, Dinnerstein alleged. They develop a devastating desire to control not only women but what women represent—nature. The title of her book metaphorically bears the meaning of this opposition: "The treacherous mermaid, seductive and impenetrable female representative of the dark and magic underwater world from which our life comes and in which we cannot live, lures voyagers to their doom. The fearsome minotaur, gigantic and eternally infantile offspring of a mother's unnatural lust, male representative of mindless, greedy power, insatiably devours live human flesh." Maternal omnipotence produces not only gender asymmetry but "the human malaise," that is, the estrangement of man from woman and both from nature. In emphasizing the male projection of the "bad mother," Dinnerstein fabricated a Kleinian analysis of civilization and its discontents.

The Mermaid and the Minotaur vividly conveys Dinnerstein's premonition of doom. Although this "sense of deep strain between women and men has been permeating our species' life as far back into time as the study of myth and ritual permits us to trace human feeling," the brooding author acknowledged, the situation had grown acute with the advent of the nuclear age. Equipped with weapons of total destruction, men could now fully realize their desire to domineer by destroying civilization itself. What greater danger could possibly lurk in maternal omnipotence?[23]

Nancy Chodorow might agree with Dinnerstein on many points, especially on the deleterious consequences of gender asymmetry. Sketching the diverging developmental paths of boys and girls, she too noted that boys face a unique psychological situation. By age three the boy must not only separate from his mother but identify with a father he rarely sees. Because the breadwinning father of Western society is so remote, the boy achieves his masculine identity only indirectly, mainly by rejecting and devaluing that which is "other." Masculinity therefore remains unstable, forcing a continuous reaffirmation of its integrity by defining femininity as both different and inferior. Although working within a slightly different relational matrix, Chodorow came to the same conclusion as Dinnerstein: men perceive all women as objects of domination.[24]

Chodorow also explicated the precise relationship between psychological and sociological asymmetries. Masculine traits, she explained, complement men's role in the public sphere, in the competitive and ruthless world of capitalist production; feminine traits serve women in the reproductive realm and, by functioning as the opposite of masculinity, prepare boys and girls to accept and excel in their differentiated roles. Talcott Parsons had himself underscored the significance of this difference. Chodorow, however, had come to an opposite conclusion. Like Dinnerstein, she judged the prevailing division of labor as detrimental not only to women but to the entire civilization.[25]

To help bring about an end to this dangerous asymmetry, Chodorow and Dinnerstein endorsed a common strategy: dual parenting. Dinnerstein assumed that if mothers and fathers participated equally in childrearing, maternal omnipotence would be curtailed. Consequently, boys would no longer develop in opposition to their mothers, and men would no longer feel psychologically compelled to dominate woman and nature alike. Chodorow similarly believed that ending the extreme disparities in the care of children would bring men and women into emotional harmony and concurrently dislodge the psychic underpinnings of industrial capitalism.

These similarities aside, Dinnerstein and Chodorow cut across post-Freudian psychoanalytic theory from opposite directions. While Dinnerstein followed Klein to insist that it is the child who creates the relational drama through its own fantasies, Chodorow borrowed extensively from Winnicott to stress the real interactions of mother and baby. Equally important, the two authors relied on different systems of developmental dynamics. Following Klein, Dinnerstein continued to rely on the dual drive theory of sex and aggression. Chodorow, in contrast, emphasized the conflict between attachment and separation.

Actually, Chodorow reworked post-Freudian principles to provide, in contrast to Dinnerstein's stark depiction of maternal omnipotence and the fears it aroused, a basically sublime description of woman's power in reproduction. Rather than Klein, she emulated the opposing group of British theorists who identified "primary object love" as the motive force of development. Rather than seeking to gratify libidinal or aggressive instincts, infants possess a basic sociality, she surmised, and chiefly crave human contact. To underscore this point Chodorow quoted Michael Balint, who insisted that infants desire most of all to "be loved and satisfied." But mothers, too, possess an instinctual attraction to their babies. Maternal love, Alice Balint proposed, "is the almost perfect counterpart to the love for the mother."[26]

It was here, in the primary object love of early infancy, that Chodorow relocated the source of femininity. Women, who never completely individuate, seek as adults to reestablish this beneficial relationship only to discover that men are poor candidates because they cannot easily regress to pre-oedipal relational modes and, moreover, devalue this "feminine" desire. Women turn to men, therefore, not to achieve emotional satisfaction but literally to reproduce primary love by giving birth to their own children. Women become mothers—the true subject of Chodorow's inquiry—not because nature suited them for this role, or because prevailing ideology and sex-role stereotyping force them to assume it. Rather, the capacity and desire for motherhood, according to Chodorow, are "built developmentally into the feminine psychic structure."[27]

Chodorow established the pre-oedipal origins of a feminine gender identity characterized as a uniquely humane capacity for relationship. Because girls routinely separate from their mothers much more slowly, often not until the fourth or fifth year, and even then less completely than do boys, they never form strong ego boundaries between "self" and "other." For this reason women, who live out their psychic lives in the reproductive realm, readily empathize with others and commonly interpret events according to the relational values of early infancy. While "the basic masculine sense of self is separate," Chodorow concluded, "the basic feminine sense of self is connected to the world."[28]

Although *The Mermaid and the Minotaur* and *The Reproduction of Mothering* both specified dire consequences of gender asymmetry for individuals and for civilization alike, the two texts cast decidedly different auras. Both authors readily agreed on the baneful trajectory of masculine development. Dinnerstein located in the conflicts of early infancy the source of men's fear of women and nature and their desire to control both. Like nature, "which sends blizzards and locusts as well as sunshine and strawberries," she explained, the mother/woman appears to men as "capricious, sometimes actively malevolent" and demanding domination.[29] Chodorow, for her part, equated masculinity with the personality prototype of industrial capitalism, of which she, a socialist, was profoundly critical. But while both writers acknowledged the constraints placed on female autonomy, Chodorow fatefully proved more ambivalent than Dinnerstein. In exploring the primary love of early infancy, she cast a fetchingly bright spotlight on the special relationship between mother and daughter and subtly recast femininity as the source of redemption.

The meaning of pre-oedipal relations depends very largely, then, upon the angle of vision. No wonder that feminist reviewers, fellow academics, popularizers, and most of the professional and lay readers who eagerly grasped these texts usually found what they were already looking for. The good mother/bad mother dichotomy of post-Freudian theory replicated a familiar set of contradictions but along the way inspired the first genuine "psychoanalytic feminism."

The Politics of Difference

This new psychoanalytic bent failed to please all feminists, especially those old enough to remember the misogyny of midcentury. The sociologist Pauline Bart charged: "It is 13 years since the second wave of the women's movement started and women who call themselves feminists are still . . . citing the very authors whose works contributed to the Freudian hegemony of the fifties, which came close to destroying an entire decade of women, myself among them." Bart was appalled by the academic praise showered on Chodorow and Dinnerstein and the robust sales of their books. The first printing of *The Reproduction of Mothering,* a narrow-marketed university press book, sold out in a short time, while its author was showered with professional accolades and prestigious fellowships. *The Mermaid and The Minotaur* was meanwhile "sanctified in the pages of *Ms.* magazine," whose controversial editor praised Dinnerstein "extravagantly" before the American Psychological Association. All this attention made Bart's feminist "blood run cold."

Other critics showed more restraint. Socialist feminists, for example, objected to both authors' seeming lack of concern with the material factors of women's oppression. While a few sociologists devalued Chodorow's reliance on psychoanalytic theory, just as many psychoanalysts found fault with her sociology. The most vocal critics across the board judged both authors insufficiently attentive to class and race. And both suffered invidious comparisons to Adrienne Rich's extraordinarily popular *Of Woman Born: Motherhood as Experience and Institution* (1976).[30]

Although often cited together, *The Mermaid and the Minotaur* and *The Reproduction of Mothering* held out dissimilar prospects even to those American feminists intrigued by their use of psychoanalysis. Publishing shortly after receiving her doctorate, the precocious Chodorow enjoyed the benefits of a timely outlook; her elder colleague hit slightly off the mark. Admittedly a slow writer, Dinnerstein had formulated her initial arguments decades earlier. Just two years younger than Betty Friedan, she had started her research when the Feminine Mystique was in full force. By the time it appeared, *The Mermaid and the Minotaur* served to cap a wave of polemics depicting the negative aspects of motherhood. *The Reproduction of Mothering*, in contrast, moved the discussion along a different path to rediscover the emancipatory potential in maternity. The tremendous popularity of Chodorow's argument signaled, at least for scholars, a major reorientation in American feminism.

When *The Mermaid and the Minotaur* and *The Reproduction of Mothering* first appeared in print, feminist writers were for the most part still emphasizing the negative aspects of motherhood, especially as manifested in the mother/daughter relationship. Nancy Friday, in her bestselling *My Mother/My Self: The Daughter's Search for Identity* (1977), maintained that "mothers are noxious to daughters," while Judith Arcana, in *Our Mothers' Daughters* (1979), made a matching case. Friday targeted specifically the "pre-oedipal alliance" between mother and daughter as the source of an enduring friction between the two parties: a daughter's desire to separate yet to remain attached; to reach out to the pleasures of the outside world and to seek security within. These emotional conflicts, according to Friday, precipitate terror, if not madness, in women. She argued her case to induce the female reader to break the maternal bond, to become, as the book jacket put it, "the vital, independent, fully sexual woman she wants to be."[31]

Several well-known feminist scholars also portrayed the relationship between mother and daughter as far from splendid. Mothers, Jane Flax argued, encourage emotional uncertainty in their daughters. Ambivalent about their own femininity, they behave erratically, pulling the daughter tightly into the mother's sphere and alternately pushing her to succeed in the father's realm. The daughter consequently grows into a woman desperately needing both nurturing and autonomy, neither of which can be satisfied, least of all by men. This fundamental ambivalence—"the conflict between warmth and intimacy and connecting with the outside world of ideas and action"—shows itself not only in the emotional conflicts recorded by Friday. It also shapes the politics of the women's movement itself, appearing rhetorically, Flax noted, as the self-contradictory slogan "sisterhood is powerful." The major splits within the women's movement such as gay/straight and radical/marxist reflect both real political differences and deep unconscious processes rooted in pre-oedipal relations. The mother-daughter relationship, Flax suggested, fosters not only women's psychological problems but discord within the women's liberation movement![32]

Assessing the literary boomlet, Chodorow herself noted a certain "level of tension and ambivalence" in current depictions of motherhood.[33] With a few qualifications, she too subscribed to this commonplace sentiment. Far from sanctifying the mother-daughter relationship, Chodorow insisted that she allowed room for plenty of conflict, going so far as to support her argument with data collected by the midcentury purveyors of psychoanalytic misogyny. As a sociologist, Chodorow appeared to feel a certain amount of intellectual kinship with the earlier neo-Freudians, including those who had argued that each culture produces a unique personality structure. She evoked the authority of Mead, Thompson, and Horney, as well as the anthropologists John and Beatrice Whiting, Herbert and Margaret Barry,

Irwin Child, and Leigh Minturn, who had continued the cross-cultural study of childrearing practices into the postwar period.

Even the notorious 1940s studies of maternal overprotection served as supporting evidence for her hypothesis that girls growing up in the twentieth century have an especially hard time achieving an "autonomous sense of self." In her own rendition of the American national character, Chodorow contended that since the 1920s American mothers have increasingly suffered the consequences of suburbanization. Isolated geographically from both female kin and their breadwinning husbands, and encouraged by experts to devote themselves entirely to childrearing, they typically turn to their children for emotional sustenance. Chodorow almost echoed Wylie in arguing that the sons of such mothers face "severe" conflicts over their masculinity, while their daughters replicate the mothers' emotional difficulties.[34]

These subtleties were, too often, lost on Chodorow's readers. While *The Mermaid and the Minotaur* occasionally elicited charges of Momism, the all-too-familiar practice of blaming women for men's mishandling of the problems of civilization, *The Reproduction of Mothering* readily escaped this complaint. One admirer did appreciate the nuances of Chodorow's argument, insisting that after the publication of *The Reproduction of Mothering* "there can be no theory of women's oppression, that does not take into account woman's role as mother of daughters and as a daughter of mothers . . . and that does not study that relationship in the wider context in which it takes place: the emotional, political, economic, and symbolic structures of family and society."[35] Many more readers, however, missed this crucial point. The majority instead judged *The Reproduction of Mothering* a celebration of motherhood. In short, what stood out was Chodorow's paean to primary love and an unintended idealization of self-in-relation—both to become legal tender for a rising generation of feminists.

By the time *The Reproduction of Mothering* appeared in print, a few writers had already begun to swim against the tide. At the forefront were African American women, angry in the aftermath of the Moynihan Report. They preceded Chodorow in issuing the earliest and most forceful maternalist missives. Angela Davis and Patricia M. Robinson provided a new narrative of African American history to accentuate the significance of matrifocal factors, naming black motherhood the chief source of resistance to the evils of white racism. Alice Walker elaborated this tenet. In her celebrated essay "In Search of Our Mothers' Gardens," the bestselling author reversed the stereotype associated with " 'Matriarchs,' 'Superwomen,' and 'Mean and Evil Bitches.' " Maternal strength has continuously nourished the community, Walker answered, making it possible for African Americans to survive the ruinous oppression that has been their lot since the slave ships first brought their ancestors to these shores. Moreover, Walker specified the empathic mother-daughter relationship as the paramount model of both inspiration and creativity.[36]

American feminists were, in fact, on the brink of a mammoth restoration project. Adrienne Rich sharply criticized Firestone for failing to recognize the constraints placed on the institution of motherhood under patriarchy. Once the system of male domination is overturned, she countered, motherhood will emerge as the ultimate transformative experience for women. "I am really asking," Rich clarified, "whether women cannot begin, at last, to *think through the body,* to connect what has been so cruelly disorganized—our great mental capacities, hardly used; our highly developed tactile sense; our genius for close observation; our complicated, pain-enduring, multi-pleasured physicality." Rich thus located in woman's reproductive capacity the source of a benevolent femininity, an identity to be cherished and enhanced throughout life. Meanwhile Jane Alpert, in her landmark document "Mother Right: A New Feminist Theory," explicitly reclaimed reproduction as "the basis of woman's power." Childbirth was not even necessary in her opinion, because the potential for motherhood, the former Weatherwoman insisted, is "imprinted in the genes of every woman." Even played out at the symbolic level, the mother/daughter relationship in particular forecast a new utopia. "Women are daughters/lovers of earth" who revel, according to Mary Daly, in the "life-loving" qualities of female energy. The popular feminist theologian defined the principal quality of femininity as the expression of "the deep mysteries of interconnectedness."[37]

The Reproduction of Mothering inadvertently nourished this trend in feminism, now distinguished by the prefix "cultural," and fed such airy journalism as Janna Malamud Smith's "Mothers: Tired of Taking the Rap" and Paula J. Caplan's *Don't Blame Mother: Mending the Mother-Daughter Relationship* (1989), a popular self-help manual.

But, more important, Chodorow's work supplied the theoretical foundation. Cultural feminists could find here a satisfying explanation of why men and women are, in Freud's terms, "a phase apart" in matters of sexuality. But they could also gain what earlier generations could not: a post-Freudian means to frame the totality of women's experiences as not only different from but superior to men's. *The Reproduction of Mothering* thus assisted what became known as "the new woman's renaissance."[38]

By the early 1980s cultural feminism reigned as the politics of identity. Just as the women's liberation movement dissolved into a multitude of warring factions, and just as issues of class, race, and sexual orientation militated ever more persuasively against a singular ideation of womanhood, cultural feminists had found a convenient means to smooth over these fissures. Motherhood, Jane Alpert insisted, fosters a "felt experience" of not only the "difference between the sexes" but an affinity with all other women.

Nowhere was this trend more evident than in the nascent interdisciplinary field of women's studies. While Dinnerstein and Chodorow were developing their ideas, a sizable contingent of feminists employed in colleges and universities had demanded new faculty positions and new courses to explore women's experiences, past and present. Inaugurated in 1970, the movement flourished. Within five years more than 150 women's studies programs were established; by 1980 the number of courses offered at the college level hovered around 30,000. Scholarship advanced at an equally fast pace, facilitated in large part by *Signs: A Journal of Women in Culture and Society,* founded in 1975. Two years later scholars came together in the National Women's Studies Association. By the end of the decade various disciplines, especially within the social sciences and humanities, were confronting the significance of what Dinnerstein had termed "sexual arrangements." *Citation Index* now listed hundreds of citations annually to *The Mermaid and the Minotaur* and *The Reproduction of Mothering.* As one scholar acknowledged, Chodorow's work in particular had encouraged American feminists "to think differently, to create alternatives to the dominant frameworks in their disciplines."[39]

The discipline of history yielded scarcely at all to psychoanalytic theory but excelled in rendering enticing narratives of women's special relational capacities and sensibilities. Historians of American women examined a multiplicity of women's friendships, networks, organizations, and institutions and emphasized their functional dissimilarity from those created by men. Pathbreaking books such as *The Female Experience: An American Documentary* (1977) by Gerda Lerner and *The Bonds of Womanhood: "Woman's Sphere" in New England, 1780–1835* (1977) by Nancy F. Cott bore the imprint of this intention. No single text surpassed Carroll Smith-Rosenberg's oft-cited "The Female World of Love and Ritual: Relations between Women in Nineteenth-Century America," which establishes an interpretive paradigm for nineteenth-century women's history that places the mother-daughter relationship at the center. A professor at the University of Pennsylvania and an expert in the psychoanalytic canon, Smith-Rosenberg provided extensive documentation of intimate relationships between nineteenth-century American women, a private world of love and friendship extending outward from the unique bonds between mothers and daughters. Published in 1975, this landmark essay inaugurated a long round of inquiry into what historians phrased "woman's culture."[40]

Literary scholars established a direct connection between cultural feminism and the post-Freudianism elaborated by Chodorow. "Mother-critics" of fiction written by women produced dozens upon dozens of books and essays on mother-daughter themes and female friendships. It became commonplace within the most prestigious literary circles to assume that texts penned by women manifested a form and content distinct from men's. The collaborators Sandra M. Gilbert and Susan Gubar produced a series of essays and several books examining those aspects of women's language, a "mother tongue," which expresses not only the unique female relational experience but women's desire to subvert the culture of patriarchy. Critics found recurring "pre-oedipal/feminine" qualities such as fluidity, mutuality, and continuity in both plot and prose. With these notions in mind, scholars avidly reinterpreted the fiction of women writers such as Louisa May Alcott, Kate Chopin, Emily Dickinson, Virginia Woolf, and Alice Walker.[41]

Chodorow's authority also informed the work of many feminist philosophers. By 1980 Sara Ruddick had argued that "out of maternal practices distinctive ways of conceptualizing, ordering, and valuing arise." Women "*think* differently": women are artistic, intuitive, integrative, subjective, playful, and above all relational in their conceptual modes. Janice D. Raymond meanwhile explored the special qualities of "Gyn/Affection" or women's friendships. Other feminist philosophers even criticized the practices of modern science for resisting "female modes of knowing." Evelyn Fox Keller thus challenged the principle of objectivity as the basis of scientific inquiry, claiming that empathy constituted an alternative and valid way.[42]

This trend reached its academic apex in the publications of yet another scholar who touted self-in-relation as the sine qua non of femininity. Following on the heels of Chodorow's commanding presentation, Carol Gilligan's *In a Different Voice: Psychological Theory and Women's Development* (1982) won even greater acclaim. Gilligan (1936–), against her own intentions, rode the coattails of an increasingly popular post-Freudian psychoanalysis. Her phenomenal success depended, however, on her uncanny ability to elude the ambiguity that marked Chodorow's interpretation. Gilligan's message could not be more clear. Women, she insisted, enjoy "a more generative view of human life."

The Harvard educator made her appealing case by comparing the different styles of moral reasoning of men and women. She took on her mentor, Lawrence Kohlberg (1927–1987), a leader in the field of developmental psychology who had sketched a topology of stages of moral development differentiated by gender. While Kohlberg equated the autonomous (masculine) self with the capacity for abstract (superior) judgment, he ranked women only at midpoint on a scale capped by men's moral position. Women, in Kohlberg's estimation, fall short because they invariably succumb to interpersonal bias.

Gilligan did not challenge this finding. She agreed, men and women are capable of achieving "only partial agreement" and consequently live out their lives in antagonistic moral domains. Not stopping here, Gilligan totally rejected Kohlberg's interpretation of this difference. The capacity to respond sensitively to a situation rather than to stick to absolute rules, she retorted, does not denote inferiority. The truly moral person is "the one who helps others, if possible without sacrificing herself." Pitting the masculine "morality of rights" against the feminine "ethic of responsibility," Gilligan had no trouble judging the latter superior.[43]

Gilligan quickly ascended to the pinnacle of popularity. Her work elicited scores of reviews, including very hostile ones from, for example, Kohlberg. For a different reason, mainly an aversion to cultural feminism, leading scholars in *Signs* and *Feminist Studies* also treated her work critically. *Ms. Magazine,* on the other hand, named Gilligan "Woman of the Year, 1984" precisely because "her work has created a new appreciation for a previously uncataloged female sensibility, as well as possibilities for new understanding between the genders." Within a decade, *In a Different Voice* sold nearly a half-million copies. Following the publication of *Making Connections: The Relational Worlds of Adolescent Girls at Emma Willard School* (1990), Gilligan's photograph appeared on the cover of the *New York Times Magazine.* In the fields of moral philosophy, linguistics, epistemology, and legal studies, Gilligan virtually transformed feminist academic practice. She also initiated an entirely new field, what one scholar described as "the study of an ethic of care."[44]

Gilligan had, in sum, effectively eliminated the contradictions in the self-in-relation paradigm elaborated in *The Reproduction of Mothering.* Few fans were aware of this accomplishment, and, moreover, they blithely conflated Gilligan's and Chodorow's perspectives. Thus, chronically associated with Gilligan's text, *The Reproduction of Mothering* sank ever deeper into the realm of cultural feminism.[45]

Chodorow did speak out. The developmental track produced by female-exclusive mothering does not, she insisted, foster goodness in either boys or girls; it spawns male dominance and denies women a sense of self or autonomy. Chodorow pointed out that she proposed dual parenting as an arrangement that would encourage boys and girls alike to develop "a sufficiently individuated and strong sense of self, as well as a positively valued and secure gender identity, that does not bog down in ego-boundary confusion, low self-esteem, and overwhelming relatedness to others, or in compulsive denial of any connection to others or dependence upon them."[46] Chodorow did not join the ranks of Gilligan's enthusiasts.

Cultural feminism actually nettled Chodorow. A celebration of the differences between the sexes, no matter how sublime the depiction of femininity, constituted, in her opinion, a "disservice" to women. She echoed Horney, who concluded that it is men, not women, who most strongly seek to accentuate gender disparities. As pointed out in *The Reproduction of Mothering*, the process of differentiation from the mother forms "one of the earliest, most basic male developmental issues." Chodorow refused to affiliate with those feminists who "would found a politics on essentialist conceptions of the feminine."[47]

That few texts in the history of second-wave feminism had afforded so much misunderstanding indicates the depth of popular desire for a theory that would make such an interpretation credible. It also suggests that *The Reproduction of Mothering* may have been especially vulnerable to misreading. Chodorow hardly helped her case when she generously endorsed *In a Different Voice*. Printed conspicuously on its back cover, her promotion of Gilligan's book as a "rich and persuasive account" undoubtedly prompted many readers to pair the two authors.

Despite Chodorow's objections, cultural feminists found in *The Reproduction of Mothering* a psychoanalytic argument to bolster their faith in an ethics of care. Its emphasis on the pre-oedipal relations of mother and daughter seemed to invite intellectual overlays such as Alpert's location of femininity in biology and Daly's in nature. Cultural feminists readily affirmed Chodorow's observation that women suffer not only from inequality but (*primarily*, some would say) from "their continuing sense of unmet emotional and relational possibilities as well."[48] Thanks to *The Reproduction of Mothering*—or at least to embellishments of its central tenets—cultural feminists could fashion a politics of identity grounded psychoanalytically in a distinctively feminine ethos of love, altruism, and cooperation.

Cultural feminists thus found in Chodorow's work the basis of a new essentialism. Not biology, not even anatomy, but the seemingly invariable processes of early development produce the dramatic differences between the sexes. The critic Toril Moi thus charged Chodorow with propagating *cultural* essentialism, with no less onerous consequences. *The Reproduction of Mothering*, Moi claimed, reintroduced the age-old patriarchal dichotomy, that is, "a specific female nature pitted against an equally specific male nature."[49]

However, the players in this confusing drama soon moved around as if in a game of musical chairs. Before she died, Dinnerstein, who had escaped these charges because of her contrary depiction of motherhood, embraced cultural feminism with a passion to become a leading proponent of ecofeminism. For her part, Chodorow entered training analysis and emerged—to the astonishment of many—a promoter of Freud's purported protofeminism. Only the celebrity Gilligan remained fixed in her paradigm.

Drawing out the full irony of the situation, the literary scholar Madelon Sprengnether pointed out that the "real liability of Chodorow's argument" was its "very success." Chodorow had depicted femininity so positively that, according to Sprengnether, she had convinced many feminists "to regard it as an inherent and desirable aspect of female identity."[50] Her own view of gender as a cultural construction was lost along the way. As a result, Chodorow's fans savored her exploration of women's relational capacities, unique sense of connectedness and empathy, and allegiance to other women and they stripped them from the theoretical core of *The Reproduction of Mothering*. No doubt, if not for Chodorow, some other theorist would have appeared to define the terms for a renewed vision of femininity as an essential quality and relatedness as its essence. It was Chodorow's fate to provide *post*-Freudian psychoanalytic grist for this contemporary mill.

A Rapprochement

Margaret S. Mahler had sketched a pattern of psychological development that contained both paradigmatic and metaphorical possibilities. She had sought to map the developmental trajectory of normal infants, that is, the interpsychic path children take to achieve a sense of individuality. She supposed that a baby passes much of the first four months of life in a symbiotic relationship with its mother and then begins slowly to gain self-recognition as a separate human being. Between four months and one year the baby experiences its first moments of differentiation and develops a body image, a process which Mahler termed "hatching." For the next six months or so the infant "practices" its evolving role as an autonomous being, returning from time to time for maternal "refueling." By the middle of the second year the toddling infant comes to emotional terms with autonomy and now wishes to share experiences with the mother. This phase, termed "rapprochement," includes intense interaction between mother and child and builds toward a crisis. Encompassing the final months of the second year of life, this third stage is marked by ambivalence and instability as the child vacillates between pushing the mother away and desperately clinging to her. It is also at this point that the child discovers anatomical sex differences and works these markers of gender into a concept of identity that develops through the processes of separation.[51]

While feminists were rediscovering psychoanalysis, a concurrent rapprochement was taking place within the psychoanalytic profession. By the mid-1970s women had created caucuses within the major societies, and femininity had become a major topic at meetings and in the leading journals. A large number of psychoanalysts conceded that Freudian formulations of development did not adequately account for the acquisition of gender identity, and they affirmed Stoller's contention that boys and girls diverge psychologically far in advance of their observation of anatomical differences.

Even those who had been unable to muster sympathy during the Great Orgasm Debate found a basis for accord in cultural feminism, and post-Freudian psychoanalysis provided an appropriate discursive field for this regrouping. These psychoanalysts built on the developmental paradigm advanced by Mahler and other post-Freudian theorists, with its focus on the mother-infant dyad, to generate an alternative free of masculine bias. As cultural feminists themselves, these analysts effected a yet more radical transformation of post-Freudian theory.[52]

Psychoanalysts following in the proud tradition of Karen Horney initiated this rapprochement. During the Great Orgasm Debate, these analysts could not connect with the radical feminists who fueled it. But now that feminist politics itself had widened, Horney's legatees found a means to refurbish her reputation. They invoked the image of a brave warrior against Freudian phallocentrism. It was Horney who had first challenged the psychic significance given to the phallus in favor of woman's unique capacity for motherhood.

Horney had eventually rejected this kind of reasoning. Undaunted, her legatees continued to fix on her early publications to pursue what Horney herself had abandoned: in Natalie Shainess's words, "a separate feminine psychology." For example, Roy Schafer, publishing in the authoritative *Journal of the American Psychoanalytic Association*, invoked Horney to set a new standard of psychological development.

He put aside anatomical factors to single out Freud's notorious contention that women, compared to men, lack a sense of justice and are more commonly swayed by their feelings. Far from rejecting this proposition, Schafer agreed with Freud. Yes, women *are* more intuitive and subjective than men. But whereas Freud and his successors interpreted these characteristics as flaws, Schafer argued to the contrary. Bowing to Horney but sounding more like Carol Gilligan, Schafer asserted that it was precisely this configuration of traits that made women better arbiters of morality.[53]

Building on these premises, Jean Baker Miller soon became the psychoanalytic profession's own preeminent cultural feminist. Trained in medicine at Columbia University, Miller had practiced psychiatry and psychoanalysis in New York before moving to Boston, where she became a clinical professor of psychiatry at the Boston University School of Medicine. She also spent two years in the early 1970s at the famed Tavistock Institute and Clinic in London. The American profession knew her well as secretary and trustee of the American Academy of Psychoanalysis and trustee of the American Orthopsychiatric Association. But it was only in the late 1970s that Miller found her niche among cultural feminists within the psychoanalytic profession.

Jean Baker Miller proceeded to make self-in-relation the signature of psychoanalytic feminism. She vigorously protested the practice of portraying one-half the world's people "as a lesser breed," but instead of targeting Freud she aimed directly at various post-Freudians who had cast development as a process by which a person separates from others to achieve an inner sense of individuated self. Thus Mahler's reigning teleology—merger to separation, dependence to autonomy—incorporates, according to Miller, a bias "tied to an image of man." But even in the case of man, this description fails to reflect reality and exists merely as a prescription. No one grows into a totally self-sufficient adult, she insisted, not even men. For women, the model of the autonomous self seriously distorts their experiences and, moreover, imposes an impossible ideal. Miller set herself to establish an alternative theory of psychological development, and she soon eclipsed Chodorow by not only affirming but intemperately celebrating "feminine" connectedness.[54]

For Miller, the phrase "self-in-relation" accurately conveys the quality of female development as triggered by maternal empathy. Because the mother perceives similarities in body and gender with a female baby, she necessarily feels more emotionally attuned to her daughter than to her son, whom she experiences as a dissimilar object. In turn, the mother's feelings facilitate different responses in boys and girls. Boys who, relative to girls, lack an early attachment and identification with their mothers thus develop a lesser sense of connection with others and capacity for intimacy. In contrast, girls develop emotional and cognitive intersubjectivity and seek relational interaction with others throughout their lives.

Both Dinnerstein and Chodorow had come to this conclusion. They had, however, argued for the necessity of breaking the nexus by bringing fathers into the development sequence. Miller, in contrast, cast her lot squarely with Gilligan and sought to make self-in-relation the universal model.

Miller thus viewed the quest for separation as emotionally deficient, a signifier of masculinity. The preferable trajectory, she insisted, is growth through and toward relationship. In her estimation, the purest example of the empathetic self follows the developmental path established in the mother-daughter relationship. Miller therefore cautioned women to cherish the strength they gained from this relationship and counseled men to "struggle to reclaim the very parts of their own experience that they have delegated to women."[55]

To advocate a view of mental health or maturity grounded in female psychology, and to promote suitable psychotherapeutic practices, Miller helped to establish the Stone Center for Development Services and Studies at Wellesley College and became its first director. She worked mainly with psychologists affiliated with McLean Hospital, a nearby psychiatric facility, or the Harvard Medical School. Refining the "Stone Center model" of self-in-relation, originating in the mother-daughter relationship, Miller and her colleagues explored empathy as a key structure in women's personality. They later established the Jean Baker Miller Training Institute to advance therapeutic programs grounded in "relational empowerment strategies." The Institute also sponsored workshops for the general public on such topics as "Mothers and Sons: Uncharted Waters" and "Overcoming the Relational Barrier of Racism."[56]

The die had been cast for cultural feminist psychoanalysis. Miller followed the publication of her successful anthology, *Psychoanalysis and Women,* with a major essay detailing woman's remarkable capacity "to encompass relations to others, simultaneous with the fullest development of the self." As a writer in *Ms. Magazine* pointed out, *Toward a New Psychology of Women* (1976) soon became "a personal bible for those concerned with preserving female cultural values, while invading a male world." Miller herself distinguished her perspective from the work of Chodorow and Dinnerstein, with whom she had been mistakenly linked, and named her true kindred spirit, Carol Gilligan. Women's oppression did not stem from exclusively female mothering, Baker insisted, but from a society that devalued the experience.[57]

Other psychoanalysts were not as discerning as Miller. By the early 1980s a significant number viewed the works of Gilligan, Chodorow, and Miller as complementary if not interchangeable. For example, the *Psychoanalytic Review* featured a symposium on *The Reproduction of Mothering* and praised Chodorow's homage to the mother-daughter relationship as the "hallmark of feminist scholarship and the source of its potentially immense creativity."[58]

Whether grounded in the early object relations employed by Chodorow or, as in Miller's view, extending across a continuous path to adulthood, the model of self-in-relation had become the new standard, the "feminine" traits of empathy and compassion the true measure of psychological well-being. These psychoanalysts, like so many other cultural feminists, thus drew authority from both Miller and Chodorow not only to underscore the differences between the sexes but to endow women with their own, perhaps superior measure of self-in-relation-hood. They could legitimately promote previously devalued "feminine" qualities. Women no longer had to suffer from low self-esteem because weak ego boundaries supposedly limited their psychological growth. To the contrary, women might revel in their unique relational capacity and know that for far too long, as one commentator noted, masculinity had reigned as "an unconscious talisman or selfobject."[59]

Soon even the most dedicated psychoanalysts confronted the contradictions that Chodorow herself had acknowledged. No matter how hard they tried, they could not comfortably contain femininity within the sphere of reproduction. It was easy enough to reject the autonomous self as the highest developmental goal, but how could psychoanalysts safely encourage women to establish their independence from men? To be self-supporting, for example, especially to work in "masculine" pursuits that pay well, demands a set of character traits that would certainly jeopardize women's uniquely "feminine" sense of self-esteem. Conventional psychoanalytic wisdom stressed for both sexes the importance of a durable sense of self or, in the terminology of object relations theory, strong ego boundaries. Now psychoanalysts had to worry that by encouraging independence they might damage their female clients' relational capacities. Achieving the correct balance between merger and separation, dependence and autonomy, proved remarkably elusive, and attempts to wrestle with the contradictions inherent in this dilemma produced a set of surprising arguments.[60]

The new interpretations of lesbianism provide a vivid illustration of this conundrum. According to classical Freudians, lesbianism results from a failure to displace penis envy by reproductive aims and presents itself in adult women as the retention of clitoral sexuality. Although early neo-Freudians like Clara Thompson had interpreted homosexuality in men or women as a cultural adaptation rather than a character flaw, the leading midcentury theorists identified it as extreme pathology. Refuting Kinsey, who reasoned that homosexual behavior occupies one place on a continuum of normal practices, a large number of psychoanalysts held their ground. Tales of valiant therapeutic efforts to cure the "illness" appeared in case studies such as Richard C. Robertiello's *Voyage from Lesbos: The Psychoanalysis of a Female Homosexual* (1959). Meanwhile the prolific writer Edmund Bergler discussed lesbianism as "a banal aberration of neurosis."[61] Only in the wake of the gay and women's liberation movements—and the American Psychiatric Association's 1973 decision to remove homosexuality from its list of disorders—did American psychoanalysts finally relent. Nevertheless, for the feminists among them, lesbianism tested the limits of post-Freudian developmental theory.

Given the validation of woman's relational capacities, lesbianism appeared to many psychoanalysts not only "normal" but logical. If, as Chodorow claimed, an adult woman seeks to re-create the experience of primary love, why should she turn to a man? Any woman would be better off seeking love from another similarly situated woman than from an emotionally autonomous man. Chodorow herself had conceded this possibility.[62] Several psychoanalysts, however, embellished this notation, while thanking Chodorow for demonstrating that lesbianism may be "the most healthy and empowered choice for the modern woman."[63]

Yet, at the same time, lesbianism became mired in the mother-daughter relation. If this primary relation facilitates homoerotic love, it also causes the majority of problems reported by lesbians in therapy. Primary love, it seems, can be too strong and enduring, forcing an unusually painful negotiation between merger and separation. Consequently, in adult relationships lesbians relive their own primordial histories and become especially vulnerable to conflicts over dependency and autonomy. And because lesbianism heightens "a woman's capacity for intensity and intimacy," it heightens other problems as well. The mother-daughter relationship thus fosters a splendid vision of lifelong primary love but simultaneously ensures the transfer of all the conflicts originating here to adult relationships.[64]

The trickiest negotiations concerned women's aspirations for careers. Although Freud had defined mental health as the ability to love and to work, he absolved women from the latter requirement and instead attributed any such striving to a masculinity complex. Early neo-Freudians challenged this dictum and, distinguishing between femininity and sex-role stereotypes, objected to the Freudian practice of conflating the two concepts. By the 1940s, though, ego psychologists were leading a relentless assault on feminism qua careerism and managed to silence all but the most steadfast. The subject of women's careers virtually disappeared from the psychoanalytic literature. Only as the women's liberation movement gained steam did the reality of the situation sink in. Between 1970 and 1980 the percentage of women working outside the home had risen from 43 to 51, and with the majority of women now in the labor force, American psychoanalysts could hardly avoid the matter. Psychoanalysts routinely reported conversations with clients who described the difficulty of coping with "dual roles." Translating into the theoretical paradigm of the day, they recorded their clients' uphill struggles to attain, as Mildred Asch put it, "a positive feeling about feminine identity apart from childbearing." Psychoanalysts thus placed themselves into the awkward position of encouraging women to pursue their worldly ambitions without, as Jean Baker Miller put it, casting off "the valuable facets of their heritage."[65]

Discussions framed around "career versus motherhood" revealed as many contradictions as the new perspective on lesbianism. Not surprisingly, given their legacy, women affiliated with the American Academy of Psychoanalysis were among the first to pursue such subjects as women's fear of success and inclinations toward neurotic dependency. Bearing the distinctive imprint of Horney, Mead, and Thompson, they acknowledged the cultural forces inhibiting women's progress in non-domestic realms, particularly the pressures inherent in a male-dominated society. They nevertheless formulated the ensuing psychological problems as a conflict between woman's sense of connectedness and the necessity to function in an autonomous, assertive manner.

Alexandra Symonds (1918–1992), a one-time trustee of the American Academy of Psychoanalysis and affiliate of the Karen Horney Clinic in New York, wrote extensively on the emotional conflicts of women who strive to combine career and marriage. An active feminist, founder and first president of the Association of Women Psychiatrists and editor of its publication, *News for Women in Psychiatry,* Symonds credited the women's liberation movement with encouraging women to take advantage of new opportunities for personal growth. Many women were successfully and happily taking on these new challenges. Despite their achievements, she noted, a sizable number were "immobilized by despair." They succumbed to stress, chronic depression, low self-esteem, and even confusion in sexual identity. Symonds intended to remove "the blockages to liberation" by overcoming their fear of self-assertion.[66]

The mother-daughter relationship proved to be, as in the case of lesbians, a major source of this conflict. Analysts like Symonds and Ruth Moulton noted that more women than men express self-doubts about their abilities, yet most women pursue therapy, at least initially, to address problems in personal relationships rather than in careers. Moulton, who had trained with Clara Thompson, traced this apparent fear of success to the patriarchal values that decree women to be "nourishing facilitators" and render them psychologically ill-equipped to enter into the masculine world of aggressive competition without severe penalties. But in the blink of an eye, she shifted interpretive gears to warn that success at a career may pose "a threat to the early symbiotic bond with the preoedipal mother."[67]

Other writers also bridged these two explanatory modes. Real structural inequalities stymie women's career aspirations, they noted, but the emotional conflict originates in pre-oedipal relations. Most often psychoanalysts discussed career women as participants in a difficult struggle against identification with their primarily domestic mothers. If these women achieve the independence and self-mastery demanded by the business world, they often feel emotionally isolated, even guilty. They interpret their success as defiance of their mothers. Emotionally overwhelmed, even the most successful women often refuse to claim their accomplishments. Thus career women, whose professional status depends on the appropriation of "masculine" traits, frequently suffer from depression. And this problem, therapists noted, appeared especially pronounced among those women who, like lesbians, had experienced a particularly "sticky" relationship with their mothers.[68]

A host of contradictions gathered here, including a not-so-subtle tendency to blame mothers for impeding their daughters' separation. As cultural feminists, psychoanalysts celebrated the distinctive female developmental track and valorized "feminine" qualities of nurturing and connectedness; but as professionals, they also sought to secure a place for women within the "masculine" sphere that favored character traits antagonistic to feminine sensibilities. Some psychoanalysts tried, without success, to straddle both realms. They described the "symptom-free successful woman" as one who had achieved a high degree of individuation without becoming too autonomous. And because a woman's self-esteem depends to a large degree on relationships, they advised those women who are unable to have children or who choose to forgo motherhood to seek to "gratify their needs for nurturing in vocational and avocational activities."[69] This argument implied that career women without children must find an outlet for their relational needs, lest they suffer emotionally. They must compensate, in other words, by choosing from a narrow range of occupations, such as the helping professions that capitalize on relational qualities and desires —and, what these psychoanalysts failed to note, that pay less than jobs "suited" to masculinity. This argument also suggested that even those women who satisfy their empathetic desires in motherhood will have a difficult time in achieving a feeling of success in careers.

Too often the resolution of this dilemma appeared frightfully simple. One writer worried that the women's liberation movement, in encouraging women to replace "passivity, dependence and submission" with "aggression, assertiveness, and independence," merely exchanged the "Stepford Wife" syndrome for an entirely new set of problems. "Is superwoman a true self or yet another false self defending against experience?" she asked. Might not such aspirations "deprive women of the wholeness, fullness, and caring of the good mother?" This writer found consolation in the about-face of former militants who succumbed to the rightward drift of the Reagan era and modified their former political stands. One psychoanalyst, for example, quoted Betty Friedan's *The Second Stage* (1982): "To deny the part of one's being that has, through the ages, been expressed in motherhood—nurturing, loving softness and tiger strength—is to deny part of one's personhood as a woman." The unexpressed thought, that only motherhood fulfills woman's emotional needs, loomed close to the surface of this new (old) argument.[70]

While affirming women's capacity to work, these feminist psychoanalysts could not relinquish the idea that women had a more pronounced need to love. Feminists at the turn of the century had promoted this idea, proclaiming motherhood as woman's singular means of self-realization. Freud himself had argued that women achieve their greatest happiness or satisfaction in the birth of a baby, particularly a boy, but only as the "consolation prize" for their own lack of a penis. Post-Freudians could now discount all anatomy-bound ideas and instead locate the origin of maternal desire in the pre-oedipal object relations. But what did it really mean that the experience of motherhood still reigned supreme? Feminism via post-Freudian psychoanalysis had come full circle, it appeared, albeit with a slight deviation.

Few psychoanalysts held such extreme views. But even those feminists concerned about the quality of relationships between mothers and daughters found it difficult to comprehend the varied and fast-changing experiences of adult women. Their female clients obviously enjoyed unprecedented control over the timing and processes of reproduction, an option desired but not easily achieved by feminists in 1910. The women's liberation movement had marked a considerable advance, insisting that women gain control over reproduction as a fundamental right. By the late 1960s feminists were campaigning hard for the repeal of all legislation barring reproductive freedom, and in 1973 the Supreme Court decision of *Roe v. Wade* legalized abortion. In 1986, amid the backlash of the Reagan-Bush years, the American Psychoanalytic Association reaffirmed its own pro-choice resolution adopted at its 1970 annual meeting. But psychoanalytic theory, running the gamut from Freudian to object relations, had not yet encompassed these all-important developments. "A woman's relationship to her reproductive capacities is fraught not only with the mysteries of her own unconscious and the conflicts of her own personal familial history, but also," one psychoanalyst admitted, "with a social, political, and economic history of patriarchy and oppression."[71] This much had long been obvious; the ramifications remained stubbornly elusive.

The historical dimensions of motherhood pushed against post-Freudian theory. Psychoanalysts arguing that femininity emanated from the mother-daughter dyad lacked the means to interpret the sharp decline in fertility in the 1970s, when an unusual number of women chose to postpone childbirth or to remain (in the uncomfortable term of the day) "unchilded." Motherhood rebounded in the 1980s but on strikingly unfamiliar terms. The new reproductive technologies, from test tubes to surrogates, had altered the context of pregnancy and childbirth for many women, raising ethical and political as well as psychological problems beyond the reach of the most talented therapists and theorists. "We are being asked to tolerate and endorse new personal freedoms, homosexual parenting, equalitarian couples," one analyst reflected. These notations on developments of staggering proportion prompted only a weak mixture of pioneering spirit and self-reassurance, the familiar promise that "we are crossing boundaries and blazing new trails."[72]

The intellectual default of post-Freudian theory also pointed to a familiar pattern of seemingly eternal return or déjà vu. The dialogue of feminism and psychoanalysis had since the dawn of the century depended largely upon a shared belief in the centrality of sexual difference. Alternative psychological theories that muted the significance of this disparity gave proponents a critical edge against the credibility gap of "difference theorists" but quickly left psychoanalysts and feminists little to say to each other. Neo-Freudians, abandoning Freud's id-driven theories for a cultural approach, challenged his anatomy-centered views but in the end substituted their own, as bad or worse, reductionism. A new generation of feminist polemicists overlaid psychoanalytic theories with a new kind of sociology, but eventually they, too, ran their intellectual course. Early relational experiences simply could not account for wide variations in maternal desires, let alone all the other aspects of a woman's life.

The rapprochement between feminism and psychoanalysis reproduced the theoretical instabilities embedded in both subjects. The ascendancy of the new developmental paradigm allowed feminist theorists to displace the Oedipus complex—thus penis envy—as the source of femininity without sacrificing unconscious formations. But, while cutting the neo-Freudian nexus, they could not escape the chronic dilemmas surrounding female subjectivity.

Psychoanalysts brought to a theoretical head the inherent tensions in this brand of identity politics. While celebrating femininity, how could theorists—or therapists—promote women's advancement into the sphere controlled and, according to their own argument, corrupted by men without risking the integrity of women's distinctive psychology? How could women honor their unique relational capacities and aspire at the same time to greater autonomy? Psychoanalysts thus underscored the dilemma of modern-day feminism: how could women be both different from and equal to men?

All this had a very postmodern flavor. What music critics termed "recontextualization," a mix-and-match of diverse systems, created a synthetic or syncretic perspective exciting in its mosaic-like qualities but devoid of strong moorings. Indeed, feminism itself became in the process less and less a centering concept, turning instead into a secondary premise shifting with the ever changing political moods of the participants. In the worst case, the claim of woman's special need to love, to connectedness over the triumphs of the world of work, seemed remarkably like an upbeat version of the familiar back-to-the-home imperatives from midcentury. But even in the best case, the women's liberation call for collective self-emancipation appeared suddenly irrelevant to the project of securing one's own relational niche.

Cynics, but not only cynics, suggested that the conservative upswing of the late 1970s and 1980s—marked by the feminization of poverty, the defeat of the Equal Rights Amendment, and a steady erosion if not all-out judicial reversal of Roe v. Wade—had turned many erstwhile activists and militant theoreticians toward a fantasy politics of difference.[73] Giving up on the apparently impossible task of changing the world, they consoled themselves with ever greater permutations of theory. And while they slept through evil days, they dreamed of an irreducible, splendid identity for all women, for all time. It was a dream so beautiful that the sleeping hardly dared to wake.

The further adventures of Erik Homberger Erikson illustrate the paradox underlying the rapprochement of feminism and psychoanalysis in the 1980s. One of the principal architects of Momism during the 1940s, Erikson stood out during the early days of the women's liberation movement as a perfect example of psychoanalytic misogyny. Ironically, to achieve redemption, he had only to hold his conceptual ground and wait for the wheel to turn again.

Erikson had also advanced a development scheme emphasizing the differences between the sexes. In observing children at play, he had noted that girls consistently configure domestic scenes of interior harmony while boys attend to outside buildings, particularly high towers, and imagine accidents and other perilous situations. This recurring pattern suggested to him that boys and girls diverge developmentally in important ways: while boys grow up to become men with "a fondness for 'what works,' " girls extend and perfect their peace-loving, life-ensuring sentiments.

Unlike Freud, Erikson did not knock the female superego or disparage femininity. To the contrary, he invested great faith in women, encouraging them to act on their rights as citizens so as to extend their beneficent influence over the public realm. He even suggested that "the representation of the mothers of the species in the council of image-making and decision" might quell the "potential for annihilation as now exists." If women shared political leadership with men, in other words, they might lower the barriers between peoples, promote cooperation against competition, and bring peace instead of war.

In the mid-1960s Erikson correctly anticipated the response to this argument. He knew that feminists would object to his, or to any man's, "attempt to help define the uniqueness of womanhood, as though by uniqueness he could be expected to mean inborn inequality." It was men who took the greater "joy in otherness," he admitted, as well as in their own "dominant identities." Yet, too much was at stake to deny the differences between the sexes, most especially woman's unique life-giving powers. "Am I saying, then, that 'anatomy is destiny'?" he asked rhetorically. Braving the anticipated storm of protest, Erikson did not budge. The "basic modalities of woman's commitment and involvement," he insisted, "naturally also reflect the ground plan of her body." The female body predisposes women to a unique biological, psychological, and moral determination to care for human life.[74]

Erikson hit the mark in predicting the objections to this causal association between women's special "inner space"—their reproductive organs—and femininity. Responding to his notorious essay on womanhood and inner space, published originally in 1964, Elizabeth Janeway and Phyllis Chesler, among others, lambasted his biologism. Kate Millett prefaced her hostile remarks by agreeing with Erikson that men were responsible for "our present predicament," the threat of nuclear annihilation, but she nevertheless refused to subscribe to his determinist perspective on the differences between the sexes. "What Erikson does not recognize," she countered, "is that the traits of each group are culturally conditioned and depend upon their political relationship."[75]

A few years later Erikson published a rejoinder in Jean Strouse's anthology, *Women and Analysis*. He appeared unmoved by the criticism of his frequently reprinted essay and refused to retract his argument or to apologize. He not only reaffirmed his thesis but underscored its broader significance: "that, as women take their share in the over-all economic and political planning of affairs so far monopolized by men, they cannot fail to cultivate a concerted attention to the whole earth as an inner space, no matter how far any of the outer spaces may reach."[76]

The continuity in Erikson's own ideas probably surprised no one. It was the readiness of many psychoanalysts and feminists to endorse his views that marked a clear and unequivocal turn. By 1982 the feminist psychoanalyst Donna Bassin employed Erikson's phrase "inner space" to call upon women to explore their bodies "as a wellspring of their unique development." Although Bassin later insisted that she chose the expression merely for metaphorical purposes, certainly not to define woman's biological destiny as motherhood, the distinction remained fuzzy at best. Bassin's proclamation was, after all, strikingly similar to that of another impatient author who blurted out "—and I all but blush to say such a thing— . . . that motherhood is a force for good in the world."[77]

Kate Millett had warned that Erikson mixed two different but not uncongenial kinds of reasoning about femininity: "Freud's chauvinism" and Erikson's own "chivalry." In the first version women lived as unequals under the ruthless law of the (missing) phallus; in the second version chivalric men made enormous concessions to women's desires and needs. Strictly speaking, the survival of the world seemed to depend upon this chivalry, in its masculine recognition and social internalization of women's sound values. But as a practical fact, this hoped-for adaptation altered very little in the biocultural facts of daily life. Freud warned that women as a group had no place in the male territory of power; Erikson had them so content with their own maternal status (including the masochistic pleasures of menses and childbirth) that they could easily yield all aspirations of "outer space" to men. "If human sexual temperament is inherent," Millett concluded her critique of Erikson, "there is really very little hope for us." Even the search for self-in-relation could not escape this possibility.[78]

8

The Crisis
in Patriarchal Authority

Chivalry and chauvinism, Kate Millett had warned, march arm in arm.
Erik Erikson had chosen to wear the knight's shining armor; his later
counterparts might treat the women's liberation movement as the real
dragon. Not surprisingly, many men did not welcome women into
their realm, and an ever accommodating psychoanalysis served just as
effectively to fortify the barriers as to lower them. If relational theory
paved the way for rapprochement with feminism, other permutations
of contemporary psychoanalysis widened the gap.

Between the publications of *The Mermaid and the Minotaur* and
The Reproduction of Mothering, a prominent scholar from another
discipline added a decidedly dissonant note to the discussion. Christopher Lasch (1932–1994), a cultural historian at the University of
Rochester, revived the time-honored tradition of psychoanalytic
misogyny. His bestselling treatise *Haven in a Heartless World: The
Family Besieged* (1977) employed psychoanalytic theory to chastise
women, particularly feminists, for abandoning their proper sphere. In
their extrafamilial pursuits, American women had helped to precipitate, according to Lasch, a "crisis in authority," that is, a breakdown
of the structures in both private and public realms that allegedly maintain the civilization.

Listening carefully, one could hear in Lasch's argument the distant strains of Philip Wylie. The prominent left critic had a lot in common with his spirited predecessor. Political journalism was likewise in his blood. His father had worked as an editorial writer for liberal newspapers; his mother, who held a doctorate in philosophy, had been an activist in the League of Women Voters. Before turning to history Lasch himself considered a career in journalism, and throughout his professional life he searched for readers "who wouldn't be only academics."[1] Major success came with a string of popular books beginning with *Haven in a Heartless World*. Although Lasch eclipsed Wylie in hyperbolic eloquence, he delivered a strikingly similar message. He repeatedly berated the citizenry for its own failures, warning against the dangers of pervasive apathy, not toward Hitler's atrocities but toward the barbarism infecting American society itself.

A lot had changed since World War II, but the flight from manhood, it seemed, more than ever hounded the best and the brightest. American men, especially young middle-class men, lacked moral rigor, Lasch complained, and for this reason backed down from civic responsibilities in a "celebration of oral sex, masturbation, and homosexuality." He traced this deficiency to the youth rebellion, which, despite its revelry in personal relationships, merely masked emotional detachment and social irresponsibility. "Unable to internalize authority," he explained, today's youth "projects forbidden impulses outward and transforms the world into a nightmare." Lasch traced the source of this ominous specter to the counterculture, New Left, and women's liberation of the 1960s.[2]

Philip Wylie lived just long enough to issue the same complaint. In his final literary effort, *Sons and Daughters of Mom* (1971), the elderly polemicist attacked the ragtag New Left, Black Power, hippie, and feminist movements for their refusal to grow up. He also renewed his charges against Mom, blaming her for producing this bumper crop of irresponsible, self-indulgent, and nihilistic young people.[3]

Lasch, with his weighty scholarly credentials, breathed new life into the discourse of Momism. He described his variation as "a muted version of [the] black 'matriarchy'" popularized earlier in the Moynihan Report. Disagreeing with Moynihan on many points, Lasch nevertheless commended the prominent liberal senator for underscoring the pathology of mother-centered households. Momism did infect

African American culture, Lasch confirmed: just consider the favorite slang of ghetto youth, the ubiquitous term of both praise and derision—"motherfucker." The problem with the Moynihan Report, Lasch grumbled, was that it exaggerated "the distance between the ghetto and the rest of American culture, which in some ways has come to resemble a pale copy of the black ghetto." The situation of African Americans was worse, of course, because slavery had long ago debased black manhood; the white middle class, in comparison, had much more to lose.

Lasch thus echoed Wylie in linking "the general deterioration of the social environment" to Momism. All American males bore its stigma as manifested in "the cult of large breasts, a fixation on oral sex, and a tendency to regard all women as mother." In middle-class white as well as black families, fathers were "weak and acquiescent at home," while mothers, Lasch complained, dominated psychologically. The American Mom, Lasch concluded à la Wylie, had imposed "her own madness on everyone else."[4]

The ultimate responsibility for this calamity lay, once again, at the feet of feminists. Lasch chastised first-wave feminists not for demanding their rights as citizens but for upsetting the natural order of the family, "the chief agency of socialization" and producer of "cultural patterns in the individual." Sounding surprisingly like his 1940s progenitors, he blamed feminists specifically for helping to remove men from their rightful jurisdiction over the family and thereby paving the way for the moral ruination of children under Mom's influence.

Skipping past the era of Mary Wollstonecraft, Lasch added a new twist to this argument. Feminists, he charged, had colluded with various reformers to transfer paternal authority to outside experts and to the impersonal state. To wit: nineteenth-century American women, in their enthusiasm for temperance, social purity, and domestic propriety, had teamed up with nascent social scientists to wrest authority away from allegedly wayward husbands and fathers; during the early part of the twentieth century they continued to foster the growth of the new "helping professions"—social workers, educators, and psychologists, among others—which, once entrenched in government agencies, proceeded to strip the family of its basic functions and the father of his rightful authority. Feminists were, in sum, responsible for the modern welfare state, which even liberals were beginning to admit failed to redress the most pressing social maladies and sometimes made them worse. Thus, thanks to feminists, the family—"the last refuge of love and decency"—no longer provided men with "a haven in private life," ever more imperative as "business, politics, and diplomacy grow more savage and warlike."[5]

To sharpen his attack against the evils of the welfare state, Lasch painted a glowing portrait of the bourgeois family of yore, highlighting its stern but well-meaning patriarch. He did concede that nineteenth-century feminists had some reasons to complain: women led a narrowly circumscribed life and, moreover, suffered a morally enervating dependence on men. Offsetting this minor injustice, however, was a salutary outcome: the production of ideal (male) citizens who were wedded to "the traditional virtues of work, thrift, and achievement." Oppressive to women, the bourgeois family had succeeded beautifully as the setting for psychosexual development, specifically by helping children to master the anxieties provoked by the famed triangulated drama of early childhood, the Oedipus complex. Authoritative at home, the powerful father could act forcefully and punitively to repress his son's incestuous impulses and thereby encourage him to internalize paternal authority and emerge with a well-organized superego. In short, the bourgeois father instilled in his sons unswerving reverence for self-mastery, the prerequisite of the responsible citizen.

The elegance of the bourgeois order contrasted sharply with the current debacle of the "fatherless society." With fathers "too shadowy and remote to challenge . . . primitive fantasies about them," Lasch clarified, "children fail to develop the self-assured, self-denying, and strong willed modal personality of the bourgeois man." Ruled by Mom's expert allies, these children are unable to internalize paternal authority and therefore enter adulthood without inner resources of their own. Lacking a firm superego, these morally pallid youth grow up to become easy prey for ideologues—hence the lure of feminism.

Captivated by Freudian theory, Lasch remained devoted to its cornerstone, the Oedipus complex. He hewed so loyally to classical psychoanalysis as he understood it that he blamed feminists for diminishing Freud's reputation, for sullying as well as misrepresenting the master's theories. He came down hard on the Culture and Personality scholars for facilitating the reformist—that is, feminist—revision of Freudianism. The chief villain was none other than Karen Horney.

According to Lasch, it was Horney who led the attack on Freud that eliminated "what was radical from his thought." Collapsing a long and complex history into the moment of Horney's original complaint against Freud's phallocentrism, Lasch attributed the major weakness in neo-Freudianism, its rejection of the libido theory, to an interwar feminist rebellion. If nineteenth-century feminists had worked to undermine paternal authority, their twentieth-century successors, according to Lasch, had tried just as hard to depreciate the one theory that had promised its redemption. One way or another, in real life or in the realm of theory, any assault on the Oedipus complex inevitably raised the specter of feminism.[6]

Although the psychoanalytic nuances of Lasch's arguments undoubtedly escaped many readers, his defense of the bourgeois moral order against the ravages of feminism did not. *Haven in a Heartless World* struck an empathetic chord among those who judged the excesses of the 1960s to have wrought lasting damage upon American society and culture. The neo-liberal *New Republic* characteristically deemed Lasch's "the best essay available today on the modern history of the family." The *New York Times* called his argument "brilliant and challenging." A few less prescient commentators were frankly puzzled by the self-avowed radical author's distaste for the welfare state but nevertheless judged the book a major accomplishment. Among the broader public Lasch gained almost overnight a celebrity rare for an academic writer.[7]

Feminists immediately interpreted the favorable reception of *Haven in a Heartless World* as a bad sign. "The nuclear family is back in favor," one writer groaned. Determined to resist the growing "nostalgia for patriarchy's heyday," feminists knew all too well that Lasch was not alone in "his sorrow for its passing."[8] The upcoming presidential election of 1980 would mark clearly the nationwide consolidation of conservatism. But what caught many feminists off-guard was the fact that Lasch's attack came from the left, not the right.

Lasch stood at the head of a coterie of radical intellectuals, male and female, who employed psychoanalysis to incite a backlash against women's liberation. There was nothing inherently remarkable about this turn of events. Through the interwar period, psychoanalysis had appealed most to left-of-center intellectuals; just as readily, it offered a conceptual haven to those fleeing Marxism for liberalism after the war. Cold War liberals had no trouble deploying psychoanalysis to wage a memorably ruthless assault on feminism as one of several dark forces threatening democracy. Now, in the late 1970s, the precipitous decline of liberalism found prominent critics who, in a doubly strange turn of history's wheel, not only blamed feminists for both the temporary triumph of liberalism and its fatal weakness but formulated their complaints in Marxist terms. The political grounds of opposition might have shifted enormously, but the underlying uneasiness with feminism remained intact.

This time feminists were well fortified to do battle with their self-declared foes. A sizable group had themselves embraced Marxism, emerging in the late 1960s as a distinct component of the women's liberation movement. Moreover, they shared Lasch's concern for the family. But unlike Lasch, who brooded over its decline, these socialist feminists targeted the patriarchal family as the principal site of women's oppression. In addition, several prominent members of this group, such as Nancy Chodorow, had also hailed psychoanalysis as an ally. Of course, their take was entirely different from Lasch's. Like their British colleague Juliet Mitchell, they envisioned psychoanalysis as "not a recommendation *for* a patriarchal society, but an analysis *of* one."[9] For these feminists, a Freudo-Marxist synthesis might just sharpen their own understanding of the nexus between the systems of reproduction and production. Spurred on by Dinnerstein and Chodorow, they made such great strides in this direction that Lasch himself found it hard to keep up.

The resulting dialogue, set into furious motion in the 1980s, exposed multiple possibilities for both feminism and psychoanalysis. The major battleground was critical theory, a psychoanalytically informed social theory and a long-standing school of European philosophy. Supplying an intellectual cachet that home-grown products could not furnish, it offered enthusiasts what earlier generations had discovered in Freud's canon: an almost sensual excitement with complex ideas. Like Freudianism proper, critical theory also offered endless options for interpretation and reinterpretation.

Critical Theory, Authority, and Domination

Previewed by Hegel and Marx as an evaluation of self and society, critical theory derives from the interdisciplinary work of the Institute of Social Research, established in 1923 in Frankfurt, Germany. Better known as the Frankfurt School, this handful of mainly German-Jewish scholars—Max Horkheimer, Theodor Adorno, Frederick Pollock, Leo Lowenthal, Erich Fromm, and Herbert Marcuse, among others—had turned to both Marxism and psychoanalysis in an attempt to understand, and ultimately to transform, the machinations of existing society. This objective remained intact while passing through the hands of several generations, eventually including both New Left and post–New Left critics as well as their feminist allies and adversaries.

Initially, critical theory took shape as a left version of Culture and Personality, that is, as an explicitly Marxist study of "the contemporary psychic make-up of men in various social groups."[10] Its German originators, troubled by the unanticipated ability of capitalism to outlast the crisis of World War I, had sought a corrective to the mechanistic Marxism bequeathed by the Second International. Russia had produced a successful revolution in 1917, Western Europe experienced a few rumblings, but the German proletariat seemed strikingly passive. Why did the working class of the most advanced industrial nation on the continent "fail" to seize power? Why did German workers remain politically apathetic despite the growing threat of fascism? Even the near-collapse of the postwar economy triggered no response. Evidently, then, the problem lay not in objective conditions, apparently ripe for revolution, so much as in the realm of culture, ideology, and psychology. Critical theory began here, as an inquiry into the processes of psychological domination.

"Lacking a satisfactory psychology," the youthful Erich Fromm clarified in 1931, "Marx and Engels could not explain *how* the material basis was reflected in man's head and heart." Psychoanalysis, he countered, could do what Marxism could not, "describe empirically the process of the production of ideologies." Where Marxism projected a "quantitative and mechanical" view of human agency, Freud's theories revealed the hidden mediations between society and the individual psyche.[11]

Working from this premise, the Frankfurt scholars reassessed the predictive power of contemporary Marxist theory and staked out new epistemological grounds in psychoanalysis. They turned to Freud specifically to interrogate "power-relationships" as reflected in an individual's "mind, his ideas, his basic concepts and judgments, but also in his innermost life, in preferences and desires." Interlacing theories of Marx and Freud, they aimed to break through the world of things to reveal the underlying relations between persons.[12]

Preserving the phylogenic and dialectical underpinnings of the theories of both Freud and Marx, the Frankfurt scholars highlighted the contradiction that would stand perennially at the center of critical theory. The possibility for agency (or selfhood) begins with the conquest of nature, they argued, at the crucial moment in human history that anticipates the triumph of reason over irrationality. But by gaining control of the forces of nature, the apparent victor unleashes a paradox, for humanity *as part of nature* becomes increasingly subject to its own domination, what Marx measured as the rise of class systems, exploitation, and war. As Theodor Adorno (1903–1969) and Max Horkheimer (1895–1973) put it: "Man's domination over himself, which grounds his selfhood, is almost always the destruction of the subject in whose service it is undertaken; for the substance which is dominated, suppressed and dissolved through self-preservation is none other than that very life as a function of which the achievements of self-preservation are defined; it is, in fact, what is to be preserved."[13]

Freud said as much. In *Civilization and Its Discontents* (1930) he restated his fundamental proposition that the victory of the ego over the id, necessary for self-preservation, can never be complete or without detrimental consequences. In sum, social progress—which the Frankfurt scholars specified as the growth of regulations and governing institutions such as the state—extracts a stiff price from the individual psyche by allowing fewer and fewer opportunities for instinctual gratification. Freud, of course, envisioned no reconciliation. He considered the commonplace contention that civilization bears the chief responsibility for human misery, that a return to primitive conditions would bring greater happiness, and he called this idea "astonishing." For those who wanted more, he could "offer them no consolation." To the contrary, he bade them to give up such notions: "But how ungrateful, how short-sighted after all, to strive for the abolition of civilization! What would then remain would be a state of nature, and that would be far harder to bear."[14] The Frankfurt scholars, following Marx, hoped for better, but they nevertheless came to this same impasse. Each step forward in controlling the forces of nature inevitably brings its counterpart in repressive social controls, and, consequently, the less constrained past always competes with a future of yet greater domination.

Ostensibly, both paths pointed away from the existing society but along opposing vectors. One aimed at a dialectical transcendence of the present moment, toward a vision of freedom perhaps never to be achieved but essential to human survival. The other led back to a "civilized" morality purportedly disintegrating too rapidly under the pressures of advancing capitalism. Later feminists would find themselves waylaid at this same crossroad, never altogether certain whether the incoming traffic was friendly or hostile.

For feminists, though, the path "backward" raised a specific problem, for the "master narrative" fashioned by the Frankfurt scholars retained the phallocentrism that troubled Freud's story of origination. More historically minded than Freud, Horkheimer and Adorno passed over the primordial beginnings of social organization in the primal horde to highlight the more recent moments of consolidation. It was the bourgeois epoch that established the basis for human self-realization, they argued, its liberal culture and philosophy fostering a vision of autonomy that, for all its limitations, remains indispensable. But despite their historicism, the Frankfurt scholars merely replicated Freud's bias. They, too, insisted that the beginning of civilization depended on the internalization of paternal authority by the sons. If Freud celebrated the overthrow of the primal father, his successors honored the emergence of the bourgeois family wherein fathers ruled supreme. In sum, the critical theorists merely transposed the crucial moment to another, more recent era and kept men at the center of the story.

The critical theorists provided the material underpinnings for the Oedipus complex, and by giving such sweeping sociological status to the personal authority of the bourgeois father they endowed the patriarchal family with a dignity in excess of Freud's more troubled model. By dint of his strength and worldly success, the father becomes the sole mediator between civil society and the family and the proper model for character development. Horkheimer did grant that the rule of the father could be tyrannical, especially when it came to depriving women and young children of happiness. But this small tragedy was nothing compared to "the self-control of the individual, the disposition for work and discipline, the ability to hold firmly to certain ideas, consistency in practical life, application of reason, perseverance and pleasure in constructive activity," that, according to Horkheimer, "could all be developed only under the dictation and guidance of the father whose own education had been won in the school of life." Horkheimer added that the very ideal of subjectivity depends on the emergence of civil society as a distinct realm of social, political, and economic interaction, that is, on the "separation of spheres" that defines bourgeois sex relations.[15]

The exaltation of paternal authority gained urgency when the Frankfurt scholars, as Marxists and as Jews, faced the premier "crisis in authority." With the consolidation of Hitler's power in 1933, the Institute for Social Research (with Horkheimer as its director from 1930) found itself concerned not with the promises of the bourgeois epoch but with the overwhelming threat to its survival posed by fascism. In response, a team of investigators supervised by Erich Fromm set themselves to discover the ways in which the modern German family fostered certain character traits—rigidity, conformity, inability to handle ambiguity, and a propensity for aggressive behavior—that not only undermined the autonomous subject but, in inhibiting class consciousness, predisposed children to fascism.

The results of this five-year study confirmed what the researchers had undoubtedly anticipated: a frighteningly positive correlation between political passivity and the father's diminished authority in both public and private spheres. With the rise of monopolistic state-guided capitalism, public institutions such as the church, state, and mass media had taken over many of the family's functions, they concluded, and the modern father, a mere wage earner rather than entrepreneur, no longer enjoyed the authority to inspire both fear and reverence in his children. This carnage had left the family an empty shell.

Recasting this melancholy development in psychoanalytic terms and applying their analysis to the contemporary political scene, the Frankfurt scholars readily discerned the sadomasochistic personality structure already prevalent among their countrymen. German fathers had responded to their reduced status, they specified, by becoming all the more authoritarian in attitude, demanding even stricter obedience and inflicting greater punishment for infringements. On the eve of Hitler's ascent, this diminished paternal figure had encouraged in his children "a strict superego, guilt feelings, docile love for paternal authority, desire and pleasure at dominating weaker people, acceptance of suffering as punishment for one's own guilt, and a damaged capacity for happiness"—in short, personality traits highly compatible with a fascist dictatorship. It was only logical, although tragic, the Frankfurt scholars surmised, that the German citizen readily submitted to authority and simultaneously derived pleasure from dominating others (including endangered Jews).

The leaps required for these conclusions might well be attributed to the severity of the crisis. The rich German cultural heritage, of which the young scholars considered themselves guardians, had given way to catastrophe, all the worse because the demonic energy of Hitler appeared to arise not from his bourgeois patrons but from the masses. But even if mass psychology held the clues (leaving aside economic, social, and racial factors), the insistence that fascist authoritarianism accompanied the decline of the patriarch better reflected the Frankfurt theorists' own presuppositions than the elegance of their argument.

The rudiments of Lasch's own critique of the crisis of authority, particularly his nostalgia for the bourgeois family, had their origin in this unique conjunction of events and ideas. But the differences are significant. Tracing the entire devolution of the bourgeois moral order from its high point in the nineteenth century, the Frankfurt scholars had in more optimistic moments viewed its internal crisis as an opportunity for a dialectical resolution. As the tyranny of the father could be justified historically only by its role in the dialectical process of development, its decline unmasked the weakness of capitalist social relations, their incapacity to provide a foundation for further human progress—much as economic crisis had exposed the fetters that decaying capitalism placed upon production. Authority, Horkheimer clarified, implies a relationship that either "favors the development of human progress" or sums up in a single word "all those social relationships and ideas which have long since lost their validity, are now artificially maintained, and are contrary to the true interests of the majority." And the difference between the two kinds of authority is as great as that between "sleeping and waking."[16]

The impulse to submission—now so slavish among the Germans—was not, according to Horkheimer, "a timeless drive." The possibility of redemption always lay ahead, a possibility that allowed no triumphant nostalgia, not even for the golden age of bourgeois society. But this position was difficult to maintain. Because neither Horkheimer nor Adorno could see beyond the patriarchal family as the best source of authority in an increasingly troubled world, they fell back upon its history as synonymous with that of the autonomous individual. Unlike Lasch, they nurtured little hope that the restoration of the father could set society aright but simply mourned the steady decline of this historic carrier of freedom.

Horkheimer and Lasch did have an important negative point in common. Neither could ask, let alone seek to answer, the question that had been posed by so many European and American political theorists since the dawn of the bourgeois epoch: Why did the advancement of women into civil society—worse, the rise of feminism—appear as part of the problem rather than as a hopeful sign of transcendence? Why must women be assigned eternally to the sphere of reproduction? In short, why must women be excluded from the dialectic of history?

Like Freud, Horkheimer did not envision a role for women outside the home and, to the contrary, linked the perpetuation of civilization to their subordination within the family. As a Marxist he might follow Friedrich Engels to pinpoint women's oppression in the overthrow of the mother-right, the earliest moment of social organization. But whereas Engels welcomed women's recent entry into the labor force as preparation for their role in the class struggle and subsequent accession of civil equality, Horkheimer believed that, despite all changes, women had best stay at home. In a strange twist of logic, he reasoned that the long history of women's oppression had a politically deleterious effect on "the female psyche." Because their welfare depended so thoroughly on their husbands' worldly success, he concluded, women could act collectively only as a conservative force. Moreover, according to Horkheimer, modern women did not really want to join men in the public realm. Why should any woman not want to trade the prospect of work as sales clerk or typist for the dream of "a happy marriage in which she will be cared for and will be able to worry about her children"? But the bottom line for Horkheimer was, simply, that the economy could not sustain the wage labor of both husband and wife. Wage-earning women would compete with men for jobs and, if they won out, men would lose yet more ground, driving the family further "into despair and decline."[17]

While the Frankfurt scholars were advancing this gloomy argument, not all Freudo-Marxists held such a dim view of women's place in modern history. In the United States, for example, the *Modern Quarterly* crowd had followed out the alternative possibility in the dialectic of history. Faithful to Engels and even more so to the readily appreciable tradition of woman's rights in the United States, V. F. Calverton and Samuel Schmalhausen had provided a mirror image of their German contemporaries. Seizing on Marxism as a corrective to Freudianism rather than the other way around, they put an entirely different spin on the implications of modernity. Resistant to European pessimism and as yet untroubled by the rise of fascism, they celebrated the Machine Age precisely because it undermined the patriarchal family. This development, bringing men and women into closer proximity in both private and public realms, had created the conditions for a genuine Sexual Revolution. Altogether in line with Engels's classic projection of "the invading socialist society," the American Freudo-Marxists welcomed the prospect of greater parity between the sexes. Reconstituted to ensure equality, the modern family would provide the mechanisms for socializing children into a new order happily bereft of the psychic forces of domination, including patriarchy.

There had, lamentably, been no grounds in the 1930s for a dialogue between the *Modern Quarterly* group and the Frankfurt School. For a time, though, the two entities shared overlapping circles of acquaintances at Columbia University, where the Institute for Social Research relocated in 1934 when forced to flee Germany. But just as the refugee scholars were settling in the United States, the *Modern Quarterly* drifted away from cultural questions and psychoanalytic concerns, fell into obscurity in the late 1930s, and died with Calverton himself in 1940. The Frankfurt School's major practitioners remained almost purposefully hermetic, locked in their own exile milieu, continuing to write in German, and remote from even noted scholars (such as Abram Kardiner) working at the same institution and with many similar interests. Erich Fromm and the communications expert Leo Lowenthal were rare prominent figures to break out of emigré insularity.

Only during World War II did cross-fertilization become a reality. The mandate to defend democracy against the worldwide threat of fascism supplied the primary initiative. Several Frankfurt scholars worked alongside American neo-Freudians and ego psychologists in the wartime investigations into national character, primarily under the auspices of the Office of Strategic Services. Best known was the project funded by the American Jewish Committee and headed by Horkheimer and Adorno, a massive and highly influential study of the potential for fascist anti-Semitism and ethnocentrism in general within both Germany and the United States.[18]

By this time American psychoanalysts were singing their own dirge over the decline of patriarchy and accusing feminists of conspiracy. For their part, leading Frankfurt scholars had lost their revolutionary aspirations and longed mainly to return home to salvage whatever remnants of bourgeois culture remained. In addition, the major outcome of their wartime research, Adorno's highly acclaimed *Authoritarian Personality* (1950), a sprawling summary of behavioral science research into the family, soon suffered the fate of the fading field of other national character studies—but not before providing a strong positive correlation between the potential for totalitarianism and the decline of paternal authority. Before they made their way back to prominent careers in postwar Germany, Horkheimer and Adorno just barely managed to contribute to the discourse on Momism.

For a brief moment, before the Institute for Social Research relocated to West Germany in 1949, the critical theorists had supplied a philosophical buttress to American psychoanalytic misogyny. Both Horkheimer and Adorno pointed to dangerous problems in the modern American family. They affirmed that paternal authority had seriously declined in the United States, opening the door to the Momism that their American peers had publicized so well. The larger corpus of critical theory, however, was to lie dormant until the next crisis in authority: the 1960s.[19]

The Return of the Repressed

The early New Left preceded Lasch to embrace critical theory with a passion. The initial introduction was, nevertheless, second-hand at best, more likely to be a reading of French existentialism or the muckraking works of Vance Packard than a careful study of the notoriously difficult passages of Horkheimer's *The Eclipse of Reason* (1947). The young radicals came a little closer in the plentiful works addressing the problems of conformity and alienation in mass society. C. Wright

Mills and especially Erich Fromm served as major conduits, the latter's *Sane Society* (1955) enjoying especially high acclaim. Building on an eclectic foundation, the young radicals of the 1960s—men and women alike—widened their scope, rescued critical theory from near-oblivion, and channeled it into revolutionary service.

For example, a version of critical theory allowed the founders of Students for a Democratic Society to specify the structures of psychological domination in their own imperialist, racist, class-ridden, yet constitutionally democratic society. The *Port Huron Statement* (1962) addresses conventional matters of domestic and foreign policy, but fully one-third of the legendary document describes the adverse consequences of mass society, including the prevailing sense of political ennui. Against the vaunted American standard of living, the authors juxtaposed the emotional wasteland of a society wherein consumer goods substitute for genuine intimacy. The ability to live in comfort, or even in luxury, does not outweigh the utter poverty of personal relations. "Loneliness, estrangement, isolation describe," they insisted, "the vast distance between man and man today."[20] In short, the drafters of the Port Huron Statement grasped intuitively, for the most part, what Horkheimer and Adorno had proposed at some length. The internalization of rules, rather than the machinations of a wicked ruling class, had created a sort of warfare-and-welfare-state mentality within each citizen, the desperate scramble for emotional security derailing the pursuit of freedom.

For similar reasons, critical theory tantalized a small number of feminists with roots in the New Left. As Marxist-feminists or socialist-feminists, they invested little faith in the liberal campaigns for equality, such as the legal initiatives around the Equal Rights Amendment championed by the National Organization for Women. Women's liberation depended, they insisted, on the destruction of the capitalist mode of production and the emergence of a socialist society. But the old answers provided by Marx and Engels no longer satisfied them. Women's status, they observed, did not correlate positively with their numbers in the workforce. The majority of American women could now expect to spend most of their adult lives earning wages, but, contrary to Engels's prediction, they were no closer to liberation. Rejecting such economistic formulas, socialist feminists turned to the legacy of the Frankfurt School to examine the psychological structures of domination. In the late 1960s, while radical feminists were assaulting Freud and his legacy, this small sector of the women's liberation movement announced a strikingly different intention.

But in embracing critical theory, the young radicals refused to give in to either pessimism or nostalgia. Instead, they caught a glimmer of transcendence, a near-utopian vision of liberation arising from within the very structures of their own repressive society, and they took the alternative path. The youth rebellion itself, even (or especially) the LSD-dropping counterculture, represented a hopeful sign. The New Left and its feminist contingent chose to celebrate these stirrings as a harbinger of an emerging protest against acquiescence to authority. The Black Power movement, women's liberation, the campaign against the war in Vietnam—all could be read as auspicious beginnings. Soon the young radicals found the one critical theorist who unabashedly held out this prospect.[21]

Herbert Marcuse (1898–1979) supplied the bridge between the original Frankfurt scholars and the liberation movements of the 1960s. After the Nazis had closed the Institute for Social Research, he had sought refuge in the United States and, like his closest colleagues, worked for the Bureau of Intelligence of the Office of War Information. Marcuse did not repatriate after World War II. He continued his research at the Russian Institute at Columbia University and the Russian Research Center at Harvard. In 1954 he joined the faculty of Brandeis University; a decade later he moved to the University of California at San Diego, where he completed his academic career.

Dubbed by the media the chief guru of the New Left, Marcuse had established his scholarly credentials in addressing the crisis in authority in his erudite *Reason and Revolution: Hegel and the Role of Social Theory* (1941) and *Soviet Marxism: A Critical Analysis* (1958). It was, however, *One-Dimensional Man: Studies in the Ideology of Advanced Industrial Society* (1964) that successfully popularized critical theory as a grand critique of the emotional poverty prevailing within technocratic American society. It was this book that radical students carried to demonstrations and worried parents read in order to understand their children. *One-Dimensional Man* sold over 100,000 copies within five years of publication and became, according to the *New York Times*, the "foremost literary symbol of the New Left."[22]

Marcuse responded to the mood of the 1960s by offering a dash of hope amid massive despair. "Throughout the world of industrial civilization," he wrote, "the domination of man by man is growing in scope and efficiency." This trend was not "an accidental, transitory regression on the road to progress." "Concentration camps, mass exterminations, world wars and atom bombs are no 'relapse into barbarism,' " he warned, but instead the logical consequences of modern science, technology, and domination. Yet, despite it all, Marcuse saw possibilities for salvation. The very forces of science and technology that created so much material and psychological devastation could, if redirected to other ends, allow humanity to break free of the reigning logic of domination. In other words, he insisted that the objective conditions existed for a socialist society and he welcomed the stirrings of the 1960s as the precursor to that new order. Critical theory, Marcuse proclaimed, "wants to remain loyal to those who, without hope, have given and give their life to the *Great Refusal.*"[23]

It was precisely this phrase—the Great Refusal—that resonated most clearly with those sectors of the New Left, including feminists, whose strategy for revolution involved in the first instance their own, individual resistance to authority. It was also on this point that Christopher Lasch would make his strongest criticism. But in the heady days of the 1960s, Marcuse struck gold in shifting the political focus from the forces of domination to the prospects for liberation.

Marcuse's timing—and his angle of approach—could not have been better. Resuscitating Freud's drive theory, he singled out sexuality as the primary site of liberation. And what could be more appealing to the youthful celebrants of Eros? Not surprisingly, they discovered in the 1962 mass-market edition of Marcuse's *Eros and Civilization: A Philosophical Inquiry into Freud* (1955) a thoroughly alluring synthesis of Marx and Freud. They responded enthusiastically to his suggestion that, because the "organization of sexuality" mirrors the "organization of society, a strike at one necessarily helps to undermine the other." Despite its difficulty, the text soon became a banner of revolution, explicating precisely why the personal is indeed political.

Equally important, Marcuse gave a new spin to the old dialectic—the history of man is the history of his repression—by linking the increasing "desexualization of the organism" to the requirement of its "social utilization as an instrument of labor." In other words, he agreed with Freud but only to a point. Sexual repression, he affirmed, had accompanied the rise of *this* civilization wherein all value is based on labor. But there were now timely and compelling reasons to reject Freud's ironclad "identification of civilization with repression."[24]

Marcuse proceeded to translate Freud's Reality Principle via Marx into the historically contingent Performance Principle that is wholly repressive under advanced capitalism. In organizing humanity into an instrument of labor, the capitalist mode of production extracts far too much energy from the libido; it demands, in fact, "surplus repression" (a concept Marcuse coined from Marx's "surplus value," the source of profits and subsequent grief for the commodified world). Humanity now suffers extreme alienation and anxiety and moves dangerously close to the lair of Thanatos, the death instinct. The inordinate restrictions placed upon the libido, historically in place and rational-seeming, thus guide the psyche as if by natural law so that under the reigning "Logos of Domination" the individual "freely" comes to desire the submission that the system demands—all the more reason to believe in the possibility of transcendence.

Marcuse encouraged the young radicals to have faith in the possibility of "a nonrepressive civilization" as an act not only reasonable but imperative. To save itself from self-destruction, he argued, humanity must reenergize the Pleasure Principle. Not since the 1910s had anyone made this point so boldly or held out such a pleasing prospect for political action. The young radicals could find in Marcuse's interpretation of critical theory the rationale for the popular generational slogan "Make Love Not War."

It was not, however, merely Marcuse's upbeat sexual politics that ensured his celebrity among New Leftists, most especially feminists. Equally important was his alignment on the Oedipus complex. Unlike his peers, Marcuse chose not to glorify the psychic consolidation of paternal authority or to lament its decline. Instead he looked even further "backward" toward a utopia that Freud, Horkheimer, and later Lasch all avoided—the pre-oedipal.

Marcuse's special vision emerged from his unique interpretation of the ancient myth of Narcissus. For Marcuse the beautiful youth who succumbed to death while admiring his reflection in the water does not embody the danger of self-destruction. To the contrary, Narcissus expresses what modern society lacks, a libidinal cathexis of self. He holds out the hope of rehabilitation, the "image of joy and fulfillment; the voice which does not command but sings . . . the liberation from time which unites man with god, man with nature." The myth thus renders in symbolic terms the most deeply structured possibility of utopia, "the archetype of another existential relation to *reality*." In sum, Narcissus represents a sensuality not governed by the Oedipus complex but emanating instead from the archaic mother, "the Nirvana before birth."[25]

For this reason Marcuse considered the introduction of the concept of primary narcissism a turning point for Freud. Narcissism reappears in the later stages of development as not only a neurotic symptom but, in Freud's words, a "limitless extension and openness with the universe," the legendary oceanic feeling of pre-oedipal bliss. While conventionally interpreted as a withdrawal from everything external to self, that is, as a dangerous life-threatening regression, narcissism also holds out a different prospect. As Marcuse put it, narcissism suggests a new Reality Principle, a "comprehensive existential order" premised on "the transformation of sexuality into Eros":

> No longer used as a full-time instrument of labor, the body would be resexualized. The regression involved in this spread of the libido would first manifest itself in a reactivation of all erotogenic zones and, consequently, in a resurgence of pregenital polymorphous sexuality and in a decline of genital supremacy. The body in its entirety would become an object of cathexis, a thing to be enjoyed—an instrument of pleasure. This change in the value and scope of libidinal relations would lead to a disintegration of the institutions in which the private interpersonal relations have been organized, particularly the monogamic and patriarchal families.[26]

Narcissus thus reveals the strata of psychic existence aligned with the pre-oedipal nurturing mother rather than the phallus-wielding powerful father.

This formulation became Marcuse's signature as a critical theorist. From his earliest days at the Institute for Social Research, he had envisioned the revolutionary promise of transcendence in sensuality, not only in sexual love as such but in the sensual pleasure of beauty. To this end he endorsed the play impulse, including its expression in art, music, theater, poetry, humor, and even personal style. In *Eros and Civilization* he took this argument one step further, predicating the overthrow of capitalism on the restoration of sexuality to its pre-oedipal state.

Marcuse's fearless emphasis on the "fundamental relatedness" of narcissism put him at right angles to the other critical theorists who celebrated the Golden Age of Oedipus. He explicitly critiqued Freud's *Totem and Taboo*, claiming that the mother promises deliverance from the oppressive Reality Principle imposed by the paternal authority. Woman as mother, according to Marcuse, conjures up Eros/Thanatos/ Nirvana, that is, the repressed memory of the pre-oedipal "libidinous union." He also outdid Horkheimer, who admitted that matriarchal remnants did have a beneficial function in the bourgeois family, "maternal and sisterly" love helping men "resist the total dehumanization of the world."[27] Marcuse, for his part, did not hesitate to attribute to "woman" ever greater potential, even as he disclaimed any element of biological essentialism. Over the decades he reworked this formulation, suggesting that "woman" was a social construction but one whose learned traits (such as "receptivity, sensitivity, non-violence, tenderness and so on") occupy the "domain of Eros," a decisive counterpoint to masculinism. In contrast to both Freud and Horkheimer, who also subscribed to this list of descriptive adjectives, Marcuse did not seek to exclude women from the affairs of civilization. To the contrary, he became an avid promoter.[28]

Somewhat belatedly, in 1974 and at age seventy-six, the grand old philosopher pronounced the women's liberation movement "perhaps the most important and potentially the most radical political movement we have." He clearly understood that contemporary feminists aspired to something besides careers. Women were not asking merely for the right to "participate" in capitalist structures, he affirmed. This generation of feminists had moved "beyond equality" to demand a total transformation of existing social relations.[29]

Marcuse pinpointed the revolutionary potential of the women's liberation movement in its capacity to negate "the aggressive and repressive needs and values of capitalism as a form of male-dominated culture." Women's liberation serves as an antidote, in other words, by releasing the primary narcissistic bliss that Freud himself recognized as essential to human survival. As a consequence new institutions will emerge, to be sure. More important, women's liberation will force "a change in the instinctual needs of men and women, freed from the requirements of domination and exploitation." The women's liberation movement promises, in short, to bring the dream of socialism into reality by facilitating "the liberation and ascent of *specifically feminine* characteristics on a social scale."[30] Friendly critics who found such formulations more chivalrous than intellectually satisfying neverthe-less believed that Marcuse had achieved a version of critical theory that acknowledged female agency.

As the premier harbinger of a new nonrepressive order, *Eros and Civilization* provided the political context for Freudo-Marxist stir-rings in the 1960s. Norman O. Brown, himself impressed by the power of Marcuse's argument, became another favorite in many New Left and feminist quarters. The classics professor had made his debut with *Life against Death: The Psychoanalytic Meaning of History* (1959) to insist that "what the great world needs . . . is a little more Eros and less strife." A genuine cult formed around yet another proponent of sexual liberation, one of Freud's pupils and a contemporary of Mar-cuse, Wilhelm Reich (1987–1957). Considered by Reuben Fine "one of the most bizarre figures in the history of psychoanalysis," Reich had insisted that mental health depends most of all on orgasmic gratifi-cation. His popularity in the late 1960s rivaled that of any Frankfurt scholar, including the highly revered Marcuse. An underground reprint of Reich's *Mass Psychology of Fascism* (1933) circulated widely among youthful celebrants and helped them to understand, *contra* Horkheimer, that the very "basis of authoritarian ideology" depends on the "patriarchal social order."[31]

By the late 1960s a flurry of publications hailed the revolutionary possibilities of critical theory. The upbeat temper of the times moved Paul Piccone to transform *Telos,* a graduate student philosophy jour-nal at the State University of New York at Buffalo founded in 1968, into the voice of Old World theory, at first emphasizing the Marxist phenomenology closest to Marcuse's own intellectual origins. Euro-tropic by nature, *Telos* would remain for a decade or more a guide to the shifting fashions of the continental intelligentsia. Three years later the *New German Critique* appeared with a wider range of articles on aesthetics. A small cluster of other journals, notably *Radical America* and *Socialist Revolution* (later, *Socialist Review*), published occasional essays or devoted special sections of issues to Horkheimer, Adorno, and Marcuse. Throughout, the British *New Left Review* probed a melange of psychoanalytic theories. As "I ♥ Adorno" bumper-stickers began to appear in university parking lots in the 1980s, yet another cluster of periodicals, now polemically postmodern, weighed in with articles informed by a "reading" of popular culture "texts" ranging from architecture to hip hop.

Mainstream academic presses had, in the meantime, caught the bug. They began to contribute mightily to the proliferation of monographs, anthologies, and collected essays, establishing new reputations. Weighing up books and cross-referencing in fields from philosophy to African studies to film, a university catalog system might at one time register a handful of items, several years later a few dozen, and within another decade more than one hundred separate entries under "critical theory."

Despite this scholarly upsurgence, the political epiphany of the Great Refusal was short-lived. By the late 1970s, with Lasch's own appropriation of critical theory, the pendulum was clearly swinging away from (women's) liberation and toward (patriarchal) order. In the guise of critical theory, psychoanalysis was once again serving as conduit for an explicit and forceful antifeminism.

The Flight from Redemption

By the late 1970s, when Lasch began to publish his polemics, critical theory had secured itself firmly in the academy, not least in the feminist wings of English departments. But the context had changed considerably. For younger theorists eager to set their own pace, the New Left was scarcely a bittersweet memory, joined to fading images of women's liberation at its most exuberant. Meanwhile many disciples of the Frankfurt School reverted to traditional pessimism, a turn somewhat justified by the conservative clouds rising over the political horizon. The defeat of the Equal Rights Amendment, the growing challenge to reproductive rights, and the consolidation of the New Right with the Republican insurgency and the crushing defeat of the Democrats' left-liberal wing—all signaled the absolute end of an era. Furthermore, the highly publicized retrenchment of such feminist notables as Betty Friedan and Germaine Greer announced the arrival of postfeminism, with its own style of personal politics on the agenda. No wonder Herbert Marcuse, once hailed for his visionary utopianism, was singled out for vituperation by critics from the near left to the far right. Outnumbered and outgunned, those critical theorists steadfastly loyal to their youthful predilections aptly described this vivid shift as a "flight from redemption."

Seeking their own redemption over the corpse of the 1960s, erstwhile radicals struck out against women's liberation. Not a few revamped the popular caricature of feminism-as-careerism and proceeded to blame the bulk of social disorder on women's individualistic strivings, that is, on their selfish pursuit of masculine entitlements at the expense of the family. They also revived the basic elements of the psychoanalytic misogyny that had flourished at midcentury. Such sentiments now played surprisingly well with an influential group of disgruntled academics who set themselves to defend American manhood. Without missing a beat, they continued to lament the decline of parental authority and accused mothers directly of endangering the psychic well-being of their families. An influential number of these critics cleverly updated the psychoanalytic nosology, targeting not the authoritarian personality documented by the early Frankfurt scholars but the narcissist rescued by Marcuse.

Lasch himself had charted the theoretical path in *Haven in a Heartless World*. Although he had gleaned his description of the admirable bourgeois personality straight from the works of the classically Freudian Frankfurt scholars, he was no intellectual slouch. A lot had changed since Horkheimer and Adorno first cataloged the traits of the authoritarian personality. The youth rebellion alone forced a reassessment. The predominant personality type is no longer the rigid and passive authoritarian that plagued Nazi Germany, Lasch readily granted, but instead the capricious and lawless narcissist.

Here Lasch identified a perfect culprit. Bemoaned and denounced across otherwise formidable geographic, class, and even racial divisions, this creature seemed to stalk the 1970s, the unchecked product of a time gone wrong, the 1960s. A combination of annoying suburban teenager, alienated radical intellectual, black mugger, and materialistic wife, the narcissist proved incapable of empathy and was painfully self-absorbed and determined to avoid both intimacy and commitment. To fill this emotional vacuum, the narcissist builds on the legacy of that earlier era to search for ever greater sensations and titillations in the realm of sexuality. To underscore his point Lasch lumped together the counterculture, the student New Left, and women's liberation as the principal indicators of the prevailing "absence of inner restraints."[32]

Lasch was not alone in noting the upswing in narcissism. Psychoanalysts themselves had long been uncertain whether clinical data reflected a shift in pathology or merely a new diagnostic paradigm. Combing the archival obscurantia of the Vienna Psychoanalytic Society of 1906, some psychoanalysts found evidence that even the first generation of practitioners had discussed numerous cases of "excessive self-assertion." Speaking to Freud's inner circle, Ernest Jones once reported on "The God Complex," a common type of narcissism that inspires loquacious monologists and verbose after-dinner speakers. By midcentury ego psychologists such as Hartmann and Erikson noted that few patients were seeking help for the obsessive-compulsive disorders such as ceaseless handwashing that Freud and his peers had routinely confronted. Instead, their patients were presenting an entirely different set of complaints: feelings of unreality, alienation, and unfulfillment; depression, low self-esteem, and an inability to feel love or form binding relationships; and persistent fears of sickness and death. These were not the conventional symptoms of oedipal guilt that Freud had documented so carefully in his clinical practice but, rather, manifestations of a character disorder particular to today's permissive society. The post-Freudian Heinz Kohut summed up the current situation. Narcissism had become the dominant psychopathology of the time, the Tragic Man displacing the Guilty Man, profound feelings of unfulfillment overshadowing problems of thwarted gratification.[33]

The discussion of narcissism had moved beyond the rarified circles of psychoanalysts to the mass media. Scores of popular writers had taken it upon themselves to lambaste the notorious "me generation" of the 1970s. Young Americans had become obsessively concerned with themselves, complained the neologist Tom Wolfe. And how better to characterize self-involved yuppies than as modern versions of the mythic Narcissus, apparently doomed to drown psychologically in pursuit of their own image?[34]

Lasch simultaneously disdained and capitalized upon this trend. The back cover of the paper edition of his hasty sequel to *Haven in a Heartless World* asked potential readers: "Have we fallen in love with our selves?" Apparently the sales pitch worked. *The Culture of Nar-*

cissism: American Life in an Age of Diminishing Expectations (1978) induced many Americans to share his discovery "that we are in thrall to a new enchantment—self-involvement." Rumor had it that President Carter read Lasch's bestseller and liked it so much that he invited the author to an intimate White House dinner. Although the historian John Demos cherished "the picture of Mr. and Mrs. Carter and Professor Lasch sitting around the table in some homey corner of the White House discussing narcissism," the majority of Americans did not. The president's subsequent speech on the "national malaise" proved a political disaster. Resurgent Republicans, from neoconservative Jewish intellectuals to evangelical Protestant spellbinders, took Carter's televised address as an admission of the failure of secular, oversexed, self-indulgent liberalism, which in their view only a mixture of military outlay, welfare cuts, and patriotic rectitude could remedy.[35]

Detrimental to Carter, the deployment of narcissism greatly enhanced Lasch's assault on feminism. It also allowed Lasch to refashion old gripes about Momism in the latest psychoanalytic mode. Nevertheless, there was something eerily familiar in his argument that mothers, confused by the feminist approbation of work outside the home, set off the whole chain of emotional disruption.

Lasch revived the familiar complaint that modern mothers respond awkwardly and inadequately to their babies' demands, overwhelming the infants with attention yet failing to provide genuine warmth. What appeared new was his diagnosis of these mothers as narcissistic themselves: imagining the child as an extension of herself, the modern mother thwarts the normal developmental sequence leading to separation. She encourages in her baby an exaggerated sense of his own importance and simultaneously makes it nearly impossible for him to admit his disappointments in her. And because modern fathers no longer enjoy the authority to temper dangerous fantasies, the child imagines only the omnipotent and terrifying "bad mother," in Lasch's Kleinian adaptation, "a devouring bird, a vagina full of teeth." Fearing the potential outcome of anger at such a creature, the infant internalizes aggression and develops destructive fantasies that shape his future emotional life. The resulting narcissistic personality pairs grandiose conceptions of self with feelings of impotent rage, mediated by conscious sensations of emptiness and inauthenticity.[36]

Lasch even revived and updated a noteworthy detail in Wylie's original complaint against Moms, their lack of sexual appeal. He blamed the women's liberation movement not only for encouraging women to pursue careers instead of motherhood but for transforming women into poor sexual partners. How can men respond erotically to women who demand intimacy and tenderness and simultaneously accuse men of oppressing them? A classic symptom of narcissism, these conflicting attitudes place impossible demands on men, especially in the realm of sexual performance. Even feminists are unable to handle these contradictions and, according to Lasch, respond by retreating from heterosexuality and by seeking diversion in the materialistic pleasures of capitalist society. How much better it would be if feminists would only abandon narcissistic notions, accept the post-oedipal facts of life, and live "gracefully" with sexual contradictions.[37]

Clearly, Lasch found no point of agreement with Marcuse. He denied all utopian possibilities in narcissism and recognized only the potential for pathological regression. But then even expert psychoanalysts disagree among themselves on the genesis and meaning of narcissism. Narcissism, it seems, is a very slippery concept.

Freud himself had recognized several varieties of narcissism, including a healthy complement to self-preservation as well as a perverse withdrawal of the libido from the external world. In its constructive secondary form, narcissism reemerges in adult life as the "ego ideal" and helps to bind the libido to the socially acceptable goals of larger loyalty to family, class, or nation. Freud therefore registered something of value in secondary narcissism, which is not only exemplary in normal women but the source of their charm for men. Men can only envy these women, he admitted, "for maintaining a blissful state of mind —an unassailable libidinal position which we ourselves have since abandoned."[38] Primary narcissism, in contrast, held out no such promise.

In *Civilization and Its Discontents* Freud put down his concluding thoughts on the oceanic bliss as the sublime feeling of fusion between self and the external world. He was quite taken with the idea but admitted that he simply could not "discover this 'oceanic' feeling" in himself. He granted that the archaic memory of symbiotic fusion between mother and infant serves an important function in adult life as a wishful fantasy. Even as "a shrunken residue," he added, the oceanic bliss offers consolation for the stringencies of human existence and encourages survival. But, pessimist to the end, Freud retreated. He condemned all efforts to retrieve the oceanic sensation as simple infantile regression, an irrational withdrawal from reality, and consequently "worthless for orientation in the alien, external world." No wonder scholars have judged *Civilization and Its Discontents* as "the most trenchant and devastating attack on utopian illusions . . . that has ever been delivered."[39]

By the 1980s erstwhile radicals, with Lasch at the forefront, were more than ready to both condemn narcissism and dispel all utopian sentiments. Marcuse became a favorite target. As early as 1969 the historian Paul Breines noticed that the movement had seemingly "outgrown . . . 'polymorphously perverse' politics." A decade later, when Lasch's *Culture of Narcissism* appeared, Marcuse had been silenced by death, and few came to his defense. Mark Poster, for example, who had nailed Horkheimer for his increasing accommodation to the gender-biased principles of bourgeois authority, now described Marcuse's reliance on the image of Narcissus as "the cosmic cop-out." Michael Walzer, coeditor of *Dissent* and a contributing editor to the *New Republic,* excoriated Marcuse as the intellectual source of New Left sins, from disruptive student strikes to hypersexuality to insufficient support for the state of Israel. Marcuse's writings served as a favorite butt of attack by onetime radicals who now looked upon women's liberation and the youth rebellion as emblems of 1960s excess. In his own anti-utopianism, Lasch joined those conservatives who paired the deceased philosopher with Marx and Mao in the so-called Ma-Ma-Ma uprising of the young. And meanwhile even resilient politicos scarcely remembered their hero of yore, as indicated by Marcuse's absence from the spate of publicity marking the twentieth anniversary of 1968.[40]

Among post–New Left critical theorists, Marcuse's recuperation of narcissism and elevation of feminism as wedges against the "Logos of Domination" were increasingly ignored if not scorned. Showing how much time had passed by 1980, only an occasional speaker at an academic conference on "Narcissism and the Crisis of Capitalism" endorsed Marcuse's usage. The psychoanalyst Joel Kovel carefully distinguished between primary and secondary narcissism and determinedly traced the source of potential resistance to "a rebellion of the body against its deformation into a machine." The agitator-turned-sociologist Stanley Aronowitz observed that the assault on narcissism was embedded in the "protest of those intellectuals who have been integrated into late capitalism as producers of its ideology and guardians of its moral norms."

Unmoved by these defenses, the majority of speakers sided with Lasch and his assessment of both narcissism and feminism. Russell Jacoby, well known for his writing on the history of psychoanalysis, adamantly insisted that under advanced capitalism even a protest such as feminism was "shot through with the society it rejects." After a similar presentation at another conference, the editors of the collected papers mused over his thesis that career women made less competent mothers than the homebodies of generations past. Like so many of his cohorts, Jacoby had lined up, they aptly suggested, with "the last defense of patriarchal authority against the assault of the feminist movement."[41]

As early as 1932 Marcuse himself had warned that industrial capitalism precipitated not mere social crisis but a "catastrophe of the human essence" that buried the dream of utopia. In the wake of collapsed social movements decades later, Left melancholy had become pandemic, and nostalgia bathed sections of the disoriented New Left as well as the emboldened New Right under Ronald Reagan, projecting a return to an imaginary happier past without feminism.[42]

The time was apparently ripe for a major political reorientation. The restoration of the bourgeois moral order, most emphatically including the patriarchal family, had a special appeal for scholars like the rising academic star historian Elizabeth Fox-Genovese, an erstwhile Marxist who now won the favor of many conservatives. Fox-Genovese firmly put aside the "injustices and failings" (including, it seems, slavery) of bourgeois society to sing its merits as "the firmest cornerstone for individual freedom the world has yet known." Meanwhile a remarkable group of post–New Leftists describing itself as "Friends of Families" and headed by the therapist-publisher (and later rabbi) Michael Lerner berated feminist intentions in a manifesto published in *The Nation*. Lerner charged that the family needed to be rescued not only from political conservatives but also from "feminists with emotional problems" who essentially projected their own fears onto society. Meanwhile, at *Telos,* editor Paul Piccone engaged in a memorable bit of wishful thinking with an essay entitled "A World without Feminists." From the liberal Catholic *Commonweal* to the rightward-drifting *New Republic,* defenses of the family against purported feminist abuse poured in, as journalists and scholars targeted "welfare mothers" and "working mothers" alike for society's chief ills.[43]

One could hardly distinguish this particular brand of antifeminism from personal peevishness. Since 1967 highly placed intellectuals aghast at the youth rebellion (which sometimes included their own children) had attacked women's liberation and gradually shifted politically to the right. The New Left itself had not been immune to this tendency. A sizable sector had fulminated against second-wave feminism since its inception, warning that women would never achieve equality if they detached themselves ideologically or organizationally from progressive men. By 1980 new alliances had formed across generations and old political divisions to defend the family against women's dangerous claims. Amid great rounds of hand-wringing, feminism had become for these scholars the veritable totem of disorder.

This turn in critical theory resembled, in some ways, the devolution of American-bred Culture and Personality from its radical beginnings and liberal efflorescence in the 1930s. The culturalism pioneered by Calverton and Schmalhausen and refined by Horney, Fromm, Mead, and Thompson had taken on, in the hands of Kardiner, Erikson, and Farnham, a very different character. The cultural relativism of the early generation succumbed under "hot" and "cold" wartime pressure to stringent conceptions of psychological and social normality. At the same time, rather than neutralizing the misogyny in orthodox psychoanalysis, Culture and Personality aligned with ego psychology and by 1940 became a powerful ideological weapon aimed precisely at feminism. Three decades later critical theory revealed these same possibilities.

There were, however, important differences between the two epochs. Despite the political retrenchments of the 1980s, feminism was, if not wholly well, still very much alive and flourishing in sectors of the academy. Nowhere was this resilience more apparent than among feminists who had imbibed the initial optimism of the Freudo-Marxism of the 1960s. More so than their predecessors in the 1920s and 1930s, they were well positioned to confront the misogynist excesses of their peers.

The Crisis of Feminism

Determination alone could not spare feminists from a nasty confrontation with the central paradox of critical theory. Perhaps bourgeois culture had really been, as Joel Whitebook noted, a "short, self-liquidating historical moment" in which the concepts of human emancipation were stated, partly realized, and then for all practical purposes suppressed.[44] But if so, what was its proper legacy? For those feminists who rejected "the ideal of the autonomous individual" for "relational" modes, the golden era of the patriarchal family could just as easily generate romantic fantasy about the past as hope for the future. The ambiguities of critical theory, buoyed by its legion of interpreters, now became a point of contention among psychoanalytic feminists themselves.

One group of feminists, loyal to the vision articulated by Marcuse, aimed at transcendence of the embattled liberalism by clinging to the prospect of freedom as both utopian and absolutely essential to human survival. They bristled at the blatant misogyny of the "tirade against narcissism" and rushed to their hero's defense. Stephanie Engel, for example, fought to preserve the joyous primordial images outlined in *Eros and Civilization*. Marcuse's "call back to the memory of original narcissistic bliss pushes us," she maintained, "toward a dream of the future." Jane Flax continued to find inspiration in Marcuse's rereading of Freud's primal anthropology—his association of the Performance Principle with the socially victorious Father, the Pleasure Principle with the sexually powerful Mother. Yet, by the time of Marcuse's death in 1979, most feminists, like other survivors of the 1960s, had tempered their own utopian expectations in the face of the harsh realities of retrenchment. The popular journalist Ellen Willis could grant Marcuse a past presence as "a star . . . a symbol of certain values," but she knew full well that these values were now under fire from the left as well as the right.[45]

There were feminists who harked back to a "civilized" morality of times gone by, hoping to reverse the much bemoaned decline of moral values. This group shared Lasch's antipathy to welfare capitalism. They, too, sought to relieve the stress that wage-earning women had placed on the marketplace by facilitating their return to the home. But most of all they sought to restore to women the prerogatives the modern state had usurped from them. Women, they insisted, must be allowed to live out their potential for empathy and nurture within the family. However, they had no use for the oedipal paradigm that undergirded Lasch's analysis.

Jean Bethke Elshtain (1941–) made a name for herself revamping critical theory to account for the new post-Freudian modalities. In a bold sweep, she altered the narrative line laid out by the Frankfurt School, insisting, against both Horkheimer and Lasch, that the idealized private sphere of bourgeois society had not been ruled by the authoritative father. To the contrary, the historic "separation of spheres" that had consigned women to the home and men to the marketplace had given mothers the edge in childrearing. Indeed, much that was good in the bourgeois epoch had been facilitated not by stern fathers but by nurturing mothers. Precisely because women had few distractions outside the home, the "feminine" values of care and consideration could prevail there, thus ensuring a singularly beneficial "private" space for children to develop personalities resistant to the rapacious influences of "public" culture. If advanced capitalism had blurred this distinction by driving women into the workforce—and punishing the children most terribly—the solution was readily apparent: restore the family wage. In sum, men must once again become the chief breadwinners in order to make it economically feasible for women to return home.[46]

"Many a monster," Elshtain added, "can march about flying the banner of 'freedom' or 'feminism.' " For this reason, and reassured by relational psychoanalytic theory, the political theorist presented herself as the "real" feminist. Women must subordinate their rights to the well-being of their children, she insisted. Against those feminists who had allegedly conspired with the expanding commodity system to become market-defined individuals, Elshtain advocated, Marynia Farnham–style, the elevation of women's status within the home. Any other position, such as men and women together sharing the responsibilities of breadwinning and childrearing, would bring into existence the frightening "new world" that the pessimistic futurists had warned against. With the civilization in crisis, someone had to resume responsibility for the family, and women were best suited for this Herculean task by tradition as well as temperament. Feminists should therefore resist all attempts to degrade "female-created and -sustained values" and rehabilitate their sphere "even under conditions of male domination."[47]

Elshtain's leftward critics bought none of this argument. The socialist Barbara Ehrenreich accused her of willfully constructing a fantasy family, free from market interference and the inequities that necessarily accompany all dependent relationships, including that of wife on husband. Others charged that Elshtain came perilously close to blaming feminists rather than capitalism for society's ills and closer yet to blaming social programs, rather than their inadequacy, for the poverty that plagued female-headed households. Such a position was unconscionable, they retorted, at a time when massive shifts of funds away from social services, health care, education, and public transportation left hard-pressed parents with fewer and fewer options. Less pressing but certainly ridiculous was Elshtain's caricature of maternal privilege in bourgeois society. It was clear, however, that Elshtain had staked a solid claim as, according to one critic, the "new darling" of left backlash.[48]

Elshtain treated all such criticisms as unsisterly attempts to jettison polite discussion. She refused to abandon the private sphere to either men or the state, insisting that it become once again a repository for that feminine morality which expresses "concern and responsibility for others." Nixing the entire project of personal politics, she refused to risk woman's relational capacity for "an abstract ideal of liberation."[49]

In the opposite corner, ready to rescue Marcuse, was Jessica Benjamin. Daughter of a famed American Communist leader of Depression-era unemployed movements, Benjamin had embraced feminism and psychoanalysis simultaneously in the late 1960s. "When I read *Eros and Civilization*," she wrote, "it was as if a big light went on"— and she followed it back to Frankfurt, Germany, where she studied social theory. After returning to the United States and earning a doctorate in sociology, she underwent training analysis and became a psychoanalyst. Through a series of essays and a major book, Benjamin demonstrated the utility of Marcuse's insights into the machinations of sexual domination.[50]

To make critical theory amenable to her particular feminist agenda, Benjamin added refinements from recent emanations of post-Freudian psychoanalysis. She also borrowed from the formulations of the developmental psychologist Jean Piaget as well as the more familiar contributions of D. W. Winnicott and Nancy Chodorow. Most prominent were the theories advanced by the ranking psychoanalytic interpreter of narcissism, Heinz Kohut.

Whereas Lasch turned to the psychoanalyst Otto F. Kernberg (1928–) to stress the psychopathology of narcissism, exemplified by the "borderline personality," Benjamin chose his alter ego.[51] Heinz Kohut (1913–1981), who had emigrated from Vienna at the onset of World War II, had advanced his own paradigm, "psychology of the self" or, simply, self psychology. Unlike Kernberg, he located in narcissism certain elements that could be developed therapeutically into socially useful attributes. The one-time president of the American Psychoanalytic Association appeared to share Marcuse's faith in its utopian potential. The positive unlocking of narcissistic impulses was analogous, Kohut boldly announced, to the "repeal of reticence" toward sexuality in Freud's own time.[52]

Benjamin perceived that Kohut had provided a means to avoid the developmental trap that had lured even Marcuse into a masculinist schema. Marcuse's projection of femininity as the antithesis of capitalist value, the reservoir of the prospect of freedom, had left implicit a very big question: freedom for whom? Despite his good intentions, Marcuse had pinned the utopian moment on the mother as object of the infant's desire. In short, he, too, had promoted man's self-realization at the expense of woman's subjectivity.[53] Kohut, while not abandoning Freud's drive model, provided a way out of this dilemma by hypothesizing a *second* line of development, one in which the self emerges in relation not to "objects" but to "selfobjects." The terminology is important: Kohut's self psychology, unlike object relations theory with its assumption of an initial state of undifferentiation or merger, and with its developmental emphasis on separation and individuation, envisions the self emerging through a process of empathetic mirroring, that is, recognizing from the moment of birth the subjectivity of the Other. The road to healthy development is marked by mutual empathy. Kohut thus abandoned the whole notion of the "autonomous individual" for the celebration of *interdependence* in human relations.[54]

Despite its important advantages over previous models, self psychology as developed by Kohut lacked a gender dimension, and it remained for Benjamin to do what Chodorow did for object relations theory: she added the missing categorical ingredient. Building on contributions to a series of new periodicals—*PsychCritique, New Ideas in Psychology, Psychology and Critical Theory,* and *m/f*—Benjamin rebuilt self psychology as an effective antidote to the claims popularized by Lasch and Elshtain. She also supplied a new and sturdy bridge between psychoanalysis and feminism.

In the first place, Benjamin rejected individuation and autonomy as the prize products of psychological development. Admitting that the infant strives for the assertion of self, she insisted that the infant simultaneously seeks the other "for connection, attachment and closeness." These two processes are intertwined from birth and in tandem define our human nature. The issue, then, is not "only how we separate from oneness, but also how we connect to and recognize others; . . . not how we become free of the other, but how we actively engage and make ourselves known to the other." Psychological development thus begins not merely as a fearful response to the authoritative oedipal father but as a joyous respect for the subjectivity of the pre-oedipal mother.[55]

Kohut had likewise disdained the "maturational morality" embedded in the classic oedipal paradigm, deeming it one of the trouble spots of Western civilization. He held that "a move from dependence (symbiosis) to independence (autonomy) in the psychological sphere is no more possible, let alone desirable, than a corresponding move from a life dependent on oxygen to a life independent of it in the biological sphere."[56]

Building on Kohut's premise, Benjamin turned against the masculinist legacy of critical theory, claiming that the real catastrophe is *too much* patriarchal authority. A wrongful symbol of autonomy, the father teaches us "the lesson that she who nurtures us does not free us and that he who frees us does not nurture us but rather rules us." In short, the patriarchal family constructs masculinity and femininity as an absolute hierarchy, where "One is independent, the other dependent; one master, the other slave."[57] And it is precisely this polarity, she pointed out, that undergirds the false equation "oneness = mother = narcissism." According to Benjamin, the myth that only paternal authority keeps us from regressing to the state of undifferentiated infantile bliss is itself a major *result* of splitting caused by the oedipal father of advanced capitalism. Not repression nor even narcissism but gender polarity causes the deep sense of anxiety and alienation that pervades our culture and in turn provides the basis for all sorts of other hierarchies in our unconscious minds. "This means," she concluded, "that male domination, like class domination, is no longer a function of personal power relationships (although these do exist) but something inherent in the social and cultural structures, independent of what individual men and women will."[58]

Benjamin's inversion of critical theory pulled apart its major critique of the crisis of authority in the so-called fatherless society. The structural divide between public and private, which accompanies the expansion of the state apparatus, parallels an intensification of the ideological structures of domination, she agreed. But it is the *specifically masculine* principles now governing public life that threaten to crush the opposing values of mutual recognition that have been banished to the private sphere. In this view, the home cannot possibly be (as for Lasch and Elshtain) "a haven in a heartless world." To the contrary, the intensification of masculine authority threatens "to negate the mother so completely," Benjamin warned, "that there may be no home to come home to."[59]

Benjamin proposed one solution to the crisis of authority but not the one outlined by Lasch and Elshtain. Rather than seeking to "return" women to the home, she preferred the program advanced by Chodorow and Dinnerstein, that mothers and fathers share the responsibilities of childrearing. "Splitting" would lessen, children would retain nurturance and empathy as central values, and the basic binary oppositions of subject and object, private and public, and particular and universal would diminish in importance. En route, Benjamin advocated greater roles for women in the realm outside the family. To put an end to the cycle of domination, she specified, "the other" must come to mean something for men, a process already begun by the women's liberation movement. We are now in a position, she suggested, "to begin thinking about reunifying aspects of human life that have been split and preserved as antagonisms in the gender system."[60]

Benjamin could now reclaim Marcuse's utopian vision. We are ready, she wrote, "to face our narcissism, to find more constructive ways to nourish it and to satisfy our utopian longings for self-knowledge and perfection." Marcuse had specified the goal of the Great Refusal as "reunion of what has become separated." However, unlike Marcuse, Benjamin had traced this fundamental estrangement not to the sexual repression brought on by the Oedipus complex but instead to the denial of the mother's subjectivity in early development. Her vision of liberation, grounded in self psychology, depended most on "the joy of being known."[61]

Earlier critics of the masculine bias in psychoanalytic theory, such as Karen Horney, had provided a corrective by renouncing Freud's libido theory. Benjamin, as well as Chodorow, did the same. If neo-Freudian cultural theory ultimately proved insufficient, post-Freudian relational theory presented its own set of problems. Benjamin may have rescued Marcuse and his utopian vision. But she could no more spare feminists from confronting a basic conundrum than Jean Bethke Elshtain could save women from the purported horrors of liberation.

Decades earlier, Ellen Key and her disciples had advised women to stop competing with men and instead to transform motherhood and childrearing into a proper realm of self-realization. Key linked this prospect to the state's ability to support women and to thereby eradicate the enervating dependence on men. The family, she contended, had often been "a torture chamber for individuality."[62] Elshtain sought to reverse the equation by pushing back the welfare state and restoring the family wage. Relational theorists like Benjamin and Chodorow, believing that men and women alike enjoyed the psychic capacity for empathy as well as subjectivity, sought to equalize their presence in the realms of both reproduction and production. Men and women would then share the responsibility of satisfying basic human needs both within the family and without. But how would this rosy scenario come to be? In practical terms, the existing system of domination denied women the power to achieve the structural changes necessary to end the one-sidedness of both childrearing and wage earning and all their ramifications. Could the answer be found in psychoanalytic theory, however relational? At the very least, this fundamental question returned the interested parties to the same point of departure of the first wave of feminism circa 1909. Could women be both different from and equal to men?

Given the political climate, it was relatively easy for Christopher Lasch to hold his ground despite making a slight bow to the newer relational psychoanalytic modes. He went so far as to interpret the Oedipus complex as a secondary formation and to acknowledge the importance of pre-oedipal events. Nevertheless, he clung to his old faith in the Oedipus complex as the source of "a more impersonal principle of authority." In other words, Lasch refused to give an inch to feminists who extolled the alternative, a moral system configured as self-in-relation.[63]

In *The Minimal Self: Psychic Survival in Troubled Times* (1984), Lasch made major concessions to post-Freudian theory. He even allowed that "normal psychological development cannot be understood simply as the substitution of patriarchal authority for the pleasure principle or as an absolute separation from the mother." But he did not yield on the ideal of the autonomous self. Instead Lasch renewed his attack on the "party of Narcissus" (which now included the current environmental and peace movements as well as feminists) for their contributions to the "deterioration of public life." In his final monograph, *The True and Only Heaven: Progress and Its Critics* (1991), Lasch dropped the psychoanalytic trappings for ruminations on American cultural history. While crediting certain ideologues, Reinhold Niebuhr in particular, for explicating the necessity to preserve order and authority at the expense of abstract notions of freedom, he once again lambasted the liberation movements of the 1960s. He blamed them for promoting such detrimental public policies as forced busing, legalized abortion, and affirmative action. Social survival depended, he insisted, on the consensual acceptance of certain forms of authority, especially those forms invested in the patriarchal family.[64]

Unlike those neo-conservatives and neo-liberals who found a place for themselves on the rightward-rushing bandwagon of American politics, Lasch could neither celebrate the erosion of the welfare state nor witness the increasing division between rich and poor. He maintained a sturdy melancholy until his death in 1994.

For feminists, the road ahead remained rocky. On the one hand, the whole question of the autonomous self versus self-in-relation exploded amid an entirely new theory of domination wherein reason and reality counted less than explorations of the imaginary. On the other hand, the way out scripted by the relational theorists no longer seemed credible. The timeworn strategy—renounce the libido theory—played poorly among feminists determined to restore the original energy to the psychoanalytic paradigm. "Can the language of sexuality," one interrogator asked, "be entirely subsumed within the language of mutual recognition? Can the pleasure of the whole body be derived theoretically from intersubjectivity only?" Or, as Freud himself observed: "Where they love they do not desire and where they desire they cannot love."[65] There were quite a few American feminists, located in the academy and enamored of the French theorist Jacques Lacan and his disciples, who revived psychoanalysis as a means to acknowledge the body as the source of desire. For them, sexuality reigned as the prime and powerful motivational force.

9

In the Age
of the Vanishing Subject

In April 1979 the sixth conference on "The Scholar and the Feminist" forecast a sea change in second-wave feminism. Sponsored by Barnard College's Women's Center, this meeting drew several hundred scholars and activists together to discuss "The Future of Difference," a topic that provoked many arguments but none so intense as those concerning the "feminist appropriation of psychoanalysis." This event raised the curtain not only on the novel hybrid known as "French feminism" but also on a wholly new scenario—postmodernism.

The proceedings bewildered quite a few participants. Those with memories dating to the early years of the women's liberation movement still mistrusted psychoanalysis and found little solace in learning that their French sisters glorified it. The reporter from the journal *Off Our Backs* voiced her personal reservations about its "heterosexist" male founder, although she admitted that the presentations themselves were very stimulating. Unfortunately, she wrote by way of apology, she could offer readers only a sketchy summary of the discussions. The names and ideas of the speakers were so alien that she could neither spell them nor make sense of them for her readers. Although well versed in the works of Nancy Chodorow and Dorothy Dinnerstein, the reporter succumbed under the weight of the psychoanalytic speculations of Monique Wittig, Julia Kristeva, Hélène Cixous, and Luce Irigaray. Questions of language and aesthetics, so central to these French thinkers, also struck her as peculiar and somewhat remote from American political concerns. Even when published appropriately in a scholarly edition, the papers and commentaries from the Barnard Conference required numerous prefatory remarks.[1]

The ideas imported from France were, the interlocutor Carolyn Burke admitted, "largely inaccessible to American readers." To understand them, she suggested, Americans would have to undergo "an intellectual detoxification." Jane Gallop, an American scholar of French literature, agreed with Burke's assessment. There was, she noted, a decidedly "alien" quality about them.

These obstacles represented—as so often in earlier confrontations with European psychoanalytic theory—not so much a problem as an opportunity to replace the domestic model with a supercharged import. Anticipating an unfavorable reception for all the right reasons, Gallop asked coyly at first, "What is the difference, and is there *a* difference, between French and American feminism?" And further: "What use is psychoanalysis to feminism? Why learn another patriarchal discourse?" Her answers, and even more so her manner of answering, went far to establish the sensationalistic style that would stamp future discussions. Setting out the merits of French feminism, Gallop insinuated that the American version suffered by comparison. American feminists "incensed by the Freudian equation of anatomy and destiny," Burke explained, had mistakenly renounced psychoanalysis as "an inimical discourse." Moreover, unlike the French, they had distorted fact to minimize the differences between the sexes. The "French detour," Burke and Gallop promised, would simultaneously show these skeptics how to "think 'difference' differently" and prime them to approach psychoanalysis as "an important strategic weapon" against patriarchy.[2]

Burke and Gallop could not have been more prescient, at least in the short run. During the 1980s, among academic feminists especially, debates continued to intensify concerning the merits of "equality" versus "difference" as the constitutive term of women's liberation. As the Barnard Conference revealed, those who would succeed cultural feminists to become known as "difference feminists" already represented a formidable bloc. The *Off Our Backs* reporter, for example, clung to her suspicions about Freud but nevertheless cast her lot with the proponents of difference. She even complained about the organizers' selection of Chodorow for the keynote panel. More suited to represent American feminism, she protested, was that home-grown champion of womanhood, Mary Daly.[3]

There was a grain of truth here, despite Daly's well-known animosity toward all ideas psychoanalytic. In their affirmation of femininity and attention to language, cultural feminists like Daly and Adrienne Rich appeared, at least on the surface, as kindred spirits of the French. Chodorow, by contrast, could finally appear in her true colors as a feminist who sought to diminish rather than accentuate the distinctions between the sexes. Her victory was pyrrhic, however. More was at stake than the chronic opposition of "difference" and "equality." Chodorow lost status because she allegedly reduced psychical reality to social reality. As one critic put it, she interpreted the differences between the sexes as "the result of the social order rather than the foundation of the symbolic order."[4]

The Barnard Conference had placed psychoanalysis and feminism on a new terrain, the common ground of *discourse*. French theorists, Burke and Gallop tried to explain, located the point of sexual differentiation at "the intersection of language and our existence as social beings." Or as Gallop put it, under the auspices of the French, the two theories came together to expose "the functioning upon and within us of patriarchy as discourse."[5] These assumptions, which would be hotly contested by resistant American feminists, dramatically reconfigured the relationship between psychoanalysis and feminism.

French theory also put postmodernism at the center of the picture by making the subjectivity long sought by modernists a disputed category of being. If critical theorists fretted that the modern self was insufficiently fortified by oedipal ritual and therefore seriously endangered, francophile postmodernists prepared to abandon the project altogether. American feminists now found themselves at yet another border of the unknown.[6]

When feminism and psychoanalysis debuted together circa 1909, the appropriators had staked out their territory with the avant-garde. Almost three-quarters of a century later, it was as if the avant-garde had overtaken the entire scene. Those pre–World War I radicals who claimed the right to determine their own sexuality could hardly have pictured themselves on the covers of their major treatises, photographed giving birth—or could they? Had the excess and parodic impulse so rampant in the last decades of the century been inherent in the enterprise, form rather than substance the real message all along? If so, the careful observer might ask, was postmodernism the necessary successor to modernism? Had both feminists and psychoanalysts been destined to flounder repeatedly on a mistaken search for self? Meanwhile, the cynic might ask, had the whole project become merely an academic exercise, a prerequisite for tenure and little else?

For sharp observers, recurring themes gleamed through the intellectual fog. No less than in the world of art or music, the postmodernist synthesis of psychoanalysis and feminism invented the future by projecting familiar themes from the past through a fun-house mirror. The images appeared weirdly distorted, even hilarious for those with a strong sense of humor.

In confronting psychoanalysis for the first time, feminists generations ago had quickly, if not amicably, come to terms with the significance of the opposition of "equality" and "difference." The debates inaugurated at the Barnard Conference not only recapitulated the earlier arguments, now transferred to the realm of discourse, but restored much of the original energy. The new emphasis on language did not advance the arguments significantly. The familiar dichotomy "biology versus culture" continued to plague both psychoanalysts and feminists, and they once again quarreled about the implications of determinist assumptions now characterized as "essentialist." The debates that resonated well into the 1990s paraphrased some of the most time-worn arguments. Even the term "feminism" rekindled distinctly familiar controversies. The source of inspiration might have shifted from Vienna to Paris, but an aura of déjà vu hung in the air.

The Return to Freud

This new synthesis of feminism and psychoanalysis originated in the remarkable and ineffable theories of Jacques Lacan (1901–1981), who, in the decade before the Barnard Conference, had reached the pinnacle of his acclaim. "Jacques Marie Emile Lacan . . . may well be the most important thinker in France since René Descartes," one zealot attested, "and the most innovative and far-ranging thinker in Europe since Friedrich Nietzsche and Sigmund Freud."[7] Such tributes to a theorist seen as an overflowing fount of wisdom on the differences between the sexes lit a very hot but fast-burning fire.

If one assesses Lacan's contribution to matters that concern feminists, it is only proper that this kind of praise materialized late in his life and career. On questions of female sexuality and femininity, Lacan, like Freud, had offered only a few notations in his foundational writings. For the most part he had simply accepted Freud's dictum that sexual differentiation accompanies the tortuous processes of psychosexual development. He added a few embellishments, no less intricate, enigmatic, and tangled than the rest of his corpus. Only after three decades of practice did Lacan begin to consider seriously the specifics of female sexuality. By this time feminists had issued their own proclamations. Lacan then rushed forward and, like Freud, rode the crest of his celebrity speaking dramatically on femininity.

The similarity between Lacan and Freud was not merely fortuitous. Lacan himself frequently underscored the likeness. According to his own lights, the French theorist had singlehandedly rescued Freudian theory from its Anglo-American corruptors. In a paper demeaning American ego psychologists, Lacan announced that he had effected a "return to Freud." It was a strikingly immodest claim, as the contemporary philosopher Louis Althusser noted.[8] But Lacan did in fact rehabilitate basic elements of Freud's original system, most emphatically the unconscious, sexuality, and the Oedipus complex. This achievement alone, his admirers contended, positioned him as the French Freudian messiah. Ultimately, Lacan did much more.

But despite his intellectual vitality, Lacan did not make an immediate impact on either the international psychoanalytic movement or French intellectual life. Tinged by its Germanic origins, psychoanalysis made little headway in France. The Association Psychoanalytique de France organized only in 1926, fully seventeen years after Freud's visit to the United States. Lacan, who had received a doctorate in psychiatry in 1927, became one of the first members of this small group. In 1936 he introduced his basic formulations at a meeting of the International Psycho-Analytic Association, and for the next decade he worked in relative obscurity, refining a unique and complex account of human subjectivity.

Finally, in 1951, Lacan began a course of weekly seminars that attracted France's leading intellectuals, including Sartre, Beauvoir,

Lévi-Strauss, Merleau-Ponty, Barthes, and Althusser. Encouraged by such luminous patronage, he became increasingly audacious in his practice, so much so that he fell from grace in the eyes of the IPA. In 1964 the renegade theorist gathered his supporters and founded the autonomous Freudian School of Paris (L'École Freudienne de Paris). Two years later the publication of his titanic *Écrits* broadened the audience not only for his own theories but for psychoanalysis in general.

G. Stanley Hall had promised Freud that the year 1909 would be a favorable "psychological moment" for a visit to the United States, and the decade that followed Freud's presentation at Clark University supplied just the right conditions for a major breakthrough. In 1968, amid the tumultuous events of May and June, Lacan finally found his moment.

Revolutionary Paris far surpassed Freud's Vienna in providing a fertile climate. Whereas both theorists discovered their earliest champions not among their professional peers but among youthful celebrants of cultural revolution, Freud observed his at a distance, across the Atlantic in the United States. Lacan, in contrast, met his admirers face-to-face in neighborhood coffeehouses or cafés and in college classrooms. Psychoanalysis had suddenly become a radical totem, as the initiators of the mass protest movement echoed their American New Left counterparts in identifying a connection between the "personal" and the "political" and proceeded to reverse the long-standing opposition to psychoanalysis. To a far greater degree, French radicals summoned psychoanalysis as a political partner. They even demanded a program of government-subsidized therapy for all university students. Slogans and graffiti appeared: "Take your desires for reality"; "A policeman dwells in each of our heads, he must be killed"; "Liberate psychoanalysis." Students petitioned psychoanalysts to join them at the barricades, and many responded, temporarily shifting their practice from the couch to the street. Lacan, who by this time stood prominently outside the ranks of both authority and orthodoxy, became the ranking hero.[9]

The French theorist, unlike his chronically ambivalent predecessor, reveled in his acclaim. By the late 1960s Lacan had become, according to an American scholar, "the revolutionary figure of French psychoanalysis." His seminars became massively popular. Buoyed up by academic prestige, he sought to enlarge his audience. Whereas Freud turned down offers to consult on Hollywood films, Lacan flirted with the media and appeared on French television. According to the philosopher and psychoanalyst Catherine Clément, Lacan had personally made the psychoanalyst into the ideal celebrity of the age, the cultural savant.[10]

Lacan had finally managed to break through the French resistance to psychoanalysis because, the historian H. Stuart Hughes pointed out, in his structuralist and linguistic revisions he appeared to be an "indigenous heretic." He had borrowed resourcefully—notions of kinship from Lévi-Strauss, aspects of phenomenology from Merleau-Ponty, surrealist aesthetics from Breton, linguistics from Saussure, and, above all, a boundless fascination with mind-body dualism from Descartes. In short, he nearly equaled Freud in fashioning a formidable and sweeping synthesis. As Catherine Clément noted, for Freud, too, "the culture of the psychoanalyst was a little bit of mythology, of history, of literature, a little bit of everything," the product of the physician who began with the expectation of curing patients and ended with a "mission to transform culture."[11]

Nevertheless, to this point, Lacan had offered no great pronouncements on female psychology as such. Like Freud, he had gathered his data from clinical experiences primarily with women (who suffered from the postmodern malady of paranoia rather than the hysteria Freud associated with Victorian repression). But matters specific to female sexuality and femininity remained incidental to his larger theories—until the feminist advance.

Actually, Lacan's interest in female sexuality had been piqued two decades earlier with the publication of Simone de Beauvoir's *The Second Sex* (1949). Few French psychoanalysts could disregard Beauvoir's spirited commentary on their profession's mishandling of female sexuality. Lacan himself helped to organize a small congress on the subject, which convened in Amsterdam in 1960, the same year that Helene Deutsch recanted before the International Psycho-Analytic Association. Lacan admitted that the sexuality of woman loomed as "a remarkable oversight" in psychoanalytic theory; he even outlined a brief plan of redress. However, several women analysts stole the initiative. Their first collection of essays, *La Sexualité Féminine: Nouvelles Recherches* (1964), not only lauded Lacan's rival, Melanie Klein, but inveighed against the masculine bias of both Freud and Lacan.

Finally, after the events of May–June 1968, indifference was no longer an option. The Parisian women's movement had embraced psychoanalysis with fervor. *Psychanalyse et Politique (Psych et Po)* had grown from its origins in 1968 in a women's study group at the University of Paris at Vincennes to become, with ample funding, the most visible and powerful sector of the larger *Mouvement de libération des femmes*. Grounded theoretically in both Marxism and psychoanalysis, *Psych et Po* placed female sexuality at the center of all discussions. Its members described their work as "using ourselves, our bodies, our unconscious, our sexuality at the starting point, always trying to link subjectivity to history and the political to the sexual."

Much like Freud's own feminist contemporaries, *Psych et Po* admired the local psychoanalytic hero but also recognized that he had replicated the founder's own shortcoming: with even less excuse, Lacan had provided few insights into female sexuality. The leader Antoinette Fouque, herself a psychoanalyst, led the charge, encouraging her co-workers to redraw the Lacanian paradigm to "bring the feminine into existence."[12]

Like Freud, Lacan responded to such criticism and belatedly prepared to address the theoretical issues surrounding female sexuality and femininity. In 1972–1973, with considerable fanfare, he conducted his famous *Encore* seminar on the Freudian theme "What does Woman want?" By this time his unabashed pursuit of celebrity, compounded by political urgency, prompted a rapid escalation of arcane formulations. Still, the septuagenarian charmed the participants to become, as Freud had, the master of all ceremony. Indeed, much that followed had a familiar ring.

Lacan positioned himself squarely at the heart of the dilemma that had taunted psychoanalysts from their first moment of confrontation with feminists: did the differences between the sexes originate primarily in anatomy or in its psychic representation? Having toyed with this question since Beauvoir issued her challenge, he now found himself compelled to answer.

Characteristically, Lacan aligned himself with Freud. He backtracked to the great debates of the 1920s and 1930s but cast the principal contenders as men, thereby subsuming the contributions of Horney, Deutsch, Müller, Lampl-de-Groot, and Klein under what he considered the more "suggestive" assessments of Freud and Jones. The so-called Freud-Jones controversy, according to Lacan, revealed that Freud had all along distinguished between anatomical differences and their psychic representation, while Jones had fallen into the feminist trap. Rushing to establish "the equality of natural rights," according to Lacan, Jones had failed to appreciate the "function of the phallus" in determining the sexual relationship.[13]

Lacan claimed that he had not only retained the essence of Freud's nonreductionist interpretation but improved it. Freud, he explained, had clearly appreciated the significance of the symbolic register because he had consistently privileged psychic representation over anatomy or biology as such. But, having developed his theses before the advent of modern linguistics, Freud could not recognize the overarching significance of language. The founder of psychoanalysis therefore failed to perceive the "passion of the signifier." The French theorists, however, possessed the necessary theoretical equipment to explicate the "meaning of the phallus," the processes by which the "universal signifier" distinguishes between the sexes.

Lacan's most famous edict—that the unconscious is structured like a language—far exceeds any hypothesis of Freud's. The originator of the "talking cure" had been very interested in language, of course; in one of his most acclaimed books, *The Psychopathology of Everyday Life* (1901), he imaginatively examined errors and omissions in both speech and writing as expressions of unconscious wishes and desires. But for Lacan the meaning of language went beyond its function in communication. Unlike Freud, he considered language a preexisting structure that integrated the psyche into culture.

Working from this premise, Lacan redrew the Oedipus complex, the cornerstone of Freudian theory, as a linguistic imperative. He preserved much of Freud's original narrative of psychosexual development but recast the child's submission to the "Law of the Father" as a gradual compliance with the law of language. According to Lacan the father enjoys the authority to mandate society's norms both socially and linguistically because, in possessing the phallus, he reigns as the carrier of speech. Familiar is the contention that the father regulates the child's sexual drive, specifically his access to the mother, through the usual mechanism of castration anxiety. But for Lacan internalization of paternal authority means taking on both the father's "no" *(le non-du-père)* and the father's "name" *(le nom-du-père)*. In sum, the child comes to terms with the trauma of separation through the intertwined processes of repression and naming. Or, to put it another way, the child resolves the Oedipus complex by exchanging the gratification promised by the mother for the privileges of a new psychic register, the Symbolic Order. It is language, then, specifically the father's language, that serves as the agency through which the child gains access to civilization.

By translating the Oedipus complex into a linguistic event, Lacan could formulate a theory of sexual difference that fully evades the lure of biologism. He cautioned that the phallus is definitely *not* the penis or any object; neither is it a fantasy nor a phenomenon or force directly knowable. The phallus "can only play its role as veiled," he specified, and can never be uncovered. The phallus is, simply, that which functions to produce a subjectivity that is sexed. Thus the power of the phallus, like the allure of the penis, remains fixed, a priori. It operates to structure the relations between the two sexes, he clarified, and thereby ensures that the subject, in entering the Symbolic Order, takes a place as either "man" or "woman."[14]

Lacan's specific theory of femininity depended, however, on a dramatic alteration of Freud's model, the creation of a new stage that precedes the Oedipus complex and profoundly affects its outcome— the mirror stage. Somewhere between the ages of six and eighteen months, Lacan proposed, the infant emerges from the primary narcissism where ego boundaries are unknown. Metaphorically speaking, what triggers this major event is a first-time encounter with a mirror. Observing both his own image and that of the person holding him, the infant achieves a joyous sense of self-recognition while realizing, paradoxically, that this sense of self depends on the Other for validation. Here, in the mirror stage, in what Lacan calls the realm of the Imaginary, the mother and child appear trapped together within a mutually defining order that is not altogether pleasant. Moreover, the image of the self, as reflected in the mirror, is a distortion, a misrecognition. The unsettling effects of the mirror stage never completely dissipate, according to Lacan, not even after the Father intervenes to break the dual imaginary relation between mother and child.

Lacan agreed with Freud that this triangulated drama cannot conclude in a truly happy ending. For Freud the self is doomed to teeter dangerously between pre-oedipal and post-oedipal pleasures, between thanatos and eros; for Lacan the individual must constantly reckon with the coexistence in psychic life of the Imaginary and Symbolic orders. But whereas Freud hesitated to speculate on pre-oedipal formations, Lacan chose to enumerate the pre-oedipal hangovers, or specular images. For example, he argued that the individual despairs over the permanent deprivation of the first object of gratification and suffers additionally from the twisted self-awareness produced during the mirror stage. The Symbolic Order, that is, the configuration of received social meanings, may save the subject from psychosis but not from all the lingering, distorted images of the imaginary hall of mirrors. The best psychoanalysis can do is to facilitate an understanding of subjectivity as the emotional experience of "something missing," which Lacan describes as the origin of desire. In this major overhaul of Freud's instinct theory, it is only through alienated desire that the self comes into existence.[15]

It is here, in the lingering power of the Imaginary, that Lacan positioned femininity. His boldest articulation to this end is "God and the *Jouissance* of The Woman," an oft-quoted yet enigmatic text. The term *jouissance* enjoys no English equivalent, and, in any case, *jouissance* operates by definition outside the realm of the Symbolic and therefore cannot be articulated or, really, known. Nevertheless, it generally refers to the extreme pleasure configured around pre-oedipal Oneness and conveys nonphallic orgasmic joy. To gain insight into this possibility, Lacan advised, "you only have to go and look at Bernini's statue [of Saint Theresa] in Rome to understand immediately that she's coming, there is no doubt about it. And what is her *jouissance*, her *coming* from? It is clear that the essential testimony of the mystics is that they are experiencing it but know nothing about it." But the bottom line is that *jouissance* gives definition to "Woman" because, according to Lacan, in man's fantasy, she who does not suffer the fear of castration comes to represent the site of this ineffable bliss.[16]

Lacan's speculations thus resemble Freud's own notion that what men find so appealing in women is their capacity to retain the primary narcissism denied to the civilizing sex. Underscoring the fantastic quality of this idea, Lacan provided the context for his most illustrious statements. "Woman," he declared, is "not all"; she is the "empty set." "Woman" herself "does not exist and . . . signifies nothing." Lacan did not mean, as his admirers have repeatedly pointed out, that women do not exist. Rather, he speculated that the ideation of "Woman" is a creation, an expression specifically of man's own psychic distance from the site of ineffable bliss and interminable desire to return. "Believing a woman is, thank God, a widespread state—which makes for company," Lacan noted, "one is no longer all alone, about which love is extremely fussy."[17] Woman is, in sum, a man-made construction, a product of his castration complex.

Lacan had definitively answered the tenacious question that Beauvoir had posed so succinctly: Why is woman always man's other? Like Freud, Lacan refused to yield to any alternative proposition. Speaking directly to those feminists who claim equality as their goal, "God and the *Jouissance* of The Woman" serves as a rejoinder by adamantly rejecting the notion that "man" and "woman" are complementary categories. Presenting this argument several years after the formation of the French women's movement, Lacan quipped: "There is woman only as excluded by the nature of things which is the nature of words, and it has to be said that if there is one thing they themselves are complaining about enough at the moment, it is well and truly that—only they don't know what they are saying, which is all the difference between them and me." Like Freud, Lacan appeared to delight in jostling those feminists who pursued—futilely in his opinion—equality.

If Lacan resembled Freud in answering feminists from a remote yet elevated position, he likewise came late to the discussion and jealously guarded his territory. His manner of argument, however, was incomparable. Unlike Freud's finely-crafted narratives and engaging case studies, Lacan's writings and lectures appear intentionally impenetrable. Epigrams replace narratives; jokes, word plays, and puns supplant declaratives. "I don't have a conception of the world: I have a style," Lacan once informed his audience.[18]

Lacan enjoyed an extremely high opinion of himself and shared Freud's expectation of complete fidelity from disciples. The philosopher and psychoanalyst Monique David-Menard, who trained under him, offered the almost comically exaggerated claim that without Lacan "psychoanalysis would have been erased from the map of the Latin world, transformed into normative psychoanalysis, as it was in Eastern Europe and North America." She admitted that Lacan's self-image, "Master in the seat of Truth," was due in no small part to "a role the Zen-like style of his famous Seminar did nothing to discourage." When he faced criticism and deviation, Lacan precipitously disbanded the institute he had founded. In general, though, his authoritarian manner, similar to Freud's own imperious style, merely enhanced his personal magnetism.[19]

All in all, the "return to Freud" via Lacan produced, as one observer put it, an "atmosphere of totemic fantasy." Having usurped the "myth of Freud as primitive father," Lacan now awaited the rebellion of not his sons but his daughters.[20]

French Psychoanalytic Feminism

If Lacan resembled Freud, first, in his reticence to take up questions of female sexuality and, second, in his construction of Woman from the male point of view, he also spawned female admirers as well as critics. David-Menard herself was such a loyalist that one detractor accused her of reenacting "the role of a personally successful, non-rebellious, comfortably critical, constructively reinforcing helper to the father—playing, as it were, Electra to Lacan's Agamemnon."[21] Freud had produced his own group of female disciples, including Lou Andreas-Salomé, Marie Bonaparte, and Helene Deutsch, who, on some points, surpassed the master in presenting a diminished view of female sexuality. He had also witnessed remarkable efforts to invert his formulations so that femininity would figure more positively.

In the 1970s a handful of luminaries, several with ties to *Psych et Po,* aimed to advance the exploration of female sexuality by correcting for Lacan's masculine bias. The leading figures—Hélène Cixous, Catherine Clément, Luce Irigaray, and Julia Kristeva—had attended Lacan's seminars, trained under him, or taught at the Freudian School of Paris. Despite significant disagreements with Lacan, as well as among themselves, these interpreters affirmed his fundamental proposition that, as Cixous put it, all hierarchies "come back to the man/woman opposition." The "problematic of difference" thus became, as it was for Freud's critics in the 1920s, the "watchword for 'New French Feminism.' "[22]

Like Karen Horney, Cixous and Irigaray set out to rehabilitate the meaning of femininity. "What's a desire originating from lack? A pretty meagre desire," Cixous echoed her forerunner. A psychoanalyst and one-time member of the Freudian School of Paris, Luce Irigaray

(1932–) seconded Cixous's demand for a theory of sexual difference that emanates not from man's fantasy but from the female body. Indeed, Irigaray, who became as unrelenting as Horney in her criticism, lost professional standing: she was fired from her teaching position shortly after publishing an irreverent and caustic critique of Freud. A few years later she extended her commentary to Lacan, the phallocrat. Freud and Lacan had both taken it upon themselves to define "woman," she charged, and had managed, in different ways, to portray her only as a flawed version of "man." Like Horney, who traced the problem to Freud's concept of penis envy, the French critics targeted Lacan's "dominant phallic economy" and similarly sought an autonomous source of femininity.[23]

Once again the Oedipus complex proved the point of contention. Lacan had reaffirmed Freud's reasoning that girls never completely resolve the Oedipus complex and retain a special and limiting relationship to the Imaginary. Building on this premise, Cixous and Irigaray fashioned an alternative schema by heightening the significance of the pre-oedipal stage. Neither denied the function of the phallus, but, just as Horney reduced Freud's concept of penis envy to a secondary formation, Lacan's revisionists sought to redeem the sphere beyond its operation. Irigaray thus reclaimed the "feminine feminine," that is, the relationship to language and selfhood established in the Imaginary and never entirely regulated by the phallus. More cautiously, Julia Kristeva also approached the Imaginary as "time" before the imposition of the Law of the Father and the reign of symbolic discourse. She sought, as Carolyn Burke tried to explain to American novices, "the return of the unconscious as a different, an *other*, site of meaning which flows counter to the symbolic use of language."[24]

In sum, Lacan's revisionists focused on the Imaginary because it held, even for Lacan, the secrets of a subjectivity outside the Law of the Father. "Woman's desire most likely does not speak the same language as man's desire," Irigaray concluded, "and it probably has been covered over by the logic that had dominated the West since the Greeks."[25] Clearly it had eluded the master theorist Lacan.

Irigaray, like Horney, cast female sexuality as exemplary. She skipped past the debate sparked by Freud's notion of genital transference, refusing to delimit the site of female sexuality to only two particulars. Unlike man, who "needs an instrument in order to touch himself," woman requires no mediation. "A woman 'touches herself' constantly without anyone being able to forbid her to do so," Irigaray insisted, "for her sex is composed of two lips which embrace continually. Thus, within herself she is already two—but not divisible into ones—who stimulate each other." She went on to say that woman's sexuality, at least double, is actually *plural:* "woman has sex organs just about everywhere. She experiences pleasure almost everywhere . . . the geography of her pleasure is much more diversified, more multiple in its differences, more complex, more subtle, than is imagined —in an imaginary centered a bit too much on one and the same."[26] Woman's body, not man's fantasy, held the key to a sexuality that clearly surpassed the male.

This somewhat strained effort to recover the libidinal economy of femininity, a sexuality that does not, in Cixous's phrase, gravitate around the penis, entailed a major linguistic endeavor. Lacan's revisionists steadfastly abided by his basic proposition that the laws of the psyche act analogously to the laws of language. They sought therefore to fashion a form of discourse grounded in the pre-oedipal semiotic. This new "language" would express the boundless pleasures of early infancy, the *jouissance* embedded in the continuity of self and other that is repressed by the Law of the Father but never totally destroyed. To carry out this strategy, the French theorists set their sights on women's writing and speech, hoping to recover the "feminine" ordinarily buried in patriarchal culture.

This novel practice, *l'écriture féminine*—the strategy of "writing with the body"—thus affirmed difference, "*their* difference," in Cixous's emphatic formulation. In "The Laugh of the Medusa," Cixous implored women to explore the Dark Continent:

Write your self. Your body must be heard. Only then will the immense resources of the unconscious spring forth . . .
To write. An act which will not only "realize" the decensored relation of woman to her sexuality, to her womanly being, giving her access to her native strength; it will give her back her goods, her pleasures, her organs, her immense bodily territories which have been kept under seal.

In a refrain worthy of Havelock Ellis, Cixous invidiously compared the narrowly genitalized male libido to the female. Woman's sexuality is never phallic, neither subjective or objective, but is "cosmic, just as her unconscious is worldwide." This discrepancy, Cixous added, accounts for the antagonism between "masculine" and "feminine" discourses. Woman's language "can only keep going, without ever inscribing or discerning contours ... She lets the other language speak—the language of 1,000 tongues which knows neither closure nor death ... Her language does not contain, it carries; it does not hold back, it makes possible."[27] In advancing the novel strategy of *l'écriture féminine,* Cixous simultaneously illustrated and carried out the practice.

These assumptions, unknown to Horney's generation, facilitated an imaginative reassessment of Freud's fragmentary yet influential study of Dora. This case had long perturbed those feminists who envisioned Dora, a pawn in her father's adulterous love affair, as the quintessential victim of psychoanalysis. Lacan himself provided a new framework. He proclaimed hysteria the maximum contest with gender, a sexual vacillation between the masculine and the feminine, an inability to grasp the signifier that represents the difference between the sexes. Dora, who refused to make this choice, suddenly became a hero, a portender of women's liberation.

Cixous, for example, redefined hysteria as a discourse of revolt against men's power over women's bodies and women's language and cleverly reinterpreted Freud's case history. Freud had carefully noted the inconsistencies in Dora's story, gaps in her memory, slippages in her language, as well as her refusal to produce a coherent narrative. Whereas he had despaired, Cixous celebrated what she perceived Dora's stubborn resistance to therapy. She personally identified with Dora and, furthermore, claimed sisterhood with all hysterics whose language simultaneously confounds men and reveals precious glimpses of femininity.[28]

Julia Kristeva (1941–), an emigrée from Bulgaria and a founder of the one-time Maoist and avant-garde journal *Tel Quel,* took up the question of discourse from yet another angle. She did not privilege alternative forms as much as challenges to the dominant Symbolic mode. She intended to discover and bring forward those fragments of femininity that lay hidden within the realm of the Symbolic.

A linguist and by 1979 a practicing psychoanalyst, Kristeva based her interpretations as much on the discourse theory of Mikhail Bakhtin and Roland Barthes as on the speculations of her friend Lacan. She focused on the dynamic interplay between the symbolic and the semi-otic, that is, between formal systems of language and the somatic and rhythmic impulses that originate in the pre-oedipal. She designated her special interest as the primordial "chora," a term borrowed from Plato to define the experiential site of the pre-Imaginary undifferentiated somatic dyad of mother and child. The chora, according to Kristeva, is the receptacle of the infant's pre-symbolic libidinous impulses that, following the Oedipus complex, become repressed by the Symbolic.

What is central to Kristeva's system is the dialogic relationship that defines these two realms. Because the symbolic attains its energy or status through its regulatory function, Kristeva contends, the semiotic necessarily persists as a powerful factor and regularly breaks through the barriers. For illustrations, Kristeva turned to avant-garde literature, especially the writings of Joyce, Mallarmé, and Artaud that, in the breaks in the structure of their language, allegedly allow the repressed or feminine aspects of subjectivity to reveal themselves. In political terms, these ruptures, which may also be discerned in visual art and music, do not cause or reflect social formations but rather foreshadow or coincide with them. It is in this manner, Kristeva explained, that "*jouissance* works its way into the social." Although she disagreed with Cixous on many matters, Kristeva shared with her the basic Lacanian contention that "it is at the level of sexual pleasure *(jouissance)* . . . that the difference makes itself most clearly apparent."[29]

Like the first generation of feminist revisionists, the post-Lacanians extolled the differences between the sexes to such an extent that they—like Lacan but for opposite reasons—disdained the goal of equality with men. They renounced contemporary campaigns for equal rights because they were not only utterly bourgeois but masculinist. Kristeva condoned only those political struggles such as abortion rights that signaled "difference and specificity." Irigaray simply advised: "French-women, stop trying." They even rejected "feminism" itself as Symbolic discourse, like any other, determined by the Law of the Father.[30]

Lacan's critics, like Freud's, intended to rehabilitate femininity, and in doing so they came full circle to find the ultimate means in motherhood. Following the path of earlier generations of feminists, they inverted psychoanalytic theory—this time Lacan's version—to trace *différance* to the "primal object." Cixous, for example, echoed Horney's complaint against the focus on the father-son dyad to the virtual exclusion of the mother-daughter. All forms of knowledge, from philosophy and science to theology, take as their premise, she protested, the "abasement of woman." This phallic economy is so totalistic that it masks the true source of female sexuality. Female sexuality originates, Cixous asserted, in the daughter's experience of her mother's body and desire.[31]

In these discussions, especially during the formative years of the 1970s, Kristeva appeared in some respects a reincarnation of Ellen Key. She took other feminists to task for their avoidance of motherhood and preference for careers. Antinatalism cannot serve as an effective political strategy, Kristeva warned, because the majority of women continue to value motherhood and seek fulfillment, "if not entirely at least to a large degree, in bringing a child into the world." Kristeva did not wholly deny Freud's configuration of motherhood as a sublimated desire for the penis but nonetheless insisted that women add a unique quality to this experience. "The arrival of the child . . . leads the mother into the labyrinths of an experience that, without the child, she would only rarely encounter: love for another. Not for herself, nor for an identical being, and still less for another person with whom 'I' fuse (love or sexual passion). But the slow, difficult, and delightful apprenticeship in attentiveness, gentleness, forgetting oneself."[32]

Kristeva supplied the psychoanalytic framework that Key had lacked, valorizing the orgasmic pleasure of unity with the maternal body, the incomparable joy of libidinal fusion. "It is the reunion of a woman-Mother with the body of her Mother" that Kristeva celebrated. "This cannot be verbalized; it is a whirl of words, rhythm," she added.[33] For Kristeva, as well as for other French feminists, motherhood represented the radical alterity of woman's body.

Kristeva and her contemporaries thus bore a distinct resemblance to Freud's earliest critics. Both groups of revisionists, albeit in remarkably different ways and separated by a half-century, set off the realm of reproduction as the definitive source of female subjectivity and agency. Kristeva even described masculinity as a fearful and envious response to the maternal body. Whereas Horney presented womb envy as that which boys seek to overcome by deprecating femininity and figuratively elevating their penis, Kristeva imagined patriarchal culture as the product of the masculine effort to repress the memory of, and a continuing desire for, pre-oedipal fusion. French feminists thus replayed a familiar theme, refusing to view the Oedipus complex as the source of femininity.

In remedying the masculine bias of Lacan's theories, his revisionists enlarged the audience for French psychoanalysis. Their imaginative revision of its linguistic underpinnings appealed most to a sector of American feminists already intrigued by the Word.[34] For a moment, theories imported from France fashioned an entirely new relationship between feminism and psychoanalysis. In this round, however, the excitement rarely extended beyond the hallowed walls of the academy.

Feminism as Theory

Unlike Freud, Lacan failed to take America by storm, although he managed not one but two visits to the United States. In 1966 Lacan participated in a symposium at Johns Hopkins University, delivering a lengthy lecture with the imponderable title "Of Structure as an Inmixing of an Otherness Prerequisite to Any Subject Whatever." In 1975, at age seventy-four, he returned to speak before an audience of distinguished scientists at the Massachusetts Institute of Technology. At neither occasion did American psychoanalysts pay their respects. Nor did Lacan overwhelm the other participants with his brilliance. In contrast to the reception given to Freud's lectures at Clark University, Lacan's presentations struck Americans as somewhere between muddled and loony. When he began a colloquy on the comparative merits of human, cat, and elephant excrement—"Civilization means shit, *cloaca maxima*," he concluded—several in attendance questioned not only his sense of propriety but his grasp on reality. Few Americans were ready to accede to Lacan's claims for the scientific elegance of his theories, least of all the ego psychologists, who bore the brunt of his insults. For the most part American psychoanalysts responded to Lacan, according to one scholar, by stating openly "their annoyance and even outrage." It would take at least another decade before his theories found their way to practicing analysts, and even then the majority remained equivocal at best.[35]

Psychoanalysis in the aftermath of Lacan reached its stride less as a theory of the psyche than of belles lettres, less as a curative therapy than an academic enterprise. Lacan's popularity on these shores, somewhat like Freud's, emanated initially from those litterateurs of various types who defined themselves as the avant-garde—but this time the self-styled professorial avant-garde rather than the Greenwich Village bohemians. Flurries around French structuralism, which overtook departments of English and modern languages in the 1970s, prepared the way. In elite universities such as Yale, Cornell, and Johns Hopkins, theories of language and representation and practices of deconstruction, all informed to some degree by Lacanian psychoanalysis, soon became staples of scholarly life. But whereas Freudianism in various forms spread to distant outposts of American culture, Lacanianism rarely escaped the dense prose of the scholarly journal or the narrow confines of the academy. Lacan's formulations did not lend themselves to easy explanation, let alone popularization by the advice columnist, sexologist, or film writer.[36]

Even for American academic feminists, the significance of Lacanian psychoanalysis dawned slowly. But once day broke, everything seemed to change at once. By the mid-1970s only a few scholarly journals, such as *Telos*, had translated or interpreted the major works of Lacan and his feminist disciples and revisionists. Juliet Mitchell had provided a brief introduction in her pathbreaking *Psychoanalysis and Feminism* (1974), while the anthropologist Gayle Rubin announced that psychoanalysis after Lacan was no longer "a feminist theory *manqué*." Meanwhile, the media scholar Laura Mulvey imaginatively critiqued the visual representation of femininity as governed by the phallic economy of narrative film. But it was not until 1976, when *Signs* published an English translation of Cixous's "The Laugh of the Medusa," that academic feminists outside modern language departments gained access to the writings of French feminists. Then, within a decade, as the sociologist and conservative cultural critic Edith Kurzweil later noted, Lacanian-derived feminist theories achieved nothing less than "godlike status."[37]

The theories imported from France, expertly wielded by American feminists, soon drove a wedge down the center of their scholarly community. At least one Ivy League English department became known as "Little Beirut." Many American scholars, including significant numbers of dyed-in-the-wool feminists, sought to turn back the new enterprise because they felt, as the philosopher Nancy Fraser put it, "a disaffinity as much intellectual as political" with the Lacanian-based project.[38] Those who embraced it did so with fervor and treated critics as fuddy-duddy has-beens. True to form, psychoanalysis could be either friend or foe, depending on its alliances.

Almost immediately the contrast between French and indigenous practices appeared striking. Like Lacan, French feminists were notorious for their flamboyant style. They usually effected a similarly brash manner, conducting bitter debates in public and attacking one another "as scandalous and outrageous." Whereas the polemical tradition struck many Americans as, at best, "unsisterly," the French women's dedication to fashion seemed decidedly retrograde. For example, Cixous, who established the first doctoral degree program in women's studies in France in 1974, was known to enter the run-down classrooms of the radical branch of the University of Paris VIII at Vincennes dressed to the nines, complete with ermine coat. While the Lacanians flaunted their femininity and went out of their way to differentiate themselves visually from men, many American feminists clung to an opposite political tactic, shunning cosmetics and similarly stigmatized apparel.[39]

Jane Gallop led the onslaught of American imitators. Her clever book *The Daughter's Seduction: Feminism and Psychoanalysis* (1982)—audaciously presented as a contribution not to American but to French psychoanalytic thought—became emblematic of the *outré* style that would prevail. Because Lacan's work was "virtually unknown to American feminists," Gallop thought it necessary to inform her allegedly parochial Anglo-American readers that she had "taken a constant care not to mystify the uninitiated by esoteric reference or jargon." She succeeded in avoiding both the hermetic terms of Lacanian psychoanalysis and a simple exegesis of a complex subject without muting the polemical, overbearing, and self-assured character of her own pitch. Framing her study as a corrective, Gallop took to task all interpreters, beginning with Mitchell and ending with Cixous. Her irreverence extended to Lacan himself, who appeared in her text alternately as "the ladies' man" and "the prick," in jests nevertheless hinting at phallic flattery of the master.

Gallop's sequel, *Reading Lacan* (1985), its title borrowed from Althusser's *Reading Marx,* employed this same tactic, emphasizing the errors of other interpreters. Gallop drove home one central and familiar message: whereas Lacan had read Freud's "most radical movements against his most conservative . . . Freud's lot in America has been cooptation, the bold Freud silenced, the timid Freud intoned." With this phrase, she sought to wipe out all the past contradictions, cross-currents of more than a half-century in duration that made no appearance even as footnotes. She either knew nothing about them or, knowing, attached no significance.[40]

Despite her professed faith in psychoanalysis, Gallop often seemed to rely on shock therapy. Sharing lecture-circuit panache with the pronounced antifeminist Camille Paglia, Gallop likewise rendered her academic event into performance art, complete with sexy dress, fishnet stockings, and stiletto heels. Clearly she was toying with images, but she was also a *French* feminist.

More than style was at stake, of course. As Gallop later noted, after 1981 few departments of English or modern languages would be the same. In that year special issues of *Critical Inquiry* and *Yale French Studies* celebrated the debut of feminist theory continuous with French poststructuralist and psychoanalytic techniques, and the alleged dialectic between the semiotic and symbolic took over as the operative principle of cutting-edge scholarship. Literary critics now fixed on textual analysis, often disregarding historical context and even authorship. They searched for traces of pre-oedipal energies, for ruptures in the phallocentric symbolic order in such signal Anglo-American texts as Kate Chopin's *The Awakening*, Louisa May Alcott's *Little Women*, Alice Walker's *The Color Purple*, Virginia Woolf's *To the Lighthouse* or, in a purposefully exemplary exercise, Edgar Allan Poe's *The Mystery of Marie Roget*.[41]

A far larger number began to replicate the French convention, bypassing the examination of literary texts for the production of theory itself. Alice A. Jardine, a professor of romance languages and literature at Harvard University, provided a clear-cut example in her well-received *Gynesis: Configurations of Woman and Modernity* (1985). The author, acting as interlocutor between the French and the Americans, opened by identifying her primary concern with "women as speaking and writing subjects, their relationship to language, and how sexual difference operates linguistically in a literary text." She provided remarkably few illustrations of actual fiction by women and instead worked her way through the intricate speculations of Gilles

Deleuze, Derrida, and Lacan to forge her own feminist theory of discourse and difference.[42]

Similar texts proliferated in the university presses at an astonishing rate. Interweaving assorted strands of French theory, the literary scholars Judith Butler, Margaret Whitford, Gayatri Chakravorty Spivak, and Diana J. Fuss, among many others, produced hundreds of related essays and dozens of monographs, each quoting French writers such as Derrida, Barthes, and Lacan in search of authority or an original twist. Altogether, such scholars effected a transmutation of their discipline, at least in the most prestigious quarters, from a study of literature to a philosophy or political theory of language.

The mark of discernment became theory itself. Ushering in the imperious tone that governed these discussions, Elaine Marks and Isabelle de Courtivron produced an anthology of translations, *New French Feminisms* (1980), carefully distinguishing between French and American practices. Although the editors hoped no one would interpret their introductory remarks to mean that "all French feminists are theoreticians and all American feminists are activists," they certainly implied as much. Marks and Courtivron put out a clear signal. Ironically, the French women who had fostered this "theory" had strongly rejected such designation, along with "feminism," as symptomatic of phallogocentric discourse. American francophiles were well aware of the French aversion to these terms but not only refused to relinquish them but exalted them by making "feminist" continuous with "theory." The American interpreters invariably grouped the writings of Cixous, Irigaray, and Kristeva under the misleading heading "French Feminist Theory." In turn, French feminist theory took its place in the American academy, as the literary scholar Janet Todd observed, by rendering American interpretive practices "parochial and naive."[43]

Here at last the Franco-American contingent had found, they presumed, a real dragon to slay. In the recent past, American feminist scholars had painstakingly established a literary practice far outside the parameters of psychoanalytic theories of any kind. Beginning in the late 1960s, with the advance of second-wave feminism, they challenged the sex-biased standards of their discipline by examining the portrayal of women characters in canonical works of fiction and by recovering "lost" women writers in order to challenge the existing definition of the canon itself. The formation of the Modern Language

Association's Commission on the Status of Women in 1970 lent added legitimacy to this enterprise, while new publications, such as *Women's Studies Quarterly* and *Feminist Studies,* and new publishing houses, such as the Feminist Press founded by Florence Howe and Paul Lauter, provided forums for feminist scholars. Nina Baym, Annette Kolodny, Nina Auerbach, Sandra Gilbert, Susan Gubar, and Patricia Meyer Spacks were among the most distinguished scholars to retrieve from oblivion, and provide insightful commentary about, scores of women writers.[44]

The francophile critics aimed their fire precisely at this restoration project, particularly its sociohistorical premises, as decidedly reargarde. American feminists, Marks and Courtivron alleged, obsessively documented and futilely attempted to measure the actual contributions of women in the past. Americans guilelessly assumed

> that women have been present but invisible and that if they look they find themselves. American feminists tend also to be focused on problem solving, on the individual fact, on describing the material, social, and psychological conditions of women and devising ways for improving it. Their style of reasoning, with few exceptions, follows the Anglo-American empirical, inductive, anti-speculative tradition. They are often suspicious of theories and theorizing.[45]

This writing of "herstory," Marks and Courtivron condescendingly noted, suffered in comparison with the superior techniques employed by the likes of Cixous or Irigaray.

In effect, American literary scholars had positioned themselves on what was becoming an increasingly sharp division between, in Elizabeth A. Meese's phraseology, "Feminist Literary Criticism" (a proper noun) and "women's studies feminism"; or, as Nancy K. Miller rephrased it metaphorically, between the elegant high-heeled shoes worn by Cixous and the "sturdy, sensible sort worn by American feminists."[46]

When psychoanalysis becomes a theory of literary criticism, Todd aptly commented, "it seems to grow supremely arrogant." French psychoanalysis, energized by Derridean deconstruction, succeeded in dividing academic feminists into opposing camps. Those who followed the French linguistic turn became known as "theorists," while those who held their ground in sociohistorical studies earned the now derisive designation "empiricists" or "humanists." This opposition—peculiar in that it was the French, not the Americans, who condemned "theory" as the sine qua non of the patriarchal Symbolic Order—soon played itself out in several other disciplines. Ironically, as the linguistic premises became steadily more pronounced, their origins in Lacanian psychoanalysis became ever more obscure. Nevertheless, the main product was acrimony. Nina Baym reproached these "theorists" for seeking approval from male academicians and, in turn, excoriating "their deviating sisters."[47]

A sizable number of feminist scholars, even those whose livelihoods depended on the examination of texts, fought the attempt to transform their disciplines into theory-mills. They saw little value in creating prose "designed to stress," in one reviewer's opinion, "the inscrutable brilliance of the writer and to make extreme demands upon the reader." Or, another reviewer asked: "Aren't there whole groups of American feminists who are left in the position of only overhearing the theoretical debates of middle-class academic feminism?" These scholars held out against the Lacanian-assisted modes primarily because they continued to value the actual role of women in literary production.[48]

The Lacanian "return to Freud" had, in a way, returned American feminists to the moment of their initial confrontation with psycho-analysis. While scores leapt at the chance to popularize the imported theories, others clung to indigenous traditions. The context had certainly changed, shifting from the sites of pre–World War I cultural radicalism to the more prosaic halls of the academy. There was, however, enough similarity to allow the distinguished American literary scholar Elaine Showalter to step comfortably into the role played decades earlier by the arch-materialist Charlotte Perkins Gilman. Just as Gilman had refused to abandon inquiries into political economy and natural science, Showalter would not give up the restoration project. She defended what Kolodny had described as its "playful pluralism" of approaches. In contrast, French theory, least of all *l'écriture féminine*, held little appeal. As a means to interpret literature, psycho-analysis had proven, she concluded, both too rigid and too narrow. Psychoanalytic criticism—and here Showalter sounded most like Gilman—"cannot explain historical change, ethnic difference, or the shaping force of generic and economic factors." Moreover, rather than alleviating the pressures of gender, a goal that Showalter shared with Gilman, psychoanalytic theory could not help accentuating them.[49]

Essentialism with a Difference

Despite—or because of—this altercation, feminists helped Lacan realize the destiny he had charted for himself. In celebrating his "return to Freud," the French theorist made clear that he was not simply restoring Freudian doctrine to its proper form, although he did in fact make this claim. Lacan intended to reinstate the "meaning of Freud," or what Freud meant to the entire history of Western civilization. In other words, he hoped to recall the revolutionary moment of Freud's ascent, the epochal "cultural break," the shattering of paradigm or episteme (in Foucault's term) that psychoanalysis had enabled. But whereas Freud and his feminist contemporaries helped to usher in modernism and "consciousness of the self," Lacan and his cohorts found their own moment in postmodernism and its peculiar rejection of the very possibility of selfhood.

Like modernism, postmodernism eludes precise definition. The relevant entry in Elizabeth Wright's handy *Feminism and Psychoanalysis: A Critical Dictionary* (1992) defines postmodernism as "a highly unstable concept, used to designate either a particular mapping of contemporary experience, a movement in the arts and literature or a theoretical critique of the Western foundations of philosophical modernity." Quite a few writers used postmodernism to identify the *condition* of what they wishfully described as "late capitalism"; others used the term interchangeably with poststructuralism, as an interpretive strategy or practice.[50]

For feminists and psychoanalysts alike, however, the defining quality of postmodernism was its new conception of subjectivity or selfhood. Unlike modernism, which embodies the Enlightenment proposition that humanity is not only "knowable" but, once properly invested with truth, moving progressively toward self-realization, postmodernism is distinguished by the denial of this possibility. Not only is there no "knowable" self; there is no telos or grand emancipatory plan. Postmodernism represents, therefore, yet another new paradigm governing the meaning of human existence.

True to form, psychoanalysts were ready to claim that Freud had not only ushered in modernism but also postmodernism. The founder of psychoanalysis, they pointed out, had likened his own discoveries to the revelations of Copernicus and Darwin. By showing that neither is the earth the center of the universe nor are humans privileged beings in the scheme of creation, Freud explained, the revolutionary scientists had delivered two severe blows to "human megalomania." Psychoanalysis issued "the most wounding blow," its theory of the unconscious proving that the ego "is not even master in its own house." Chodorow summarized Freud's argument as "we are not who or what we think we are: we do not know our own centers; in fact, we probably do not have a center at all. Psychoanalysis radically undermines notions about autonomy, individual choice, will, responsibility, and rationality, showing that we do not control our own lives in the most fundamental sense. It makes it impossible to think about the self in any simple way, to talk blithely about the individual." Nonetheless, she herself did not consider Freud's intentions postmodern and preferred to save this designation for Lacan.[51]

There is a big difference between Freud and Lacan, Chodorow insisted. Freud "wanted to resolve the paradox he created, to use the scrutiny of individual and self not to celebrate fragmentation but to restore wholeness." Postmodernists head in the opposite direction. Whereas Freud "wanted to reconstitute the individual and the self he had dissected," Lacan, according to Chodorow, dismissed the whole idea of the so-called bourgeois individual subject as bogus and perhaps one of the grandest delusions ever perpetrated. Lacan, not Freud, put the psychoanalytic stamp on postmodernism by advancing the tenet that the self cannot be constituent in itself. It was Lacan who claimed that the self *is constituted* through language and, in its necessary relations to others and the Other, is subject to a law that rules out even the complex processes that Freud had charted.[52]

Despite Chodorow's clarifications, many American feminists honored Lacan as Freud's rightful successor and condoned the conflation of postmodernism and psychoanalysis because this particular alignment facilitated a new and improved approach to the question of the female self. If postmodernism signaled, as one enthusiast alleged, "resistance to any form of reified meaning," this imperative also put the brakes on gender as the principal organizing category of human existence. Lacan had already disaffirmed the existence of Woman; feminist theorists could now take another giant step to untangle once and for all the relationship between the physical body and its psychic representation as "sexed." Gender, a discursive category, has no more meaning than does "the self": both reflect the instability of the human condition.[53]

And yet, for all the theoretical innovations and the revelry they prompted in the academy, close listeners swore they could hear eerily familiar strains. According to die-hard skeptics, even the Lacanians had evaded rather than met the old challenges concerning the limitations of psychoanalysis. They might have switched the locus of sexual differentiation from anatomy to language and even projected the impossibility of a coherent self. But did they really point the way out of the tangle of gender? Perhaps they merely created their own form of determinism, an essentialism that even their inventive discursive mode failed to conceal. The link between body and psyche remained stubbornly intact.[54]

Because Lacan wrote so little on female sexuality or femininity, his own French critics more readily illustrated this vice. In general, *l'écriture féminine* employs such literal descriptions and repeated references to sexual organs, several skeptics charged, that it ultimately serves as an exercise in direct representation. Irigaray's "lips," for example, seem "dangerously essentialist," to say the least. Cixous's choice of metaphors was so sorely overdetermined that, despite her professed obeisance to language, her tributes to female genitalia succeeded in refurbishing the realm of biology. In sum, Cixous's signifying practices lyrically saluted "the body" in such literal fashion that the French writer appeared to have surpassed Freud in her preoccupation with anatomy. As one critic tartly noted, the French feminists risked "a fetishization of the female body, a privileging of maternity at the expense of non-procreative sexuality, or even an *equation* of feminine creativity with maternity (as Kristeva seems to do), coming full circle to the worst of Freud." Cixous might assert that "everything turns on the Word: everything is the Word and only the Word," but she and her cohorts, through their graphic and often excessive evocations of the physical body, actually fructified the long-standing dualism of "biology vs. culture." As Elizabeth Abel summed up, Lacan and the post-Lacanians "essentialize a dishistoricized paternal law, derived from the symbolic Father."[55]

Francophile feminists answered these charges predictably by bolstering their own claims. They insisted ever more adamantly that the principal virtue of Lacanian theory, its emphasis on language, frees psychoanalysis of such reductionism, which is, they retorted, much more characteristic of American practices. The very elegance of French theory, they contended, depends to a large degree on its repudiation of biologism. After all, Lacan presented Woman as "a signifier." Or, as Gallop confirmed, the phallus is neither a fantasy nor an object, much less the organ that it symbolizes. Indeed, it is precisely this *non*-correspondence between anatomical and psychic structures that transforms the body into text, perhaps the premier text of the avid textualists.[56]

This incessant volley between feminists, played on the court of postmodernism, registered the distant sounds of Charlotte Perkins Gilman at intellectual match point against Ellen Key. It also recalled Horney's protest against Freud—and Freud's charges against Horney. At first, psychoanalysts proved just as eager to fend off the charge of biologism as did their feminist critics. And they seemed just as likely at other times to claim a direct correspondence between the biological and psychic realms. For example, Marynia Farnham and Theodor Reik did not hesitate to trace femininity directly and literally to woman's reproductive organs. Two decades later second-wave feminists quite reasonably reviled Freudian psychoanalysis for its heinous biological determinism. Yet almost simultaneously cultural feminists began to celebrate the differences between the sexes to such an extent that several luminaries were willing not only to acknowledge biology as a major organizing factor but to exalt woman's unique reproductive capacity. Postmodernists aspired to render both sides of this historic debate null and void.

Judith Butler ran away with this logic to criticize Lacanians in the name of postmodernism itself. Her *Gender Trouble: Feminism and the Subversion of Identity* (1990), one of the most cited books of the decade, argues that psychoanalytic theory, be it Freudian or Lacanian, inevitably reifies gender identity through its metanarrative of psychosexual development. Butler readily acknowledged that even Kristeva, considered by many Americans the most sophisticated of the lot, failed to evade the logic of the binary system. "The female body that she seeks to express," Butler observed, "is itself a construct produced by the very law it is supposed to undermine." For his part, Lacan had depicted a paternal law that reigns with such force that human existence without it appears impossible. In other words, French psychoanalysis, much like the Freudian version, wavers dangerously between exposing the functional relations of patriarchy and reinforcing them.

According to Butler, psychoanalytic theory errs in forcing a conceptual coherence between sex, gender, and desire when, in contrast, gender does not "express" sexuality but rather functions culturally as a "regulatory ideal." She bade feminists to abandon gender altogether as the organizing principle of their politics. Writing specifically on the relationship between psychoanalysis and feminism, she urged her colleagues to forsake the category of "woman" precisely because it presumes an "ontological integrity that needs to be dispelled." Gender, she countered, is "a fabrication," a fantasy "inscribed on the surface of bodies."[57]

In drawing out the strategic implications, Butler paired well with Donna J. Haraway, a philosopher of science at the University of California at Santa Cruz. Haraway pronounced as "eminently" political the "refusal to become or to remain a 'gendered' man or a woman." She asked everyone to imagine a "post-gendered world" populated by "cyborgs" who transgress boundaries and disassemble and reassemble cultural symbols into a "postmodern, collective and personal self." In an extended and strangely mixed metaphor, she described the reigning phallogocentrism as the "egg ovulated by the master subject, the brooding hen to the permanent chickens of history." The outsider in that nest would take wing as a phoenix "that will speak in all the tongues of a world turned upside down." If veteran Marxist readers detected formulations borrowed from Leon Trotsky's "permanent revolution," and from the historian Christopher Hill's description of the English revolution, they could shake their heads about the long-awaited commonwealth: in Haraway's utopian vision, the overthrow not of capitalism but binary dualism, that is, a future without gender.[58]

This feminist postmodern move suited a surge of the cultural avant-garde amid the deepening political conservatism of the 1980s and early 1990s. Queer Theory, whose roots in parodic identities ran deep, found in Butler a way to reinterpret cross-dressing, drag, and the stylized roles embedded in the butch/femme relationship. Butler, equally eager to claim this territory as her own, cited the fluidity between anatomy and gender as identity and gender as performance. If the gender meanings were admittedly "part of hegemonic, misogynist culture," they had been so effectively "denaturalized and mobilized" through parodic performance as to thoroughly subvert and displace the original and even "imitate the myth of originality itself." Such practices, she maintained, challenged the artificial coherence imposed by the binarism of gender and thereby opened the possibility of greater complexity, hence liberation.[59]

Or did they? In denying the efficacy of gender as an organizing category, did postmodern feminists outdistance even Lacanian psychoanalysts in drawing attention to the differences between the sexes? One young writer, educated in Women's Studies at the University of California-Santa Cruz, thus bared the centrality of gender even as she denied its fixity:

> i am transgendered, Jewish, boy, lesbian. My sex is female. I feel gendered male: i identify with the social construction of masculinity; i often wish that my body looked like a boy's and i am sad that i have big breasts and that i don't have a boy butt; i like it when i am confused for a boy; i enjoy it when my lesbian friends and lovers call me little boy. But i am not a man. I do not consider myself a man. I have been gendered male, participate in constructing my own male gender, but i have been hurt because *i am girl* who crosses the gender lines.[60]

Neither feminism nor psychoanalysis, however postmodern, could cast out the "difference" bogey. The struggles over gender, unrelenting since the 1960s, had merely become increasingly abstract in an era of marked political frustration and generational uncertainty.

Perhaps the most damning assessment possible was that the very attempt to unfix gender evolved into an extraordinary reification. Skeptics suggested that the incessant scrutiny—what became known as "theorizing"—actually tightened the grip of gender as an organizing category of human existence. Rather than a strategy for personal liberation en route to a larger collective transformation, the practice became the pivot around which the wounded and wearied subject endlessly turned.

As the historian Linda Gordon noted, *difference* ruled as "the dominant motif" of feminist theory in the twentieth century. Although first-wavers did not employ this term, they had managed to convert misogynistic discourses about the differences between the sexes into positive statements about the distinctive qualities of womanhood that deserve recognition. It was this project that occasionally aligned feminists with psychoanalysts and, at other times, set them apart. But the central paradox—the pursuit of equality on the grounds of woman's difference from man—remained firmly intact through various waves of psychoanalytic and also feminist theory.[61]

By the late 1930s Horney concluded that the very concern with the differences between the sexes benefited men more than women. Like the postmodernists, she decided that gender is not an absolute but a relative category of human existence. Each society maintains its own system for "producing" men and women, she surmised, not simply through discursive structuring but through cultural conditioning. Disputing the significance of "female psychology," she abandoned the field altogether. A half-century later, postmodernists once again waved the flag of relativism but, in proclaiming the indeterminacy of gender, appeared dangerously obsessed with it. It could be said that feminist theory was becoming a victim of its own binarism, so much so that oppositional thinking advanced as (ironically), in Butler's words, "a kind of 'slave morality.' "[62]

But could feminists give up gender or the category of woman and continue to function as political strategists? Could the politics of difference be replaced, as Linda Alcoff suggested, by "a plurality of difference where gender loses its position of significance"? Or, as Butler put it: "If there is no subject, who is left to emancipate?"[63]

Although Butler provided a forceful answer, she could not satisfy all feminists, including some postmodernists. Elizabeth Grosz, a close student of Lacan, asked the intransigent questions: "If women cannot be characterized in any general way, if all there is to femininity is socially produced, how can feminism be taken seriously? What justifies the assumption that women are oppressed as a sex? What does it mean to talk about women as a category? If we are not justified in taking women as a category, what political grounding does feminism have?"

Quite a few scholars had concluded that feminists minimally required a functional essentialism, an admittedly opportunistic assumption of woman as a category. Theirs would be, however, an "essentialism with a difference." Fumbling for another way out of the various blind alleys, scholars associated with Brown University's Pembroke Center concluded that attacking essentialism had become an exercise in futility. They staked out instead an equally imaginative and murky solution, an *anti*-anti-essentialism. If not a realistic goal, this variation gave some scholars at least the prospect of a fresh target.[64]

The late 1990s found intellectual exhaustion on both (or, rather, all) sides of the debate. As the search for a female/feminine subject had "died," the historic link between feminism and psychoanalysis also seemed to evaporate into thin air. Even to explore the origins of femininity, the summa of the joint project, appeared retrograde: such a task assumed that subjectivity exists. As the British scholar Patricia Waugh tartly observed, the old slogan of women's liberation—"the personal is political"—had yielded to the postmodern imperative—"let us wage war on totality."[65]

But for those American feminists who could not be convinced, the whole postmodern project, including Lacanian psychoanalysis however misplaced, seemed no less spurious than when it debuted in the 1970s. Skeptics questioned whether the exclusive masculine pantheon of Derrida, Barthes, Lyotard, Foucault, and Lacan himself could effectively serve feminists. Could woman be, one cynic asked, merely "the subject of man's postmodern discourse," never to become a "speaking subject" herself? Could feminists embrace postmodern discourse without making "the man's theories into an object of her seduction"? Psychoanalysis suffered chronically from phallocentrism, as Horney alleged, or phallogocentrism, as Lacan's critics charged. The perceptive critic Jane Flax concluded that Lacan's theories were "profoundly misleading" and more tainted by "masculinist assumptions" than Freud's. The bottom line, to many so-called Anglo-American feminists, was clear. Harking back to Marks and Courtivron, Flax stated the grievance that would not die:

The lack of attention to concrete social relations and the qualitative differences among them, such as the distribution of power, results, as in Lacan's work, in the obscuring of relations of domination, including those *among* women, such as race. Treated this way, relations of domination tend to acquire an aura of inevitability or become equated with language as such. Attention shifts from the many and varied sources of women's oppression to "whether or not we can in fact escape from the structuring imposed by language."

Flax refused to yield the fundamental proposition, that gender is not merely or even primarily a discourse but gains its power and definition as a social relation.[66]

In early 1996 the San Francisco *Examiner* (under the subtitle "Why is psychoanalysis still driving critics crazy after all these years?") announced the opening of the very first Lacanian institute in the United States. Leon Patsalides, who personally launched the school—comprising just 15 students, two-thirds of them women—after conducting evening seminars on Lacan in Berkeley for six years, stated his mission in the fashion typical of the master: "Lacan *is* Freud. But he took Freud from a Cartesian, Newtonian paradigm and put him in an Einsteinian quantum paradigm." Patsalides, a native Belgian who trained with Lacan but admitted to leanings toward Eastern religions, conducted his own practice in the French fashion: $150 per fifty-minute session, halting without refund if and when the analyst achieves "a moment of discovery." Asked by a reporter if the Lacanian mode did not encourage the analyst to be authoritarian and manipulative, Patsalides responded, "Sometimes a patient needs a little shock to see."[67]

Not surprisingly, American analysts showed little inclination to follow the path of the Lacanian School of Psychoanalysis and its advocacy of emotional shock therapy. Among the growing number of women who filled the professional ranks, Melanie Klein and D. W. Winnicott were more influential. Even those feminist practitioners like Jessica Benjamin who welcomed the challenge to modernist notions of subjectivity demanded that psychoanalysis "retain some notion of the subject as a self, a historical being that preserves its history in the unconsciousness, whatever skepticism we allow about reaching the truth of that history." Whereas in France *Anti-Oedipus: Capitalism and Schizophrenia* (1972) by the philosopher Gilles Deleuze and the psychoanalyst Félix Guattari and endorsed by Michel Foucault became the emblematic post-1968 celebration of the revolutionary potential of fragmented subjectivity, psychoanalysts in the United States remained cautious. The imploded self or the experience of multiple personalities exacted, in one critic's estimation, "terrible psychological costs." It was a matter of opinion if decentering was pleasurable or, as others contended, intolerable and potentially deadly.[68] The future of Lacanian theory, like its past, seemed to be in the lecture room or scholar's study rather than the therapist's office.

Soon psychoanalysis itself experienced a major decentering. Several prominent American scholars began to view psychoanalysis less as a means of recovering memory than as an interpretation of the fictions of early development. Roy Schafer, who scrutinized the published case histories of eminent analysts, declared that he had discovered the fictional element. The narrative coherence they had imposed on the patient's story represented, he warned, only "a version of the past," albeit a very important one. Other commentators, such as Donald Spence, similarly highlighted the role of the analyst in uncovering not factual but "artistic truth" about the patient's past life. The goal of analysis thus became not the emergence of insight into the previously unconscious past but the production of new stories.[69]

Suffering from its own contingencies, psychoanalysis faced a new spate of iconoclasm. Powerful critics once again targeted Freud, challenging his fundamental tenets, clinical techniques, and even professional ethics and personal morality. From the popular presentation by the research psychiatrist E. Fuller Torrey, *Freudian Fraud: The Malignant Effect of Freud's Theory on American Thought and Culture* (1992), to the unrelenting *Why Freud Was Wrong: Sin, Science, and Psychoanalysis* (1995) by Richard Webster and the erudite *The Memory Wars: Freud's Legacy* (1995) by the literary scholar Frederick Crews, there seemed no place to turn except the hallowed halls of the academy.

It could be said, then, that Lacan did not really return to Freud as much as abrogate his entire teleology, a move that proved as detrimental to psychoanalysis as to feminism. But such an interpretation would fail to account for the extraordinary curiosity aroused by Lacan and the post-Lacanians. The ramifications of the connection between French theory and American feminism reached far beyond their common linguistic and postmodern signature. They shared the fate of other social theories at the end of the twentieth century, vulnerable to most of the same strains and putative solutions.

All that remained, at least in the realm of the speculative, was the possibility of new performances. And here Lacan had offered Anglo-American feminists something more than deliverance from the old master's revisionists and critics. In complementing the French post-structuralist exaltation of language or discourse, and in promoting the postmodern anti-teleology of the fragmented self, Lacan and his followers successfully reconfigured the whole meaning of sexual difference. The so-called French feminists, positioning subjectivity solely in relation to the imaginary and symbolic orders, only carried the Lacanian formulation to its logical conclusion.

The Lacanian impulse was clearest in the pursuit of "multiple subject positions," an attempt to dissolve the Hegelian notion of self altogether. Keen observers would notice how closely this notion resembled the modernist search for subjectivity in the feminist camp more than a half-century earlier. Beginning with Freud's visit, feminists had determinedly attached themselves to the project of self-realization. They had also added their own qualifier, its true nature contested even among the firmest believers: a woman's self. And they turned to psychoanalysis as the vehicle precisely appropriate for this pursuit.

In a moment of innocence, it seemed that feminists had nearly succeeded in turning the timeworn denial of women's subjectivity on its head. When Freudianism began to enchant Americans circa 1909, feminism as a theory of selfhood achieved definition in contradistinction to the world view of an older generation who steadfastly clung to formalistic notions of natural rights, civil equality, and social service. With great audacity, young avant-gardists hailed what would later be called a new epistemic order, describing themselves as the true revolutionaries. Rebellious youngsters demanding control of their bodies and minds breathed vitality into the very notion of the "modern." The most philosophically minded observers imagined that they saw the living application of Hegel's apotheosis of a romantic art that realizes its identity through successive (and perhaps endless) dialectical negations.

It was an unforgettably exciting moment, for themselves as well as for the new century—and one fraught with controversy. The hard awakening began as soon as the new notion of feminine self up-ended the foundations of the older vision. The old-guard materialist Charlotte Perkins Gilman could readily see in the fresh idealism a flight from all that three generations of activists had sought for women. Her complaint, in large part a rejection of the increasing (and distinctly radical) emphasis on the differences between the sexes, exposed what would stand as the central contradiction of modern feminism.

Future generations, whether they embraced or shunned the label "feminist," found themselves again and again on the horns of this dilemma. By the 1930s women in American psychoanalytic ranks had repudiated the notion of a feminine self. Amid the quest for a common humanity on the one hand, the rise of methodological relativism on the other, they seemed to have made great strides in that direction. Femininity was culturally conditioned, a sense of self inherent in neither sexual anatomy nor social arrangements, and definitely not dictated by the Oedipus complex.

Against the backdrop of World War II and the Cold War, psychoanalysts and their allies turned back toward a reductionist/functionalist argument, downgrading or even replacing self. Its successor, "identity," emphatically including *feminine* identity, now corresponded properly with idealized social roles. Ordained by nature to be nurturing, women achieved femininity by wielding a broom, changing diapers, and blissfully complying with their subservient status. Those who thought differently were not only rear-guard but potentially subversive to the security of the home, the rising generations, and perhaps even the rational traditions of the West now threatened by Communism.

The 1960s tore up this prescription, identifying psychoanalysis as archenemy for its presumption to define femininity and naming patriarchy the main actor behind the curtain. However mistaken the bill of particulars, second-wave feminists had set themselves the goal of complete equality. And then, as hopes dimmed, the turn toward post-Freudian psychoanalysis changed everything again—or did it?

If feminists hoped to escape the oedipal paradigm to displace paternal authority for the subtle and sub rosa influence of the mother, they continued to meet resisters. There were those psychoanalysts and social critics who preferred to salvage that older notion of selfhood, the highly differentiated and distinctly *male* self revived and memorialized by the Frankfurt scholars and their American successors. Feminists found themselves struggling hard to offer an alternative model, the self-in-relation that appealed both to cultural feminists and to those who sought a nuanced critique of the possessive individualism that bolstered industrial capitalism. Here the bonds of mother and infant valorized a different notion of selfhood, one that exalted attachment and empathy and provided a source of value outside the patriarchal system of domination and greed.

The "French turn," aligned with postmodernism, inevitably called into question the entire notion of self or subjectivity, describing it as something unknowable and in any case never stable. This is difficult to see at first glance from the documents and practices of *l'écriture féminine*, which in exonerating the female libidinal economy actually provides new mechanisms for essentializing femininity. But if only through repeated insistence, the French linguistic theorists revealed the ephemeral quality of the whole project. Self/subjectivity always disappears in the last instance, leaving nothing tangible in its aftermath.

Rather than putting to bed perennial problems, postmodern psychoanalysis succeeded in reviving the controversies that had persisted in one form or another since the early part of the century. If any lessons had been learned from the first rounds, few carried over. Much that initially appeared new and marvelous proved painfully familiar. Even in the postmodern mode, where "history" had apparently vanished, historic themes held fast.

Always at the center and however disguised by refracted discussions were the competing notions of subjectivity articulated by Marx and Freud: the placement of "woman" along the axes of work and sex, production and reproduction. Neither psychoanalysts nor feminists could stray far from the boundaries or limits of these two fundamental but seemingly opposing possibilities. The aspiration for selfhood, for both psychoanalysts and feminists, could swing either way: the right to enter into "civilization" and become producers; and the right to validate women's unique ability to reproduce the species and rear it according to the values emanating from this particular capacity. Postmodernism added no new solutions.

As the new fin de siècle approached, a handful of erstwhile postmodern feminists began to rethink their views. Perhaps the most distinguished "materialist" of the field, Teresa L. Ebert, interpreted patriarchy as the "primary site for the ideological construction of individuals as gendered subjects," and as a historically determined structure embedded in a particular mode of production. "Patriarchal capitalism," in her formulation, tends to use men and women interchangeably as sources of wage-labor and non-wage domestic labor, introducing a diminution in the "differentiation between masculine and feminine" while at the same time ensuring male privilege. It remains for the feminist theorist, then, to explain how patriarchy can "successfully maintain and reproduce the domination of one gender over the other." Ebert's latest work, offering a sharp critique of what she regards as an outdated and failed perspective, returns the feminist theoretical agenda to its beginnings in production and reproduction by shucking off the hull of the discursive.

In *Ludic Feminism and After: Postmodernism, Desire and Labor in Late Capitalism* (1996) Ebert argues that linguistic play has turned out to be a blind alley after all. Theory that can never transcend the "politics of representation" inevitably regresses to the familiar idealist and individualist philosophies of the middle classes, updated to the late-twentieth-century romance of the cyber-slinging artist-entrepreneur. Even the notion of "women's oppression," lately condemned by feminists like Gayle Rubin as useless and mystifying, is destined to be jettisoned. In what may be the final theoretical phase, lust or desire is pronounced *the* prime materialist force, generating profit on a world scale and promising the possibility of truly untrammeled individual freedom.

Most of the postmodernists moving to the outward limits of gender-bending theory by this time rejected the Freudian basis of their intellectual maneuvers, but here, too, they had made a telling return. Any theory that poses "desire" as the building block of material reality recalls Freud's thesis that sex is the primary drive, the infant's greedy passion for pleasure the organizing principle of humanity. Freud, of course, believed profoundly in men's capacity to sublimate their strongest desires and thereby ensure the march of civilization. Generations later, when expectations of progress had soured, sublimation seemed beside the point. Only desire remained, a desire that allegedly knew no sex.

Such postmodernist musings seemed ever further from the reality of women's lives. By the middle 1990s social theorists increasingly mulled the consequences of rampant nationalism, unprecedented stresses on the natural environment, skyrocketing corporate profits, and huge populations facing catastrophic drops in their living standards. The continued forced restructuring of societies, rather than increasing women's status (as in many developmental models) worked relentlessly in the opposite direction. Even the middle classes of the West found their hard-won gains now unexpectedly precarious. Thirty years down the road from their initial embrace of Lacan, feminist theorists might realize that the discursive mode was losing its relevance. To be blunt: its theorists had reached a dead end.

The "freedom of pleasure," or the freedom to pleasure oneself, so basic to postmodern feminism must finally yield, Ebert insisted, to "the founding freedom: *freedom from necessity.*" Her appeal for a feminist "resistance modernism" rooted in a social struggle over "material differences" of sex, race, and class is unlikely to win any popularity contests among resolute postmodernists. But it catches a straw in the current European intellectual winds and predicts a turn in the United States as well.[70]

If post-Freudian theory had reconfigured the old conceptual stalemate, it might be said more charitably that the controversies around self-in-relation had produced indispensable dialogue. Decades of research and discussion at the highest (as well as the lowest) levels had been devoted to the competing possibilities of women at home or in the workplace, reproducing the species or advancing the civilization. The dual possibilities for female agency were explored widely, although often at the expense of women themselves. The most damning complaint to be made against the linguistic phase is not that its theorists lacked sympathy for their subject, but that they fled the field of study without seriously addressing the problems. Yet this long moment in feminism (and anti-feminism) could also have been seen as inevitable at a time when the weight of history seemed to so many people to have given way to something unfamiliar. The recognition of the limitations of postmodernism would unburden its successors of the history-free illusion as well.

Marx and Freud, it may be noted once more, had divided over whether labor or sexuality provides the chief lever by which the instincts for survival come into play. They nevertheless both deemed production the prime sphere of *Homo sapiens,* the locus of civilization. Reproduction, in contrast, represented a sphere *outside* history, necessary to the perpetuation of the species but not the source of progress. Feminists and their psychoanalytic allies/opponents had over the course of a century established at least this much: without an understanding of the relationship between reproduction and production no social theory would go very far. Theorists have continued to come back to the conceptual problems again and again, as if to underline the conclusion that the solution does not lie in theory alone. Nonetheless, the history of such theories, described at length in these pages, suggests that ideas do count.

Notes
Acknowledgments
Index

Notes

Abbreviations

AJP   *American Journal of Psychoanalysis*
IJP   *International Journal of Psycho-Analysis*
JAAP   *Journal of the American Academy of Psychoanalysis*
JAH   *Journal of American History*
JAPA   *Journal of the American Psychoanalytic Association*
PQ   *Psychoanalytic Quarterly*
PR   *Psychoanalytic Review*
PSC   *Psychoanalytic Studies of the Child*
SE   *Standard Edition of the Complete Psychological Works of Sigmund Freud*, ed. and trans. James Strachey (London: Hogarth Press, 1953–1974).

Introduction

1. *Boston Evening Transcript,* Sept. 10, 1909, 4. Ernest Jones, *Sigmund Freud: Life and Work* (London: Hogarth Press, 1955), vol. 2, 63. Sigmund Freud, "Five Lectures on Psycho-Analysis" (1910), SE 11: 54. See also Nathan G. Hale Jr., *Freud and the Americans: The Beginnings of Psychoanalysis in the United States, 1876–1917* (New York: Oxford University Press, 1971).

2. Emma Goldman, "The Hypocrisy of Puritanism," in *Anarchism and Other Essays* (New York: Mother Earth Publishing Association, 1911), 178; and *Living My Life* (abridged), ed. Richard and Anna Maria Drinnon (New York: New American Library, 1977), 173, 455.

3. Edna Kenton, "Feminism Will Give. . . ." *Delineator,* 85 (July 1914), 17. Jenney Howe, "Feminism," *New Review,* 2 (Aug. 1914), 441. For the etiology of the term feminism, see Nancy F. Cott, *The Grounding of American Feminism* (New Haven: Yale University Press, 1987); Mari Jo Buhle, *Women and American Socialism, 1870–1920* (Urbana: University of Illinois Press,

1981); Leslie Fishbein, *Rebels in Bohemia: The Radicals of the "Masses," 1911–1917* (Philadelphia: Temple University Press, 1982).

4. Elizabeth Cady Stanton, "Solitude of Self," address before the U.S. Senate Committee on Woman Suffrage, Feb. 20, 1892, in Mari Jo Buhle and Paul Buhle, eds., *The Concise History of Woman Suffrage* (Urbana: University of Illinois Press, 1978), 325. George Burman Foster, "The Philosophy of Feminism," *The Forum*, 52 (July 1914), 16.

5. Warren I. Susman, " 'Personality' and the Making of Twentieth-Century Culture," in *Culture as History: The Transformation of American Society in the Twentieth Century* (New York: Pantheon, 1973), 271.

6. Margaret Homans noted this imbalance in her review of Jane Gallop's *The Daughter's Seduction*, "Daddy's Girl," *Yale Review*, 72 (Spring 1983), 445. Freud quoted in Ernest Jones, *Sigmund Freud: Life and Work* (London: Hogarth Press, 1953), vol. 1, 176. Thomas Laqueur, *Making Sex: Body and Gender from the Greeks to Freud* (Cambridge, Mass.: Harvard University Press, 1990), 195. See also Edith Kurzweil, *Freudians and Feminists* (Boulder: Westview, 1995); Charlotte Krause Prozan, *Feminist Psychoanalytic Psychotherapy* (Northvale, N.J.: Jason Aronson, 1992).

7. *Boston Evening Transcript*, Sept. 11, 1909, pt. 3, 3. *The Nation*, 89 (Sept. 23, 1909), 285.

8. Quoted by Jones, *Freud*, vol. 2, 67.

9. Boris Sidis quoted by Hendrick N. Ruitenbeek, *Freud and America* (New York: Macmillan, 1966), 35. Freud's five lectures appeared as "The Origins and Development of Psychoanalysis," trans. A. A. Brill, *American Journal of Psychology*, 21 (April 1910). Hale, *Freud and the Americans*, 397–398.

10. Mark Sullivan, *Our Times: The United States, 1900–1925* (New York: Scribner, 1932), vol. 4, 170–171. Max Eastman, "Exploring the Soul and Healing the Body," *Everybody's Magazine*, 32 (June 1915), 743; and *Enjoyment of Living* (New York: Harper, 1948), 491. Floyd Dell quoted by Frederick J. Hoffman, *Freudianism and the Literary Mind* (Baton Rouge: Louisiana State University Press, 1945), 58. Susan Glaspell, *Road to the Temple* (New York: Frederick A. Stokes, 1927), 250.

11. Eastman, "Exploring the Soul," 744. Mabel Dodge Luhan, *Movers and Shakers* (New York: Harcourt Brace, 1936), 440.

12. Edith Kurzweil, *The Freudians: A Comparative Perspective* (New Haven: Yale University Press, 1989), 25.

13. Sigmund Freud, " 'Civilized' Sexual Morality and Modern Nervous Illness" (1908), SE 9: 197. Floyd Dell, "How It Feels to Be Psychoanalyzed," quoted in Robert E. Humphrey, *The Children of Fantasy: The First Rebels of Greenwich Village* (New York: Wiley, 1978), 226. See also Floyd Dell, "Speaking of Psycho-Analysis: The New Boon for Dinner Table Conversa-

tionalists," *Vanity Fair*, 5 (Dec. 1915). F. H. Matthews, "The Americanization of Sigmund Freud: Adaptations of Psychoanalysis before 1917," *Journal of American Studies*, 1 (April 1967).

14. Nathan G. Hale Jr., "From Berggasse XIX to Central Park West: The Americanization of Psychoanalysis, 1919–1940," *Journal of the History of the Behavioral Sciences*, 14 (1978).

15. Stephen Farber and Marc Green, *Hollywood on the Couch* (New York: Morrow, 1993).

16. See, e.g., Russell Jacoby, *Social Amnesia: A Critique of Conformist Psychology from Adler to Laing* (Boston: Beacon, 1975); and *The Repression of Psychoanalysis: Otto Fenichel and the Political Freudians* (New York: Basic Books, 1983).

17. Joan Kelly, "Early Feminist Theory and the Querelle des Femmes, 1400–1789," in Kelly, *Women, History and Theory* (Chicago: University of Chicago Press, 1984).

18. Florence Guertin Tuttle, *The Awakening of Woman: Suggestions from the Psychic Side of Feminism* (New York: Abingdon, 1915), 16.

19. Karen Offen, "Defining Feminism: A Comparative Historical Approach," *Signs*, 14 (Autumn 1988). See also Deborah L. Rhode, ed., *Theoretical Perspectives on Sexual Difference* (New Haven: Yale University Press, 1990); Gisela Bok and Susan James, eds., *Beyond Equality and Difference: Citizenship, Feminist Politics and Female Subjectivity* (New York: Routledge, 1992).

20. Suzanne M. Marilley, "Frances Willard and the Feminism of Fear," *Feminist Studies*, 19 (Spring 1993).

21. Karl Marx and Friedrich Engels, *The German Ideology*, in Robert C. Tucker, ed., *The Marx-Engels Reader* (New York: Norton, 1972), 114, 119–120. Sigmund Freud, *Civilization and Its Discontents* (1930), SE 21: 117, 118; and "The Future of an Illusion" (1928), SE 21: 8.

22. Marx, "Critique of the Hegelian Dialectic and Philosophy as a Whole" and "Estranged Labour," in Tucker, ed., *Marx-Engels Reader*, 90, 61. G. W. F. Hegel, *The Phenomenology of Mind*, trans. J. B. Baillie (New York: Harper and Row, 1967), 238.

23. Sigmund Freud, *Three Essays on a Theory of Sexuality* (1905), SE 7: 238–239.

24. Herbert Marcuse, *Eros and Civilization: A Philosophical Inquiry into Freud* (Boston: Beacon, 1955), 17.

25. Freud, *Civilization and Its Discontents*, 103.

26. On this division see Eli Zaretsky, *Capitalism, the Family, and Personal Life*, rev. ed. (New York: Perennial Library, 1986).

27. Karl Marx and Friedrich Engels, *Manifesto of the Communist Party*, in Tucker, ed., *Marx-Engels Reader*, 349–350.

28. Freud, *Civilization and Its Discontents*, 103–104.

29. Alice Jardine, "Notes for an Analysis," in Teresa Brennan, ed., *Between Feminism and Psychoanalysis* (London: Routledge, 1989), 15.

30. Joan Wallach Scott, *Gender and the Politics of History* (New York: Columbia University Press, 1988), 42.

1. Feminism, Freudianism, and Female Subjectivity

1. Edwin B. Holt, *The Freudian Wish and Its Place in Ethics* (New York: Henry Holt, 1915), vi. Emma Goldman, *Anarchism and Other Essays* (New York: Mother Earth Publishing Association, 1911), 178. Floyd Dell, "Speaking of Psycho-Analysis: The New Boon for Dinner Table Conversationalists," *Vanity Fair*, 5 (Dec. 1915), 53.

2. Dr. William S. Sadler, *Worry and Nervousness* (Chicago: McClurg, 1914), 357.

3. Gertrude Atherton, "Mrs. Atherton Tells of Her 'Perch of the Devil,' " *Current Opinion*, 57 (Nov. 1914), 349. Kathy Peiss, *Cheap Amusements: Working Women and Leisure in Turn-of-the-Century New York* (Philadelphia: Temple University Press, 1986). James McGovern, "The American Woman's Pre–World War I Freedom in Manners and Morals," *JAH*, 55 (Sept. 1968).

4. Michel Foucault, *The History of Sexuality*, trans. Robert Hurley (New York: Pantheon, 1978), vol. 1, 17.

5. G. Legman, *No Laughing Matter: An Analysis of Sexual Humor* (Bloomington: Indiana University Press, 1968), vol. 1, 432. Carl N. Degler, "What Ought to Be and What Was: Women's Sexuality in the Nineteenth Century," *American Historical Review*, 79 (Dec. 1974). See John D'Emilio and Estelle B. Freedman, *Intimate Matters: A History of Sexuality in America* (New York: Harper and Row, 1988).

6. The poems were rpt. in Genevieve Taggard, ed., *May Days: An Anthology of Verse from Masses-Liberator* (New York: Boni and Liveright, 1925), 87, 170. On this phase of feminism in New York, see Judith Schwarz, *Radical Feminists of Heterodoxy: Greenwich Village, 1912–1940* (Lebanon, N.H.: New Victoria, 1986). June Sochen, *The New Woman: Feminism in Greenwich Village* (New York: Quadrangle, 1972), focuses on women rebels. Robert E. Humphrey, *The Children of Fantasy: The First Rebels of Greenwich Village* (New York: Wiley, 1978), examines the outlook of six prominent men. Leslie Fishbein, "Freud and the Radicals: The Sexual Revolution Comes

to Greenwich Village," *Canadian Review of American Studies,* 12 (Fall 1981), draws the connection between lifestyle and Freud.

7. Margaret Sanger, *My Fight for Birth Control* (New York: Farrar and Rinehart, 1931), 50. See *The Story of a Lover* (New York: Boni and Liveright, 1919), published anonymously by Hutchins Hapgood; Ellen Kay Trimberger, ed., *Intimate Warriors: Portraits of a Modern Marriage, 1899–1944* (New York: Feminist Press, 1991); Candace Falk, *Love, Anarchy, and Emma Goldman* (New York: Holt, Rinehart, and Winston, 1984).

8. Agnes Repplier, "The Repeal of Reticence," *Atlantic Monthly,* 113 (Feb. 1914). Elsie Clews Parsons, "Varia," PR, 2 (Oct. 1915), 477. Mabel Dodge Luhan, *Movers and Shakers* (New York: Harcourt Brace, 1936), 69–71; Emma Goldman, *Living My Life* (abridged), ed. Richard and Anna Maria Drinnon (New York: New American Library, 1977), 173. See Ellen Herman, "The Competition: Psychoanalysis, Its Feminist Interpreters and the Idea of Sexual Freedom, 1910–1930," *Free Associations,* 3 (1992).

9. Sigmund Freud and Josef Breuer, *Studies on Hysteria* (1895), SE 3: 246.

10. George Burman Foster, "The Philosophy of Feminism," *The Forum,* 52 (July 1914), 21.

11. The designation comes from Paul Robinson, "Havelock Ellis and Modern Sexual Theory," *Salmagundi,* 21 (Winter 1973), 28. Benjamin Brody, "Freud's Case Load," *Psychotherapy: Theory, Research and Practice,* 7 (Spring 1970), 11. On Freud's reluctance to make the differences between men and women a central component of his theory of sexuality, see Lisa Appignanesi and John Forrester, *Freud's Women* (New York: Basic Books, 1992).

12. Sigmund Freud, "Fragment of an Analysis of a Case of Hysteria" (1905), SE 7.

13. Sigmund Freud, " 'Civilized' Sexual Morality and Modern Nervous Illnesses" (1908), SE 9.

14. Sigmund Freud, *Three Essays on the Theory of Sexuality* (1905), SE 7: 207, 219, 220.

15. Letter to Wilhelm Fliess, July 24, 1904, in *The Complete Letters of Sigmund Freud to Wilhelm Fliess, 1887–1904,* ed. and trans. Jeffrey Moussaieff Masson (Cambridge, Mass.: Harvard University Press, 1985), 467.

16. Sigmund Freud, "The Sexual Theories of Children" (1908), SE 9: 211–212, 215, 218.

17. Putnam quoted by Brill in his intro. to *The Basic Writings of Sigmund Freud,* ed. and trans. A. A. Brill (New York: Modern Library, 1938), 15.

18. Foucault, *History of Sexuality,* 64. See Cynthia Eagle Russett, *Sexual Science: The Victorian Construction of Womanhood* (Cambridge, Mass.: Harvard University Press, 1989).

19. Edward Carpenter, *Love's Coming of Age: A Series of Papers on the Relations of the Sexes* (New York: Mitchell Kennerley, 1911), 26. Havelock Ellis, *The New Spirit* (New York: Boni and Liveright, 1921 [1892]), 129, 279.

20. Floyd Dell, *Homecoming: An Autobiography* (New York: Farrar and Rinehart), 288–289. Margaret Sanger, *What Every Boy and Girl Should Know* (New York: Brentano's, 1928), 59.

21. Havelock Ellis, *Studies in the Psychology of Sex* (New York: Random House, 1942 [1905]), vol. 1, pt. 2, 189, 249, 256. On Ellis's relations with Freud see Nathan G. Hale Jr., *Freud and the Americans: The Beginnings of Psychoanalysis in the United States, 1876–1917* (New York: Oxford University Press, 1971), 259–267; Vincent Brome, *Havelock Ellis: Philosopher of Sex* (London: Routledge and Kegan Paul, 1979).

22. Carpenter, *Love's Coming of Age,* 68, 77.

23. Ellis, *Studies in the Psychology of Sex,* vol. 1, pt. 2, 253.

24. Freud, *Three Essays,* 207.

25. Katharine S. Anthony, *Feminism in Germany and Scandinavia* (New York: Henry Holt, 1915), 6.

26. Ellen Key, *Love and Marriage* (New York: Putnam, 1911), 71, 99, 172. Anthony, *Feminism in Germany and Scandinavia,* 94.

27. Cheri Register, "Motherhood at Center: Ellen Key's Social Vision," *Women's Studies International Forum,* 5 (1982); Kay Goodman, "Motherhood and Work: The Concept of the Misuse of Women's Energy, 1895–1905," in Ruth-Ellen Joeres and Mary Jo Maynes, eds., *German Women in the Eighteenth and Nineteenth Centuries: A Social and Literary History* (Bloomington: Indiana University Press, 1986). See Barbara Taylor Allen, *Feminism and Motherhood in Germany, 1800–1914* (New Brunswick: Rutgers University Press, 1991).

28. Norman Hapgood, "What Women Are After," *Harper's,* 58 (Aug. 16, 1913). Anthony, *Feminism in Germany and Scandinavia,* v. Floyd Dell, *Women as World Builders: Studies in Modern Feminism* (Chicago: Forbes, 1913), 81, 83. H. L. Mencken, "The Flapper," *Smart Set,* 45 (1915), 1–2. Fannie Hurst, *Star-Dust* (New York: Harper, 1921).

29. William J. Robinson, *Woman: Her Sex and Love Life* (New York: Eugenics Publishing, 1925 [1917]), 28.

30. Sanger, *My Fight for Birth Control,* 57; and *Woman and the New Race* (New York: Brentano's, 1920), 98–99.

31. Foster, "Philosophy of Feminism," 22.

32. Walter Lippmann, "The Woman's Movement," *The Forum,* 52 (Aug. 1914), 156–157; "Freud and the Layman," *New Republic,* 2, supp. 9–10 (April 17, 1915), 9–10. W. L. George, "Feminist Intentions," *Atlantic*

Monthly, 112 (Dec. 1913), 730. Emma Goldman, "The Tragedy of Woman's Emancipation," in *Anarchism and Other Essays*, 223, 225. Anthony, *Feminism in Germany and Scandinavia*, 213.

33. Carpenter, *Love's Coming of Age*, 60. Sanger, *Woman and the New Race*, 99. Goldman, "The Tragedy of Woman's Emancipation," 225. Floyd Dell, *Intellectual Vagabondage: An Apology for the Intelligentsia* (New York: George H. Doran, 1926), 165. See also Henry F. May, *The End of American Innocence* (New York: Knopf, 1959).

34. Eliza Burt Gamble, *The Evolution of Woman: An Inquiry into the Dogma of Her Inferiority to Man* (New York: Putnam, 1894), 61.

35. Louis C. Fraina, "Socialism and Psychology," *New Review*, 3 (May 1915), 10–12; Marie Jenney Howe, "Feminism," *New Review*, 2 (Aug. 1914), 441. Louis C. Fraina, "Lydia Kyasht—Spirit of Beauty," *Modern Dance*, 2 (Aug.–Sept. 1917), 12–13.

36. Quoted by Larry Ceplair, *Charlotte Perkins Gilman: A Nonfiction Reader* (New York: Columbia University Press, 1991), 2.

37. Ellen Key, *The Woman Movement* (New York: Putnam, 1912), 176. See also Ellen Key, "Motherliness," *Atlantic Monthly*, 110 (Oct. 1912).

38. Charlotte Perkins Gilman, "On Ellen Key and the Woman Movement," *Forerunner*, 4 (Feb. 1913), 35; "The New Mothers of a New World," ibid. (June 1913), 149; "Education for Motherhood," ibid. (Oct. 1913), 262.

39. Gilman, "Ellen Key and the Woman Movement," 36.

40. Charlotte Perkins Gilman, *Human Work* (New York: McClure, Phillips, 1904), 368.

41. Gilman, "Ellen Key and the Woman Movement," 35.

42. Rheta Childe Dorr, *A Woman of Fifty* (New York: Funk and Wagnalls, 1924), 224. In *Current Opinion*: "Ellen Key's Attack on 'Amaternal' Feminism," 54 (Feb. 1913), 138–140; "A New Conception of Maternity," 54 (March 1913), 220–221; "The Conflict between 'Human' and 'Female' Feminism," 56 (April 1914), 291–292. Gilman, "Ellen Key and the Woman Movement," 36.

43. See Nancy F. Cott, *The Grounding of Modern Feminism* (New Haven: Yale University Press, 1987), on the debate between Gilman and Key.

44. G. Stanley Hall, "The Question of Co-Education," *Munsey's*, 34 (Feb. 1906), 588; and "Flapper Americana Novissima," *Atlantic Monthly*, 129 (June 1922), 780. Phyllis Blanchard, *The Adolescent Girl: A Study from the Psychoanalytic Viewpoint* (New York: Moffat, Yard, 1920), 105. Charlotte Perkins Gilman, "The New Generation of Women," *Current History*, 18 (Aug. 1923), 736.

45. Brill quoted by Bruce Barton, "You Can't Fool Your Other Self," *American Magazine*, 92 (Sept. 1921), 13.

2. Dissent in Freud's Ranks

1. Sigmund Freud to Martha Bernays, 15 Nov. 1883, in *The Letters of Sigmund Freud, 1873–1939,* ed. Ernst L. Freud, trans. Tania and James Stern (London: Hogarth Press, 1970), 90–91.

2. *Minutes of the Vienna Psychoanalytic Society,* ed. Herman Nunberg and Ernst Federn, trans. M. Nunberg, (New York: International Universities Press, 1962–1976), vol. 1, 35.

3. Sigmund Freud, "On the History of the Psycho-Analytic Movement" (1914), SE 14.

4. See Lisa Appignanesi and John Forrester, *Freud's Women* (New York: Basic Books, 1992); Constance M. McGovern, "Psychiatry, Psychoanalysis, and Women in America," PR, 71 (Dec. 1984).

5. Nellie L. Thompson, "Early Women Psychoanalysts," *International Review of Psychoanalysis,* 14 (1987), estimates that women represented about 20 percent of the membership of all psychoanalytic organizations by 1930. George MacLean and Ulrich Rappen, *Hermine Hug-Hellmuth: Her Life and Work* (London: Routledge, 1991).

6. Robert Fliess, ed., *The Psycho-Analytic Reader: An Anthology of Essential Papers with Critical Introductions* (New York: International Universities Press, 1969), 159.

7. Dorothy Dunbar Bromley, "Feminist—New Style," *Harper's,* 155 (Oct. 1927), 522, 556. Ernest Jones, "Early Female Sexuality," IJP, 16 (July 1935), 273. Ray Strachey, ed., *Our Freedom and Its Results* (1936), 9–10.

8. Harriet Anderson, *Utopian Feminism: Women's Movement in Fin-de-siècle Vienna* (New Haven: Yale University Press, 1991), 10–11.

9. Berthe Pappenheim quoted in Appignanesi and Forrester, *Freud's Women,* 79. See also Lucy Freeman, *The Story of Anna O* (New York: Walker, 1972); M. A. Kaplan, "Anna O and Berthe Pappenheim: An Historical Perspective," in M. Rosenblum and M. Muroff, eds., *One Hundred Years of Psychoanalysis* (New York: Collier Macmillan, 1984); Mikkel Borch-Jacobsen, *Remembering Anna O.: A Century of Mystification,* trans. Kirby Olson (New York: Routledge, 1996).

10. On Eckstein, see Jeffrey Moussaieff Masson, *The Assault on Truth: Freud's Suppression of the Seduction Theory* (New York: Viking Penguin, 1985); and Appignanesi and Forrester, *Freud's Women.*

11. Grete Meisel-Hess, *The Sexual Crisis: A Critique of Our Sex Life,* trans. Eden and Cedar Paul (New York: Critic and Guide Co., 1917), 212, 316, 322. See also Harriet Anderson, "Psychoanalysis and Feminism: An Ambivalent Alliance. Viennese Feminist Responses to Freud, 1900–1930," in Ed-

ward Timms and Ritchie Robertson, eds., *Psychoanalysis in Context* (Edinburgh: Edinburgh University Press, 1992).

12. Freud quoted by John Boyer, "Freud, Marriage, and Late Viennese Liberalism: A Commentary from 1905," *Journal of Modern History*, 50 (March 1978), 92.

13. See Biddy Martin, *Woman and Modernity: The (Life)Style of Lou Andreas-Salomé* (Ithaca: Cornell University Press, 1991); Appignanesi and Forrester, *Freud's Women*.

15. Lou Andreas-Salomé, "The Feminine Type," abstracted from *Zeitschrift fur Anwendung der Psychoanalyse auf die Geisteswissenschaften*, 3, no. 1, by Louise Brink, PR, 6 (April 1919).

15. Lou Andreas-Salomé, *The Freud Journal*, trans. Stanley A. Leavy, intro. Mary-Kay Wilmers (London: Quartet, 1987), 118. Sigmund Freud, "On Narcissism: An Introduction" (1914), SE 14: 88–89.

16. Freud to Andreas-Salomé, letter, Nov. 22, 1917, in *Sigmund Freud and Lou Andreas-Salomé: Letters*, ed. Ernst Pfeiffer, trans. William and Elaine Robson-Scott (London: Hogarth Press and Institute of Psycho-Analysis, 1972), 67.

17. Freud, "On Narcissism," 94, 80–81, 88–89.

18. Letter to Fliess, Nov. 14, 1897, in *The Complete Letters of Sigmund Freud to Wilhelm Fliess, 1887–1904*, trans. and ed. Jeffrey Moussaieff Masson (Cambridge, Mass.: Harvard University Press, 1985), 280. Sigmund Freud, *Three Essays on a Theory of Sexuality* (1905), SE 7: 220, 221.

19. Sigmund Freud, "On Transformations of Instinct as Exemplified in Anal Erotism" (1917), SE 17; "The Taboo of Virginity" (1918), SE 11: 205; "A Child Is Being Beaten: A Contribution to the Study of Sexual Perversions" (1919), SE 17.

20. Paul Roazen, *Freud and His Followers* (New York: Knopf, 1975). Martin Grotjahn, in Franz Alexander, Samuel Eisenstein, and Martin Grotjahn, eds., *Psychoanalytic Pioneers* (New York: Basic Books, 1966).

21. Karl Abraham, "Manifestations of the Female Castration Complex," IJP, 3 (March 1922), 2.

22. Ibid., 9, 13–15, 19–22.

23. J. H. W. Van Ophuijsen, "Contributions to the Masculinity Complex in Women," IJP, 5 (Jan. 1924), 41, 48. Hermine Hug-Hellmuth, "Psychoanalytic Findings about Women" (1921), in MacLean and Rappen, eds., *Hermine Hug-Hellmuth*, 250–251.

24. Sigmund Freud, "The Psychogenesis of a Case of Female Homosexuality" (1920), SE 18: 169.

25. Sigmund Freud, "Female Sexuality" (1932), SE 21: 241.

26. Karen Horney, "The Flight from Womanhood: The Masculinity Complex in Women as Viewed by Men and by Women," IJP, 7 (July–Oct. 1926). See also Susan Quinn, *A Mind of Her Own: The Life of Karen Horney* (New York: Summit, 1987); Bernard J. Paris, *Karen Horney: A Psychoanalyst's Search for Self-Understanding* (New Haven: Yale University Press, 1994); Appignanesi and Forrester, *Freud's Women*.

27. Entry, Reinbeck, 27 Aug. 1904, *The Adolescent Diaries of Karen Horney* (New York: Basic Books, 1980), 90–93.

28. Janet Sayers, *Mothers of Psychoanalysis: Helene Deutsch, Karen Horney, Anna Freud, and Melanie Klein* (New York: Norton, 1991). Marianne Horney Eckardt, "Karen Horney's Feminine Psychology and the Passions of Her Time," in Milton M. Berger, ed., *Women Beyond Freud: New Concepts of Feminine Psychology* (New York: Brunner/Mazel, 1994).

29. Karen Horney, "On the Genesis of the Castration Complex in Women," IJP, 6 (Jan. 1924), 50.

30. See Nancy J. Chodorow, "Freud on Women," in Jerome Neu, ed., *The Cambridge Companion to Freud* (New York: Cambridge University Press, 1991).

31. Sigmund Freud, *The Interpretation of Dreams* (1900), SE 4: 257. See also Masson, *Assault on Truth*.

32. Sigmund Freud, *The Ego and the Id* (1923), SE 19; and "The Dissolution of the Oedipus Complex," (1924), SE 19: 178–179.

33. Sigmund Freud, "Infantile Genital Organization" (1923), SE 19: 142; and "Dissolution of the Oedipus Complex," 178.

34. Sigmund Freud, "Some Psychical Consequences of the Anatomical Distinction between the Sexes" (1925), SE 19: 252–256, 258.

35. See Zenia Odes Fliegel, "Feminine Psychosexual Development in Freudian Theory," PQ, 42 (1973).

36. Josine Müller, "A Contribution to the Problem of Libidinal Development of the Genital Phase in Girls," IJP, 13 (July 1932), 362–368. Horney, "Genesis of the Castration Complex," 65.

37. Horney, "Flight from Womanhood," 328, 329, 330, 331, 338. See Ruth Moulton, "Early Papers on Women: Horney to Thompson," AJP, 35 (1975).

38. Jones, "Early Female Sexuality," 264; Ernest Jones, "The Early Development of Female Sexuality," IJP, 8 (Oct. 1927), 459. Melanie Klein, "Early Stages of the Oedipus Conflict," IJP, 9 (April 1928). Helene Deutsch, "The Psychology of Women in Relation to the Functions of Reproduction," IJP, 6 (Oct. 1925), 405.

39. Marjorie Brierley, "Some Problems of Integration in Women," IJP, 13 (Oct. 1932), 438; Ernest Jones, "The Phallic Phase," IJP, 14 (Jan. 1933), 1.

40. Letters, Abraham to Freud, Dec. 3, 1924; Freud to Abraham, Dec. 8 and 29, 1924, in *A Psycho-Analytic Dialogue: The Letters of Sigmund Freud and Karl Abraham, 1907–1926*, ed. Hilda C. Abraham and Ernst L. Freud, trans. Bernard Marsh and Hilda Abraham (New York: Basic Books, 1965), 375–379.

41. Freud, "Female Sexuality," 225, 228, 230, 243.

42. Sigmund Freud, "Femininity," in *New Introductory Lectures on Psycho-Analysis* (1933), SE 22: 116–117, 119, 125, 132, 135.

43. Sigmund Freud, "Analysis Terminable and Interminable" (1937), SE 23.

44. Helene Deutsch, *Psychoanalysis and the Sexual Functions of Women*, ed. Paul Roazen, trans. Eric Mosbacher (London and New York: Karnac, 1991), 81.

45. Helene Deutsch, "The Psychology of Women in Relation to the Functions of Reproduction," IJP, 6 (Oct. 1925), 417.

46. Letter, Freud to Dr. Carl Müller-Braunschweig, July 21, 1935, published as "Freud and Female Sexuality: A Previously Unpublished Letter," *Psychiatry*, 34 (Aug. 1971), 329.

47. Freud, "Female Sexuality," 240.

48. Freud, "Femininity," 116.

49. Freud, "Analysis Terminable and Interminable," 252.

50. Horney, "Flight from Womanhood," 337; see also Karen Horney, "Denial of the Vagina: Contribution to the Problem of Genital Anxieties Specific to Women," IJP, 14 (Jan. 1933).

51. Karen Horney, "The Dread of Woman: Observations on the Specific Difference in the Dread Felt by Men and by Women Respectively for the Opposite Sex," IJP, 13 (July 1932).

52. Karen Horney, "Book Review," IJP, 7 (Jan. 1926), 99.

3. Culture and Feminine Personality

1. Dee Garrison, "Karen Horney and Feminism," *Signs*, 6 (Summer 1981).

2. Karen Horney, "Woman's Fear of Action" (1935), rpt. in Bernard J. Paris, *Karen Horney: A Psychoanalyst's Search for Self-Understanding* (New Haven: Yale University Press, 1994), 237.

3. Mead quoted in Jack L. Rubins, *Karen Horney: Gentle Rebel of Psychoanalysis* (New York: Dial, 1978), 167–168. Karen Horney, *New Ways in Psychoanalysis* (New York: Norton, 1939), 12. See also Marcia Westkott, *The Feminist Legacy of Karen Horney* (New Haven: Yale University Press, 1986).

4. Maria Jahoda, "The Migration of Psychoanalysis: Its Impact on American Psychology," in Donald Fleming and Bernard Bailyn, eds., *The Intellectual Migration: Europe and America, 1930–1960* (Cambridge, Mass.: Harvard University Press, 1969), 428. See also Nathan G. Hale Jr., *The Rise and Crisis of Psychoanalysis in the United States: Freud and the Americans, 1917–1985* (New York: Oxford University Press, 1995).

5. John C. Burnham, "The Influence of Psychoanalysis on American Culture," in Burnham, *Paths into American Culture: Psychology, Medicine and Morals* (Philadelphia: Temple University Press, 1988), 98. *New York Times* quoted in Frederick J. Hoffman, *Freudianism and the Literary Mind* (Baton Rouge: Louisiana State University Press, 1967 [1945]), 68.

6. Franz Alexander, *Our Age of Unreason: A Study of the Irrational Forces in Social Life,* rev. ed. (Philadelphia: Lippincott, 1952 [1942]), 190.

7. Clara Thompson, with Patrick Mullahy, *Psychoanalysis: Evolution and Development* (New York: Grove, 1950). On the larger movement away from biology and toward culture as prime determinants of human nature, see Carl N. Degler, *In Search of Human Nature: The Decline and Revival of Darwinism in American Social Thought* (New York: Oxford University Press, 1991).

8. Karen Horney, "Tenth Anniversary," AJP, 11 (1951), 3. See Martin Birnbach, *Neo-Freudian Social Philosophy* (Stanford: Stanford University Press, 1961).

9. André Siegfried, *America Comes of Age: A French Analysis,* trans. H. H. Hemming and Doris Hemming (New York: Harcourt, Brace, 1927), 347.

10. Floyd Dell, *Love in the Machine Age: A Psychological Study of the Transition from Patriarchal Society* (New York: Farrar and Rinehart, 1930), 138, 139. Foreword [to *Adventures in Womanhood*], Ruth Fulton Benedict Papers, Vassar College Library, quoted in Margaret M. Caffrey, *Ruth Benedict: Stranger in This Land* (Austin: University of Texas Press, 1989), 91. See Christina Simmons, "Modern Sexuality and the Myth of Victorian Repression," in Kathy Peiss and Christina Simmons, eds., *Passion and Power: Sexuality in History* (Philadelphia: Temple University Press, 1989).

11. Quoted by John D'Emilio and Estelle B. Freedman, *Intimate Matters: A History of Sexuality in America* (New York: Harper and Row, 1988), 240.

12. Lillian Wald, *Windows on Henry Street* (Boston: Little, Brown, 1934), 322. Jane Addams, *Second Twenty Years at Hull House* (New York: Macmillan, 1930), 192–193. Charlotte Perkins Gilman, "Toward Monogamy," in Freda Kirchwey, ed., *Our Changing Morality* (New York: Albert and Charles Boni, 1930), 58, 59.

13. Phyllis Blanchard and Carolyn Manasses, *New Girls for Old* (New York: Macaulay, 1930), 240. See also Blanchard, *The Adolescent Girl: A Study from the Psychoanalytic Viewpoint* (New York: Moffat, Yard, 1920).

14. Beatrice Forbes-Robertson Hale, "Women in Transition," in Calverton and Schmalhausen, eds., *Sex in Civilization*, 69, 67. See also Elaine Showalter, ed., *These Modern Women: Autobiographical Essays from the Twenties* (Old Westbury, N.Y.: Feminist Press, 1978).

15. Samuel D. Schmalhausen and V. F. Calverton, "Preface," in *Sex in Civilization*, 11; Schmalhausen, "The Sexual Revolution," ibid., 360; Calverton, "Sex and Social Struggle," ibid., 280; A. A. Roback, "Sex in Dynamic Psychology," ibid., 146. Dell, *Love in the Machine Age*, 406.

16. André Tridon, *Psychoanalysis and Love* (Garden City, N.Y.: Garden City Publishing, 1922), vi, 275, 281. Dell, *Love in the Machine Age*, 6. On Tridon see Hale, *Rise and Crisis of Psychoanalysis*.

17. Schmalhausen, "Sexual Revolution," 402. Leonard Wilcox, *V. F. Calverton: Radical in the American Grain* (Philadelphia: Temple University Press, 1992).

18. Leonard Wilcox, "Sex Boys in a Balloon: V. F. Calverton and the Abortive Sexual Revolution," *Journal of American Studies*, 23 (April 1989).

19. Samuel D. Schmalhausen, *The New Road to Progress* (New York: Falcom, 1934), 212, 248–249, 251, 255. Calverton and Schmalhausen, "Preface," 9. Calverton, "Sex and Social Struggle," 283.

20. Abraham Myerson, "Freud's Theory of Sex: A Criticism," in Calverton and Schmalhausen, eds., *Sex in Civilization*, 519.

21. Schmalhausen, "Sexual Revolution," 399, 401, 406. V. F. Calverton, *The Bankruptcy of Marriage* (New York: Macaulay, 1928), 13.

22. Robert Briffault, "The Evolution of Woman," in V. F. Calverton and Samuel D. Schmalhausen, eds., *Woman's Coming of Age: A Symposium* (New York: Liveright, 1931), 16.

23. Mathilde and Mathias Vaerting, *The Dominant Sex: A Study in the Sociology of Sex Differentiation*, trans. Eden and Cedar Paul (New York: Doran, 1923), 224–225; for a popular review, see Miriam Allen deFord, "The Feminist Future," *New Republic*, 56 (Sept. 19, 1928). Roback, "Sex in Dynamic Psychology," 154; Schmalhausen, "Sexual Revolution," 361; Alice Beal Parsons, "Man-Made Illusions about Women," in Calverton and Schmalhausen, eds., *Woman's Coming of Age*. Alexander Goldenweiser, "Woman and Culture or the Seven Tasks of Woman," *Modern Monthly*, 5 (Nov. 1928), 99.

24. *New York Times*, May 28, 1929, 17.

25. Calverton, "Sex and Social Struggle," 282.

26. Edward Sapir, *Culture, Language and Personality*, ed. David G. Mandelbaum (Berkeley: University of California Press, 1960 [1949]), 185. See *Edward Sapir: Appraisals of His Life and Work*, ed. Konrad Koerner (Amsterdam: John Benjamins, 1984).

27. *Worcester Daily Telegram* (Worcester, Mass.), Sept. 8, 1909, 6.

28. Franz Boas, "The Aims of Ethnology" (1888), in *Race, Language and Culture* (New York: Macmillan, 1940), 636. Boas, *Anthropology and Modern Life* (New York: Norton, 1928), 11.

29. Alexander Goldenweiser, *History, Psychology, and Culture* (London: Kegan Paul, Trench, Trubner, 1932), 71, 59. For an overview, see Marvin Harris, *The Rise of Anthropological Theory: A History of Theories of Culture* (New York: Thomas Y. Crowell, 1968). Clyde Kluckhohn, "The Influence of Psychiatry on Anthropology in America during the Past One Hundred Years," in J. K. Hall, G. Zilboorg, and H. A. Bunker, eds., *One Hundred Years of American Psychiatry* (New York: Columbia University Press, 1944).

30. Sigmund Freud, *Totem and Taboo* (1912–1913), SE 13: 1. See also Robert A. Paul, "Freud's Anthropology: A Reading of the 'Cultural Books,' " in Jerome Neu, ed., *The Cambridge Companion to Freud* (Cambridge: Cambridge University Press, 1991).

31. Franz Boas, "The Methods of Ethnology" (1920), in *Race, Language and Culture*, 288–289. See Edward Sapir, "Cultural Anthropology and Psychiatry" (1932), in *Culture, Language and Personality;* A. L. Kroeber, "*Totem and Taboo:* An Ethnologic Psychoanalysis," *American Anthropologist,* 22 (1920).

32. Bronislaw Malinowski, *Sex and Repression in Savage Society* (London: Routledge and Kegan Paul, 1953), 31.

33. Edward Sapir, "The Discipline of Sex," *American Mercury,* 16 (1929), 413. Havelock Ellis, "Introduction," in Calverton and Schmalhausen, eds., *Sex in Civilization,* 20, 25.

34. Thomas Haweis quoted by Christopher Herbert, *Culture and Anomie: Ethnographic Imagination in the Nineteenth Century* (Chicago: University of Chicago Press, 1991), 179. Bronislaw Malinowski, *A Diary in the Strict Sense of the Term,* trans. Norbert Guterman (New York: Harcourt, Brace and World, 1967), 255. Ellis, "Introduction," 20.

35. Dell, *Love in the Machine Age,* 298. Blanchard quoted in *New York Times,* June 9, 1929, 7.

36. Malinowski, *Sex and Repression,* 2; Malinowski, "Psychoanalysis and Anthropology," *Psyche,* 4 (April, 1924), 294, 295, 331.

37. Ernest Jones, "Mother-Right and the Sexual Ignorance of Savages," IJP, 6 (April 1925), 109–111, 130. See also Anne Parsons, "Is the Oedipus Complex Universal? The Jones-Malinowski Debate Revisited" in Parsons, *Belief, Magic, and Anomie: Essays in Psychosocial Anthropology* (New York: Free Press, 1969); Rosalind Coward, *Patriarchal Precedents: Sexuality and Social Relations* (London: Routledge and Kegan Paul, 1983).

38. Marie Bonaparte, "Some Psychoanalytic and Anthropological Insights Applied to Sociology," trans. Vera Dammann, in Hendrik M. Ruitenbeek, ed., *Psychoanalysis and the Social Sciences* (New York: Dutton, 1965). Geza Roheim, *Psychoanalysis and Anthropology: Culture, Personality and the Unconscious* (New York: International Universities Press, 1950). Melford E. Spiro, *Oedipus in the Trobriands* (Chicago: University of Chicago Press, 1982).

39. Sigmund Freud, *Civilization and Its Discontents* (1930), SE 21: 87, 89, 131. On Freud's avoidance of theories of matriarchy, see Ann Douglas, *Terrible Honesty: Mongrel Manhattan in the 1920s* (New York: Farrar, Straus and Giroux, 1995).

40. Freud, *Civilization and Its Discontents*, 86.

41. Jane Howard, *Margaret Mead: A Life* (New York: Simon and Schuster, 1984), 248. Mead, *Blackberry Winter: My Earliest Years* (New York: Simon and Schuster, 1972).

42. Mead tested some of Freud's hypotheses and reported the primacy of cultural variables in "An Ethnologist's Footnote to 'Totem and Taboo,' " PR, 17 (July 1930).

43. Mead, *Blackberry Winter*, 196.

44. Margaret Mead, *Sex and Temperament in Three Primitive Societies* (New York: New American Library, 1950 [1935]), 190–191.

45. Sigmund Freud, "Some Psychical Consequences of the Anatomical Distinctions between the Sexes" (1925), SE 19: 257–258. Ruth Benedict, *Patterns of Culture* (Boston: Houghton Mifflin, 1934), 237.

46. Mead, *Blackberry Winter*, 221. Mead, *Sex and Temperament*, "Preface to the 1950 Edition."

47. George D. Stocking Jr., "Essays on Culture and Personality," in Stocking, ed., *Malinowski, Rivers, Benedict and Others: Essays on Culture and Personality* (Madison: University of Wisconsin Press, 1986), 8.

48. Margaret Mead, *Coming of Age in Samoa* (New York: William Morrow, 1928), 233. Mead, *Sex and Temperament*, 199, 208, 211.

49. Benedict, *Patterns of Culture*, 278. See also Ruth Benedict, "Anthropology and the Abnormal," *Journal of General Psychology*, 10 (1934).

50. Karen Horney, *New Ways in Psychoanalysis* (New York: Norton, 1939), 12–13.

51. Marianne Eckardt, "Feminine Psychology Revisited: A Historical Perspective," AJP, 51 (1991), 242. Karen Horney, *Feminine Psychology* (New York: Norton, 1967), 182–183.

52. Helene Deutsch, "The Significance of Masochism in the Mental Life of Women" (1930), in Robert Fliess, ed., *The Psycho-Analytic Reader* (New

York: International Universities Press, 1948), 200. Horney, *Feminine Psychology*, 231.

53. Horney, *Feminine Psychology*, 231.

54. Laura Fermi, *Illustrious Immigrants: The Intellectual Migration from Europe, 1930–41* (Chicago: University of Chicago Press, 1968), 144. Helen Swick Perry, "Introduction" in Harry Stack Sullivan, *The Fusion of Psychiatry and Social Science* (New York: Norton, 1964), xviii. Mead quoted in Howard, *Margaret Mead*, 176.

55. Rubins, *Karen Horney*, 193, 236–237.

56. Thompson, *Psychoanalysis*, 211. On cultural conditioning in childhood, see Ruth Benedict, "Continuities and Discontinuities in Cultural Conditioning," *Psychiatry*, 1 (May 1938). On Sullivan see A. H. Chapman and Miriam C. M. S. Chapman, *Harry Stack Sullivan's Concepts of Personality Development and Psychiatric Illness* (New York: Brunner/Mazel, 1980); Philip Cushman, *Constructing the Self, Constructing America: A Cultural History of Psychotherapy* (Reading, Mass.: Addison-Wesley, 1995).

57. Gordon W. Allport, in Hadley Cantril, ed., *Tensions That Cause Wars* (Urbana: University of Illinois Press, 1950), 135.

58. Horney, *New Ways in Psychoanalysis*, 8–11, 87, 119.

59. Karen Horney, "Culture and Neurosis," *American Sociological Review*, 1 (1936), 227.

60. Horney, *New Ways in Psychoanalysis*, 118.

61. Ibid., 119.

62. Horney, "Woman's Fear of Action," 233, 238.

63. Hale, *Rise and Crisis of Psychoanalysis*.

64. Susan Quinn, *A Mind of Her Own: The Life of Karen Horney* (New York: Summit, 1987).

65. Franz Alexander, "Psychoanalysis Revisited" (1940), in Alexander, *The Scope of Psychoanalysis, 1921–1961* (New York: Basic Books, 1961), 145, 155.

66. Horney, *Feminine Psychology*, 116.

67. Erich Fromm, Foreword to Clara M. Thompson, *On Women*, ed. Maurice R. Green (New York: Mentor, 1971), xiv. See also Ruth Moulton, "Early Papers on Women: Horney to Thompson," *AJP*, 35 (1975); Moulton, "The Role of Clara Thompson in the Psychoanalytic Study of Women," in Jean Strouse, ed., *Women and Analysis: Dialogues on Psychoanalytic Views of Femininity* (Boston: G. K. Hall, 1985).

68. Thompson, *Psychoanalysis*, 38–39. Thompson, *On Women*, 74, 77, 73.

69. Ibid., 111–112.

70. Dorothy D. Bromley and Florence H. Britten, *Youth and Sex* (New York: Harper and Row, 1938), 8.

71. Gretta Palmer, "A Truce with Men," *Saturday Evening Post*, 209 (June 5, 1937), 37.

72. Thompson, *On Women*, 121.

73. Mead, *Sex and Temperament*, 219.

74. Harold E. Stearns, *America: A Re-appraisal* (New York: Hillman-Curl, 1937), 17–18.

75. Thompson, *Psychoanalysis*, 17. See also Edward A. Purcell Jr., *The Crisis of Democratic Theory: Scientific Naturalism and the Problem of Value* (Lexington: University of Kentucky Press, 1973).

76. Rubins, *Karen Horney*, 240. Quinn, *A Mind of Her Own*, 331.

4. Momism and the Flight from Manhood

1. Philip Wylie, *Generation of Vipers*, rev. ed. (New York: Pocket Books, 1955), 298, 1.

2. John Erskine, *The Influence of Women and Its Cure* (Indianapolis: Bobbs-Merrill, 1936), 17. Wylie, *Generation of Vipers*, 184–186.

3. Wylie, *Generation of Vipers*, 184, 201–202, 184n. For typical reviews, see *Time*, 41 (Jan. 18, 1943), 100; *New Yorker*, 52 (Jan. 2, 1943), 18. On its impact, see Truman Frederick Keefer, *Philip Wylie* (Boston: Twayne, 1977); Robert Howard Barshay, *Philip Wylie: The Man and His Work* (New York: University Press of America, 1979).

4. Wylie, *Generation of Vipers*, ix–x.

5. Lionel Trilling, *Beyond Culture* (New York: Viking, 1965), 108–109, 104.

6. Thomas S. Szasz, *Ideology and Insanity: Essays on the Psychiatric Dehumanization of Man* (Garden City, N.Y.: Doubleday, 1969), 4; and "The Problem of Psychiatric Nosology," *American Journal of Psychiatry*, 114 (Nov. 1957), 405–413.

7. Wylie, *Generation of Vipers*, 299. For examples of this line of reasoning, see Harold D. Laswell, *Psychopathology and Politics* (Chicago: University of Chicago Press, 1930); and esp. Erich Fromm, *The Sane Society* (New York: Holt, Rinehart and Winston, 1955).

8. Wylie, *Generation of Vipers*, 76n, xv.

9. Ray H. Abrams, reviewing Edward A. Strecker, *Their Mothers' Sons*, in *Annals of the American Academy of Social and Political Science*, 251 (May 1947), 187.

10. Peter Gay, *Freud: A Life for Our Time* (New York: Norton, 1988), 310.

11. Sigmund Freud, *Beyond the Pleasure Principle* (1920), SE 18: 38.

12. Paul Federn, in "The Reality of the Death Instinct, Esp. in Melancholia," PR, 19 (April 1932), 129–130, claims that Franz Alexander was the first psychoanalyst to establish the validity of Freud's hypothesis.

13. See Nathan G. Hale Jr., "From Berggasse XIX to Central Park West: The Americanization of Psychoanalysis, 1919–1940," *Journal of the History of the Behavioral Sciences,* 14 (1978), 308.

14. Freud, *The Ego and the Id* (1923), SE 19: 36, 56.

15. Ibid., 12–28.

16. Ernst Kris, "The Development of Ego Psychology," *Simiksa: The Indian Journal of Psychoanalysis* (1952), quoted by Daniel Yankelovich and William Barrett, *Ego and Instinct: Psychoanalytic View of Human Nature—Revised* (New York: Random House, 1970), 54. Fromm's assessment appears in his *The Crisis of Psychoanalysis* (New York: Holt, Rinehart, and Winston, 1970), 37, 39.

17. Sigmund Freud, "Female Sexuality" (1932), SE 21: 226; "Femininity," in *New Introductory Lectures on Psycho-Analysis* (1933), SE 22: 130. See esp. Ruth Mack Brunswick, "The Preoedipal Phase of the Libido Development," PQ, 9 (1940).

18. Anna Freud, "Links between Hartmann's Ego Psychology and the Child Analyst's Thinking," in Rudolph F. Loewenstein et al., eds., *Psychoanalysis: A General Psychology* (New York: International Universities Press, 1966), 18. See also Elisabeth Young-Bruehl, *Anna Freud* (New York: Summit, 1988); Janet Sayers, *Mothers of Psychoanalysis* (New York: Norton, 1991).

19. Sigmund Freud, "Analysis: Terminable and Interminable" (1937), SE 23: 250, 240.

20. Anna Freud and Dorothy Burlingham, *Infants without Families* (New York: International Universities Press, 1944), 103. Anna Freud, Foreword to Edith Buxbaum, *Your Child Makes Sense* (London: George Allen and Unwin, 1951), vii.

21. Heinz Hartmann, Ernst Kris, and Rudolph M. Lowenstein, "Some Psychoanalytic Comments on 'Culture and Personality' " (1951), in *Psychological Issues,* vol. 4, no.2, monograph 14 (New York: International Universities Press, 1964), 111.

22. Paul Roazen, *Freud and His Followers* (New York: De Cap, 1975), 520. See also H. Stuart Hughes, *The Sea Change* (New York: Harper and Row, 1975).

23. René Spitz, "Hospitalism: An Inquiry into the Genesis of Psychiatric Conditions in Early Childhood," PSC, 1 (1945), 53–75; Spitz and K. Wolf, "Anaclytic Depression," PSC, 2 (1946), 313–342. Although criticized severely in the mid-1950s for not controlling for contagious diseases like measles, Spitz stood by his principles and summarized three decades of research in *The First*

Year of Life (New York: International Universities Press, 1965). For biographical material, see René A. Spitz, *A Genetic Field Theory of Ego Formation: Its Implications for Pathology* (New York: International Universities Press, 1959).

24. David M. Levy, "Psychosomatic Studies of Some Aspects of Maternal Behavior" (1932), in Clyde Kluckhohn and Henry A. Murray with David M. Schneider, eds., *Personality in Nature, Society, and Culture* (New York: Knopf, 1967), 104–110. Margaret A. Ribble, *The Rights of Infants: Early Psychological Needs and Their Satisfaction* (New York: Columbia University Press, 1943), 10, 14. The earliest cited study of maternal rejection is N. W. Newell, "The Psychodynamics of Maternal Rejection," *American Journal of Orthopsychiatry*, 4 (1934), 387–401. See also Diane E. Eyer, *Mother-Infant Bonding: A Scientific Fiction* (New Haven: Yale University Press, 1992).

25. Wylie, *Generation of Vipers*, 50, 197–198, 18.

26. Helene Deutsch, *The Psychology of Woman* (New York: Grune and Stratton, 1944), vol. 1, 318; Deutsch, "Freud and His Pupils," PR, 9 (1940), 85. Nathan W. Ackerman, *The Psychodynamics of Family Life* (New York: Basic Books, 1958), 40.

27. Hughes, *Sea Change*, 192.

28. Richard M. Brickner, *Is Germany Incurable?* (Philadelphia: Lippincott, 1943), intro. Margaret Mead.

29. Ruth Benedict, "Psychological Types in the Culture of the Southwest," *Proceedings of the International Congress of Americanists*, 23 (1928), 572–581; and "Configurations of Culture in North America," *American Anthropologist*, 34 (1932), 1–27. Edward Sapir, "The Emergence of the Concept of Personality in a Study of Cultures" (1934), in *Culture, Language, and Personality* (Berkeley: University of California Press, 1949).

30. Ralph Linton, *The Cultural Background of Personality* (New York: D. Appleton-Century, 1945), 50.

31. Geoffrey Gorer, "The Scientific Study of National Character," quoted in Ellen Herman, *The Romance of American Psychology: Political Culture in the Age of Experts* (Berkeley: University of California Press, 1995), 34. See Victor Barnouw, *Culture and Personality*, rev. ed. (Homewood, Ill.: Dorsey, 1973); Thomas L. Hartshorne, *The Distorted Image: Changing Conceptions of the American Character since Turner* (Cleveland: Case Western Reserve University Press, 1968).

32. Margaret Mead, *And Keep Your Powder Dry: An Anthropologist Looks at America* (New York: William Morrow, 1942), 12, 14; and "The Study of National Character," in Daniel Lerner and Harold D. Lasswell, eds., *The Policy Sciences* (Stanford: Stanford University Press, 1951).

33. Geoffrey Gorer, "Themes in Japanese Culture" (1943), in Douglas G. Haring, ed., *Personal Character and Cultural Milieu* (Syracuse: Syracuse Uni-

versity Press, 1949), 278. Weston La Barre, "Some Observations on Character Structure in the Orient: The Japanese," *Psychiatry,* 8 (Aug. 1945), 326.

34. Edward A. Strecker, *Their Mothers' Sons: The Psychiatrist Examines an American Problem* (Philadelphia: Lippincott, 1946), 137–139. Lauren H. Smith, "Edward A. Strecker, M.D.: A Biographical Sketch," *American Journal of Psychiatry,* 101 (July 1944).

35. Strecker, *Their Mothers' Sons,* 135.

36. Erik H. Erikson, *Childhood and Society,* rev. ed. (New York: Norton, 1963), 16. Robert Coles, *Erik H. Erikson: The Growth of His Work* (Boston: Little, Brown, 1970). The litany of psychoanalytic descriptions of Hitler appears on 329.

37. Erikson, *Childhood and Society,* 339, 328–329. A study conducted for the OSS contains similar interpretive themes: Walter C. Langer, *The Mind of Adolf Hitler* (New York: Signet, 1973).

38. Amram Scheinfeld, "Are American Moms a Menace?" *Ladies' Home Journal,* 62 (Nov. 1945), 138.

39. See essays on Japan by Edward Norbeck, Margaret Norbeck, and Betty B. Lanham in Haring, ed., *Personal Character and Cultural Milieu.*

40. Hartmann, Kris, and Loewenstein, "Comments on 'Culture and Personality,'" 102–111.

41. Geoffrey Gorer, *The American People: A Study in National Character* (New York: Norton, 1948), 27–28.

42. Arthur J. Brodbeck and David M. White, "How to Read 'Li'l Abner' Intelligently," in Bernard Rosenberg and David Manning White, eds., *Mass Culture: The Popular Arts in America* (New York: Free Press, 1957), 218. Gorer, *American People,* 48–49, 61.

43. Gorer, *American People,* 55–60.

44. For overviews of this development see Gerald N. Grob, "World War II and American Psychiatry," *Psychohistory Review,* 19 (Fall 1990); John C. Burnham, "The Influence of Psychoanalysis upon American Culture," in Burnham, *Paths into American Culture: Psychology, Medicine and Morals* (Philadelphia: Temple University Press, 1988). See also Nathan G. Hale Jr., *The Rise and Crisis of Psychoanalysis in the United States: Freud and the Americans, 1917–1985* (New York: Oxford University Press, 1995).

45. Strecker, *Their Mothers' Sons,* 23, 25, 30, 128.

46. Floyd Dell, *Love in the Machine Age: A Psychological Study of the Transition from Patriarchal Society* (New York: Farrar and Rinehart, 1930), 101. John B. Watson, *Psychological Care of Infant and Child* (New York: Norton, 1928).

47. Sigmund Freud, *Three Essays on the Theory of Sexuality* (1905), SE 7: 160–161. See also Freud, *Leonardo da Vinci and a Memory of His*

Childhood (1910), SE 11. Jerome Neu, "Freud and Perversion," in Neu, *Cambridge Companion to Freud* (Cambridge: Cambridge University Press, 1991).

48. See Kenneth Lewes, *The Psychoanalytic Theory of Male Homosexuality* (New York: Simon and Schuster, 1988). See also Ronald Bayer, *Homosexuality and American Psychiatry: The Politics of Diagnosis* (New York: Basic Books, 1981).

49. Walter E. Barton, *The History and Influence of the American Psychiatric Association* (Washington: American Psychiatric Press, 1987), 134. Edmund Bergler, *Homosexuality: Disease or Way of Life* (New York: Hill and Wang, 1957). Statistics of discharge appear in John D'Emilio, "The Homosexual Menace: The Politics of Sexuality in Cold War America," in Kathy Peiss and Christina Simmons, eds., *Passion and Power: Sexuality in History* (Philadelphia: Temple University Press, 1989), 226–240. See also Lewes, *Psychoanalytic Theory of Male Homosexuality*; Allan Berube, *Coming Out under Fire: The History of Gay Men and Women in World War Two* (New York: Penguin, 1990).

50. Gorer, *American People*, 49, 54, 64, 129. A Mother, "Was Our Boy a Sissy?" *Parents' Magazine*, 26 (April 1952), 44–45, 66, 68–69.

51. Abram Kardiner, *Sex and Morality* (London: Routledge and Kegan Paul, 1955), 160–192.

52. Irving Bieber et al., *Homosexuality: A Psychoanalytic Study of Male Homosexuals* (New York: Basic Books, 1962), 319, 220, 44, 114–117. Charles W. Socarides, *Homosexuality* (New York: Jason Aronson, 1978), makes the ultimate case for homosexuality, especially pre-oedipal homosexuality, as pathological.

53. E. Franklin Frazier, *The Negro Family in the United States* (Chicago: University of Chicago Press, 1939).

54. Park quoted by Patricia Morton, *Disfigured Images: The Historical Assault on Afro-American Women* (New York: Praeger, 1991), 70. See also Herman, *Romance of American Psychology*.

55. John Dollard, *Caste and Class in a Southern Town* (New York: Harper, 1937).

56. Reuben Fine, *A History of Psychoanalysis* (New York: Columbia University Press, 1979), 107.

57. William C. Manson, "Abram Kardiner and the Neo-Freudian Alternative in Culture and Personality," in George W. Stocking Jr., ed., *Malinowski, Rivers, Benedict and Others: Essays on Culture and Personality* (Madison: University of Wisconsin Press, 1986), 72–94; William C. Manson, *The Psychodynamics of Culture: Abram Kardiner and Neo-Freudian Anthropology* (Westport, Conn.: Greenwood, 1988).

58. Abram Kardiner, *The Psychological Frontiers of Society* (New York: Columbia University Press, 1945), 12.

59. Abram Kardiner and Lionel Ovesey, *The Mark of Oppression: A Psychosocial Study of the American Negro* (New York: Norton, 1951), 381–382, 54, 65.

60. Lee Rainwater and William L. Yancy, *The Moynihan Report and the Politics of Controversy* (Cambridge, Mass.: MIT Press, 1967), 62.

61. Andre Fontaine, "Are We Staking Our Future on a Crop of Sissies?" *Better Homes and Gardens*, 29 (Dec. 1950), 154–160. The articles by D. Ashbaugh and C. C. Bowman respectively appeared in *Parents' Magazine*, 24 (Dec. 1949), 36–37, and *Coronet*, April 1950, 11–14. Editors of *Look*, *The Decline of the American Male* (New York: Random House, 1958). Arthur Schlesinger Jr., "The Crisis of American Masculinity," *Esquire*, Nov. 1958, 63–65.

62. Philip Wylie, "More Musings on Mom," *Saturday Review of Literature*, 29 (Dec. 7, 1946), 21. Strecker, *Their Mothers' Sons*, 13, 133.

63. Hughes, *Sea Change*, 196–198. Fromm, *Sane Society*, 72. See also Martin Birnbach, *Neo-Freudian Social Philosophy* (Stanford: Stanford University Press, 1961).

64. Strecker, *Their Mothers' Sons*, 219. Wylie, "More Musings on Mom," 22.

65. See, e.g., Mirra Komarovsky, *The Unemployed Man and His Family: The Effect of Unemployment upon the Status of the Man in Fifty-Nine Families* (New York: Dryden, 1940).

66. Edith Vowinckel Weigert, "Women in Wartime: Disabilities and 'Masculine' Defense Reactions," *Psychiatry*, 6 (Nov. 1943), 375, 378, 377.

67. Elaine Tyler May, *Homeward Bound: American Families in the Cold War Era* (New York: Basic Books, 1988).

68. Wylie, *Generation of Vipers*, 199. Erikson, *Childhood and Society*, 295, 291. Gerald Sykes, *The Hidden Remnant* (New York: Harper, 1962), 17.

69. Spitz, "Hospitalism," 72; Hoover quoted by May, *Homeward Bound*, 137.

70. William G. Niederland, "Some Psychological Disorders of Femininity and Masculinity," in Johnson E. Fairchild, ed., *Women, Society and Sex* (New York: Sheridan, 1952), 129.

71. E. Fuller Torry, *Freudian Fraud: The Malignant Effect of Freud's Theory on American Thought and Culture* (New York: HarperCollins, 1992), 132, 35. See also Lynn Z. Bloom, *Dr. Spock: Biography of a Conservative Radical* (Indianapolis: Bobbs-Merrill, 1972); Fred Matthews, "The Utopia of Human Relations: The Conflict-Free Family in American Social Thought,

1930–1960," *Journal of the History of the Behavioral Sciences,* 24 (Oct. 1988); A. Michael Sulman, "The Humanization of the American Child: Benjamin Spock as a Popularizer of Psychoanalytic Thought," *Journal of the History of the Behavioral Sciences,* 9 (July 1973).

72. Fine, *History of Psychoanalysis,* 160. John Bowlby, *Maternal Care and Mental Health* (Geneva: World Health Organization Monograph Series no. 2, 1951), 11, 13, 67, 157. On "Bowlbyism," see Denise Riley, *War in the Nursery: Theories of the Child and Mother* (London: Virago, 1983).

73. Margaret Mead, "Some Theoretical Considerations of the Problem of Mother-Child Separation" (1954), in Haring, ed., *Personal Character and Cultural Milieu,* 642.

74. Cynthia Harrison, *On Account of Sex: The Politics of Women's Issues, 1945–1968* (Berkeley: University of California Press, 1988), 23. *New York Times,* July 20, 1946, 12.

75. Abram Kardiner, "Social and Cultural Implications of Psychoanalysis," in Sydney Hook, ed., *Psychoanalysis, Scientific Method, and Philosophy* (New York: New York University Press, 1959), 100, 101.

5. Ladies in the Dark

1. Bosley Crowther, " 'Lady in the Dark,' with Ginger Rogers, Opens at Paramount," *New York Times,* Feb. 23, 1944, 17. Stephen Farber and Marc Green, *Hollywood on the Couch: A Candid Look at the Overheated Love Affair between Psychiatrists and Moviemakers* (New York: William Morrow, 1993), 55–58.

2. Andrea S. Walsh, *Women's Film and Female Experience, 1940–1950* (New York: Praeger, 1984), 161. See also Krin Gabbard and Glen O. Gabbard, *Psychiatry and the Cinema* (Chicago: University of Chicago Press, 1987); Mary Ann Doane, *The Desire to Desire: The Woman's Film of the 1940s* (Bloomington: Indiana University Press, 1987); E. Ann Kaplan, *Motherhood and Representation: The Mother in Popular Culture and Melodrama* (London: Routledge, 1992).

3. Hendrik M. Ruitenbeek, *Freud and America* (New York: Macmillan, 1966). John C. Burnham, "The Influence of Psychoanalysis upon American Culture," in Burnham, *Paths into American Culture: Psychology, Medicine and Morals* (Philadelphia: Temple University Press, 1988).

4. Prologue from *Spellbound* quoted in Gabbard and Gabbard, *Psychiatry and the Cinema,* 64. Lawrence S. Kubie, "Psychiatry and the Films," *Hollywood Quarterly,* 2 (Jan. 1947), 116.

5. Viola Klein, *The Feminine Character: History of an Ideology* (Urbana: University of Illinois Press, 1972 [1946]), 71. John Schultheiss and Mark

Schaubert, eds., *To Illuminate Our Time: The Blacklisted Teleplays of Abraham Polonsky* (Los Angeles: Sadanlaur, 1994), 177.

6. Nathan G. Hale Jr., *The Rise and Crisis of Psychoanalysis in the United States* (New York: Oxford University Press, 1995). For a contemporary assessment, see Thomas A. C. Rennie and Luther E. Woodward, *Mental Health in Modern Society* (New York: Commonwealth Fund, 1948). Brill's remarks were published in the *American Journal of Psychiatry*, 91 (1935).

7. Clarence P. Oberndorf, *A History of Psychoanalysis in America* (New York: Harper and Row, 1964 [1953]), 207.

8. Karen Horney, *Self-Analysis* (New York: Norton, 1942), 82. See also Marcia Westkoff, *The Feminist Legacy of Karen Horney* (New Haven: Yale University Press, 1986).

9. Francis S. Wickware, "Psychoanalysis," *Life,* 22 (Feb. 3, 1947), 98–108. William H. Chafe, *The Paradox of Change: American Women in the 20th Century* (New York: Oxford University Press, 1991), 176. "American Woman's Dilemma," *Life,* 22 (June 16, 1947), 101–110.

10. Gregory Zilboorg, "Masculine and Feminine: Some Biological and Cultural Aspects," *Psychiatry,* 7 (Aug. 1944), 261.

11. Philip Wylie, "Masculinesque Womenfolk," *Saturday Review,* 30 (Feb. 1, 1947), 13.

12. Ferdinand Lundberg and Marynia F. Farnham, *Modern Woman: The Lost Sex* (New York: Grosset and Dunlap, 1947), 10, 235.

13. Ibid., 23, 3.

14. Ibid., 143.

15. Ibid., ch. 7.

16. Ibid., 149.

17. Ibid., 149–150.

18. Ibid., 151, 160.

19. Marynia F. Farnham, "The Tragic Failure of America's Women," *Coronet* (Sept. 1947), 4.

20. Frederic Wertham, "Ladies in the Dark," *New Republic,* 116 (Feb. 10, 1947), 38. Mildred Burgum, review in *Science and Society,* 11 (1947), 388. Dorothy Parker, quoted by Frances Levison, "What the Experts Say: Books, Articles Debate the 'Woman Question,' " *Life,* 22 (June 16, 1947), 112.

21. Wylie, "Masculinesque Womenfolk," 13; Donald W. Calhoun, review in *Social Forces,* 26 (1948), 351. David Dempsey, "Talk with Dr. Farnham," *New York Times Book Review* (Sept. 30, 1951), 24.

22. Joanne Meyerowitz, "Beyond the Feminine Mystique: A Reassessment of Postwar Mass Culture, 1946–1958," JAH, 79 (March 1993), 1475–76. Review by Arnold W. Green, *Annals of the American Academy of Political and Social Science,* 251 (May 1947), 188. Review by Mabel B. Cohen, *Psy-*

chiatry, 11 (Feb. 1948), 101. Abraham Myerson's review appeared in *American Journal of Psychiatry,* 104 (March 1948), 589–591.

23. The quotation from the *New York Herald* appears in Helene Deutsch, *Confrontations with Myself* (New York: Norton, 1973), 173. Margaret Nordfeldt, review of *The Psychology of Women, Survey,* 82 (Jan. 1946), 27.

24. Helene Deutsch, *The Psychology of Women: A Psychoanalytic Interpretation* (New York: Bantam, 1973 [1944]), vol. 1, xiv, 248.

25. Ibid., 305, 310, 298. See also Helene Deutsch, "George Sand: A Woman's Destiny," *International Review of Psycho-Analysis,* 9 (1982).

26. Sigmund Freud, "Femininity," in *New Introductory Lectures on Psycho-Analysis* (1933), SE 22: 133.

27. Lundberg and Farnham, *Modern Woman,* 319. See also Marynia Farnham, "Battles Won and Lost," *Annals of the American Academy of Political and Social Science,* 251 (May 1947).

28. Erik H. Erikson, *Childhood and Society,* rev. ed. (New York: Norton, 1963 [1950]), 279. Lundberg and Farnham, *Modern Woman,* 9.

29. Erich Fromm, *Escape from Freedom* (New York: Holt, Rinehart and Winston, 1941), 265; *The Sane Society* (New York: Holt, Rinehart and Winston, 1955), 111.

30. Arthur Schlesinger Jr., *The Vital Center: The Politics of Freedom* (Boston: Houghton Mifflin, 1949), 1. Nathan W. Ackerman, *The Psychodynamics of Family Life: Diagnosis and Treatment of Family Relations* (New York: Basic Books, 1958), 3. Robert Linder, *Prescription for Rebellion* (New York: Rinehart, 1952), 99.

31. Eric and Mary Josephson, eds., *Man Alone: Alienation in Modern Society* (New York: Dell, 1962), n.p. Lundberg and Farnham, *Modern Woman,* 201.

32. Philip Wylie, "Liberty and the Ladies," *American Scholar,* 19 (Spring 1950), 174–175. William Appleman Williams, *The Great Evasion* (Chicago: Quadrangle, 1964), 112.

33. Reuben Fine, *A History of Psychoanalysis* (New York: Columbia University Press, 1979), 492. Warren I. Susman, " 'Personality' and the Making of Twentieth-Century Culture" (1979), in Susman, *Culture as History: The Transformation of American Society in the Twentieth Century* (New York: Pantheon, 1984), 284.

34. Review by Martin Grotjahn, PQ, 20 (1951). Erikson, *Childhood and Society,* 42.

35. Erikson, *Childhood and Society,* 281, 282. The reference to Freud's "Jewish identity" is found in his "Address to the Society of B'nai B'rith" (1926), SE 20.

36. Erikson, *Childhood and Society,* 249.

37. Ibid., ch. 2.

38. Parsons introduced his functionalist theory of sex roles in "The Kinship System of the Contemporary United States," *American Anthropologist,* 45 (1943); and filled out the framework within the terms of ego psychology in "The Superego and the Theory of Social Systems," *Psychiatry,* 15 (Feb. 1952).

39. Freud, *New Introductory Lectures,* 133–134.

40. Jacques S. Gottlieb and Gary Tourney, "Being a Boy—Being a Girl," *National Parent Teacher,* 50 (Feb. 1956), 11.

41. Ibid., 10.

42. Lundberg and Farnham, *Modern Woman,* 228.

43. Haim Ginott, *Between Parent and Child: New Solutions to Old Problems* (London: Staples, 1965), 176. Daniel G. Brown, "Sex-Role Development in a Changing Culture," *Psychological Bulletin,* 55 (July 1958), 233. O. Spurgeon English and Constance J. Foster, "How to Raise Better Husbands," *Parents' Magazine,* 23 (Nov. 1948), 22. See also Robert R. Sears, Eleanor E. Maccoby, and Harry Levin, *Patterns of Child Rearing* (New York: Harper, 1957).

44. D. Barclay, "Trousered Mothers and Dishwashing Dads," *New York Times Magazine* (April 28, 1957), 48.

45. Marynia F. Farnham, "Helping Boys to Be Boys . . . Girls to Be Girls," *Parents' Magazine,* 28 (Jan. 1953), 34, 35.

46. Abram Kardiner, *Sex and Morality* (Indianapolis: Bobbs-Merrill, 1954), 47, 226, 225.

47. Frieda Miller, Women's Bureau, quoted in Chafe, *Paradox of Change,* 161.

48. On women in psychoanalysis, see Laura Fermi, *Illustrious Immigrants: The Intellectual Migration from Europe, 1930–41* (Chicago: University of Chicago Press 1969), 170. See also Elaine Tyler May, *Homeward Bound: American Families in the Cold War Era* (New York: Basic Books, 1988). Wini Breines, *Young, White, and Miserable: Growing Up Female in the Fifties* (Boston: Beacon, 1992), summarizes these findings from *Americans View Their Mental Health* (1957).

49. Clara M. Thompson, *On Women* (New York: New American Library, 1971), 159, 160, 17.

50. Edward R. Strecker and Vincent T. Lathbury, *Their Mothers' Daughters* (Philadelphia: Lippincott, 1954), 144.

51. Kardiner, *Sex and Morality,* 46, 49, 209, 231.

52. Margaret Mead, *Sex and Temperament in Three Primitive Societies* (New York: William Morrow, 1935), 321.

53. Margaret Mead, *Male and Female: A Study of the Sexes in a Changing World* (New York: William Morrow, 1949), 9–10, 160, 300–301, 372.

54. Clyde Kluckhohn, *Mirror for Man: The Relation of Anthropology to Modern Life* (New York: McGraw-Hill, 1949), 20. See Carl N. Degler, *In Search of Human Nature: The Decline and Revival of Darwinism in American Social Thought* (New York: Oxford University Press, 1991).

55. Milton H. Miller, "On Building Bridges," in Norman S. Greenfield and William C. Lewis, eds., *Psychoanalysis and Current Biologist Thought* (Madison: University of Wisconsin Press, 1965), 3. On the WHO-sponsored conference, see J. M. Tanner and Barbel Inhelder, eds., *Discussions on Child Development* (New York: International Universities Press, 1958), vol. 3.

56. John Bowlby, "The Nature of the Child's Tie to His Mother," IJP, 34 (Sept.–Oct. 1958), 355–372. On the relationship between ethology and ego psychology, see Daniel Yankelovich and William Barrett, *Ego and Instinct: The Psychoanalytic View of Human Nature—Revised* (New York: Random House, 1970).

57. Harry Harlow, "The Nature of Love," *American Psychologist,* 15 (1958), 673–685.

58. Deutsch, *Psychology of Woman,* vol. 2, 15, 17, 20.

59. Therese Benedek, "Adaptation to Reality in Early Infancy," PQ, 7 (1938), 200–215; Benedek, *Insight and Personality Adjustment: A Study of the Psychological Effects of War* (New York: Ronald Press, 1946), 15.

60. Therese Benedek, *Psychosexual Functions in Women* (New York: Ronald Press, 1952), vi.

61. Franz Alexander, *Psychosomatic Medicine: Its Principles and Applications* (New York:. Norton, 1987 [1950]), 34. Idem., *Fundamentals of Psychoanalysis* (New York: Norton, 1948), 139.

62. See Mary Jane Lupton, *Menstruation and Psychoanalysis* (Urbana: University of Illinois Press, 1993).

63. Erich Fromm, "Freud's Model of Man and Its Social Determinants" (1969), in Fromm's *The Crisis in Psychoanalysis,* (New York: Holt, Rinehart and Winston, 1970). Judd Marmor, quoted in Jules H. Masserman, ed., *Sexuality of Women* (New York: Grune and Stratton, 1966), v.

64. Kardiner, *Sex and Morality,* 221, 226. Lionel Ovesey, "Masculine Aspirations in Women: An Adaptation Analysis," *Psychiatry,* 19 (Nov. 1956), 341–342.

65. Paul Roazen, *Freud and His Followers* (New York: Knopf, 1975), 326–327.

66. Theodor Reik, "Emotional Differences of the Sexes," *Psychoanalysis,* 2 (Summer 1953), 4, 5, 7.

67. Idem., *Of Love and Lust: On the Psychoanalysis of Romantic and Sexual Emotions* (New York: Farrar, Straus, 1949), 451.

68. Amram Scheinfeld, commentary, *Psychoanalysis,* 2 (Summer 1953), 15. See also Philip Wylie, "An Introductory Hypothesis to a Psychology of Women," *Psychoanalysis,* 1 (Spring 1952).

69. Lundberg and Farnham, *Modern Woman,* 147. Farnham, "Helping Boys to Be Boys," 34.

70. Sigmund Freud, "The Unconscious" (1915), SE 14: 168; and *Beyond the Pleasure Principle* (1920), SE 18: 60.

71. Fine, *History of Psychoanalysis,* 159.

72. "Aberrations of the Sexual Instinct," *Quarterly Journal of Psychological Medicine and Medical Jurisprudence,* 1 (July 1867), 89.

6. Feminists versus Freud

1. Mary R. Beard, *Woman as Force in History: A Study in Traditions and Realities* (New York: Collier, 1962 [1946]), unnumbered preface, 81.

2. Letter to Betty Friedan, July 23, 1970, quoted in Wini Breines, *Young, White, and Miserable: Growing Up Female in the Fifties* (Boston: Beacon, 1992), 78.

3. Betty Friedan, *The Feminine Mystique* (New York: Dell, 1974 [1963]), 115, 116.

4. "Who We Are: Descriptions of Women's Liberation Groups," handout at the Lake Villa Conference, Nov. 1968, quoted in Alice Echols, *Daring to Be Bad: Radical Feminism in America, 1967–1975* (Minneapolis: University of Minnesota Press, 1989), 97.

5. Edward J. Bardon, *The Sexual Arena and Women's Liberation* (Chicago: Nelson-Hall, 1978), 7.

6. Kate Millett, *Sexual Politics* (New York: Doubleday, 1970), 178; Shulamith Firestone, *The Dialectic of Sex: The Case for Feminist Revolution* (New York: William Morrow, 1970), 42; Eva Figes, *Patriarchal Attitudes: The Case for Women in Revolt* (New York: Fawcett World Library, 1970), 133; Germaine Greer, *The Female Eunuch* (New York: Bantam, 1972 [1971]), 93.

7. Mary Roth Walsh, ed., *The Psychology of Women: Ongoing Debates* (New Haven: Yale University Press, 1987), 19; Josephine Donovan, *Feminist Theory: The Intellectual Traditions of American Feminism* (New York: Frederick Ungar, 1985), 101.

8. Ramona X, "Looking Backwards . . . and Forwards," *Sojourner* (Boston), June 1989, 15.

9. Alix Kates Shulman, "Sex and Power: Sexual Bases of Radical Feminism," *Signs,* 5 (Summer 1980), 590.

10. Millett, *Sexual Politics*, 23. "The Feminists: A Political Organization to Annihilate Sex Roles," in Anne Koedt and Shulamith Firestone, eds., *Notes from the Second Year: Women's Liberation, Major Writings of the Radical Feminists* (New York: New York Radical Feminists, 1970), quoted by Shulman, "Sex and Power," 597.

11. Richard Gilman, "The FemLib Case against Sigmund Freud," *New York Times Magazine* (Jan. 31, 1971), 10.

12. Helene Deutsch, *The Psychology of Women* (New York: Grune and Stratton, 1945), vol. 2. Marie Bonaparte, *Female Sexuality* (New York: International Universities Press, 1953). Ferdinand Lundberg and Marynia F. Farnham, *Modern Woman: The Lost Sex* (New York: Grosset and Dunlap, 1947), 265, 275. See, e.g., an excerpt from Lundberg and Farnham's book in Edwin M. Schur, ed., *The Family and the Sexual Revolution* (Bloomington: Indiana University Press, 1964).

13. Millett, *Sexual Politics*, 117, 182. Judith Hole and Ellen Levine, *Rebirth of Feminism* (New York: Quadrangle, 1971), 178.

14. Sigmund Freud, *New Introductory Lectures on Psycho-Analysis* (1933), SE 22: 118; quoted, e.g., in Lonnie Garfield Barbach, *For Yourself: The Fulfillment of Female Sexuality* (Garden City, N.Y.: Anchor, 1976), 17. See also Cynthia Jayne, "The Dark Continent Revisited: An Examination of the Freudian View of the Female Orgasm," *Psychoanalysis and Contemporary Thought*, 3 (1980); Carole Groneman, "Nymphomania and the Freudians," *Psychohistory Review*, 23 (Winter 1995).

15. Edward E. Hitschmann and Edmund Bergler, *Frigidity in Women: Its Characteristics and Treatment* (New York: Nervous Disease Monograph Series no. 60, 1936), 20; quoted by Burness E. Moore, "Frigidity: A Review of Psychoanalytic Literature," PQ, 33 (1964), 324. Edmund Bergler, *Neurotic Counterfeit-Sex* (New York: Grune and Stratton, 1951). Sándor Lorand, "Contribution to the Problem of Vaginal Orgasm" (1939).

16. Lundberg and Farnham, *Modern Woman*, 266. Dr. Marie M. Robinson [Marie Nyswander], *The Power of Sexual Surrender* (New York: Signet, 1962 [1959]), 22, 111. Frank S. Caprio, *The Sexually Adequate Female* (Greenwich, Conn.: Fawcett, 1966 [1955]), 64, quoted in Hole and Levine, *Rebirth of Feminism*, 178. See also Alice Rossi, "Sex Equality: The Beginning of Ideology," in Betty Roszak and Theodore Roszak, eds., *Masculine/Feminine: Readings in Sexual Mythology and the Liberation of Women* (New York: Harper and Row, 1969); Julie Weiss, "Womanhood and Psychoanalysis: A Study of Mutual Construction in Popular Culture, 1920–1963," Ph.D. diss., Brown University, 1990.

17. Robert Latou Dickinson and Lura Beam, *A Thousand Marriages: A Medical Study of Sex Adjustment* (Baltimore: Williams and Wilkins, 1932

[1931]), 129. See also Gilbert V. Hamilton, *A Research in Marriage* (New York: Albert and Charles Boni, 1929); Katherine Bemont Davis, *Factors in the Sex Life of Twenty-two Hundred Women* (New York: Harper, 1929).

18. Alfred C. Kinsey, *Sexual Behavior in the Human Female* (New York: Pocket, 1965 [1953]), 582.

19. William Masters and Virginia Johnson, *Human Sexual Response* (New York: Bantam, 1966). See also Janice M. Irvine, *Disorders of Desire: Sex and Gender in Modern American Sexology* (Philadelphia: Temple University Press, 1990).

20. Susan Lydon, "Understanding Orgasm," *Ramparts*, 7 (Dec. 1968).

21. Echols, *Daring to Be Bad*. See, e.g., Annie Popkin's reminiscences on reading this essay, in Joan Morrison and Robert K. Morrison, eds., *From Camelot to Kent State: The Sixties Experience in the Words of Those Who Lived It* (New York: Times Books, 1987), 184.

22. Anne Koedt, "The Myth of the Vaginal Orgasm" (1971), in Anne Koedt, Ellen Levine, and Anita Rapone, eds. *Radical Feminism* (New York: Quadrangle, 1973), 204, 206.

23. Ruth Bleier, *Science and Gender: A Critique of Biology and Its Theories on Women* (New York: Pergamon, 1984), 173; Barbach, *For Yourself*, 198.

24. Boston Women's Health Book Collective, *Our Bodies, Ourselves: A Course By and For Women* (Boston: New England Free Press, 1971), 12. Rossi, "Sex Equality," 181. Alix Shulman, "Organs and Orgasms," in Vivian Gornick and Barbara K. Moran, eds., *Woman in Sexist Society* (New York: Basic Books, 1971), 292, 302.

25. Cited by Lisa Appignanesi and John Forrester, *Freud's Women* (New York: Basic Books, 1992), 457.

26. Anne Koedt, "Lesbianism and Feminism," *Notes from the Third Year: Women's Liberation* (New York: Radical Feminists, 1971). Jill Johnston, *Lesbian Nation: The Feminist Solution* (New York: Simon and Schuster, 1973), 166, 167. The slogan is usually attributed to Ti-Grace Atkinson.

27. Koedt, "Lesbianism and Feminism," 257. Lucy Komisar, testimony, *Green Hearings,* quoted in Hole and Levine, *Rebirth of Feminism,* 192. Firestone, *Dialectic of Sex,* 8.

28. Hole and Levine, *Rebirth of Feminism,* 171. Firestone, *Dialectic of Sex,* 11.

29. Sigmund Freud, *The Question of Lay Analysis* (1926), SE 12: 212.

30. Maxwell Gitelson, "On the Identity Crisis in American Psychoanalysis" (1964), in Gitelson, *Psychoanalysis: Science and Profession* (New York: International Universities Press, 1973). Reuben Fine, *History of Psychoanalysis* (New York: Columbia University Press, 1979), 577. See also Arnold A. Rogow, *The Psychiatrists* (New York: Putnam, 1970).

31. Robert R. Sears, *Survey of Objective Studies of Psychoanalytic Concepts*, Bulletin 51 (New York: Social Science Research Council, 1941); H. J. Eysenck, *Uses and Abuses of Psychology* (Harmondsworth: Penguin, 1953); Sydney Hook, ed., *Psychoanalysis, Scientific Method, and Philosophy* (New York: New York University Press, 1959). Naomi Weisstein, Virginia Blaisdell, and Jesse Lemisch, *The Godfathers: Freudians, Marxists, and the Scientific and Political Protection Societies* (New Haven: Belladonna, 1975), 75.

32. Leading works in anti-psychiatry include Thomas S. Szasz, *The Myth of Mental Illness: Foundations of a Theory of Personal Conduct* (New York: Hoeber-Harber, 1961); Szasz, *The Manufacture of Madness* (New York: Harper and Row, 1970); David Cooper, *The Death of the Family* (New York: Pantheon, 1970); Ronald D. Laing and A. Esterson, *Sexuality, Madness and the Family* (New York: Pelican, 1970). For an overview, see Peter Segwick, *Psycho Politics: Laing, Foucault, Goffman, Szasz and the Future of Mass Psychiatry* (New York: Harper and Row, 1982). Carol Hanisch, "The Personal Is Political," *Notes from the Second Year;* rpt. in Radical Therapist Collective, *The Radical Therapist* (New York: Ballantine, 1971), 153.

33. Virginia L. Clower, "Feminism and the New Psychology of Women," in Toksoz B. Karasu and Charles W. Socarides, eds., *On Sexuality: Psychoanalytic Observations* (New York: International Universities Press, 1979), 297; Mildred Ash, "Freud on Feminine Identity and Female Sexuality," *Psychiatry*, 34 (Aug. 1971), 324; Lucy Freeman and Herbert S. Strean, *Freud and Women*, (New York: Frederick Ungar, 1981), 230.

34. Edmund Bergler and William Kroger, *Kinsey's Myth of Female Sexuality: The Medical Facts* (New York: Grune and Stratton, 1954). Ruitenbeek, ed., *Psychoanalysis and Female Sexuality*, 11–13.

35. The 1960 meeting was summarized by Burness E. Moore, "Frigidity in Women," JAPA, 9 (1961). Deutsch's opening remarks were published as "Frigidity in Women," in Helene Deutsch, *Neuroses and Character Types: Clinical Psychoanalytic Studies* (New York: International Universities Press, 1965). Moore, "Frigidity: A Review of Psychoanalytic Literature," 325.

36. Mary Jane Sherfey, "On the Nature of Female Sexuality," in Jean Baker Miller, ed., *Psychoanalysis and Women* (Baltimore: Penguin, 1973), 151–152, 153, 139.

37. Ibid., 148.

38. Discussions of Sherfey's paper were printed in the JAPA, 16 (July 1968). Burness E. Moore, "Psychoanalytic Reflections on the Implications of Recent Physiological Studies of Female Orgasm," JAPA, 16 (July 1968), 582. William H. Gillespie, "Concepts of Vaginal Orgasm," IJP, 50 (1969), 497. See also Gillespie, "Woman and Her Discontents: A Reassessment of Freud's Views on Female Sexuality," *International Review of Psycho-Analysis*, 2 (1975);

Hannah Lerman, *A Mote in Freud's Eye: From Psychoanalysis to the Psychology of Women* (New York: Springer, 1986).

39. Mary Jane Sherfey, "The Rib Belongs to Eve," *New York Times*, Nov. 13, 1972, 37; and Nov. 14, 1972, 47. Sherfey, "A Theory on Female Sexuality," in Robin Morgan, ed., *Sisterhood Is Powerful: An Anthology of Writing from the Women's Liberation Movement* (New York: Vintage, 1970).

40. Rogow, *Psychiatrists*.

41. Cary Cherniss, "Personality and Ideology: A Personalogical Study of Women's Liberation," *Psychiatry*, 35 (May 1972), 125. Irving Howe, "On Sexual Politics: The Middle-Class Mind of Kate Millett," in Howe, *The Critical Point: On Literature and Culture* (New York: Horizon, 1973). Carolyn Stoloff, "Who Joins Women's Liberation?" *Psychiatry*, 36 (Aug. 1973), 338. Robert Seidenberg, "Psychoanalysis and the Feminist Movement," in Marie Coleman Nelson and Jean Ikenberry, eds., *Psychosexual Imperatives: Their Role in Identity Formation* (New York: Human Sciences Press, 1979), 323.

42. Kate Millett, *Sexual Politics*, 187. Sylvia A. Manalis, "The Psychoanalytic Concept of Feminine Passivity: A Comparative Study of Psychoanalytic and Feminist Views," *Comprehensive Psychiatry*, 17 (Jan.–Feb. 1976), 244. Ash, "Freud on Feminine Identity," 326.

43. Judd Marmor, "Some Considerations Concerning Orgasms in the Female," and Leon Salzman, "Sexuality in Psychoanalytic Theory," in Marmor, ed., *Modern Psychoanalysis: New Directions and Perspectives* (New York: Basic Books, 1968), 134, 135; see also Salzman, "Psychology of the Female: A New Look," in Miller, ed., *Psychoanalysis and Women*. See also Seymour Fisher, *The Female Orgasm: Psychology, Physiology, Fantasy* (New York: Basic Books, 1973).

44. Ruth Moulton, "Multiple Factors in Frigidity," in Jules H. Masserman, ed., *Sexuality of Women* (New York: Grune and Stratton, 1966).

45. Natalie Shainess, "A Re-assessment of Feminine Sexuality and Erotic Experience," in Masserman, ed., *Sexuality of Women*. Natalie Shainess, "Let's Bury Old Fictions," *Psychiatric Opinion*, 9 (June 1972).

46. Natalie Shainess, "Authentic Feminine Orgasmic Response," in Edward T. Adelson, ed., *Sexuality and Psychoanalysis* (New York: Brunner/Mazel, 1975), 148, 153–154. See also Shainess, "The Problem of Sex Today," *American Journal of Psychiatry*, 124 (1968); and "Sexual Problems of Women," *Journal of Sex and Marital Therapy*, 1 (Winter 1974), which reaffirms the "dual nature of female orgasm."

47. Ann Ruth Turkel, "The Impact of Feminism on the Practice of a Woman Analyst," AJP, 36 (1976), 126. On the Horney revival see Karen Horney, *Feminine Psychology*, ed. Harold Kelman (New York: Norton, 1967); Robert Coles, "Karen Horney's Flight from Orthodoxy"; Rona Cherry

and Laurence Cherry, "The Horney Heresy," *New York Times Magazine* (Aug. 26, 1973).

48. Miller, ed., *Psychoanalysis and Women*, xi, xiii.

49. Ronald A. LaTorre, "Psychological Correlates of Preferences for Clitoral or Vaginal Stimulation," *American Journal of Psychiatry*, 136 (Feb. 1979). On the "G" Spot, see Cynthia Jayne, "Freud, Grafenberg, and the Neglected Vagina," *Journal of Sex Research*, 20 (May 1984).

50. Roy Schafer, "Problems in Freud's Psychology of Women," JAPA, 22 (July 1974), 483. Robert J. Stoller, "Overview: The Impact of New Advances in Sex Research on Psychoanalytic Theory," *American Journal of Psychiatry*, 130 (March 1973).

51. Juliet Mitchell, *Woman's Estate* (New York: Vintage, 1973), 167; and *Psycho-Analysis and Feminism: Freud, Reich, Laing, and Women* (New York: Vintage, 1975), xiii. Firestone, *Dialectic of Sex*, 44.

52. Margaret Mead, "On Freud's View of Female Psychology," in Jean Strouse, ed., *Women and Analysis: Dialogues on Psychoanalytic Views of Femininity* (Boston: G. K. Hall, 1985), 98.

53. Clower, "Feminism and New Psychology of Women," 319. See also Peter Barglow and Margaret Schaefer, "A New Female Psychology?" in Harold P. Blum, ed., *Female Psychology: Contemporary Psychoanalytic Views* (New York: International Universities Press, 1977); Howard J. Haymes, "Postwar Writing and the Literature of the Women's Liberation Movement," *Psychiatry*, 38 (Nov. 1975).

54. Betty Yorburg, "Psychoanalysis and Women's Liberation," PR, 61 (Sept. 1974), 72. See also Ruth Moulton, "Psychoanalytic Reflections on Women's Liberation," *Contemporary Psychoanalysis*, 8 (Spring 1972).

55. Clara Thompson, "Some Effects of the Derogatory Attitude toward Female Sexuality" (1950), in Wendy Martin, ed., *The American Sisterhood* (New York: Harper and Row, 1972), 314. Ruth Moulton, "A Survey and Reevaluation of the Concept of Penis Envy" (1970), in Miller, ed., *Psychoanalysis and Women*, 241. Friedan, *Feminine Mystique*, 107–109; Figes, *Patriarchal Attitudes*, 136, 137.

56. Millett, *Sexual Politics*, 202–203; Firestone, *Dialectic of Sex*, 43. Erich Fromm, *Sigmund Freud's Mission: An Analysis of His Personality and Influence* (New York: Harper, 1959), 22.

57. Clara Thompson, "Role of Women in This Culture" *Psychiatry*, 4 (Feb. 1941), 1. Lerman, *Mote in Freud's Eye*, 42. Lerman also tabulated the number of cases and ratio of women to men in Freud's practice from 1890 to 1939. See also Charles Berneimer and Claire Kahane, eds., *In Dora's Case: Freud-Hysteria-Feminism* (New York: Columbia University Press, 1985); Salvadore R. Maddi, "Freud's Most Famous Patient: The Victimization of Dora," *Psy-*

chology Today, 8 (Sept. 1974); Diane Hunter, "Hysteria, Psychoanalysis, and Feminism: The Case of Anna O.," *Feminist Studies,* 9 (Fall, 1983).

58. Florence Rush, "The Freudian Coverup: Sexual Abuse of Children," *Chrysalis,* 1 (1977), 39, 44. Jeffrey Moussaieff Masson, *The Assault on Truth: Freud's Suppression of the Seduction Theory* (New York: Viking, 1985), made a similar, fuller, and more popular case. Masson did not cite the voluminous feminist literature on sexual abuse of children; the second edition belatedly attributed the surge in interest to feminist efforts.

59. Ellen Frankfort, *Vaginal Politics* (New York: Quadrangle, 1972), 182. See also Jim Swan, "Mater and Nannie: Freud's Two Mothers and the Discovery of the Oedipus Complex," *American Imago,* 31 (1974).

60. Friedan, *Feminine Mystique,* 108–109.

61. Letter to Bernays, quoted in Ernest Jones, *Sigmund Freud, Life and Work* (London: Hogarth Press, 1935), vol. 1, 320. Letter to Fliess, Oct. 3, 1897, in *The Complete Letters of Sigmund Freud to Wilhelm Fliess, 1887–1904,* trans. and ed. Jeffrey Moussaieff Masson (Cambridge, Mass.: Harvard University Press, 1985), 268.

62. Jones, *Freud,* vol. 2, 456.

63. Fromm, *Freud's Mission,* 10. Judith Bernays Heller, "Freud's Mother and Father" (1956), in Hendrick M. Ruitenbeek, ed., *Freud as We Knew Him* (Detroit: Wayne State University Press, 1973), 336, 337–339.

64. Marianne Krüll, *Freud and His Father,* trans. Arnold J. Pomerans (New York: Norton, 1986), 118, 117. Lucy Freeman and Herbert S. Strean, *Freud and Women* (New York: Frederick Ungar, 1981), 11, 14. In the wake of object-relations theory, a few writers have incorporated elements of the relational model of psychoanalysis to explain Freud's misogyny; see, e.g., Ruth Abraham, "Freud's Mother Conflict and the Formulation of the Oedipal Father," PR, 69 (1982); Herbert Lehmann, "Reflections on Freud's Reaction to the Death of His Mother," PQ, 52 (April 1983); Samuel Slipp, *The Freudian Mystique: Freud, Women, and Feminism* (New York: New York University Press, 1993); Deborah P. Margolis, *Freud and His Mother: Preoedipal Aspects of Freud's Personality* (Northvale, N.J.: Jason Aronson, 1996).

65. Friedan, *Feminine Mystique,* 108–109; Paul Roazen, *Freud and His Followers* (New York: Knopf, 1975), 45.

66. Jones, *Freud,* vol. 2, 443–445. On the Jewish context of Freud and psychoanalysis, see, e.g., Sander L. Gilman, *Freud, Race, and Gender* (Princeton: Princeton University Press, 1993); and Estelle Roith, *The Riddle of Freud: Jewish Influences on the History of Female Sexuality* (London: Tavistock, 1987).

67. Friedan, *Feminine Mystique,* 109.

68. Roazen, *Freud and His Followers,* 56. Jones, *Freud,* vol. 2, 468.

69. Lerman, *Mote in Freud's Eye;* Freeman and Strean, *Freud and Women.*

70. Friedan, *Feminine Mystique*, 111, 71. Jones, *Freud*, vol. 2, 469. Alan C. Elms, "Freud and Minna," *Psychology Today*, 16 (Dec. 1982), speaks to the sensationalistic treatments in the *New York Times, London Times*, and *Newsweek*. Fromm, *Freud's Mission*, 28–31.

71. Lerman, *Mote in Freud's Eye*, 29.

7. Feminine Self-in-Relation

1. Simone de Beauvoir, *The Second Sex*, ed. and trans. H. M. Parshely (New York: Modern Library, 1968 [1949]), 38. Jane Lazarre, "What Feminists and Freudians Can Learn from Each Other" (1974), in Uta West, ed., *Women in a Changing World* (New York: McGraw-Hill, 1975), 74. See also Edith Kurzweil, *Freudians and Feminists* (Boulder: Westview, 1995); and esp. Hannah Lerman, *A Mote in Freud's Eye: From Psychoanalysis to the Psychology of Women* (New York: Springer, 1986).

2. Proceedings of the Business Meeting quoted by Reuben Fine, *A History of Psychoanalysis* (New York: Columbia University Press, 1979), 118.

3. Stephen A. Mitchell, *Relational Concepts in Psychoanalysis: An Integration* (Cambridge, Mass.: Harvard University Press, 1988), 2. See also Morris N. Eagle, ed., *Recent Developments in Psychoanalysis: A Critical Evaluation* (Cambridge, Mass.: Harvard University Press, 1984); Rubin and Gertrude Blanck, *Beyond Ego Psychology: Developmental Object Relations Theory* (New York: Columbia University Press, 1986); Neil J. Skolnick and Susan C. Warshaw, eds., *Relational Perspectives in Psychoanalysis* (Hillsdale, N.J.: Analytic Press, 1992).

4. Interview with Dinnerstein, Winter 1986, in Elaine Hoffman Baruch and Lucienne J. Serrano, eds., *Women Analyze Women in France, England, and the United States* (New York: New York University Press, 1988), 300. Dorothy Dinnerstein, *The Mermaid and the Minotaur: Sexual Arrangements and Human Malaise* (New York: Harper Colophon, 1977), xi. Nancy J. Chodorow, *The Reproduction of Mothering: Psychoanalysis and the Sociology of Gender* (Berkeley: University of California Press, 1978), 40.

5. *Choice*, 15 (Nov. 1978), 1280. See also Josephine Donovan, *Feminist Theory: The Intellectual Traditions of American Feminism* (New York: Frederick Ungar, 1985).

6. Roy Schafer, "Problems in Freud's Psychology of Women," JAPA, 22 (1974), 468–469. See also Philip Rieff, *Freud: The Mind of a Moralist* (New York: Viking, 1959).

7. This phrase comes from Daniel N. Stern, *The Interpersonal World of the Infant: A View from Psychoanalysis and Developmental Psychology* (New York: Basic Books, 1985), 104.

8. Joel Kovel, "The Castration Complex Reconsidered," in Jean Strouse, comp., *Women and Analysis* (Boston: G. K. Hall, 1985 [1974]), 137.

9. Ethel S. Person, "The Influence of Values in Psychoanalysis: The Case of Female Psychology" (1983), in Claudia Zanardi, ed., *Essential Papers on the Psychology of Women* (New York: New York University Press, 1990).

10. John Money and Anke A. Ehrhardt, *Man and Woman, Boy and Girl: The Differentiation and Dimorphism of Gender Identity from Conception to Maturity* (Baltimore: Johns Hopkins University Press, 1972), 16. For a measure of change in paradigm, see John Money, ed., *Sex Research: New Developments* (New York: Holt, Rinehart and Winston, 1965).

11. Robert J. Stoller, "The Sense of Femaleness" (1968), and "The 'Bedrock' of Masculinity and Femininity: Bisexuality" (1972), in Jean Baker Miller, ed., *Psychoanalysis and Women* (Baltimore: Penguin, 1973). The main argument is summarized in Robert J. Stoller, *Sex and Gender: On the Development of Masculinity and Femininity* (New York: Science House, 1968).

12. Martin J. Silverman, "Cognitive Development and Female Psychology," JAPA, 29 (1981), 583. On gender differentiation, see Irene Fast, *Gender Identity: A Differentiation Model* (Hillsdale, N.J.: Analytic Press, 1984); Ethel S. Person and Lionel Ovesey, "Psychoanalytic Theories of Gender Identity," JAAP, 13 (1983).

13. Stoller, "The Sense of Femaleness," 272, and "Femininity," 132.

14. See, e.g., Peter Barglow and Margaret Schaefer, "A New Female Psychology?" in Harold P. Blum, ed., *Female Psychology* (New York: International Universities Press, 1977).

15. For an overview see Sylvia Brody, *Patterns of Mothering: Maternal Influence during Infancy* (New York: International Universities Press, 1956). Herman Roiphe and Eleanor Galenson, *Infantile Origins of Sexual Identity* (New York: International Universities Press, 1981). Edith Jacobson, *The Self and the Object World* (New York: International Universities Press, 1964).

16. Margaret Mahler, interview by Dr. Bluma Swerdloff, 1969, Psychoanalytic Movement Project: Oral History, 1963–1982, Oral History Office, Columbia University, Transcript. See also Mahler, *Memoirs of Margaret Mahler* (New York: Free Press, 1988). Alice Balint, *The Early Years of Life: A Psychoanalytic Study* (New York: Basic Books, 1954). Margaret Mahler, Fred Pine, and Ani Bergman, *The Psychological Birth of the Human Infant* (New York: Basic Books, 1975).

17. Margaret S. Mahler, "Thoughts about Development and Individuation" (1962), quoted in John B. McDevitt and Calvin F. Settlage, eds., *Separation-Individuation: Essays in Honor of Margaret S. Mahler* (New York: International Universities Press, 1971), 2–3. Ani Bergman and Steven Ellman, "Margaret S. Mahler: Symbiosis and Separation-Individuation," in Joseph

Reppen, ed., *Beyond Freud: A Study of Modern Psychoanalytic Theorists* (Hillsdale, N.J.: Analytic Press, 1985).

18. Heinz Lichtenstein, *The Dilemma of Human Identity* (New York: Jason Aronson, 1977), 17. George S. Klein, "The Ego in Psychoanalysis: A Concept in Search of Identity," PR, 56 (Winter 1969–1970).

19. Miller, ed., *Psychoanalysis and Women,* 381, xiii. Strouse, comp., *Women and Analysis,* 3, 6.

20. "Splitting" is well defined in Mahler, Pine, and Bergman, *Psychological Birth of the Human Infant.* See also Ani Bergman, "Considerations about the Development of the Girl During the Separation-Individuation Process," in Dale Mendell, ed., *Early Female Development: Current Psychoanalytic Views* (New York: SP Medical and Scientific Books, 1982).

21. The phrase "good enough mothering" appears in D. W. Winnicott, "The Relationship of a Mother to Her Baby at the Beginning" (1960), quoted in Madeleine Davis and David Wallbridge, *Boundary and Space: An Introduction to the Work of D. W. Winnicott* (London: Penguin, 1983), 104. On the British psychoanalytic community, see Judith M. Hughes, *Reshaping the Psychoanalytic Domain: The Work of Melanie Klein, W. R. D. Fairbairn, and D. W. Winnicott* (Berkeley: University of California Press, 1989).

22. Hester Eisenstein, *Contemporary Feminist Thought* (Boston: G. K. Hall, 1983), 95. See Joyce Trebilcot, ed., *Mothering: Essays in Feminist Theory* (Totowa, N.J.: Rowman and Allenheld, 1983).

23. Dinnerstein, *Mermaid and Minotaur,* 5–6.

24. Nancy Chodorow, "Family Structure and Feminine Personality," in Michele Zimbalist Rosaldo and Louise Lamphere, eds., *Woman, Culture, and Society* (Stanford: Stanford University Press, 1974). This article and others by Chodorow cited below are rpt. in Nancy J. Chodorow, *Feminism and Psychoanalytic Theory* (New Haven: Yale University Press, 1989).

25. Chodorow, *Reproduction of Mothering,* 38.

26. Michael Balint, "Early Developmental States of the Ego: Primary Object-Love" (1937), in Balint, *Primary Love and Psycho-Analytic Technique* (London: Tavistock, 1965), 82. Alice Balint, "Love for the Mother and Mother Love" (1939), ibid., 101.

27. Chodorow, *Reproduction of Mothering,* 39.

28. Ibid., 169.

29. Dinnerstein, *Mermaid and Minotaur,* 95.

30. Pauline Bart, "Review of Chodorow's *The Reproduction of Mothering,*" in Trebilcot, ed., *Mothering,* 152. See also Bart, "*The Mermaid and the Minotaur:* A Fishy Story That's Part Bull," *Contemporary Psychology,* 22 (Nov. 1977). For commentary by socialist feminists see Sandra Harding, "What Is the Real Base of Patriarchy and Capital?" in Lydia Sargent, ed.,

Women and Revolution (Boston: South End Press, 1981). See also Roger Gottlieb, "Mothering and the Reproduction of Power: Chodorow, Dinnerstein, and Social Theory," *Socialist Review,* 14 (Sept.–Oct. 1984). For special issues of feminist journals, see *Feminist Studies,* 4 (June 1978), "Toward a Feminist Theory of Motherhood"; and the forum with Judith Lorber, Rose Laub Coser, Alice S. Rossi, and Nancy Chodorow, "On *The Reproduction of Mothering:* A Methodological Debate," *Signs,* 8 (Summer 1981).

31. Nancy Friday, *My Mother/My Self: The Daughter's Search for Identity* (New York: Dell, 1977), 196.

32. Jane Flax, "Mother-Daughter Relationships: Psychodynamics, Politics, and Philosophy," in Hester Eisenstein and Alice Jardine, eds., *The Future of Difference* (Boston: Beacon, 1980), 23, 37; and "The Conflict between Nurturance and Autonomy in Mother-Daughter Relationships and within Feminism," *Feminist Studies,* 4 (June 1978), 178, 184, 185.

33. Nancy Chodorow and Susan Contratto, "The Fantasy of the Perfect Mother," in Barrie Thorne with Marilyn Yalom, eds., *Rethinking the Family: Some Feminist Questions* (New York: Longman, 1982), 55, 56.

34. Chodorow's citations of neo-Freudian analysis appear in *Reproduction of Mothering,* 41, 212–213. See also Chodorow, "Being and Doing: A Cross-Cultural Examination of the Socialization of Males and Females," in Vivian Gornick and Barbara K. Moran, eds., *Woman in Sexist Society* (New York: New American Library, 1971).

35. Marianne Hirsch, "Mothers and Daughters," *Signs,* 7 (Autumn 1981), 202.

36. Angela Davis, *The Black Woman's Role in the Community of Slaves* (Somerville, Mass.: New England Free Press, 1971). Patricia M. Robinson, "A Historical and Critical Essay for Black Women of the Cities (Excerpts)," in Sookie Stambler, ed., *Women's Liberation: Blueprint for the Future* (New York: Ace, 1970). Alice Walker, *In Search of Our Mothers' Gardens: Womanist Prose* (San Diego: Harcourt Brace Jovanovitch, 1983), 237. See also Patricia Hill Collins, "The Meaning of Motherhood in Black Culture and Black Mother/Daughter Relationships," *Sage,* 4 (Fall 1987). On writings on motherhood during this period, see Lauri Umansky, *Motherhood Reconceived: Feminism and the Legacies of the Sixties* (New York: New York University Press, 1996).

37. Adrienne Rich, *Of Woman Born: Motherhood as Experience and Institution* (New York: Norton, 1976), 284. Jane Alpert, quoted and interpreted by Alice Echols, *Daring to Be Bad: Radical Feminism in America, 1967–1975* (Minneapolis: University of Minnesota Press, 1989), 250. Alpert's "Mother Right" appeared in *Ms. Magazine,* 2 (Aug. 1973). Mary Daly, *Gyn/Ecology: The Metaethics of Radical Feminism* (Boston: Beacon, 1978), 400. See also

Susan Griffin, *Woman and Nature: The Roaring inside Her* (New York: Harper and Row, 1978); Ynestra King, "Healing the Wounds: Feminism, Ecology, and Nature/Culture Dualism," in Alison M. Jaggar and Susan R. Bordo, eds., *Gender/Body/Knowledge: Feminist Reconstructions of Being and Knowing* (New Brunswick: Rutgers University Press, 1989); Eva Feder Kittay, "Womb Envy: An Explanatory Concept," in Trebilcot, ed., *Mothering*.

38. Janna Malamud Smith, "Mothers: Tired of Taking the Rap," *New York Times Magazine*, June 10, 1990. Paula J. Caplan, *Don't Blame Mother: Mending the Mother-Daughter Relationship* (New York: Harper and Row, 1989). For "Momism" criticism of Dinnerstein, see Ann Snitow, "Thinking about *The Mermaid and the Minotaur*," *Feminist Studies*, 4 (Summer 1978). See also Barbara Johnson, "My Monster/My Self," *Diacritics*, 12 (Summer 1982). Gayle Kimball, ed., *Women's Culture: The Women's Renaissance of the Seventies* (Metuchen, N.J.: Scarecrow, 1981), 3.

39. Jane Wyatt, *Reconstructing Desire: The Role of the Unconscious in Women's Reading and Writing* (Chapel Hill: University of North Carolina Press, 1990), 15. On women's studies, see Winifred D. Wandersee, *On the Move: American Women in the 1970s* (Boston: Twayne, 1988).

40. Carroll Smith-Rosenberg, "The Female World of Love and Ritual: Relations between Women in Nineteenth-Century America," *Signs*, 1 (Autumn 1975). See also Ellen DuBois, Mari Jo Buhle, Temma Kaplan, Gerda Lerner, and Carroll Smith-Rosenberg, "Politics and Culture in Women's History: A Symposium," *Feminist Studies*, 6 (Spring 1980). The phenomenon is reviewed by Linda K. Kerber, "Some Cautionary Words for Historians," *Signs*, 11 (Winter 1986); and Carol B. Stack, "The Culture of Gender: Women and Men of Color," *Signs*, 11 (Winter 1986).

41. Examples in literary criticism: Cathy N. Davidson and E. M. Broner, *The Lost Tradition: Mothers and Daughters in Literature* (New York: Frederick Ungar, 1980); Elizabeth Abel, "(E)Merging Identities: The Dynamics of Female Friendship in Contemporary Fiction by Women," *Signs*, 6 (Spring 1981); Abel, *Virginia Woolf and the Fiction of Psychoanalysis* (Chicago: University of Chicago Press, 1989); Shirley Nelson Garner, Claire Kahane, and Madelon Sprengnether, eds., *The (M)other Tongue: Essays in Feminist Psychoanalytic Interpretation* (Ithaca: Cornell University Press, 1985); Margaret Homans, *Bearing the Word: Language and Female Experience in Nineteenth-Century Women's Writing* (New Haven: Yale University Press, 1986); and *Diacritics* (Summer 1982), a special issue entitled "Cherchez la Femme." Sandra M. Gilbert and Susan Gubar's best-known works are *The Madwoman in the Attic: The Woman Writer and the Nineteenth-Century Literary Imagination* (New Haven: Yale University Press, 1979) and *No Man's Land: The Place of the Woman Writer in the Twentieth Century* (New Haven: Yale

University Press, 1988), vol. 1. See also Patricia Bell-Scott et al., *Double Stitch: Black Women Write about Mothers and Daughters* (Boston: Beacon, 1991); Susan Cahill, ed., *Mothers: Memories, Dreams and Reflections by Literary Daughters* (New York: New American Library, 1988); Marianne Hirsch, *The Mother/Daughter Plot: Narrative, Psychoanalysis, Feminism* (Bloomington: Indiana University Press, 1989).

42. Sara Ruddick, "Maternal Thinking," *Feminist Studies*, 6 (Summer 1980), 359; Janice G. Raymond, *A Passion for Friends: Toward a Philosophy of Female Affection* (Boston: Beacon, 1966). See also Ruddick, *Maternal Thinking: Toward a Politics of Peace* (Boston: Beacon, 1989). Evelyn Fox Keller, *Reflections on Gender and Science* (New Haven: Yale University Press, 1985); and *A Feeling for the Organism: The Life and Work of Barbara McClintock* (San Francisco: Freeman, 1983). For an example in sociology, see Jessie Bernard, *The Female World* (New York: Free Press, 1981).

43. Carol Gilligan, *In a Different Voice: Psychological Theory and Women's Development* (Cambridge, Mass.: Harvard University Press, 1982), 8, 164, 165.

44. Lawrence Kohlberg, Charles Levine, and Alexandra Hewer, *Moral Stages: A Current Formulation and a Response to Critics* (New York: Karger, 1983). Lindsey Van Gelder, "Carol Gilligan: Leader for a Different Kind of Future," *Ms.*, 12 (Jan. 1984), 38. See also Mary Roth Walsh, ed., *The Psychology of Women* (New Haven: Yale University Press, 1987). For feminist opposition to Gilligan's assumptions, see Judy Auerbach et al., "Commentary: On Gilligan's *In a Different Voice*," *Feminist Studies*, 11 (Spring, 1985); Linda K. Kerber et al., "On *In a Different Voice*: An Interdisciplinary Forum," *Signs*, 11 (Winter 1986). Francine Prose, "Carol Gilligan Studies Girls Growing Up: Confident at 11, Confused at 16," *New York Times Magazine*, Jan. 7, 1992. Carol Gilligan, Nona P. Lyons, and Trudy J. Hanmer, *Making Connections: The Relational Worlds of Adolescent Girls at Emma Willard School* (Cambridge, Mass.: Harvard University Press, 1990). Mary Jeanne Larrabee, ed., *An Ethic of Care: Feminist and Interdisciplinary Perspectives* (New York: Routledge, 1993), collects commentaries on Gilligan's work.

45. See Katha Pollitt, "Are Women Morally Superior to Men?" *The Nation* (Dec. 28, 1992).

46. Chodorow, "Family Structure and Feminine Personality," 66.

47. Nancy Chodorow, "Gender, Relation, and Difference in Psychoanalytic Perspective," in Eisenstein and Jardine, eds., *Future of Difference*, 4, 14, 15, 16. See also Chodorow, "Feminism and Difference: Gender, Relation, and Difference in Psychoanalytic Perspective" (1979), in Walsh, ed, *Psychology of Women*.

48. Nancy Chodorow, "Mothering, Object-Relations, and the Female Oedipal Configuration," *Feminist Studies,* 4 (Feb. 1978), 155.

49. Toril Moi, "Patriarchal Thought and the Drive for Knowledge," in Teresa Brennan, ed., *Between Feminism and Psychoanalysis* (London: Routledge, 1989), 190. See also Patricia Elliott, *From Mastery to Analysis: Theories of Gender in Psychoanalytic Feminism* (Ithaca: Cornell University Press, 1991).

50. Madelon Sprengnether, *The Spectral Mother: Freud, Feminism, and Psychoanalysis* (Ithaca: Cornell University Press, 1990), 190, 194.

51. Mahler et al., *Psychological Birth of the Human Infant.*

52. See, e.g., Adria E. Schwartz, "Psychoanalysis and Women: A Rapprochement," *Women and Therapy,* 3 (Spring 1984).

53. Natalie Shainess, "Is There a Separate Feminine Psychology?" *New York State Journal of Medicine,* 70 (Dec. 1970). Schafer, "Problems in Freud's Psychology of Women." For a different reading, see Alexandra Symonds, "Gender Issues and Horney Theory," AJP, Special Issue on Karen Horney, 51 (Sept. 1991).

54. Miller, ed., *Psychoanalysis and Women,* 383, 387, 89–90.

55. Jean Baker Miller, *Toward a New Psychology of Women* (Boston: Beacon, 1976), 46, 95.

56. "Jean Baker Miller Training Institute Spring Courses," Wellesley Centers for Women, *Research Report,* 1 (Fall 1996), 2.

57. Suzanne Gordon, "Anger, Power, and Women's Sense of Self," *Ms.,* 14 (July 1985), 42. Janet L. Surrey, "Relationship and Empowerment," in Judith V. Jordan, Alexandra G. Kaplan, Jean Baker Miller, Irene P. Stiver, and Janet L. Surrey, eds., *Women's Growth in Connection: Writings from the Stone Center* (New York: Guilford, 1991), 180.

58. Mary Brown Parlee, Carol Nadelson, and Jessica Benjamin, "Chodorow's *Reproduction of Mothering:* An Appraisal," PR, 69 (Sept. 1982), 151. See also Muriel Laskin, JAPA, 30 (1982); Mariam J. Wimpfheimer and Bonnie Kaufman, PQ, 50 (1981); Hannah Lerman, "From Freud to Feminist Personality Theory: Getting Here from There," in Walsh, ed., *Psychology of Women.*

59. Susan Spieler, "The Gendered Self: A Lost Maternal Legacy," in Judith L. Alpert, ed., *Psychoanalysis and Women: Contemporary Reappraisals* (Hillsdale, N.J.: Analytic Press, 1986), 39. For another example, see Schwartz, "Psychoanalysis and Women: A Rapprochement."

60. Malkah T. Notman, Joan J. Zilbach, Jean Baker Miller, and Carol C. Nadelson, "Themes in Psychoanalytic Understanding of Women: Some Reconsiderations of Autonomy and Affiliation," JAAP, 14 (April 1986). Dorothy Litwin, "Autonomy: A Conflict for Women," in Alpert, ed., *Psycho-*

analysis and Women. Judith V. Jordan and Janet L. Surrey, "The Self-in-Relation: Empathy and the Mother-Daughter Relationship," in Toni Bernay and Dorothy W. Cantor, eds., *The Psychology of Today's Woman: New Psychoanalytic Visions* (Hillsdale, N.J.: Analytic Press, 1986).

61. Clara M. Thompson, "Changing Concepts of Homosexuality in Psychoanalysis" (1947), in *On Women,* ed. Maurice R. Green (New York: New American Library, 1971). Richard C. Robertiello, M.D., *Voyage from Lesbos: The Psychoanalysis of a Female Homosexual* (New York: Citadel, 1959), 15. Edmund Bergler and William S. Kroger, *Kinsey's Myth of Female Sexuality* (New York: Grune and Stratton, 1954), 142.

62. Chodorow, *Reproduction of Mothering,* 200. See also Chodorow, "Oedipal Asymmetries and Heterosexual Knots," *Social Problems,* 23 (April 1976); Gayle Rubin, "The Traffic in Women: Notes on the 'Political Economy' of Sex," in Rayna R. Reiter, ed., *Toward an Anthropology of Women* (New York: Monthly Review Press, 1975).

63. Eileen Starzecpyzel, "The Persephone Complex," in Boston Lesbian Psychologies Collective, *Lesbian Psychologies: Explorations and Challenges* (Urbana: University of Illinois Press, 1978), 262.

64. Beverly Burch, "Barriers to Intimacy: Conflicts over Power, Dependency, and Nurturing in Lesbian Relationships," in Boston Lesbian Psychologies Collective, *Lesbian Psychologies,* 140. See also Sue Vargo, "The Effects of Women's Socialization on Lesbian Couples," ibid. Barbara Ponse, "Finding Self in the Lesbian Community," in Martha Kirkpatrick, ed., *Women's Sexual Development* (New York: Plenum, 1980).

65. Mildred Ash, "Freud on Feminine Identity and Female Sexuality," *Psychiatry,* 34 (Aug. 1971), 326. Adrienne Applegarth, "Women and Work," in Bernay and Cantor, eds., *Psychology of Today's Woman,* 212. Miller, ed., *Psychoanalysis and Women,* 389.

66. Alexandra Symonds, "The Liberated Woman: Healthy and Neurotic," AJP, 34 (Fall 1974), 177, 182.

67. Ruth Moulton published several key articles on this theme: "Professional Success: A Conflict for Women," in Alpert, ed., *Psychoanalysis and Women;* "The Fear of Female Power: A Cause of Sexual Dysfunction," JAAP, 5 (Oct. 1977); "Women with Double Lives," *Contemporary Psychoanalysis,* 13 (Jan. 1977); "Some Effects of the New Feminism," *American Journal of Psychiatry,* 134 (Jan. 1977); "Ambivalence about Motherhood in Career Women," JAAP, 7 (1979). See also Natalie Shainess, "The Working Wife and Mother: A New Woman?" *American Journal of Psychotherapy,* 34 (July 1980); Mimi Grand-Jean Crowell, "Feminism and Modern Psychoanalysis: A Response to Feminist Criticism and Psychoanalysis," *Modern Psychoanal-*

ysis, 6 (1981); Alexandra Symonds, "Separation and Loss: Significance for Women," AJP, 45 (Spring 1985).

68. Ethel Spector Person, "Working Mothers: Impact on the Self, the Couple, and the Children," in Bernay and Cantor, eds., *Psychology of Today's Woman.*

69. Anne E. Berstein and Gloria Marmar Warner, *Women Treating Women: Case Material from Women Treated by Female Psychoanalysts* (New York: International Universities Press, 1984), 179. See also Julie Firman and Dorothy Firman, *Daughters and Mothers: Healing the Relationship* (New York: Continuum, 1989).

70. Toni Bernay, "Reconciling Nurturing and Aggression: A New Feminine Identity," in Bernay and Cantor, eds., *Psychology of Today's Woman.* See also Jane B. Abramson, *Mothermania* (Lexington, Mass.: D. C. Heath, 1987); Elizabeth Debold, Marie Wilson, and Idelisse Malave, *Mother Daughter Revolution* (Reading, Mass.: Addison-Wesley, 1993).

71. Susan L. Williams, "Reproductive Motivations and Contemporary Feminine Development," in Joan Offerman-Zuckerberg, ed., *Gender in Transition: A New Frontier* (New York: Plenum, 1989), 167.

72. Joan Offerman-Zuckerberg, "Reflections," ibid., 297.

73. See Echols, *Daring to Be Bad.*

74. Erik Erikson, "Womanhood and Inner Space" (1974), in Strouse, comp., *Women and Analysis.*

75. Kate Millett, *Sexual Politics* (Garden City, N.Y.: Doubleday, 1970), 211, 220.

76. Erik H. Erikson, "Once More the Inner Space," in Strouse, comp., *Women and Analysis,* 340. See also Helen Block Lewis, *The Psychic War in Men and Women* (New York: New York University Press, 1976).

77. Donna Bassin, "Women's Images of Inner Space: Data toward Expanded Interpretive Categories," *International Review of Psychoanalysis,* 9 (1982). Interview in Elaine Hoffman Baruch and Lucienne J. Serrano, eds., *Women Analyze Women* (New York: New York University Press, 1988). Barbara Katz Rothman, *Recreating Motherhood: Ideology and Technology in a Patriarchal Society* (New York: Norton, 1989), 214.

78. Millett, *Sexual Politics,* 212, 219.

8. The Crisis in Patriarchal Authority

1. "History as Social Criticism: Conversations with Christopher Lasch," interviews by Casey Blake and Christopher Phelps, JAH, 80 (March 1994), 1320.

2. Christopher Lasch, *Haven in a Heartless World: The Family Besieged* (New York: Basic Books, 1979 [1977]), 183, 178.

3. Philip Wylie, *Sons and Daughters of Mom* (Garden City, N.Y.: Doubleday, 1971).

4. Lasch, *Haven in a Heartless World,* 165, 156.

5. Ibid., xix, 3, and ch. 1.

6. Ibid., 80, and ch. 4.

7. David Hacket Fisher, "This Year's Books, Part II," *New Republic,* 177 (Dec. 3, 1977), 24. Christopher Lehmann-Haupt, "All in the Family," *New York Times,* Nov. 28, 1977, 29.

8. Wini Breines, Margaret Cerullo, and Judith Stacey, "Social Biology, Family Studies, and Antifeminist Backlash," *Feminist Studies,* 4 (Feb. 1978), 59. See also Berenice M. Fisher, "The Wise Old Men and the New Women: Christopher Lasch Besieged," *History of Education Quarterly,* 19 (Spring 1979).

9. Juliet Mitchell, *Psychoanalysis and Feminism* (New York: Vintage, 1975), xiii.

10. Max Horkheimer, "Authority and the Family" (1936), in *Critical Theory: Selected Essays,* trans. Matthew J. O'Connell (New York: Continuum, 1982), 54.

11. Erich Fromm, *The Crisis of Psychoanalysis* (Greenwich, Conn.: Fawcett, 1970), 155. See also Martin Jay, *The Dialectical Imagination: A History of the Frankfurt School and the Institute of Social Research, 1923–1950* (Boston: Little, Brown, 1973); Rolf Wiggershaus, *The Frankfurt School: Its History, Theories and Political Significance,* trans. Michael Robertson (Cambridge: Polity, 1994).

12. Horkheimer, "Authority and the Family," 69.

13. Max Horkheimer and Theodor W. Adorno, *Dialectic of Enlightenment,* trans. John Cumming (New York: Herder and Herder, 1972 [1947]), 57. See also Trent Schroyer, *The Critique of Domination: The Origins and Development of Critical Theory* (New York: George Braziller, 1973).

14. Sigmund Freud, *Civilization and Its Discontents* (1930), SE 21: 86, 145; *The Future of an Illusion* (1928), SE 21: 15.

15. Horkheimer, "Authority and the Family," 105.

16. Ibid., 70–71, 101, 111, 114. See also Erich Fromm, *The Working Class in Weimar Germany: A Psychological and Sociological Study,* trans. Barbara Weinberger, ed. Wolfgang Bonss (Cambridge, Mass.: Harvard University Press, 1984).

17. Horkheimer, "Authority and the Family," 118–119, 122–123.

18. Wiggershaus, *Frankfurt School.*

19. Theodor W. Adorno, Else Frankel-Brunswik, Daniel J. Levinson, and R. Nevitt Sanford, *The Authoritarian Personality* (New York: Harper, 1950). Max Horkheimer, "Authoritarianism and the Family Today," in Ruth Nanda Anshen, ed., *The Family: Its Function and Destiny* (New York: Harper, 1949). See also Stephen Eric Bronner, *Of Critical Theory and Its Theorists* (Oxford: Blackwell, 1994).

20. Students for a Democratic Society, *The Port Huron Statement* (New York, 1964 [1962]), 5.

21. See Theodore Roszak, *The Making of a Counter Culture: Reflections on the Technocratic Society and Its Youthful Opposition* (Berkeley: University of California Press, 1995 [1968]).

22. *New York Times* quoted on back cover of Herbert Marcuse, *One-Dimensional Man: Studies in the Ideology of Advanced Industrial Society* (Boston: Beacon, 1991 [1964]). Barry Katz, *Herbert Marcuse and the Art of Liberation: An Intellectual Biography* (London: Verso, 1982). Douglas Kellner, *Herbert Marcuse and the Crisis of Marxism* (Berkeley: University of California Press, 1984).

23. Herbert Marcuse, *Eros and Civilization: A Philosophical Inquiry into Freud* (Boston: Beacon, 1955), 4. Marcuse, *One-Dimensional Man*, 257. See also Jurgen Habermas, "Psychic Thermidor and the Rebirth of Rebellious Subjectivity," in Robert Pippin, Andrew Feenberg, Charles P. Webel, et al., *Marcuse: Critical Theory and the Promise of Utopia* (South Hadley, Mass.: Bergin and Garvey, 1988). See also Bruce Brown, *Marx, Freud, and the Critique of Everyday Life: Toward a Permanent Cultural Revolution* (New York: Monthly Review Press, 1973); Jeremy J. Schapiro, "One-Dimensionality: The Universal Semiotic of Technological Experience," in Paul Breines, ed., *Critical Interruptions: New Left Perspectives on Herbert Marcuse* (New York: Herder and Herder, 1970).

24. Marcuse, *Eros and Civilization*, 4.

25. Ibid., 147, 168, 171, 184, 187, 193. For Marcuse's celebration of the youth movement, see *An Essay on Liberation* (Boston: Beacon, 1969).

26. Marcuse, *Eros and Civilization*, 201. For the quotation from Freud, Marcuse cites *Civilization and Its Discontents* (London: Hogarth Press, 1949), 14.

27. Horkheimer, "Authority and the Family," 118–119.

28. Marcuse, *Eros and Civilization*, 59–62. Herbert Marcuse, *Counterrevolution and Revolt* (Boston: Beacon, 1972), 75.

29. Herbert Marcuse, "Marxism and Feminism," *Women's Studies*, 2 (1974), 279, 281; Margaret Cerullo, "Marcuse and Feminism," *Telos*, no. 41 (Fall 1979), 185. See also Trudy Steuernagel, "Marcuse, the Women's Movement, and Women's Studies," in John Bokina and Timothy J. Lukes, eds.,

Marcuse: From the New Left to the Next Left (Lawrence: University Press of Kansas, 1994).

30. Marcuse, "Marxism and Feminism," 281, 282.

31. Reuben Fine, *A History of Psychoanalysis* (New York: Columbia University Press, 1979), 108. Wilhelm Reich, *The Mass Psychology of Fascism* (n.p.: Albion Press, 1970 [1933]), 74. Introduction to "Wilhelm Reich on Marx and Freud," *Studies on the Left*, 6 (July–Aug. 1966), 3. See also Joel Kovel, "From Reich to Marcuse," in Sohnya Sayers, Anders Stephanson, Stanley Aronowitz, and Fredric Jameson, eds., *The 60s without Apology* (Minneapolis: University of Minnesota Press, 1984). Mihaly Vajda and Agnes Heller, "Family Structure and Communism," trans. Andrew Arato, *Telos*, no. 7 (Spring 1971). Mark Poster, "Freud's Concept of the Family," *Telos*, no. 30 (Winter 1976–77); Poster, *Critical Theory of the Family* (New York: Seabury, 1978).

32. Lasch, *Haven in a Heartless World*, 156, 140.

33. Jesse F. Battan, "The 'New Narcissism' in 20th-Century America: The Shadow and the Substance in Social Change," *Journal of Social History*, 17 (Winter 1983). Ralph J. Kahana, "Reflections on Narcissism in Boston," in Joseph D. Lichtenberg and Samuel Kaplan, eds., *Reflections on Self Psychology* (Hillsdale, N.J.: Analytic Press, 1983), 5. See also Stephen Frosh, *The Politics of Psychoanalysis: An Introduction to Freudian and Post-Freudian Theory* (New Haven: Yale University Press, 1987).

34. Prominent examples: Tom Wolfe, "The 'Me' Decade and the Third Great Awakening," *New York*, 9 (Aug. 23, 1976); Jim Hougan, *Decadence: Radical Nostalgia, Narcissism, and Decline in the Seventies* (New York: Morrow, 1975); Edwin M. Schur, *The Awareness Trap: Self-Absorption instead of Social Change* (New York: Quadrangle–New York Times, 1976); Shirley Sugerman, *Sin and Madness: Studies in Narcissism* (Philadelphia: Westminster, 1976); Richard Sennett, *The Fall of Public Man* (New York: Knopf, 1977).

35. John Demos, "Introduction of Dr. Heinz Kohut," in Lichtenberg and Kaplan, eds., *Reflections on Self Psychology*, 10, 11.

36. Christopher Lasch, *Culture of Narcissism* (New York: Norton, 1978), 172, 175, 176.

37. Ibid., 198–199, 206. See also Christopher Lasch, "The Flight from Feeling," *Marxist Perspectives*, 1 (Summer 1978).

38. Sigmund Freud, "On Narcissism: An Introduction" (1914), SE 14: 73–74, 88, 89, 90. See also Reuben Fine, *Narcissism, the Self, and Society* (New York: Columbia University Press, 1986).

39. Freud, *Civilization and Its Discontents*, 65. Letter from Freud to Romain Rolland, Jan. 19, 1930, quoted in David James Fisher, "Reading

Freud's Civilization and Its Discontents," in Dominick LaCapra and Steven L. Kaplan, eds., *Modern European Intellectual History: Reappraisals and New Perspectives* (Ithaca: Cornell University Press, 1982), 262. Frank E. and Fritzie P. Manuel, *Utopian Thought in the Western World* (Cambridge, Mass.: Harvard University Press, 1979), 788.

40. Paul Breines, "From Guru to Specter: Marcuse and the Implosion of the Movement," in Breines, ed., *Critical Interruptions: New Left Perspectives on Herbert Marcuse* (New York: Herder and Herder, 1970), 19. Poster, *Critical Theory of the Family*, 61. Michael Walzer, *The Company of Critics: Social Criticism and Political Commitment in the Twentieth Century* (New York: Basic Books, 1988). See also Alfons Sollner, "Marcuse's Political Theory in the 1940s and 1950s," *Telos*, no. 74 (Winter 1987–88).

41. Joel Kovel, "Narcissism and the Family," *Telos*, no. 44 (Summer 1980), 95, 99; Stanley Aronowitz, "On Narcissism," ibid., 70, 73; Russell Jacoby, "Narcissism and the Crisis of Capitalism," ibid., 65; John Alt and Frank Hearn, "Symposium on Narcissism: The Cortland Conference on Narcissism," ibid.. See also Joel Kovel, *The Age of Desire: Reflections of a Radical Psychoanalyst* (New York: Pantheon, 1981). John P. Diggins and Mark E. Kann, eds., *The Problem of Authority in America* (Philadelphia: Temple University Press, 1981), 181–182.

42. Herbert Marcuse, "Neue Quellen zur Grundlegung des historischen Materialismus," in *Philosophie und Revolution: Aufsatze von Herbert Marcuse* (Berlin, 1967), 96–97, quoted in Brown, *Marx, Freud, and the Critique of Everyday Life*, 14. David Gross, "Left Melancholy," *Telos*, no. 65 (Fall 1985). See also Paul Breines, "Redeeming Redemption," ibid.; C. Fred Alford, "Nature and Narcissism: The Frankfurt School," *New German Critique*, no. 36 (Fall 1985); Janice Doane and Devon Hodges, *Nostalgia and Sexual Difference: The Resistance to Contemporary Feminism* (New York: Methuen, 1987); Joel Whitebook, *Perversion and Utopia: A Study in Psychoanalysis and Critical Theory* (Cambridge, Mass.: MIT Press, 1995).

43. Elizabeth Fox-Genovese, "The Personal Is Not Political Enough," *Marxist Perspectives*, 8 (Winter 1979–80), 109. The manifesto appeared in *The Nation*, Feb. 6, 1982. Michael Lerner, "Mass Psychology and Family Life: A Response to Epstein and Philipson," *Socialist Review*, 69 (May–June 1983), 109–110. Jan Rosenberg, "Social Policy: Conflicts and Solutions," *Democratic Left* (July–Aug. 1989), 15–16. See also Alexander Delfini, "Remaking Love: Undoing Women?" *Telos*, no. 76 (Summer 1988); Paul Piccone, "Narcissism after the Fall: What's on the Bottom of the Pool?" *Telos*, no. 44 (Summer 1980).

44. Joel Whitebook, "Saving the Subject: Modernity and the Problem of the Autonomous Individual," *Telos*, no. 50 (Winter 1981–82), 90.

45. Stephanie Engel, "Femininity as Tragedy: Re-examining the 'New Narcissism,' " *Socialist Review*, 53 (Sept.–Oct. 1980), 81. Jane Flax, "Mother-Daughter Relationships: Psychodynamics, Politics, and Philosophy," in Hester Eisenstein and Alice Jardine, eds., *The Future of Difference* (Boston: Beacon, 1980), 21. Ellen Willis, *Beginning to See the Light: Pieces of a Decade* (New York: Knopf, 1981), 141. See also Joan B. Landes, "Marcuse's Feminist Dimension," *Telos*, no. 41 (Fall 1979); Nancy Fraser, *Unruly Practices: Power, Discourse, and Gender in Contemporary Social Theory* (Minneapolis: University of Minnesota Press, 1989).

46. Jean Bethke Elshtain, "Feminism, Family, and Community," *Dissent* (Fall 1982). See also Elshtain, "The Family in Civil Life," in David G. Blakenhorn, Steven Bayme, and Jean Bethke Elshtain, eds., *Rebuilding the Nest: A New Commitment to the American Family* (Milwaukee: Family Service America, 1990).

47. Jean Bethke Elshtain, *Public Man, Private Woman: Women in Social and Political Thought* (Princeton: Princeton University Press, 1981), 216–217, 448. See also Elshtain, "An Open Letter to Marshall Berman," *Dissent* (Spring 1984); Elshtain and John Buell, "Families in Trouble," *Dissent* (Spring 1991).

48. Barbara Ehrenreich, "On Feminism, Family and Community," *Dissent* (Winter 1983); Ehrenreich, "Through a Glass Darkly," *Tikkun*, 6 (Sept. 1991). Arlie Hochschild, "Is the Left Sick of Feminism?" *Mother Jones*, 8 (June 1983). Jean Bethke Elshtain, "Single Motherhood," with a reply by Iris Marion Young, *Dissent* (Spring 1994). See also Kathleen B. Jones, "Socialist-Feminist Theories of the Family," *Praxis International*, 8 (Oct. 1988); Linda Nicholson, *Gender and History: The Limits of Social Theory in the Age of the Family* (New York: Columbia University Press, 1986).

49. Elshtain, "Open Letter to Marshall Berman," 254. See also Theodore Mills Norton, "Contemporary Critical Theory and the Family: Private World and Public Crisis," in Elshtain, ed., *The Family in Political Thought* (Amherst: University of Massachusetts Press, 1982); and Elshtain, *Power Trips and Other Journeys: Essays in Feminism as Civic Discourse* (Madison: University of Wisconsin Press, 1990).

50. Interview with Jessica Benjamin, in Elaine Hoffman Baruch and Lucienne J. Serrano, eds., *Women Analyze Women in France, England, and the United States* (New York: New York University Press, 1988), 318.

51. See Otto Kernberg, *Borderline Conditions and Pathological Narcissism* (New York: Jason Aronson, 1975); Monica Carsky, "Otto Kernberg: Psychoanalysis and Object Relations Theory: The Beginnings of an Integrative Approach," in Joseph Reppen, ed., *Beyond Freud: A Study of Modern Psychoanalytic Theorists* (Hillsdale, N.J.: Analytic Press, 1985). On the problems

of applying narcissism to social theory, see C. Fred Alford, *Narcissism: Socrates, the Frankfurt School, and Psychoanalytic Theory* (New Haven: Yale University Press, 1988).

52. Heinz Kohut, "Thoughts on Narcissism and Narcissistic Rage" (1972), in Paul H. Ornstein, ed., *The Search for the Self: Selected Writings of Heinz Kohut: 1950–1978*, vol. 2 (New York: International Universities Press, 1978), 620. Kohut, *The Analysis of the Self: A Systematic Approach to the Psychoanalytic Treatment of Narcissistic Personality Disorders* (New York: International Universities Press, 1971); and *The Restoration of the Self* (New York: International Universities Press, 1977). See also Salman Akhtar, "Kernberg and Kohut: A Critical Comparison," in Douglas W. Detrick and Susan P. Detrick, eds., *Self Psychology: Comparisons and Contrasts* (Hillsdale, N.J.: Analytic Press, 1989).

53. For these feminist post-Freudian critiques, see Patricia Jagentowicz Mills, *Woman, Nature, and Psyche* (New Haven: Yale University Press, 1987), 163; Nancy J. Chodorow, "Beyond Drive Theory: Object Relations and the Limits of Radical Individualism" (1985), in Chodorow, *Feminism and Psychoanalytic Theory* (New Haven: Yale University Press, 1989).

54. Several other psychoanalysts have noted a basic compatibility between feminism and self psychology. See, e.g., Kay Knox, "Women's Identity: Self Psychology's New Promise," *Women and Therapy*, 4 (Fall 1985); Judith Kegan Gardiner, "Self Psychology as Feminist Theory," *Signs*, 12 (Summer 1987); Joan A. Lang, "Notes toward a Psychology of the Feminine Self," in Paul E. Stepansky and Arnold Goldberg, eds., *Kohut's Legacy: Contributions to Self Psychology* (Hillsdale, N.J.: Analytic Press, 1984); Christiane Brems, "Self-Psychology and Feminism: An Integration and Expansion," AJP, 51 (June 1991).

55. Jessica Benjamin, "The Oedipal Riddle: Authority, Autonomy, and the New Narcissism," in Diggins and Kann, eds., *Problem of Authority in America*, 204; *The Bonds of Love: Psychoanalysis, Feminism, and the Problem of Domination* (New York: Pantheon, 1988), 18, 47; "The Decline of the Oedipus Complex," in John M. Broughton, ed., *Critical Theories of Psychological Development* (New York: Plenum, 1987), 216–217; "Sameness and Difference: Toward an 'Overinclusive' Model of Gender Development," *Psychoanalytic Inquiry*, 15 (1995).

56. Heinz Kohut, "Reflections on Advances in Self Psychology," in Arnold Goldberg, ed., *Advances in Self Psychology* (New York: International Universities Press, 1980), 480; Kohut, *How Does Analysis Cure?* ed. Arnold Goldberg with Paul E. Stepansky (Chicago: University of Chicago Press, 1984), 47. See also Jessica Benjamin, "An Outline of Intersubjectivity: The Development of Recognition," *Psychoanalytic Psychology*, 7 (supp., 1990).

57. Benjamin, "Decline of the Oedipus Complex," 221; *Bonds of Love,* 162; "Oedipal Riddle," 210. See also Benjamin, "Master and Slave: The Fantasy of Erotic Domination," in Ann Snitow, Christine Stansell, and Sharon Thompson, eds., *Powers of Desire: The Politics of Sexuality* (New York: Monthly Review Press, 1983).

58. Benjamin, *Bonds of Love,* 147–148, 171, 186–187.

59. Benjamin, *Bonds of Love,* 185, 205, 184. See also Jessica Benjamin, "Authority and Family Revisited: or, A World without Fathers?" *New German Critique,* no. 13 (Winter 1978).

60. Jessica Benjamin, "The End of Internalization: Adorno's Social Psychology," *Telos,* no. 32 (Summer 1977), 42–43; *Bonds of Love,* 217, 221; "Decline of the Oedipus Complex," 234, 235.

61. Benjamin, "Oedipal Riddle," 220–221.

62. Ellen Key, *The Woman Movement* (New York: Putnam, 1912), 183.

63. Christopher Lasch and Discussants, "Family and Authority," in Barry Richards, ed., *Capitalism and Infancy: Essays on Psychoanalysis and Politics* (Atlantic Highlands, N.J.: Humanities Press, 1984), 24–25.

64. Christopher Lasch, *The Minimal Self: Psychic Survival in Troubled Times* (New York: Norton, 1984); and *The True and Only Heaven: Progress and Its Critics* (New York: Norton, 1991). For a compatible statement, see Elizabeth Fox-Genovese, *Feminism without Illusions: A Critique of Individualism* (Chapel Hill: University of North Carolina Press, 1991).

65. Gad Horowitz, "Psychoanalytic Feminism in the Wake of Marcuse," in Bokina and Lukes, eds., *Marcuse,* 122. Sigmund Freud, "A Special Type of Object Choice Made by Men" (1910), SE 11: 183. See also Stephen A. Mitchell, *Relational Concepts in Psychoanalysis: An Integration* (Cambridge, Mass.: Harvard University Press, 1988), pt. 2.

9. In the Age of the Vanishing Subject

1. Lois A. West, "French Feminist Theorists and Psychoanalytic Theory," *Off Our Backs* (July 1979).

2. Jane Gallop and Carolyn Burke, "Psychoanalysis and Feminism in France," in Hester Eisenstein and Alice Jardine, eds., *The Future of Difference* (Boston: G. K. Hall, 1980), 106, 107, 108.

3. West, "French Feminist Theorists," 5.

4. Teresa Brennan, "Introduction," in Brennan, ed., *Between Feminism and Psychoanalysis* (London: Routledge, 1989), 8.

5. Gallop and Burke, "Psychoanalysis and Feminism in France," 110, 106.

6. See Linda J. Nicholson, ed., *Feminism/Postmodernism* (New York:

Routledge, 1990), for essays by leading scholars in several disciplines on this subject. The definition of postmodern as a "cultural break" bringing together "feminism, deconstruction, and Lacanian psychoanalysis" comes from the preface to E. Ann Kaplan, ed., *Postmodernism and Its Discontents: Theories and Practice* (London: Verso, 1988), 4.

7. Ellie Ragland-Sullivan, *Jacques Lacan and the Philosophy of Psychoanalysis* (Urbana: University of Illinois Press, 1986), ix.

8. Louis Althusser, "Freud and Lacan," *New Left Review*, 55 (May–June 1969), 54.

9. Sherry Turkle, *Psychoanalytic Politics: Freud's French Revolution* (New York: Basic Books, 1978).

10. David James Fisher, *Cultural Theory and Psychoanalytic Tradition* (New Brunswick: Transaction, 1992), 4. Turkle, *Psychoanalytic Politics*, 238; Catherine Clément, *The Weary Sons of Freud*, trans. Nichole Ball (London: Verso, 1987), 86; Stuart Schneiderman, *Jacques Lacan: The Death of an Intellectual Hero* (Cambridge, Mass.: Harvard University Press, 1983), vi.

11. H. Stuart Hughes, *The Obstructed Path: French Social Thought in the Years of Desperation, 1930–1966* (New York: Harper and Row, 1966), 290. Clément, *Weary Sons of Freud*, 84, 86.

12. Quoted from *Le Torchon brûle* (no. 4, 1972), in Claire Duchen, *Feminism in France: From May '68 to Mitterand* (London: Routledge and Kegan Paul, 1986), 32.

13. Jacques Lacan, "The Meaning of the Phallus" (1958), in Juliet Mitchell and Jacqueline Rose, eds., *Feminine Sexuality: Jacques Lacan and the école freudienne*, trans. Jacqueline Rose (New York: Norton, 1985).

14. Ibid. See also Stephen Frosh, "Masculine Mastery and Fantasy, or the Meaning of the Phallus," in Anthony Elliott and Stephen Frosh, eds., *Psychoanalysis in Contexts* (London: Routledge, 1995).

15. See Anthony Elliott, *Social Theory and Psychoanalysis in Transition: Self and Society from Freud to Kristeva* (Oxford: Blackwell, 1992).

16. Lacan, "God and the *Jouissance* of The Woman," in Mitchell and Rose, eds., *Feminine Sexuality*, 147.

17. Jacques Lacan, "Seminar of 21 Jan. 1975," in Mitchell and Rose, eds., *Feminine Sexuality*, 170.

18. Lacan, quoted in Turkle, *Psychoanalytic Politics*, 239.

19. Monique David-Menard, "Lacanians against Lacan," *Social Text*, no. 6 (Fall 1982), 87, 91. See also Shoshana Felman, *Jacques Lacan and the Adventure of Insight: Psychoanalysis in Contemporary Culture* (Cambridge, Mass.: Harvard University Press, 1989); Fisher, *Cultural Theory and Psychoanalytic Tradition*.

20. Charles Levin, "Lacanian Psychoanalysis and Feminist Metatheory," in Arthur and Marilouise Kroker, eds., *The Hysterical Male: New Feminist Theory* (New York: St. Martin's, 1991), 236. See also Elliott, *Social Theory and Psychoanalysis in Transition*.

21. Gillian C. Gill, "Dubious Diagnoses," *Women's Review of Books*, 8 (Jan. 1991), 7.

22. Hélène Cixous, "Castration or Decapitation?" (1976), trans. Annette Kuhn, *Signs*, 7 (Autumn 1981), 44. Constance Penley, *The Future of an Illusion: Film, Feminism, and Psychoanalysis* (Minneapolis: University of Minnesota Press, 1989), xii.

23. Hélène Cixous, "The Laugh of the Medusa" (1975), trans. Keith Cohen and Pamela Cohen, in Elaine Marks and Isabelle de Courtivron, eds., *New French Feminisms: An Anthology* (New York: Schocken, 1980), 262. Luce Irigaray, "This Sex Which Is Not One," trans. Claudia Reeder, in Marks and de Courtivron, eds., *New French Feminisms*. The similarity between Horney and Irigaray has been noted by Janet Sayers, *Biological Politics: Feminist and Anti-Feminist Perspectives* (London: Tavistock, 1992).

24. Julia Kristeva, "Women's Time," trans. Alice Jardine and Harry Black, *Signs*, 7 (Autumn 1981). Gallop and Burke, "Psychoanalysis and Feminism," 112.

25. Irigaray, "Sex Which Is Not One," 101.

26. Ibid., 100, 103. On Irigaray's theories, see Margaret Whitford, *Luce Irigaray: Philosophy in the Feminine* (London: Routledge, 1991).

27. Cixous, "Castration or Decapitation?" 50. Cixous, "Laugh of the Medusa," 250, 259–260. See also Ann Roslind Jones, "Writing the Body: Toward an Understanding of *L'Ecriture Féminine*," *Feminist Studies*, 7 (Summer 1981).

28. Hélène Cixous and Catherine Clément, *The Newly Born Woman*, trans. Betsy Wing (Minneapolis: University of Minnesota Press, 1986). See also Monique David-Menard, *Hysteria from Freud to Lacan*, trans. Catherine Porter (Ithaca: Cornell University Press, 1989); Ellie Ragland-Sullivan, "Dora and the Name-of-the-Father: The Structure of Hysteria," in Marleen Barr and Richard Felstein, eds., *Discontented Discourses* (Urbana: University of Illinois Press, 1989).

29. Julia Kristeva, *The Revolution in Poetic Language*, trans. Margaret Waller (New York: Columbia University Press, 1984 [1974]), 80. Hélène Cixous, "Sorties" (1975), trans. Ann Liddle, in Marks and Courtivron, eds., *New French Feminisms*, 95.

30. Kristeva, "Woman's Time," 21.

31. Cixous, "Sorties."

32. Kristeva, "Woman's Time," 30–31. See also Janice Doane and Devon

Hodges, *From Klein to Kristeva: Psychoanalytic Feminism and the Search for the "Good Enough" Mother* (Ann Arbor: University of Michigan Press, 1992).

33. Julia Kristeva, *Desire in Language,* trans. T. Gora, A. Jardine, and L. S. Roudiez, ed. L. S. Roudiez (New York: Columbia University Press, 1980), 239. See also Kristeva, *Black Sun: Depression and Melancholia,* trans. Leon S. Roudiez (New York: Columbia University Press, 1990).

34. See, e.g.,, Chris Weedon, *Feminist Practice and Poststructuralist Theory* (London: Blackwell, 1987).

35. Lacan quoted in Turkle, *Psychoanalytic Politics,* 238. See also Stuart Schneiderman, ed. and trans., *Returning to Freud: Clinical Psychoanalysis in the School of Lacan* (New Haven: Yale University Press, 1980); Elisabeth Roudinesco, *Jacques Lacan and Co.: A History of Psychoanalysis in France, 1925–1985,* trans. Jeffrey Mehlman (Chicago: University of Chicago Press, 1990).

36. Jane Gallop, *Reading Lacan* (Ithaca: Cornell University Press, 1985), 24. See also Clément, *Weary Sons of Freud.*

37. Juliet Mitchell, *Psychoanalysis and Feminism: Freud, Reich, Laing, and Women* (New York: Vintage, 1975). Gayle Rubin, "The Traffic in Women: Notes on the 'Political Economy' of Sex," in Rayna R. Reiter, ed., *Toward an Anthropology of Women* (New York: Monthly Review Press, 1975), 185. Laura Mulvey, "Visual Pleasure and Narrative Cinema," *Screen,* 16 (Autumn 1975), 6. Edith Kurzweil, *Freudians and Feminists* (Boulder: Westview, 1995), 125. See also Elizabeth Grosz, *Jacques Lacan: A Feminist Introduction* (London: Routledge, 1990).

38. Nancy Frazer, "The Uses and Abuses of French Discourse Theories for Feminist Politics," in Nancy Fraser and Sandra Lee Bartky, eds., *Revaluing French Feminism: Critical Essays on Difference, Agency, and Culture* (Bloomington: Indiana University Press, 1992), 177.

39. Verena Andermatt, "Hélène Cixous and the Uncovery of a Feminine Language," *Women and Literature,* 7 (Winter 1979), 41–42. See also Morag Shiach, *Hélène Cixous: A Politics of Writing* (London: Routledge, 1991); Verena Andermatt Conley, *Hélène Cixous* (London: Harvester/Wheatsheaf, 1992).

40. Jane Gallop, *The Daughter's Seduction: Feminism and Psychoanalysis* (Ithaca: Cornell University Press, 1982), 5, xi. Gallop and Burke, "Psychoanalysis and Feminism in France," 114, 115.

41. Jane Gallop, *Around 1981: Academic Feminist Literary Theory* (New York: Routledge, 1992). This psychoanalytic approach occasionally combined pre-oedipal facets of American and French theory: see, e.g., Jean Wyatt,

Reconstructing Desire: The Role of the Unconscious in Women's Reading and Writing (Chapel Hill: University of North Carolina Press, 1990); Shirley Nelson Garner, Claire Kahane, and Madelon Sprengnether, eds., *The (M)other Tongue* (Ithaca: Cornell University Press, 1985). Poe's story is interpreted by Naomi Schor, "Female Paranoia: The Case for Psychoanalytic Feminist Criticism," *Yale French Studies,* 62 (1981).

42. Alice Jardine, *Gynesis: Configurations of Woman and Modernity* (Ithaca: Cornell University Press, 1985), 13.

43. Janet Todd, *Feminist Literary History* (New York: Routledge, 1988), 63, 15. See also Iris Marion Young, "Humanism, Gynocentrism, and Feminist Politics," *Women's Studies International Forum,* 8 (1985).

44. For a survey of early practices, see Josephine Donovan, ed., *Feminist Literary Criticism: Explorations in Theory* (Lexington: University of Kentucky Press, 1975).

45. Marks and de Courtivron, eds., *New French Feminisms,* x, xi.

46. Elizabeth A. Meese, *(Ex)Tensions: Re-Figuring Feminist Criticism* (Urbana: University of Illinois Press, 1990), 3, 4; see also *Tulsa Studies in Women's Literature,* 3 (1984). Nancy K. Miller, "The Text's Heroine: A Feminist Critic and Her Fictions," *Diacritics,* 12 (Summer 1982), 49. See also Elaine Showalter, ed., *The New Feminist Criticism: Essays on Women, Literature and Theory* (New York: Pantheon, 1985); Seyla Benhabib, "On Contemporary Feminist Theory," *Dissent,* 36 (Summer 1989).

47. Todd, *Feminist Literary History,* 51. Nina Baym, "The Madwoman and Her Languages: Why I Don't Do Feminist Literary Theory," *Tulsa Studies in Women's Literature,* 3 (1984), 45. See also Teresa Brennan, "Controversial Discussions and Feminist Debates," in Edward Temin and Naomi Segal, eds., *Freud in Exile: Psychoanalysis and Its Vicissitudes* (New Haven: Yale University Press, 1988).

48. Gill, "Dubious Diagnoses," 7. Sharon Willis, "Feminism's Interrupted Genealogies," *Diacritics,* 18 (Spring 1988), 32. Madelon Sprengnether, *The Spectral Mother: Freud, Feminism, and Psychoanalysis* (Ithaca: Cornell University Press, 1990), 195.

49. Elaine Showalter, "Feminist Criticism in the Wilderness," *Critical Inquiry,* 8 (Winter 1981), 182, 197; Annette Kolodny, "Dancing through the Minefield: Some Observations on the Theory, Practice, and Politics of a Feminist Literary Criticism," *Feminist Studies,* 6 (Spring 1980), 19–20.

50. Elizabeth Wright, ed., *Feminism and Psychoanalysis: A Critical Dictionary* (Oxford: Blackwell, 1992), 341. See also E. Ann Kaplan, ed., *Postmodernism and Its Discontents, Theories, Practices* (London: Verso, 1988), which includes "Postmodernism and Consumer Society" by the most-cited authority, Fredric Jameson; Judith Grant, *Fundamental Feminism: Contesting the Core Concepts of Feminist Theory* (New York: Routledge, 1993).

51. Sigmund Freud, *Introductory Lectures on Psycho-Analysis* (1915–1916), SE 16: 285. Nancy Chodorow, "Toward a Relational Individualism: The Mediation of Self Through Psychoanalysis," in Chodorow, *Feminism and Psychoanalytic Theory* (New Haven: Yale University Press, 1989), 154. See also Barnaby B. Barratt, *Psychoanalysis and the Postmodern Impulse: Knowing and Being since Freud's Psychology* (Baltimore: Johns Hopkins University Press, 1993).

52. Chodorow, "Toward a Relational Individualism," 155. See also Eli Zaretsky, "Psychoanalysis and Postmodernism," *American Literary History*, 8 (Spring 1996).

53. Elizabeth Wright, "Thoroughly Postmodern Feminist Criticism," in Brennan, ed., *Between Feminism and Psychoanalysis*, 146.

54. See, e.g., Toril Moi, *Sexual/Textual Politics: Feminist Literary Theory* (New York: Methuen, 1985). See also Rachel Bowlby, "The Feminine Female," *Social Text*, no. 7 (Spring/Summer 1983).

55. Maggie Berg, "Luce Irigaray's 'Contradictions': Poststructuralism and Feminism," *Signs*, 17 (Fall 1991). Cixous, "Castration or Decapitation," 44. Jerry Aline Flieger, "The Female Subject: (What) Does Woman Want?" in Richard Feldstein and Henry Sussman, eds., *Psychoanalysis and . . .* (New York: Routledge, 1990), 59; emphasis in the original. Elizabeth Abel, "Race, Class, and Psychoanalysis? Opening Questions," in Marianne Hirsch and Evelyn Fox Keller, eds., *Conflicts in Feminism* (New York: Routledge, 1991), 185. See Mary Poovey, "Feminism and Deconstruction," *Feminist Studies*, 14 (Spring 1988); Laura E. Donaldson, "(ex)Changing (wo)Man: Towards a Materialist-Feminist Semiotics," *Cultural Critique*, no. 11 (Winter 1988–1989); Dorothy Leland, "Lacanian Psychoanalysis and French Feminism: Toward an Adequate Political Psychology," *Hypatia*, 3 (Winter 1989).

56. Gallop, *Reading Lacan*, 136; ch. 6 examines this controversy. See also Arleen B. Dallery, "The Politics of Writing (the) Body: *écriture féminine*," in Alison M. Jaggar and Susan R. Bordo, eds., *Gender/Body/Language* (New York: Routledge, 1989); Patricia Elliot, *From Mastery to Analysis: Theories of Gender in Psychoanalytic Feminism* (Ithaca: Cornell University Press, 1991).

57. Judith Butler, "The Body Politics of Julia Kristeva," in Fraser and Bartky, eds., *Revaluing French Feminism*, 175. Butler, "Gender Trouble, Feminist Theory, and Psychoanalytic Discourse," in Nicholson, ed., *Feminism/Postmodernism*, 332. See also Butler, "Variations on Sex and Gender: Beauvoir, Wittig and Foucault," in Seyla Benhabib and Drucilla Cornell, eds., *Feminism as Critique: On the Politics of Gender* (Minneapolis: University of Minnesota Press, 1987).

58. Donna J. Haraway, *Simians, Cyborgs, and Women: The Reinvention of Nature* (New York: Routledge, 1991), 148, 150, 154.

59. Judith Butler, "Gender Trouble, Feminist Theory, and Psychoanalytic Discourse," 329, 338, 339. See also Butler, "Phantasmatic Identification and the Assumption of Sex," *Psyke and Logos,* 15 (1994).

60. Tamar Avishur, "Letters to the Staff," *City on a Hill Press* (Santa Cruz), Nov. 9, 1995, 5.

61. Linda Gordon, "On 'Difference,' " *Genders,* 10 (Spring 1991), 91.

62. Linda Alcoff, "Cultural Feminism versus Post-Structuralism: The Identity Crisis in Feminist Theory," *Signs,* 13 (Spring 1988), 407. Judith Butler, *Gender Trouble: Feminism and the Subversion of Identity* (New York: Routledge, 1990), 57. See also Butler, *Bodies That Matter: On the Discursive Limits of "Sex"* (New York: Routledge, 1992).

63. Butler, "Gender Trouble, Feminist Theory, and Psychoanalytic Discourse," 327.

64. Elizabeth Grosz, "Sexual Difference and the Problem of Essentialism," in Naomi Schor and Elizabeth Weed, eds., *The Essential Difference* (Bloomington: Indiana University Press, 1994), 93.

65. Patricia Waugh, "Postmodernism," in Wright, ed., *Feminism and Psychoanalysis,* 342.

66. Ruth Salvaggio, "Psychoanalysis and Deconstruction and Woman," in Feldstein and Sussman, eds., *Psychoanalysis and . . .,* 152, 155–156. Jane Flax, *Thinking Fragments: Psychoanalysis, Feminism, and Postmodernism in the Contemporary West* (Berkeley: University of California Press, 1990), 91, 178, 182.

67. Margret Schaefer and Raymond Barglow, "Return of the Repressed," *San Francisco Examiner Magazine,* Jan. 21, 1996, 8, 16.

68. Jessica Benjamin, *Like Subjects, Love Objects: Essays on Recognition and Sexual Difference* (New Haven: Yale University Press, 1995), 13. James M. Blass, *Shattered Selves: Multiple Personality in a Postmodern World* (Ithaca: Cornell University Press, 1993), 59. See also K. Leary, "Psychoanalytic 'Problems' and Postmodern 'Solutions,' " PQ, 63 (1994).

69. Roy Schafer, *Narrative Actions in Psychoanalysis* (Worcester, Mass.: Clark University Press, 1980), 3. Donald Spence, *Narrative Truth and Historical Truth* (New York: Norton, 1982), 269–270. See also Anthony Elliott and Charles Spezzano, "Psychoanalysis and Its Limits: Navigating the Postmodern Turn," PQ, 65 (1996).

70. Teresa L. Ebert, *Ludic Feminism and After: Postmodernism, Desire and Labor in Late Capitalism* (Ann Arbor: University of Michigan Press, 1996), 300. Ebert cites Derrida's shift, in his last book before his death, back to Marxism. See also Kevin Anderson, "Western Europe, Spring 1966: New Labor Battles, Intellectual Ferment," *News and Letters* (Chicago), June 1996, 1, 9.

Acknowledgments

Because my interest in psychoanalysis dates to my teens, I am now beholden to many people. My social studies teacher at North Chicago Community High School, Roger Johnson, introduced me to Freud's theories and suggested the possibility of my becoming, if not a psychoanalyst, a clinical psychologist. This aspiration became at once more concrete and more elusive at the University of Illinois, Champaign-Urbana, where I majored in psychology. At the time the Department of Psychology was a leader in experimental psychology and, to my regret, offered no courses in the clinical area. Fortunately, I found two kindred spirits among the faculty. Foremost was Leigh Minturn, an anthropologist who studied childrearing patterns cross-culturally and taught Culture and Personality to frustrated Freudians. Earl E. Davis, a social psychologist, employed me as a student assistant on his project derived from Theodor Adorno's *Authoritarian Personality*. From Professor Davis I learned first-hand about F-scales, which he was adapting to measure the potential for racial prejudice among white male college students. Although I soon left psychology for history, the imprint of these early teachers is indelible.

My fascination with the history of feminism came later, when I entered graduate school in American history at the University of Wisconsin–Madison. Women's history had not yet become a part of the curriculum, but I found distant mentors through reading the pioneering books and articles of Gerda Lerner and Anne Firor Scott. Since 1970 professors Lerner and Scott have assisted me in many ways, and I thank them for their unceasing generosity. In Madison two collaborators and dear friends educated me in women's history: Nancy Schrom Dye, now president of Oberlin College; and Ann D. Gordon, editor of the papers of Elizabeth Cady Stanton and Susan B. Anthony.

At Brown University, funds from the Odyssey program for faculty-student collaboration encouraged me to integrate the histories of psychoanalysis and American feminism. Thanks to Dean Karen Romer, Debbie Bercuvitz found a summer's employment preparing the initial bibliographies that became the core research for this book. Debbie and I also worked together to design an undergraduate seminar on the topic, which provided a forum for testing some of my early ideas.

Many friends and colleagues helped me with the research along the way. I owe great debts to Nan Alamilla Boyd, Phil Brown, Peter Cohen, Ruth Feldstein, David James Fisher, Elizabeth Francis, Carol Frost, Jane Gerhard, Todd Gernes, Linda Gordon, Louise Newman, Kathy Peiss, Donna Penn, Uta Poiger, Tricia Rose, Gina Rourke, Jessica Shubow, Mary Trigg, Lauri Umansky, Elizabeth Weed, Julie Weiss, Eli Zaretsky, and Natasha Zaretsky.

Careful readings of chapters at various stages were provided by Paul Breines, Nancy F. Cott, Ellen Carol DuBois, Jane Gerhard, Nell Irwin Painter, and Judith E. Smith. These distinguished scholars saved me from embarrassing errors and offered astute advice for rewriting. Dee Garrison provided just the right mix of criticism and reassurance. Joel Kovel applied his vast knowledge of psychoanalysis to a thorough critique. Thanks to Sybil Mazor, of the Department of American Civilization at Brown University, for printing all the drafts that these folks read.

I had the truly memorable pleasure of finishing this book in Santa Cruz, California. Michael Cowan, who chairs the American Studies program at the University of California, Santa Cruz, kindly made me a visiting scholar for the year. The John D. and Catherine T. MacArthur Foundation provided the crucial financial (and psychological) support.

One could not hope for a more enthusiastic editor than Lindsay Waters of Harvard University Press. Thanks, too, to Kimberly Steere for timely assistance on technical matters; and to Camille Smith for expert manuscript editing.

I am also grateful to Paul Buhle, who a long time ago browbeat me out of becoming a psychologist. He persuaded me to join him in the discipline of history and ended up paying a stiff price: he read all the drafts of this book.

Index

Index

Strouse, Jean, 249, 278
Students for a Democratic Society, 294
Studies in the Psychology of Sex (Ellis), 36
Studies on Hysteria (Freud and Breuer), 29–30, 232
sublimation, 19, 30–31
Sullivan, Harry Stack, 114–115, 151, 225, 244
Susman, Warren I., 3, 185
Symbolic Order, 327, 328, 333–334, 342
Symonds, Alexandra, 272
Szasz, Thomas, 129, 220

"Taboo of Virginity" (Freud), 66
Tannenbaum, Samuel, 6
Telos, 300, 307, 337
Their Mothers' Daughters (Strecker and Lathbury), 194–195
Their Mothers' Sons (Strecker), 156
Thomas, Norman, 224
Thompson, Clara, 13, 88, 114, 130, 159, 206, 232, 257, 270, 272; on Farnham, 193; theories of femininity, 119–122
Three Essays on a Theory of Sexuality (Freud), 31–32, 35, 66, 71
Tichenor, Edward Bradford, 7
Todd, Janet, 340, 341–342
Totem and Taboo (Freud), 100–101; Marcuse on, 299
Toward a Psychology of Women (Miller), 269
Tridon, André, 93
Trilling, Lionel, 128
Trobriand Islanders, 102–104, 156
True and Only Heaven (Lasch), 316
Turkel, Ann Ruth, 229

Uses and Abuses of Psychology (Eysenck), 220

vaginal orgasm, 213, 214, 215, 217, 222, 223, 224, 227, 240
Vaginal Politics (Frankfort), 233
Van Ophuijsen, J. H. W., 68

Vienna Psychoanalytic Society, 54, 55, 80, 118, 137, 181, 303
Vienna Society for Individual Psychology, 55
Vindication of the Rights of Women (Wollstonecraft), 59
Voyage from Lesbos (Robertiello), 270

Waisbrooker, Lois, 24
Wald, Lillian, 91
Walker, Alice, 259, 261
Walzer, Michael, 306
Watson, John B., 150
Waugh, Patricia, 350
Weininger, Otto, 32–33
Weisstein, Naomi, 220
welfare state: Key on, 41; Lasch on, 282–283, 317–318
White, William Alanson, 5
Whitebook, Joel, 309
Whiting, Beatrice, 257
Whiting, John, 257
Willard, Frances, 15, 44–45
Williams, William Appleman, 185
Willis, Ellen, 309
Winnicott, Donald W., 135, 250, 253
Wittels, Fritz, 118
Wolfe, Tom, 303
Wollstonecraft, Mary, 23, 59; in *Modern Woman*, 176–177
Woman as Force in History (Beard), 206–207
Woman Movement (Key), 47
Woman Question, 2, 12, 18; Freud on, 53–54; Gilman on, 46–50; Horkheimer on, 291; Key on, 39–40; *Modern Woman* on, 176–178; New Moralists on, 38–39
Woman Rebel, 43
Woman's Coming of Age (Calverton and Schmalhausen), 94
Woman's Estate (Mitchell), 230
Woman: Her Sex and Love Life (Robinson), 42
womb envy, 83
Women and Analysis (Strouse), 249, 278

— 431 —